D0856386

The Missing Link in Cognition

The Missing Link in Cognition

Origins of Self-Reflective Consciousness

Edited by
Herbert S. Terrace and Janet Metcalfe

OXFORD
UNIVERSITY PRESS

2005

OXFORD
UNIVERSITY PRESS

Oxford   New York
Auckland   Bangkok   Buenos Aires   Cape Town   Chennai
Dar es Salaam   Delhi   Hong Kong   Istanbul   Karachi   Kolkata
Kuala Lumpur   Madrid   Melbourne   Mexico City   Mumbai   Nairobi
São Paulo   Shanghai   Taipei   Tokyo   Toronto

Copyright © 2005 by Oxford University Press, Inc.

Published by Oxford University Press, Inc.
198 Madison Avenue, New York, New York 10016

www.oup.com

Oxford is a registered trademark of Oxford University Press

Library of Congress Cataloging-in-Publication Data

The missing link in cognition : origins of self-reflective consciousness /
edited by Herbert S. Terrace and Janet Metcalfe.
p. cm.
Includes bibliographical references and index.
ISBN-13 978-0-19-516156-4
ISBN 0-19-516156-4
1. Self-perception.   2. Cognition in animals.   3. Psychology, Comparative.
I. Terrace, Herbert S., 1936–   II. Metcalfe, Janet.

BF697.5.S43M58 2004
156'.3—dc22   2004010567

9 8 7 6 5 4 3 2 1

Printed in the United States of America
on acid-free paper

Contents

Contributors

Josep Call
Max Planck Institute for Evolutionary Anthropology
Deutscher Platz 6
D-04103 Leipzig
Germany
call@eva.mpg.de

Robert R. Hampton
Laboratory of Neuropsychology
National Institute of Mental Health
Building 49, Room 1B-80
Bethesda, MD 20892–4415
robert@ln.nimh.nih.gov

E. Tory Higgins
Professor of Psychology and Professor of Management
Columbia University
406 Schermerhorn Hall
New York, NY 10027
tory@psych.columbia.edu

Marcel Kinsbourne
Professor of Psychology
New School University
New York, NY
Kinsbourne@aol.com

Patricia Kitcher
Professor and Chair of Philosophy
Mark van Doren Professor of the Humanities
Columbia University
Department of Philosophy
New York, NY 10027
Pk206@columbia.edu

Hedy Kober
Columbia University
Department of Psychology
406 Schermerhorn Hall
New York, NY 10027
hedy@psych.columbia.edu

Nate Kornell
Columbia University
Department of Psychology
406 Schermerhorn Hall
New York, NY 10027
nkornell@psych.columbia.edu

Charles Menzel
Language Research Center
Georgia State University
3401 Panthersville Road
Decatur, GA 30034
lrccrm@langate.gsu.edu

Janet Metcalfe
Professor of Psychology and of Neurobiology and Behavior
Columbia University
406 Schermerhorn Hall
New York, NY 10027
jm348@columbia.edu

Katherine Nelson
Distinguished Professor of Psychology (Emerita)
City University of New York Graduate Center
50 Riverside Drive #4B
New York, NY 10024
knelson@gc.cuny.edu

Bennett L. Schwartz
Associate Professor
Department of Psychology
Florida International University
bennett.schwartz@fiu.edu

J. David Smith
University at Buffalo, State University of New York
Department of Psychology
346 Park Hall
Buffalo, NY 14260
psysmith@buffalo.edu

Lisa K. Son
Barnard College
Department of Psychology
3009 Broadway
New York, NY 10027
lson@barnard.edu

Herbert S. Terrace
Professor of Psychology and Psychiatry
Columbia University
406 Schermerhorn Hall
New York, NY 10027
terrace@columbia.edu

Endel Tulving
Rotman Research Institute of Baycrest Centre
3560 Bathurst Street
North York, Ontario, Canada M6A 2A1
tulving@psych.utoronto.ca

Introduction: From Descartes to Darwin and Beyond

Herbert S. Terrace & Janet Metcalfe

> We must . . . admit that there is a much wider interval between one of
> the lowest fishes . . . and one of the higher apes, than between and ape
> and man; yet this interval . . . is filled up by numberless gradations.
>
> Darwin, *The Descent of Man*

The central issue in this volume is where self-reflective consciousness
should be situated among the numberless gradations hypothesized
by Darwin. One can ask, perhaps too simplistically, did self-reflective
consciousness evolve before or after language? A better question would
be, which gradations of self-reflective consciousness require language
and which do not?

Discussions of self-reflective consciousness inevitably refer to Descartes's dictum, "I think, therefore I am":

> because our senses sometimes deceive us, I wanted to focus exclusively on
> the search for truth, I thought it was necessary to do the exact opposite,
> and reject as absolutely false everything in which I could imagine the
> slightest doubt and to see, as a result, if anything remained among my
> beliefs that was completely indubitable. Thus, because our sense some-
> times deceives us, I decided to assume that nothing was the way the senses
> made us imagine it. And because there are some people who make mis-
> takes in reasoning and commit logical fallacies even in the simplest geo-
> metrical proofs, and I thought that I was as subject to mistakes as any-
> one else, I rejected as false all the arguments that I had previously accepted
> as demonstrations. Finally, since I thought we could have all the same
> thoughts while asleep, as we have while we are awake, although none of
> them is true at the same time, I decided to pretend that nothing that ever
> entered my mind was any more true than the illusions of my dreams. But
> I noticed immediately afterwards, that, while I thus wished to think that
> everything was false, it was necessarily the case that I, who was thinking
> this, was something. When I noticed this truth—*I think, therefore I am*—was

so firm and certain that all the most extravagant assumptions of the sceptics were unable to shake it. (Descartes, 1637/1999, pp. 24–25)

What we would like to explore in this book is, how and when did the kind of self-reflective consciousness that led Descartes to his "I think, therefore I am" evolve? To what extent is the ability to doubt what one knows, to deny or affirm one's beliefs, to judge one's own memories and percepts, to comment on one's dreams, to recollect and reflect upon one's own past uniquely human? Can animals, other than humans, think in this manner, or is their "thinking" utterly bound to their stimulus environments? Our goal is a rapprochement between the Cartesian view, emphasizing the critical importance of this particular kind of consciousness but according it only to humans, and the Darwinian view, which sees all human capabilities, including this one, as having discoverable precursors in other animals.

Descartes maintained that animals are unable to engage in the kind of self-reflection that led to his own "I think, therefore I am" because they lack language:

> For it is very noticeable that there are no human beings so unintelligent and stupid, including even mad people, who are incapable of arranging different words and composing from them an utterance by which they make their thoughts understood; whereas there is no other animal, no matter how perfectly and favourably born it may be, which acts similarly. (Descartes, 1637/1999, p. 41)

He argued that an animal's behavior consists entirely of instinctive and mechanical reactions to their environments. The fluent use of language was taken, by Descartes, as both evidence for self-reflective consciousness and proof that only humans have it. In this volume, we contest the tight linkage between language and self-reflection assumed by Descartes. Even though animals lack the ability to communicate grammatically, they may be able to examine features of their own mental life and then respond to them appropriately. Language and self-reflection need not be synonymous.

Darwin wrote sparingly about the evolution of language, but he argued that animals are intelligent creatures and that there was a continuum of cognitive abilities across species, humans included. So confident was Darwin (1859) about the overlap between human and animal intelligence that he predicted, "In the distant future ... Psychology will be based on a new foundation ... Light will be thrown on the origin of man and his history" (p. 311).

Darwin was right about the distant future. It took more than 100 years for cognitive psychology to show much interest in the theory of evolution. It is, of course, true that comparative psychology is based on the theory of evolution and that many comparative psychologists have argued that the principles of conditioning could explain all behavior and cognition, including language (e.g., Thorndike, Pavlov, Hull, and Skinner). Indeed, behaviorism was so influential during the first half of the twentieth century that many investigators of human cognition applied the terminology of conditioning to their own subject matter (e.g., weakening of a stimulus-response bond instead of forgetting; mediated generalization instead of semantic network, etc.).

It is now widely recognized that the assumptions of behaviorism were grandiose, even in the case of animal behavior. As many chapters of this book attest, the thriving subdiscipline of animal cognition owes more to the conceptual language of human cognition than it does to principles of conditioning. There remains, however, the question that has haunted the theory of evolution from its earliest moments: How did this pinnacle of human mental life—self-reflective consciousness—evolve, and how much does it depend on language?

In recent years, negative results of various ape language projects (Terrace, 1985; Terrace, Petitto, Sanders, & Bever, 1979) and broad advances in animal cognition suggest that Descartes was right about the uniqueness of language but that he was wrong about an animal's capacity for thought and self-reflection. Animals have been shown to engage in some kinds of thinking without language (Roberts, 1998; Shettleworth, 1998; Wynne, 2001). Even so, that is a far cry from a claim that any animal, other than the human one, would ever arrive at the conclusion "I think, therefore I am." But once the tight relationship between thought and language is relaxed, Darwin's continuity hypothesis becomes testable. Recent research about primate metacognition—much of which is presented and discussed in this volume—lends credence to Darwin's conjecture that psychologists may eventually identify gradations in animal intelligence, even those from which human self-reflective consciousness evolved.

The idea of this book emerged from discussions we (HT and JM) had about the implications of experiments on metacognition in primates for a rapprochement between animal and human cognition. To be clear about our usage of cognition and metacognition, we will start by defining our terms. By *cognition*, we are referring to the science of representations, specifically to theories about the features of various types of representations and about how they are used. Representations free us from the constraints of the present environment in the sense that they allow us to think of objects that are not physically present. They have properties that philosophers describe as "intentional," not in the sense of one's motivations, but rather in the sense that representations can be differentiated from the objects in the world to which they refer. Thus, at a minimum, cognition implies that a person or an animal is able to represent some object or event (X) and then use its representation of X, in the absence of X, to solve a problem. A familiar example is the representation of a sample that a subject uses when performing a delayed matching-to-sample task. The only way for the subject to decide whether a probe is the same as the sample is to compare the probe with a mental representation of the sample (Blough, 1959).

There is abundant evidence that nonhuman primates (and other animals) can form representations and use them to solve problems (see Terrace, 1984, and Wasserman, 1993, for reviews). There is also evidence that animals can make judgments about the relative magnitude of environmental events, for example, that A is larger (or smaller) than B (McGonigle & Chalmers, 1996). These separate abilities can be combined to allow a person or an animal to engage in *metacognition*, a process for making judgments about a representation of X. Thus, metacognition implies representations of other representations, as opposed to representations of environmental events.

When investigating metacognition, it is important to keep in mind that the separate abilities to represent X and to make judgments about X do not automatically translate into the ability to make metacognitive judgments. At a minimum, metacognition implies the *coordination* of those abilities. Recent experiments on monkeys and dolphins have reported evidence that, some have argued, satisfy the criterion of being metacognitive (Smith, Shields, & Washburn, 2003). Whether this evidence truly qualifies for the term self-reflection, in the sense so central to human identity, provides much of the interesting subtext of the current volume.

Much of the evidence for animal metacognition parallels research on confidence judgments by humans—evidence that has been cited in theories of human metacognition and its relationship to other cognitive abilities. Should the standard be the same (or lower or higher) for accepting animals as metacognitive beings as it is for deciding that humans are acting metacognitively?

Evidence of metacognition in animals also raises the question, does metacognition require consciousness? Finally, if one can reflect upon one's own thought processes, perhaps, by extension, one can also reflect on the thought processes of conspecifics—thereby exhibiting what has been called theory of mind, the attribution of a thinking mind to creatures other than oneself. This ability to understand and take the perspective of the other is, perhaps, the most fundamental requirement of language, being even more basic than grammatical capabilities. One would expect to see this particular metacognitive capability emerge prior to language, and to be the basis for the latter.

When viewed against the background of behaviorism, evidence of cognition in animals, let alone metacognition, is a remarkable development that requires a redefinition of the boundary between animal and human cognition. Defining the nature of that boundary and the territories that lie on either side was the focus of a conference we organized on that topic, The Missing Link in Cognition: Origins of Self-Reflective Consciousness, which was held at Columbia University on April 20–22, 2002. Each chapter of this book was written by a participant in that conference.

Why organize a conference on self-knowing consciousness? We had two reasons. One was the recent surge of interest in metacognition in nonhuman primates and children. The second was the concept of self-knowing or autonoetic consciousness that Endel Tulving (2002) introduced to describe the human ability to move back in time to recollect past events, and forward in time to anticipate future events.

The concept of autonoetic consciousness, as Tulving calls it, seemed tantalizingly close to the construct of self-reflective consciousness and metacognition with which we were initially concerned. Was this just a clang association, or is Tulving's autonoetic consciousness, which depends critically on episodic memory, really tightly related to what was being studied as metacognitive ability? We suggest that the evolution of metacognition, and preliminary forms of remembering past events, sets the stage for the appearance of theory of mind and eventually full-blown self-reflective consciousness, episodic memory, and language, which presupposes both the ability to take the other person's perspective and the ability to travel mentally in time through one's own past and future. Thus, instead of focusing on language, we here consider the more fundamental capabilities from which language emerged—the origins of self-reflective consciousness.

In the interest of full disclosure, we should make clear that we lack a crisp definition of self-reflective consciousness. Finding one was one of the main goals of the conference we organized. To help us achieve that goal, we invited participants who had expertise in various aspects of the phylogenetic and/or ontogenetic development of self-reflective consciousness. Roughly half of the participants were investigators of primate cognition: Josep Call, David Smith, Robert Hampton, Lisa Son and Nate Kornell, and Herbert Terrace. The remaining participants approached the topic of self-knowing consciousness from empirical, theoretical, and philosophical analyses of the human cognition: Tory Higgins, Marcel Kinsbourne, Patricia Kitcher, Janet Metcalfe, Katherine Nelson, and Endel Tulving. From these lineups, it may be tempting to assume that the participants coalesced into rival "animal" and "human" camps, each advocating their own party line. That no such party lines emerged is a testament to the open minds with which conference participants discussed the concept of self-knowing consciousness and its potential as a bridge between animal and human cognition. Not that there was complete agreement. That everything was open for debate is perhaps the only point on which there was complete consensus. But these disputes were nondogmatic, always productively honing in on the issues at stake.

Chapter 1, by Endel Tulving, describes the link between episodic memory and self-reflective consciousness (or, in his terminology, autonoetic consciousness). Autonoetic conscious is needed to allow a person to travel mentally through his or her own personal past, free of the immediate stimulus environment. Tulving also delineates the relation between this kind of episodic memory and the ability to project into the future. In Tulving's view, the latter is the kernel of consciousness that is necessary for culture. Accordingly, the evolutionary significance of the ability to think about the future and its importance for human society cannot be overestimated. Tulving also suggests a practical test, the "spoon test," as a method for determining, without the use of language, whether a person or animal possesses autonoetic consciousness.

Chapter 7, by Patricia Kitcher, provides a philosophical perspective on self-consciousness, contributing a historical grounding for modern theories. Kitcher assesses the extent to which animals might be self-conscious by applying two epistemological criteria to their behavior. The first relates to episodic memory (cf. chapters 1, 8, and 9) and was originally suggested by Locke in his discussion of human memory and its relation to "moral responsibility." The second relates to metacognition as an example of Kant's concept of "epistemic self-improvement" (cf. chapters 2, 10, 12, and 13). In the case of moral responsibility, Kitcher asks whether an animal could think back to a past action that was punished and try to make amends if given the opportunity. She discusses de Waal's observations of reconciliation by chimpanzees following various fights, some recent, others not so recent. In the case of epistemic self-improvement, Kitcher asks whether animals can notice when they lack sufficient information to solve a problem and then proceed to obtain that information. Josep Call (chapter 13) presents empirical evidence of that ability in chimpanzees and other apes.

In chapter 2, Janet Metcalfe and Hedy Kober discuss an animal's capacity for self-reflective consciousness by assessing an overarching capability that they call the "projectable self." Animals that have a projectable self can travel mentally in time (back into their personal past or forward into their imagined future) and also in space (e.g., taking the mental position of another animal and thereby exhibiting theory of mind). Interestingly, the ability to deceive is thought to require projection, insofar as one must know what another individual knows (an individual that has both a different mind and spatial perspective from one's own), in order to mislead it. Metcalfe and Kober argue that the first step in the attainment of projectable self is metacognition—the ability of one mental subsystem to view another. This coordinated system, then, further develops so that it can mentally view mental representations that are not part of the here and now.

Thus, simple metacognition should evolve before episodic memory and theory of mind as, in fact, seems to be the case.

In chapter 4, Katherine Nelson details how self-reflective consciousness, as one particular kind of consciousness among several others, emerges during the development of the child. She stresses the importance of language, and particularly that it is narrative structure that promotes the emergence of this kind of consciousness. Episodic memory is thought to depend, in this view, on a self-narrative that is itself dependent upon sophisticated language abilities that do not display themselves until at least late toddlerhood. Nelson skillfully weaves the interconnection between language and self-reflective consciousness, with episodic memory, in Tulving's sense of the capability of traveling into one's personal past. Together they help to define a sense of self.

Marcel Kinsbourne, in chapter 5, strongly supports the continuity view of the evolution of self-consciousness. He argues that self-reflective consciousness is not an autonomous "add on" that is controlled by a particular module of the brain. Instead, he presents a gradualist view of the emergence of self-reflective consciousness that is based on increments in freedom from the control of stimuli from the immediate environment, in sustainable attention, in self-control, and in working memory. Kinsbourne also argues that awareness and self-reflective consciousness occur when diffuse cortical networks are activated long enough to function as a representation that an organism can discriminate. Kinsbourne concludes that it is the sustainability of activity in particular networks of the brain in combination with a bodily sense of self that underlies self-reflective consciousness.

Chapter 6, by Tory Higgins, is devoted to the self implied by one's personality. Higgins does not relate this concept of self to Descartes's. It is therefore unclear how the self of one's personality is related to one's phenomenological self or to a person's remembered past experiences, as formulated in Tulving's concept of autonoetic consciousness. Higgins's chapter does, however, pose the question: Is knowing about one's self—in the sense of a self digest or even of having episodic memories, isomorphic with the state that Descartes took to be indisputable—the state of "self"-reflective consciousness?

David Smith, in chapter 10, presents evidence for metacognitive abilities of monkeys and dolphins from experiments on discrimination learning in which they can respond *yes, no,* or *uncertain.* There has been considerable controversy, both at our conference and in recent articles, as to whether an uncertainty response is really the same as Cartesian "doubt." Smith was the first researcher to systematically investigate metacognition in animals, and his and his colleagues' provocative experiments—whether we agree or not that it really is metacognition proper—remain seminal in this endeavor.

Rob Hampton (chapter 11) has devised a paradigm that many agree has the potential to reveal true metacognition in animals, if such exists. The main controversies surrounding Smith's paradigm centered on whether what he referred to as metacognitive judgments were simply judgments of extant stimuli that are present when the subject responds *uncertain*. To address this issue, Hampton used a delayed-match-to-sample paradigm in which the subject has to decide whether to submit to a test of the sample *after* the stimulus display itself has been removed but before the test has been presented. By using a modified version of the match-to-sample paradigm, Hampton showed that his star monkey (Shepard) was able to make valid metacognitive judgments.

Lisa Son and Nate Kornell further extended Hampton's approach of asking a monkey to respond metacognitively (chapter 12). Son and Kornell required their subjects to respond on all trials, easy and hard. However, a subject's reward was not contingent on the accuracy of its response but on the appropriateness of its level of confidence in the accuracy of its response. After each trial, subjects were required to select a high- or a low-confidence icon. If they chose the high-confidence icon after responding correctly to the problem at hand, they received a large reward (of tokens). If they chose that high-confidence icon after making an incorrect response, they lost a large number of tokens. Having shown that their subjects chose the high- and low-confidence icons appropriately, Son and Kornell argue that the metacognitive ability of monkeys is similar to that observed in human subjects in experiments that use the confidence judgment paradigm.

Josep Call investigated a different aspect of metacognition. He asked whether a nonhuman primate would seek information it needs to solve some problem. Call hypothesized that if a nonhuman primate knows that it needs information, it would engage in information-seeking behavior before responding. In chapter 13, Call describes experiments showing that orangutans, chimps, and gorillas systematically seek information they need to respond correctly on some task. In contrast, phylogenetically older animals such as dogs do not exhibit such behavior.

In chapter 8, Charles Menzel addresses an issue raised by Endel Tulving. Do nonhuman primates have episodic memory? As evidence that they do, Menzel describes some experiments in which a female chimpanzee (Panzee) engages in behavior that was previously thought to be possible only in human beings. For example, Panzee would watch a video monitor showing one of her trainers hiding a piece of food outside in an area with which she is familiar. Panzee then indicated to a different trainer, who was unaware of where the food was hidden, the exact location of that food, and also coaxed that trainer to go outside and get it for her. She did this even when there was a considerable delay between the time at which she observed the first trainer hiding some food and the point at which the second trainer appeared. Menzel also describes a fascinating anecdote in which Panzee, who some consider to be a genius chimp, passed Tulving's spoon test.

Bennett Schwartz (chapter 9) also investigated episodic memory in a nonhuman primate. His subject was a circus gorilla named King, who used symbols to identify several foods and to name several of his trainers. Schwartz reported that King could recall what food he ate, after delays as long as a day, in contexts that were radically different from the context in which he ate the food. King was also able to report the name of the trainer who gave him the food to another trainer (who was not aware of the correct answer) at a better-than-chance level of accuracy. Schwartz's chapter not only presents a new paradigm for studying episodic memory in a nonhuman primate but also serves to sharpen the definition of what will and will not qualify as evidence of episodic memory.

Chapter 3, by Herbert Terrace, distinguishes between two types of intelligence in human and nonhuman primates. During the last 30 years, much evidence has accumulated that animals can perform complicated tasks that, on the one hand, cannot be explained by the principles of conditioning and that, on the other hand, do not rise to the level of language. For example, Terrace describes experiments on sequence learning in which rhesus macaques learned what are arguably the most difficult lists ever mastered by a nonhuman primate, including apes that have been trained to use linguistic and numerical symbols. Terrace argues, however, that the type of intelligence used to solve a problem in a nonsocial setting, no matter how complex, is different from the kind of intelligence needed for self-reflective consciousness and language. The latter assumes some ability to read a conspecific's mental states rather than its behavior. Terrace attributes the failure of ape language projects to the failure to recognize that the major function of language is to share and exchange information and that sharing and exchanging information requires an awareness of another's mind. He concludes that the gap between animal and human intelligence is less mysterious once the significance of self-recognizing consciousness is recognized as a critical step in the evolution of human intelligence.

ACKNOWLEDGMENTS We thank Professor Robert Belknap, director of the University Seminars at Columbia University, for underwriting the major costs of the conference held at Columbia University on April 20–22, 2002, The Missing

Link in Cognition: Origins of Self-Reflective Consciousness. We also thank President George Rupp for allowing us to convene the conference in the Trustees Room and Professor Don Hood, Chair and Professor of the Psychology Department, for their generous support. Special thanks to Catherine Carlin from Oxford University Press for her help, encouragement, and fine editing. Some of the costs of this conference were provided by NIMH grants MH40462 to Herbert Terrace and MH60637 to Janet Metcalfe. We also thank Lisa Son, Brady Butterfield, and Brigid Finn for their superb logistical efforts in making the conference run as smoothly as it did.

REFERENCES

Blough, D. S. (1959). Delayed matching in the pigeon. *Journal of the Experimental Analysis of Behavior, 2*, 151–160.

Darwin, C. (1859). *On the origin of species.* London: Mercury.

Darwin, C. (1998). *The descent of man.* Amherst, NY: Prometheus. (Original work published 1874)

Descartes, R. (1999). *Discourse on method* (D. M. Clark, Trans.). New York: Penguin. (Original work published 1637)

McGonigle, B., & Chalmers, M. (1996). The ontology of order. In L. Smith (Ed.), *Critical readings on Piaget* (pp. 279–311). New York: Routledge.

Roberts, W. (1998). *Principles of animal cognition.* Boston: McGraw-Hill.

Shettleworth, S. J. (1998). *Cognition, evolution, and behavior.* Oxford, UK: Oxford University Press.

Smith, D. J., Shields, W. E., & Washburn, D. (2003). The comparative psychology of uncertainty monitoring and metacognition. *Behavioral and Brain Sciences, 26*, 317–373.

Terrace, H. S. (1984). Animal cognition. In H. L. Roitblat, T. G. Bever, & H. S. Terrace (Eds.), *Animal cognition* (pp. 7–28). Hillsdale, NJ: Lawrence Erlbaum.

Terrace, H. S. (1985). In the beginning was the name. *American Psychologist, 40*, 1011–1028.

Terrace, H. S., Petitto, L. A., Sanders, R. J., & Bever, T. G. (1979). Can an ape create a sentence? *Science, 206*, 891–902.

Tulving, E. (2002). Episodic memory: From mind to brain. *Annual Review of Physiology, 53*, 1–25.

Wasserman, E. (1993). Comparative cognition: Toward a general understanding of cognition in behavior. *Psychological Science, 4*, 156–161.

Wynne, C. D. L. (2001). *Animal cognition: The mental lives of animals.* New York: Palgrave.

The Missing Link in Cognition

1

Episodic Memory and Autonoesis: Uniquely Human?

Endel Tulving

> The mental faculties of man and the lower animals do not differ in kind, although immensely in degree.
>
> C. Darwin, *The Descent of Man*

Among the games that scientists play, one of the best known is virtual tug-of-war. Two teams position themselves at the opposite ends of an imaginary rope that represents a continuum of nature, grab their end of the rope, and try to pull the other team over the center line. If they succeed, which actually seldom happens, they would declare their end of the rope the "truth," and themselves the winners.

One long-lasting virtual tug-of-war has to do with the nature of the similarities and differences between the species, especially those between humans and other animals. The existence of the basic similarities has been accepted by intelligent people ever since Darwin's theory of "descent with modification" survived the harshest scrutiny that any set of scientific ideas has had to face, but the battle over the differences continues unabated. The differences typically have to do with humans and the species that occupy the neighboring branches on the evolutionary tree—sometimes chimpanzees and gorillas, sometimes all "greater apes," sometimes all "nonhuman primates," sometimes even other "nonhuman animals," or simply "brutes," as Darwin called all of them. And the two ends of the rope are called "qualitative" versus "quantitative," or, as Darwin put it, "kind" or "degree."

The contestants at one end of the rope believe that there are no essential differences between humans and the various "others," and that whatever differences may seem to exist are either minor or uninteresting in the broader scheme of things. Those at the other end believe that in addition to many (uninteresting or less interesting) similarities between humans and others, there are some truly fundamental differences, that there indeed may be "gaps." So they keep tugging, without realizing that even when one or the other team seems more successful at a given time, the rope itself remains unchanged.

The contributors to this volume deal with the issue of similarities and differences in the nature of consciousness, or "higher mental faculties," of humans and other animals. Many of them will feel like grabbing one end of the rope rather than the other. In my own case, I take a position that others will want to interpret as revealing a preference for differences in kind. But in this case too, the rope will remain whole.

In this essay, I argue that only human beings possess "autonoetic" episodic memory and the ability to mentally travel into the past and into the future, and that in that sense they are unique. Having thus identified myself with one end of the rope, let me hasten to clarify my position. It is important to note that my essay is not meant as delayed rearguard action in support of the myth of *scala naturae*. It is not a campaign for human superiority. It is meant simply as an acknowledgement of both similarities and differences in animal kingdom, an acknowledgment that sometimes comes hard to life scientists, as it comes hard to those who think only of human uniqueness.

At the outset, it is useful to keep in mind the fact that uniqueness is by no means unique to humans. Every species is unique in the sense that it possesses features and traits that other species do not. Some of these unique features may be more conspicuous than others, and some may be better known than others, but the basic principle remains the same: If there were no differences between Species A and B, they would be the same species.

Scorpions locate their prey by seismic vibrations; bats can catch small insects by echolocation in midflight in the darkness of the night; electric fish can perform comparable feats through electrolocation, in ways that scientists have yet to completely fathom; migrating birds know how to reach destinations thousands of miles away. The list of these and similar kinds of spectacular achievements by creatures of nature can go on and on. But neither such unique features nor many less conspicuous differences rule out the general principle of broad phylogenetic continuity. Equally important, broad phylogenetic continuity does not rule out differences between the species, even those that to an external observer may seem like gaps. Diversity in nature can take many diverse forms.

The scientific question of interest is not whether the human mind is similar to or different from those of other animals. Nor is it whether phylogenetic evolution is continuous or whether there are gaps in it. The answer to both questions is either "neither" or "both," and neither of these answers is terribly informative. A more appropriate question is how and in what sense are the minds of two species similar and how and in what sense are they different, or, how and in what sense the phylogenetic evolution is continuous and in what sense it is not. In the context of these sorts of questions, it may even be appropriate to speculate, as some contributors to this volume do, how, why, and when the current situation might have come about.

It ought to be completely noncontroversial to say that nonhuman animals are conscious, that they have memory, that they can learn, that they can think, that they know what happens in their world—in brief, that they are "intelligent" (Weiskrantz, 1985). It ought to be equally noncontroversial to say that the consciousness of other species is probably different from ours, that their awareness of the world is different from ours, that they are more skilled at some and less skilled at other forms of behavior than we are, and that in general their intelligence is different from ours. Finally, everybody also knows, of course, that in terms of the ultimate biological criterion, survival, an overwhelming majority of the other species are as capable and successful in their world as we are in ours (Darwin, 1874/1998; Macphail, 1998; Shettleworth, 1998).

It is against the backdrop of these musings—the premises of the argument—that I present the thesis (hypothesis) of this essay: Human beings possess a form of memory (episodic memory) and a form of consciousness (autonoetic consciousness, or "autonoesis") that no other animals do. Thus, the thesis is that these two aspects of the mind are unique in humans, in the sense that the mental capacities that define them do not exist in quite the same full-fledged form in other species. They do not exist in insects, in birds, in mice or rats, in cats or dogs, and not even in gorillas and chimps.

Some see the thesis as representing self-evident truth; others may think of it as woefully misguided; still others view it as little more than idle speculation that cannot possibly get us anywhere. Indeed, it is possible to argue that no essential progress has been made toward resolving the issues involved for more than a hundred years. So why try again? There are at least two reasons. One, much of the previous debate has involved issues that have been formulated too broadly to allow an incisive approach. Narrowing it down may help. Two, today we have a bit more evidence relevant to the issues than was available yesterday. Therefore, it may be worth looking at it again.

In this essay, I narrow the issue down to one kind of consciousness (autonoetic) that characterizes the workings of one kind of memory (episodic), and discuss it in light of the empirical findings that can be seen as pertinent to it. The essay consists of five sections, plus a summary:

1. Thesis: Mental time travel exists in humans only.
2. Theory: This thesis is a part of a more comprehensive story of the human brain/mind, the theory of episodic memory.
3. Data: People exist who are fully competent mentally, who have no episodic memory, yet manage to do quite well in staying alive.
4. Analysis: What we know about episodic memory in animals.
5. Resolution: It is in principle possible to obtain solid evidence for the existence of episodic memory in nonverbal organisms.

THE THESIS

In 1983, I wrote a book titled *Elements of Episodic Memory,* in which I discussed the possibility that episodic memory is functionally different from other kinds of memory. The book opened with the following paragraph:

> Remembering past events is a universally familiar experience. It is also a uniquely human one. As far as we know, members of no other species possess quite the same ability to experience again now, in a different situation and perhaps in a different form, happenings from the past, and know that the experience refers to an event that occurred in another time and in another place. Other members of the animal kingdom can learn, benefit from experience, acquire the ability to adjust and adapt, to solve problems and make decisions, but they cannot travel back into the past in their own minds. (Tulving, 1983, p. 1)

This paragraph set out, somewhat guardedly and rather fortuitously, of course, the main point of the present chapter—*episodic memory is uniquely human.* Reading it 20 years later, it is not difficult to see that it shows its age—I would not say exactly the same thing now. By and large, however, it does not seem to be terribly out of line.

Back in 1983, the claim about the differences between humans and nonhuman animals was introduced primarily as a device of getting a head start on the formidable task of trying to explain to the reader what the new kind of memory—"episodic memory"—was all about. At the time, the study of human memory was still trying to shake the powerful behaviorist or behavioralist (Leahey, 1987) influences of the past, influences in which the idea of unity of all learning and memory, between and within the species, held a dominant position. The throwaway comment on humans sharing not quite all of their learning and memory capabilities with their furry and feathered cousins was supposed to provide a graphic description of the differences between episodic and other kinds of memory.

The casual reference to "mental time travel" similarly served as a device for distancing episodic from other forms of memory. From the beginning (Tulving, 1972) it had been useful to contrast episodic memory with what, for historical reasons, was called "semantic" memory. Because semantic memory has many features in common with episodic memory—as we will see in greater detail later in the chapter—it was easy for people not to take any proposed differences seriously. The idea of mental time travel was pressed into service as a device that might help others see the difference: Episodic memory did, whereas semantic memory did not, necessarily involve any such time travel.

Finally, the paragraph mentions, even if somewhat indirectly, an idea about episodic memory that sometimes tends to be overlooked, an idea that turns out to be relevant to the issue of the relation between episodic and "episodic-like" memory (Clayton & Dickinson, 1998; Clayton, Bussey, & Dickinson, 2003). The idea is that a happy owner of episodic memory can think about personal happenings ("what") that took place at another time ("when") and in another place ("where")—that is, thinking in Place P1 about a personal experience in Place P2. The ability to "mentally travel in space" is, as we will see, a property of semantic (declarative) memory and is therefore a precondition for mental travel in time, in keeping with the general idea that episodic memory "grows out of," and represents an extension of, semantic memory (Tulving, 1984). Mental "space travel" (imagining different spatial locations) does not require mental time travel (imagining oneself at different times). The present point is that mental time travel always occurs not only in subjective time but also in mental space, and that the mental space of the remembered past and imagined future may be different from the present space. Individuals with (autonoetic) episodic memory can, if the situation calls for it, think here and now about personal happenings in other places and other times. Therefore, if we ask whether other animals have episodic memory, we ask, among other things, whether they can also do so.

As it turned out, until recently not much fuss was made about what the 1983 paragraph said about episodic memory of other animals. Not only had similar thoughts been expressed by many others, they were peripheral to the main message of the book. Just about the only person who rose to defend the impugned repute of our furry friends was David Olton. He had proposed the distinction between working memory and reference memory (Olton, Becker, & Handelmann, 1979, 1980; Olton & Pappas, 1979), and he suggested that these two parallelled the distinction between episodic and semantic memory (Olton, 1984, 1985). At the time it was easy enough to agree with him, as I did (Tulving, 1983, pp. 118–119). Now, thirty years later, the issues have become a bit more complicated, as they frequently do in living science. Let us consider two relevant points.

First, there is no proof that the thesis is true. Indeed, because of its logical nature, it will always remain impossible to prove its truth. The thesis is based on the absence of evidence contrary to it, and its relatively smooth integration into a larger picture for which supporting evidence is available. The absence of evidence, as everyone knows, is not evidence for the absence, and that is why more evidence is needed. The fit between the thesis and the larger picture (the theory of episodic memory) can be seen as a part of "more evidence." Science does not progress by proving hypotheses true to begin with; it progresses by proving hypotheses false. In the present case, too, it is possible to prove the hypothesis false. In the final section of the essay, I make a suggestion as to what would constitute evidence that the hypothesis is untenable.

Second, the neuropsychological and developmental findings that I summarize in this chapter are relevant to the argument in at least three senses. First, they help delineate more precisely what the mental faculties are that, according to the thesis, nonhuman animals do not have. Second, they illustrate the procedures used to distinguish between different kinds of learning and memory. If there were no way to separate (autonoetic) episodic memory from other forms of memory, the claim that nonhuman animals do not have it would be hollow. No one has much doubted the usefulness of the concept of episodic memory for classificatory ("bookkeeping") purposes, but there has been considerable resistance to the idea that it represents anything special in biological reality. Nevertheless, steady progress in the accumulation of pertinent evidence makes the claim that only humans have episodic memory more readily tractable. Third, the findings are also relevant insofar as they help support the idea that episodic memory is not necessary (even) for humans. If so, the proposition that it does not exist in other animals is less shocking than it would be otherwise. It also would make more acute the question as to why episodic memory may have evolved.

It is reasonable to assume that episodic memory evolved recently, although there is as yet no way to find out whether the assumption is true and, if so, how recently. Because chimpanzees, our closest relatives on the evolutionary tree, do not have humanlike episodic memory, it makes sense to assume that our common ancestors did not have it either. The alternative possibility, that it had evolved in other species too but was somehow lost in the course of evolution, is difficult to imagine. We will return to this issue presently.

THEORY: EPISODIC MEMORY AND AUTONOETIC CONSCIOUSNESS

Most readers of this volume know that episodic memory has to do with remembering personally experienced events. But there are variations on the theme. Therefore, before we can undertake the task of evaluating the presence of episodic memory in nonhuman animals, the concept needs to be sharpened. Just saying that it concerns personal happenings is too vague and leaves too much room for nonfocused debate. We need to be as clear as possible about the kind of memory that I am denying to our feathered and furry friends.

Let us begin with a thumbnail sketch, or definition, of episodic memory. Because definitions do play a role in the study of nature, even in today's dominant Zeitgeist of "exploratory science," and because definitions have a habit of changing, it is helpful to identify definitions in a way that sets them apart from others in their class. This is why I refer to the present definition as "episodic memory—2004":

> Episodic memory is a recently evolved, late developing, and early deteriorating brain/mind (neurocognitive) memory system. It is oriented to the past, more vulnerable than other memory systems to neuronal dysfunction, and probably unique to humans. It makes possible mental time travel through subjective time—past, present, and future. This mental time travel allows one, as an "owner" of episodic memory ("self"), through the medium of autonoetic awareness, to remember one's own previous "thought-about" experiences, as well as to "think about" one's own possible future experiences. The operations of episodic memory require, but go beyond, the semantic memory system. Retrieving information from episodic memory ("remembering") requires the establishment and maintenance of a special mental set, dubbed episodic "retrieval mode." The neural components of episodic memory comprise a widely distributed network of cortical and subcortical brain regions that overlap with and extend beyond the networks subserving other memory systems. The essence of episodic memory lies in the conjunction of three concepts—self, autonoetic awareness, and subjective time.

Note that episodic memory is conceptualized as a (hypothetical) brain/mind (neurocognitive) system, as indeed is semantic memory, mentioned here in passing. The concept of "memory system" as such has been discussed elsewhere (Nadel, 1994; Schacter & Tulving, 1994; Sherry & Schacter, 1987), and attempts to describe episodic memory in system terms have been made previously (Tulving, 1985a, 1998, 2002b; Tulving & Markowitsch, 1998; Wheeler, Stuss, & Tulving, 1997; see also Nyberg et al., 2000).

Given, then, that the term *episodic memory* in this essay refers to the "episodic memory system," it is important to note what the term does not refer to. It does not refer to a particular kind of memory task, or a particular kind of performance measure in a task, or a particular kind of stored information, or a particular kind of phenomenal experience, or to any alternative sense in which it sometimes appears in the contemporary literature. All these other senses are related to episodic memory, but they are not identical with it (Tulving, 2000). A great deal of confusion and futile debate can be avoided by keeping the distinction between episodic memory and related terms firmly in mind.

Like all other systems, episodic memory consists of a number of interacting neural and cognitive components which together are capable of operating in a manner that the same components in isolation, or in different combinations, cannot. Like all other neurocognitive systems, it is complex and not easily summarized in a few words. It is defined in terms of criteria such as the system's function—what the system does, how it works, the kind of "information" that it deals with, its relations to other systems, and its neural substrates (Schacter & Tulving, 1994; Schacter, Wagner, & Buckner, 2000; for a different conceptualization of memory systems, see Eichenbaum, 2000; Gaffan, 2001). Convergent dissociations, observed across tasks or subjects, play an important role in the identification of the properties of a memory system (Nyberg & Tulving, 1997), but they are not the only features of the definition.

An alternative to the classification of memory in terms of multiple systems is classification in terms of "kinds" (or "varieties") of memory (Roediger, Marsh, & Lee, 2002). The concept of "kinds" of memory, as dealt with by Roediger and his colleagues, is not the same as the concept of memory "systems" (Schacter & Tulving, 1994). For example, Roediger and his colleagues discuss episodic memory, as one of the different "kinds" of memory, primarily in terms of retention performance of healthy adults in experiments involving verbal to-be-remembered materials. In their conceptualization of episodic memory, it would be difficult to raise coherent questions about episodic memory's existence in animals, or to claim that animals do not have it.

Properties of Episodic Memory

Because the search for the identity of the constituent components of episodic memory has barely begun, not much is yet known about these components. An initial step in the appropriate direction, however, has been taken in the form of postulation of certain "functional properties" of episodic memory. An early, not completely successful attempt at such a formulation was made in Tulving (1983, table 3.1), at a time when few research findings were available to distinguish between episodic and other varieties of memory.

A somewhat more (empirically) disciplined list of the properties, or features, of episodic and semantic memory systems, modified from Wheeler et al. (1997), Tulving and Markowitsch (1998), and Griffiths, Dickinson, and Clayton (1999), is presented in table 1.1. The list consists of a number of key terms or brief phrases, each of which could be greatly extended. It is organized into two sublists.

Both sublists are necessary to convey the full scope of episodic memory. The sublist on the left gives the properties of episodic memory that it has in common with semantic memory, whereas the sublist

Table 1.1 Features of Episodic Memory

Semantic/Episodic Memory—Common Features	Episodic Memory—Unique Features
• Key function: Knowing—Registering, storing, and using sharable knowledge of the world	• Key function: Remembering—Conscious awareness of happenings in subjective time (chronesthesia)
• Multimodal input	• Makes possible mental time travel in both temporal directions, past and future
• Transmodal storage	• Operations accompanied by autonoetic conscious awareness
• Fast encoding operations—single-trial learning possible	
• Large, complex, highly structured storage	• Operations depend on a remembering self
• Stored information is representational—isomorphic with what is, or could be, in the world	• More recently evolved than other memory systems
• Stored information is propositionalizable	• Ontogenetic development lags behind other memory systems
• Stored information has truth value	• More vulnerable to disease, injury, and aging
• Stored information can be used as a basis of inferences	• Operations require the establishment and maintenance of a special neurocognitive set—episodic retrieval mode
• Information processing is highly sensitive to context	
• Stored information can be accessed flexibly	• Operations depend on semantic memory
• Stored information is expressed symbolically	• Episodic remembering implies semantic knowing, but semantic knowing does not imply remembering
• System is cognitive—contents can be thought about	
• Behavioral expression is optional and not obligatory	• Dependent on prefrontal cortex and other neocortical regions in a way that other systems are not
• Operations do not require awareness of time	
• Operations accompanied by noetic conscious awareness	• Probably unique to humans
• System interacts closely with other neurocognitive systems, such as those involved in language, affect, and reasoning	
• Dependent on widely distributed cortical and subcortical neural networks, including temporal lobe and diencephalic structures	
• Present in a wide range of animals; highly evolved in mammals and birds	

on the right gives "unique" properties of episodic memory, properties shared neither by semantic memory nor by any other memory system. The (partial) overlap between the properties of episodic and semantic memory reflects the idea that episodic memory evolved "out of" semantic memory (Tulving, 1984).

The two sublists imply that it is possible to define episodic memory broadly or narrowly. The broad definition comprises all the properties listed in table 1.1, both those on the left and those on the right. The narrow definition includes only the properties listed on the right.

The thumbnail sketch of "episodic memory—2004" presented earlier corresponds to the narrow definition. It is important to note that the thesis of this essay also applies only to the narrow ("unique") definition of episodic memory. It does not apply to the properties that episodic memory shares with semantic memory. Quite to the contrary, the shared properties, those that define semantic memory, do very well in describing learning and memory capacities possessed by many animals, including birds and mammals. Indeed, an important part of the argument here is that many behavioral feats in nonhuman animals that tend to be attributed to humanlike episodic memory are, according to theory, manifestations of a highly complex and powerful memory system, namely semantic (or declarative) memory.

It has been suggested elsewhere (Tulving & Markowitsch, 1998) that "declarative memory" (Squire, 1992; see also Squire & Kandel, 1999) can be thought of as representing features common to episodic and semantic memory, that is, features listed on the left in table 1.1. Defined along these lines, semantic (declarative) memory is a large, complex, multimodal system capable of fast ("single-trial") encoding operations. Information that it handles is representational and can be, even if it need not be, described in propositional format. The representational information has truth value: it corresponds to objects, events, relations, and states of the world. The information is accessible and expressible flexibly, that is, through different input and output routes, and it can serve as a basis of inferences about other objects, events, relations, and states of the world, those that may not have been directly experienced. The operations of semantic (declarative) memory are cognitive (not rigidly tied to behavior) and sensitive to context.

These characteristics of semantic (declarative) memory fit reasonably closely descriptions of declarative memory in the literature (Cohen, Poldrack, & Eichenbaum, 1997; Eichenbaum, 1997; Knowlton & Squire, 1995; Squire, 1987).

It is important to note that neither semantic nor episodic memory as defined here depends on language or any other symbol system for its operations, although both systems in humans can greatly benefit from language. "Semantic memory" is a designation that is what it is for purely historical reasons; a more fitting term for it is "knowledge of the world." Language may have played an important role in the evolution (or coevolution) of human semantic memory, and probably even more so in the evolution of episodic memory, and it can greatly facilitate the operations of memory and learning systems, but it is not necessary for such operations.

Relations Between Episodic and Semantic Memory

The two sublists of table 1.1 not only distinguish between two definitions of episodic memory, broad and narrow, they also help describe the relation between episodic and semantic memory. The thumbnail sketch earlier said that "the operations of episodic memory require, but go beyond, the semantic memory system." We can now say that episodic memory represents an extension of semantic memory, both in terms of its emergence in the course of evolution and in terms of its operations. This kind of relation between the two systems, initially sketched in terms of the "embeddedness" hypothesis (Tulving, 1984, p. 260), was later reformulated as the serial parallel independent (SPI) model (Tulving, 1993a, 1995).

The structure of the SPI model reflects the assumed sequence of the two kinds of memory in both phylogenetic evolution and ontogenetic development: semantic memory precedes episodic memory (Nelson, 1993, see also chapter 4, this volume; Perner & Ruffman, 1995; Suddendorf & Corballis, 1997; Wheeler et al., 1997). The importance of this feature of the model lies in the fact that it allows those organisms that have no episodic memory to acquire knowledge of the world, but it rules out acquisition of episodic information without semantic memory. That is, episodic memory is not necessary for the operation of any other memory and learning system. This is why nonhuman animals can do perfectly well without episodic memory.

The functional relations between episodic and semantic memory in the SPI model are process-specific, that is, the relations depend on the processes. Encoding processes are organized serially (S), storage processes in parallel (P), and retrieval processes in the two systems are independent (I). The seriality of encoding of information "into" episodic memory means that the information must be first processed in semantic memory and that, therefore, impairments of semantic memory have consequences for the operations of episodic memory. However, episodic memory is not required for encoding information into semantic memory: organisms with impaired or totally missing episodic memory (nonhuman animals, young children, some brain-damaged patients) are capable of acquiring (complex) knowledge about the world even if they cannot remember (autonoetically recollect) anything of their own past lives. In other words, seriality of encoding implies that only single dissociations are possible in encoding (Tulving, 1995). Parallellity of storage means that corresponding information may be stored in both systems. And independence of retrieval means that stored information can be retrieved from one system or the other system, or both, thus allowing for both single and double dissociations between retrieval of episodic and semantic information (for more details on SPI, see Tulving, 2001a).

Uniqueness of Episodic Memory

The features listed in the right-hand column in table 1.1 define the uniqueness of episodic memory. Four of them can be thought of as being central: (1) episodic memory's function, namely that of mental time travel, or "remembering"; (2) episodic memory's dependence on a remembering "self"; (3) the expression of such remembering through the self's autonoetic consciousness, or autonoesis; and (4) episodic memory's relation to subjectively apprehended time, or "chronesthesia" (Tulving, 2002a).

First, episodic memory's function is to enable mental time travel or remembering, that is, to make it possible for the rememberer to travel back in his or her mind to an earlier occasion or situation in the rememberer's life, and to mentally relive the experienced and thought-about happenings. Semantic memory cannot do so, at least not with a comparable efficacy. Episodic memory allows the individual to remember now, at Time 2, something about what happened at an earlier Time 1, as well as know what happened. Because the output of episodic memory can serve as an input into semantic as well as episodic memory, the remembering individuals can also know what happened on an occasion, even if they do not remember the happening or the occasion.

Only individuals who have episodic memory are capable of remembering past events, in the sense of mental time travel. Other cognitive memory systems may provide access to the past, including one's personal past, but they do so in the absence of autonoesis. For example, both healthy people and those with certain kinds of brain damage can recite autobiographical facts about themselves without necessarily remembering anything. Amnesic patients can tell stories about themselves that have to do with the past, but in doing so they rely on semantic memory ("personal semantic memory" as suggested by Cermak & O'Connor, 1983).

Sherry and Schacter (1987) have proposed that new memory systems evolve when existing systems cannot satisfy the adaptive needs of the organism. The proposal that episodic memory evolved to serve a function not served by other systems, including semantic memory, fits well into Sherry and Schacter's scheme.

Second, episodic memory differs from other kinds of memory in that its operations require a self. It is the self that engages in the mental activity that is referred to as mental time travel: there can be no travel without a traveler. If it is not self that does the traveling, then who, or what? "Self" and "self-awareness" are among those terms that are indispensable for discussing phenomena of the mind, yet have many meanings that are difficult to define and explicate (Kircher & Leube, 2003). We can think of self as the traveler who engages in mental time travel. Like other components of the system that is episodic memory, self too is defined in terms of its properties, and in terms of its relations to other components of the system.

Some thinkers prefer a philosophical framework for the scientific approach to mental life in which the phenomena to be explained are expressions of processes, but in which the entities that do the processing (agents) are not permitted. Thus, thinking occurs without thinkers, knowing without knowers, and consciousness without anyone being conscious. The idea is to avoid using structural terminology, because it is not fashionable these days. Besides, "self" sounds like the dreaded homunculus that needs to be exorcised by all means possible (Noelle, 2001). But until such time that we have better ways of explaining the phenomenal existences of things such as pain, smell, and recollection of the past, we need an agent such as self for the sake of the completeness of the story (theory). Eventually, self may turn out like phlogiston or aether—a convenient temporary prop. But the problem today is that the story of the mind is incomplete and awkward to tell if a concept like "self" is omitted from it. This is why it should not be exorcised yet.

Third, the conscious awareness that characterizes remembering is different from other forms of conscious awareness, and different in an unmistakable manner. When you remember an event, however vaguely, you are aware that the present experience is related to the past experience in a way that no other kind of experience is. You do not confuse it with perceiving, or imagining, or dreaming, or hallucinating, or having thoughts about what is or could be in the world. In order to be able to refer to the kind of conscious awareness that characterizes episodic remembering, the term "autonoetic consciousness" has been proposed (Tulving, 1985b; Wheeler et al., 1997). The term "autonoesis" was introduced later as a (shorter) synonym for "autonoetic consciousness" (Tulving, 2001b). Autonoesis refers to the kind of conscious awareness that characterizes conscious recollection of personal happenings. It refers to what William James (1890) probably had in mind when he talked about the "warmth and intimacy" of remembering one's past experiences. (The relation between consciousness and awareness is discussed in Tulving, 1993c; for a somewhat different conceptualization of consciousness and awareness, see Chalmers, 1996, especially pp. 28–29.)

Many organisms without episodic memory possess a highly functional semantic memory. Retrieval (use) of information from semantic memory occurs whenever an organism thinks about, or mentally represents, something that exists or could exist in the world. Such retrieval ("knowing") is accompanied by a form of conscious awareness that I refer to as noetic awareness. Both people and animals are fully capable of knowing things about the world, including things that occurred in their own past. The essential difference is between knowing that something is such and such, or occurs so and so, on the one hand, and remembering that one had a particular experience (witnessed, or felt, or thought something) in a particular place at a particular time. Neither the knowledge of the facts nor the experiencing of past events needs to be complete or accurate in any sense, of course. Nor is it necessary to assume that the distinction between knowing and remembering is always sharp. In real life, many thoughts a person has may have elements contributed by both the semantic memory (knowing) system and the episodic memory (remembering) system.

Episodic Memory, Autonoesis, and Time

The fourth central feature of episodic memory, and most relevant in the present context, has to do with episodic memory's unique relation to time. Unlike all other forms of biological memory, or memory systems, episodic memory is oriented to time. All other forms of memory operate in time, as does everything else in life, but only episodic memory allows people to consciously reexperience past experiences. Its special relationship to time is neither widely known nor adequately appreciated. Most people naturally associate all kinds of memory with the past and are surprised to learn that this is not so.

Episodic remembering is oriented to the past. When William James (1890) and Henri Bergson (1911) wrote about the "pastness" of memory, they had in mind what we now refer to as episodic memory, even if they did not use the term. At the time, there was no need for it, because what writers meant by "memory" referred either to episodic memory or to the combination of episodic and semantic memory, that is, declarative memory (Squire & Kandel, 1999). Note that Bennett Schwartz, in chapter 9 in this volume, uses the term "palinscopy" to refer to the same idea of "pastness."

The time in which episodic memory operates is the same in which all physical and biological events occur, physical time. But the time in which remembered events occur is different. We can call it subjective time. It is related to but not identical with physical time. The relation between physical time and subjective time is analogous to the relation between the physically present stimulus energy and the psychologically experienced awareness of the corresponding aspects of this energy, as studied in the venerable science of psychophysics. A falling tree in the forest will produce a physical disturbance in the air even if no living thing is nearby, but it produces a sound only if a living thing hears it. Sound exists as surely as do moving air molecules, but it exists solely by virtue of the interaction between the moving air molecules and brains equipped with auditory systems. The same is true of subjective time—it too exists, but only by virtue of the interaction between physical time and the part of the brain/mind that we call (autonoetic) episodic memory.

Philosophers and others (Dalla Barba, 2000, 2001) sometimes write about the "paradox" that phenomenal experience of pastness emerges from an aftereffect of the past (engram, or memory trace) that itself exists in the present. How is this possible, they wonder? How is it possible for what was to be present in what is?

From the perspective of episodic theory, there are two points to be made about the paradox. First, it exists, or may appear to exist, only for episodic memory. Because there is no pastness in any other memory system in humans, and no pastness in any memory system in all other creatures, the paradox, even if it were "real" otherwise, would not be a paradox of memory in general. Second, human episodic pastness does not reside in memory traces as such; it emerges as the phenomenally apprehended product of the episodic memory system, autonoetic consciousness, in ways that are as mysterious as the emergence of other kinds of consciousness from brain activity. Dalla Barba (2000, 2001) similarly attributes the feeling of pastness to a special kind of "temporal consciousness."

Autonoetic Future

Subjective time not only covers the past; it also extends into the future. The forward-looking sense of subjective time, or "proscopic chronesthesia" (Tulving, 2002a), is especially noteworthy, because it represents a key feature of autonoesis, which plays such an important role in the human condition. Anticipation of, thinking about, and explicitly or implicitly preparing and planning for the personal future seems to be a thoroughly quintessential human activity. It pervades an individual's daily life, from early in the morning till late at night, as it pervades his or her entire life course, from childhood to old age. If we retained all our other marvelous mental capacities but lost the awareness of the future time in which our lives are going to be played out, we might still be radically different from other animals, but we would no longer be human as we understand humanness.

This remarkable ability of humans to be aware of our own future has already been subjected to thought and study (Atance & O'Neill, 2001; Clayton et al., 2003; Haith, 1997; Haith, Benson, Roberts, & Pennington, 1994; Ingvar, 1985; Klein, Loftus, & Kihlstrom, 2002; Suddendorf & Corballis, 1997), but nowhere yet near to the extent that it deserves. A major stumbling block in this study might have been the absence of a clear conceptual distinction between future-oriented be-

havior and future-oriented thought (cognition). Frequently, the two
have been treated as directly related, future-oriented behavior being
seen as based on and reflecting future-related thought. Although such
concordance between behavior and cognition, and behavior and consciousness, undoubtedly occurs, it does not follow that it always occurs. It is quite possible to imagine that some (even highly complex)
future-related behaviors, or behaviors that can be seen as such, occur
quite independently of any deliberate conscious activity. As in many
other instances of apparent concordance between behavior and cognition, the question about the nature of the relation between behavior
and thought will have to be answered on the basis of empirical study;
it cannot be solved by assumption (Tulving, 1989a).

Semantic memory, as defined by the features listed in the left-hand
column of table 1.1, cannot serve the same function of remembering,
in the sense of mental time travel, as does episodic memory. Unlike
episodic memory, semantic memory has no special relation to time.
Indeed, as already stated, and popular misconceptions notwithstanding, no kind of memory other than episodic has any special relation
to time. Semantic memory allows the individual to *know*, at Time 2,
something about what happened at an earlier time, Time 1, but it
does not allow the individual to *remember* what happened. Semantic
memory also allows an individual to construct possible future worlds,
but since it is lacking autonoetic capability, it would not allow the
individual to mentally travel into his own personal future.

Those without episodic memory can learn, retain what they have
learned, make use of what they have retained—and thus they have
memory in this sense—but they cannot remember. An event happens
and is registered at Time 1 that may have consequences for behavior
or cognition at a subsequent Time 2. But this temporal sequence of
stages of knowledge acquisition is in no way special to memory. Temporal sequencing of this kind does not distinguish semantic memory
from other temporal cause-and-effect sequences in, say, eating a meal,
or being vaccinated against malaria, or growing old as one goes
through life. There is no need whatsoever for any temporal marker to
be attached to and retained about the learned facts of the world. The
facts can be put to good use by the owner of a semantic memory
system regardless of whether episodic memory is functional or not. It
is crucial to distinguish between the consequences of an experienced
event and the remembering of the experienced event (Lockhart, 1984).

Darwin's Moral Beings

When Charles Darwin contemplated the differences in mental characteristics of his subjects in *Descent of Man*, he did make an exception in
his insistence on total continuity otherwise:

> A moral being is one who is capable of reflecting on his past actions and their motives—of approving of some and disapproving of others; and the fact that man is the one being who certainly deserves this designation, is the greatest of all distinctions between him and the lower animals. (Darwin, 1874/1998, p. 633)

Darwin's additional writing provides a rather detailed description of what he conceives of as a moral being. Interestingly, this description includes features of such a being that correspond to some of the central features of episodic memory: (1) conscious reflection, (2) self, (3) personal past, and (4) ethical judgment. Thus we see that Darwin anticipated, implicitly at least, the idea that nonhuman animals do not have what we now call autonoetic consciousness. Indeed, by adding man's "ethical aspects" to the equation, he goes beyond it.

It is especially instructive to note that Darwin's moral beings were concerned about the future. This means, by our theory, that they must have had autonoetic consciousness. This raises the question: Can one be a moral being in the absence of autonoesis?

I have to leave the exercise of determining the nature of the relation between autonoesis and moral judgment to others, although at first glance it does not seem to be unreasonable to think of autonoesis as a necessary condition for moral judgment, rather than vice versa. If this is so, then the inability of Darwin's "beasts," like that of very young children, to differentiate right from wrong has its roots in their lack of ability to mentally travel into their own personal futures. Darwin's position on human uniqueness also covers the major properties of Metcalfe and Kober's concept of projectable self—the sensing, imagining, willing, and doubting self (chapter 2, this volume).

Why Did Episodic Memory Evolve?

Why did autonoetic consciousness and episodic memory emerge in the process of evolution? Wherein lies their evolutionary payoff? What can organisms with autonoetic consciousness do that organisms without it cannot?

Robert Hampton, a contributor to this volume, and a researcher on the opposite end of the rope, put these very questions to me in e-mail correspondence some time ago:

> Thus I would like to know what the possession of episodic memory does for an individual. What additional capacity is provided when one has episodic memory? This needs to go beyond the mere ability to report "I remember that happening to me. My experience of this memory is distinct from others." In other words, what can an animal with episodic memory do that gives it an evolutionary advantage over an animal without episodic memory? Having different covert experiences by itself cannot lead to selection for episodic memory. These experiences need to be turned into adap-

tive behavior if one can specify what that adaptive behavior is—what an animal with episodic memory can do that another cannot—then one can do an experiment to test for that capacity. (Personal communication, July 2, 2002)

Questions of this kind—why did X evolve—of course are difficult to answer in any case, but when asked about mental capabilities, which do not leave any fossils, answering them becomes essentially impossible, and one can only speculate.

One possible story begins with the assumption that the common ancestors that the species that eventually became *Homo sapiens* shared with what became living pongids, some 5 or 6 million years ago, possessed capabilities that we now identify with semantic memory, but they did not possess episodic memory. Episodic memory emerged, presumably gradually, in the course of human evolution. It may have grown out of a gradual extension of the human mental reach farther and farther back into subjectively apprehended past, perhaps as a sort of temporal stretching of the duration of the subjectively experienced here and now. There are clear evolutionary advantages to being consciously aware not only of what is happening here and now, but also of what happened 5 seconds ago, 10 seconds, a minute, 10 minutes, an hour, a day ago, even if the dimness of such awareness increased monotonically with the retention interval. A special evolutionary leap may have been necessary to produce brains that were capable of bridging the remembering across the diurnal divide. But these unfathomable specifics aside, it is a fact that humans somehow acquired the ability to remember their experienced past, in addition to the earlier acquired skill of knowing of things in the present.

Along with such an expansion of the subjective time horizon toward the past in remembering occurred a similar, even if possibly more muted, expansion toward the future. Once the brain "discovered" the trick of representing subjective time and making access to it available to the evolving self, through similarly evolving autonoetic consciousness, our distant forbears came to live with the capability of awareness of subjective time in which they and their group existed, their ancestors had existed, and their children and their children were going to exist.

Evolutionary Payoff: Awareness of the Future

The truly momentous development was the emergence of autonoesis that allowed individuals to imagine and worry about their own future, because it brought with it a radical shift in humans' relation to nature. Instead of using their wits to adjust to the vagaries of nature, including the uncertainties of availability of food, shelter, and protection from predators, humans began to anticipate these problems and take steps to mitigate their unpredictability.

Other early expressions of future-oriented thought and planning consisted of learning to use, preserve, and then make fire, to make tools, and then to store and carry these with them. Furnishing the dead with grave goods; growing their own crops, fruits, and vegetables; domesticating animals as sources of food and clothing; creating the spirit world and endowing its inhabitants with powers that explained otherwise unexplainable natural phenomena, and then inventing ways of placating the spirits through rituals and other proper ways of behavior—these all represent relatively recent developments in human evolution. Every single one is predicated on the awareness of the future.

Future-oriented (proscopic) time sense (chronesthesia) was only one of the necessary conditions that had to be simultaneously satisfied for human culture and civilization to come into being and then to proceed and flourish. But, at least according to the results of the thought experiments that I mentioned, the requirement for autonoetic awareness of the future is one of the more stringent ones.

Hampton (personal communication, July 2, 2002) is right in suggesting that if inner thoughts always remain inner thoughts, that is, if they do not affect behavior, they will die with the one who thinks them. They need to be translated into action to make any difference in the world. The question therefore is, what kinds of inner thoughts, or covert experiences, lead to what kind of action. The world is full of living things that may be said to think, and then act on their thoughts. Or at least it is possible to interpret many observable activities in this way. But an overwhelming majority of these thoughts and the ensuing actions are motivated by the creatures' current needs and are directed at the environment that exists here and now. These thoughts and actions do not change the world from one to which all living creatures must adapt, to one that better satisfies their needs.

These kinds of musings do contain one possible answer to Hampton's query about the biological utility of covert experiences. Inner thoughts, phenomenal awareness of one's world, need not but in fact often do lead to overt action. One notable example of such action is doing something now that will pay off only in the future. Humans with autonoetic episodic memory think about the future, anticipate what challenges and rewards it will bring, and take action now that fit the problems and the expected rewards.

If nonhuman animals do not have autonoetic awareness that they can direct at the imagined but physically nonexistent future, they will not be able to create any culture in the sense of changing the natural world. They may act in ways that a friendly anthropologist can call "culture"—for instance, elements of deliberate instruction of the young by their parents—but that kind of culture works using the same tried-and-true method as does evolution, or development, or

learning: they increase the fitness of the animal by changing the animal. Nature is full of demonstrations that the method works, but it is
the plodder's method. The autonoetic *Homo sapiens* invented a truly
revolutionary method: They enhanced their own fitness by altering
the Earth to suit their needs.

The idea of altering the world was unrivalled by anything that had
ever happened on Earth, and it could not have happened without
thinking about the future. Creatures lacking the ability to imagine
their possible futures might still be capable of impressive feats of intelligence: semantic memory, problem solving, communication, and
the like, but they would be unable to act on the basis of their knowledge of the past and their expectations for the future.

To sum up this section, episodic memory evolved because autonoesis, its critical constituent component, added to the already existing ability to mentally travel in space the ability to mentally travel in
time, not only into the past but, more important, also into the future.
Future-oriented consciousness (proscopic chronesthesia) made possible a feat that had no precedence anywhere in nature: individuals
intentionally, voluntarily, consciously taking action in response to
something that did not exist in the physical world. As a consequence,
humans were able to create a world to fit them, rather than live in
one into which they had to fit.

AUTONOETIC EPISODIC MEMORY: DATA

In this section, I discuss two rather different but converging lines of
evidence that speak to the issues of the episodic theory and the thesis
of this essay. One line is neuropsychological. The evidence consists of
clinical and experimental observations of memory and other cognitive
capabilities of certain brain-damaged patients who exhibit dissociations on memory tasks that vary in their assumed dependence on episodic memory. The second line consists of developmental studies that
have revealed task dissociations, as a function of children's age, indicative of episodic and semantic memory.

The Case of K.C.

In 1981, going home from work, a 30-year-old man accidentally rode
his motorcycle off the road and suffered brain damage of a highly
unusual kind. In addition to dense anterograde amnesia that frequently follows traumatic brain injury, K.C. exhibits an uncommon
form of retrograde amnesia in that his previously acquired knowledge
of the world (accessibility of the "contents" of semantic memory) is
largely intact, while his ability to recollect premorbid personal, autobiographical events is, for all practical purposes, completely lost. [To-
day, K.C. lives with his parents in Mississauga, near Toronto, in the

family home where they have lived for over 40 years. As his mental capabilities have not changed greatly from the time of his accident, I describe him in the present tense, although a good deal of relevant information is provided by studies done in the past (Hayman, Macdonald, & Tulving, 1993; Tulving, 1989b; Tulving, Schacter, McLachlan, & Moscovitch, 1988). For a recent thorough report on his case, see Rosenbaum et al. (in press).]

In most ways, K.C.'s intellectual capabilities are comparable to those of healthy adults. His thinking is clear, his intelligence is normal; language is normal, he can read and write; he has no problem recognizing objects and naming them; his imagery is normal (he can close his eyes and give an accurate visual description of the CN Tower, Toronto's famous landmark); his knowledge of mathematics, history, geography, and other school subjects is about the same as that of others at his educational level; he can define and tell the difference between stalagmites and stalactites; he knows that 007 and James Bond are one and the same person; he can play the organ, chess, and various card games; his social manners are exemplary; and he possesses a quiet sense of humor.

K.C.'s memory, very broadly defined, too, is unimpaired, and can be considered normal in a number of ways. He has no great difficulty answering questions about semantic (public, objective, shared) aspects of his own past life (autobiographical knowledge), such as his date of birth, the address of his home for the first 9 years of his life, the names of the schools he attended, the make and color of the car he once possessed, and the fact that his parents owned and still own a summer cottage. He knows the location of the cottage, can easily find it on the map, and knows its distance (90 miles) from his home and how long it takes to drive there from Toronto in weekend traffic. He also knows that he has spent a lot of time there.

Note, however, that all this accessible factual (declarative, cognitive, propositional) knowledge, even if it is about his own past, is classified as semantic because it is impersonal, objective, public, and shared with others. K.C. knows things about himself and his past in the same way that he knows similar things about others, friends and family. It is knowledge of one's life from the point of view of an observer rather than that of a participant, the same kind of knowledge that people have about many other aspects of their world.

K.C.'s primary (short-term, or working) memory is normal: he remembers what happened a short-term while (1 to 2 minutes) ago, and his forward digit span is 7 to 8. He can play a whole hand of hearts, or bridge, without any apparent memory handicap. He has no particular problems with many perceptual-motor and cognitive skills, or with the retrieval of premorbidly acquired general knowledge. His perceptual priming performance, as measured by word-fragment completion, even exceeds that of an average University of Toronto student (Tulving, Hayman, & Macdonald, 1991). And although he is very slow in comparison with healthy controls, he is capable of acquiring novel semantic information (Hayman et al., 1993; Tulving et al., 1991; Westmacott & Moscovitch, 2001).

K.C.'s Episodic Memory

K.C.'s major problem is that he cannot remember anything that has happened to him. However hard he tries, and however powerfully he is prompted, he cannot bring into his conscious awareness a single event, happening, or situation that he witnessed or in which he participated. This global episodic amnesia covers the span of his whole life, the period from his birth to the present day: he cannot recollect anything from his life either before or after the accident. He knows the address and, when standing in front of it, recognizes the house where he lived for the first 9 years of his life, but does not remember a single event that took place in the house. He does not remember a single visit to the family cottage, and not a single happening there in which he participated. Nor is he capable of remembering anything ever having happened in the house where he has now lived for over 40 years. He knows that he owned a black Honda, but does not remember a single trip he ever took in it.

In the course of studying his amnesia, we collected descriptions of a number of poignant events from his life that would be regarded as highly memorable by everyone—a fight he had in a pub resulting in a broken arm that took him to the hospital, a traffic accident that caused his jaw to be wired shut for a week, the accidental death of his older brother to whom he was close, and a huge chemical spill near his home that caused a 10-day evacuation of over 100,000 people in his neighborhood, including himself. The idea was to test his autobiographical memory with increasingly complete cues about the events. (We also made up a collection of descriptions of otherwise comparable events that had not happened to him, and used them as controls.) The results were clear. Even when he was given full descriptions of the real events, his response was the same as those he gave to the fabricated events: he said he did not remember the events, and did not feel any familiarity toward them.

Thus, although K.C. *knows* a great deal about the world because he learned it before his accident, he does not *remember* anything from the same period in his life (or any other period). This striking dissociation suggests that episodic and semantic memory are subserved by at least partially distinct sets of neural mechanisms. The brain damage that K.C. suffered, a rare one-in-a-million accident, must have greatly impaired the operations of one while leaving the other largely intact.

Other Cases

Other neuropsychological cases have been described in the literature that are similar to K.C.'s in that they exhibit a disproportionate impairment of episodic memory in relation to other kinds of memory (Calabrese et al., 1996; Giovagnoli, Erbetta, & Bugiani, 2001; Kapur, 1999; Levine et al., 1998; Markowitsch et al., 1993; Rousseaux, Godfrey, Cabaret, Bernati, & Pruvo, 1997; Van der Linden, Brédart, Depoorter, & Coyette, 1996; Viskontas, McAndrews, & Moscovitch, 2000; Wheeler & McMillan, 2001).

Especially striking, both with respect to their behavioral profiles and correlated neuroanatomical pathology, are the cases of young developmental amnesia patients described by Vargha-Khadem and her colleagues (Mishkin, Suzuki, Gadian, & Vargha-Khadem, 1997; Vargha-Khadem et al., 1997, 2003). Their behavioral profiles are interesting inasmuch as they remember little of ongoing experiences and, like K.C., cannot mentally relive the past, yet learn about the world without undue difficulties. Their neuroanatomical damage is interesting inasmuch as it is largely confined to the hippocampus proper and does not extend, as it frequently does, to the subjacent cortex. Thus, despite hippocampal pathology, these young people have managed to acquire normal or near-normal levels of intelligence, including normal language skills and general knowledge of the world. These fascinating cases once again suggest that a fully functioning episodic memory system is not required for the learning of general skills and knowledge. The cases of these young patients once more suggest that episodic memory is not necessary for the learning of general skills and knowledge.

Self-Awareness and Autonoetic Awareness

What about K.C.'s consciousness? Is he conscious? Is he reflectively or self-reflectively conscious? Does he possess normal self-awareness? Is he autonoetically conscious?

The answers to these questions clearly depend on what one means by the terms. I would say that of course K.C. is conscious. Furthermore, he is self-reflectively conscious. Yet, at the same time, I would also say that he does not have normal self-awareness, and that he is not autonoetically conscious.

On the one hand, he is not in the least confused or uncertain about himself as an independently functioning individual. He knows his name, where he lives, his family, how to take care of himself, the daily routine, how to spend time in the house, and what he does when he goes for walks in the neighborhood. He knows about them in two senses: he carries out relevant actions without any hesitation and usually without any prodding by anyone else, and he can reflect on what he is doing, that is, he can answer questions appropriately about these actions, when he is asked to do so. As a result of his accident, K.C.'s personality was greatly changed (Rosenbaum et al., in press), but he has even learned his new self as revealed by trait judgments (Tulving, 1993b; see also Klein, Loftus, & Kihlstrom, 1996).

When K.C. is asked about whether his "mind is clear," he has no hesitation in stating that it is, and nothing in his ongoing everyday behavior would lead anyone to question his judgment in the matter. Thus it seems reasonable to say that he has a well-developed and properly functioning self and that he possesses self-awareness. Although he has not yet been formally tested on his understanding of the theory of mind, or metacognition (chapter 2, this volume), I and others who know him well believe that he would have no difficulty passing relevant tests. Indeed, it is not unreasonable to imagine that giving K.C. a Gallup mirror test or even Povinelli's delayed video test (Povinelli, Landau, & Perilloux, 1996) in order to check on his self-awareness would be equivalent to giving Columbia University professors a test of the alphabet.

On the other hand, K.C. is a densely amnesic person who remembers nothing of what has ever happened to him. It is difficult to imagine that these missing features have no bearing on his awareness of himself. This awareness is not "normal." What is missing is what I have referred to as autonoetic awareness. He is severely deficient when it comes to autonoesis: for all practical purposes, he has no functioning autonoetic self, or Metcalfe and Kober's (chapter 2) projectable self. On Katherine Nelson's (chapter 4) scale of consciousness, K.C. seems to be missing the lower level (3–6 years of age) narrative consciousness but, paradoxically perhaps, seems to have the higher level (5–10 years of age) cultural consciousness. The apparent paradox, however, can be resolved along the lines of the SPI model (Tulving, 1995, 2001a) by distinguishing between the processes of encoding and retrieval.

K.C. and the Future

K.C. cannot think about his own personal future. Thus, when asked, he cannot tell the questioner what he is going to do later on that day, or the day after, or at any time in the rest of his life, any more than he can say what he did the day before or what events have happened in his life. When he is asked to describe the state of his mind when he thinks about his future, whether the next 15 minutes or the next year, he again says that it is "blank." Indeed, when asked to compare the two kinds of blankness, one of the past and the other of the future, he says that they are "the same kind of blankness" (Tulving, 1985b). Thus K.C. seems to be as incapable of projecting himself mentally into his personal future as he is incapable of seeing himself in his personal past. He lacks autonoetic awareness.

It is important to note that K.C. has no greater difficulty with the concept of the future as an aspect of physical time than he has with physical space. He knows and can talk about what most other people know about physical time, its units, its structure, its measurement by clocks and calendars, and the location of events in the world in the past. But such knowledge of time in and of itself does not allow him to remember events as having happened at a particular time. It is necessary but not sufficient. Something else is needed, and this something else—the awareness of time in which one's experiences are recorded—seems to be missing from K.C.'s neurocognitive repertoire. He thus exhibits a dissociation between knowing time and experiencing time, a dissociation that parallels one between knowing the facts of the world and remembering past experiences.

When K.C. is engaged in activities that do not require mental time travel into his own past or future, his awareness is indistinguishable from what most neuropsychologists would consider normal. When he is asked the name of the capital of France, or the difference between stalagmites and stalactites, or thousands of other such facts, there is no sign of any deficiency. In these situations, he is naturally consciously aware of what he is doing, but the kind of consciousness involved is different from autonoesis: it contains no awareness of personal time. We can describe the situation by saying that there is nothing apparently wrong with or missing in his noetic consciousness. Thus, although K.C.'s autonoesis is severely impaired, his capability of conscious awareness of the world beyond subjective time, that is, his noetic consciousness or noesis, is well preserved.

It was this striking pattern of K.C.'s mental life—his extensive repertoire of conscious thoughts about the impersonal world contrasted with his essentially nonexistent conscious thoughts about his own past and future—that first suggested the distinction between noetic and autonoetic consciousness (Tulving, 1985b). K.C. possesses the former and does not possess the latter. Because he is perfectly well aware of his timeless self—self in the present—it seems reasonable to attribute his difficulties with personal past and personal future to deficient, perhaps largely lacking, autonoesis.

This brief description of K.C. can be summarized by saying that he "fails" the test of possession of the episodic memory capacity by all four criteria represented by episodic memory's defining features. He does not remember any personally experienced events; he is not self-aware in the dimension of time; he has no autonoetic awareness; and he does not seem to possess any feeling of subjective time. I concede that some of these assertions may be too strong. It is possible that he has a little left of one or more of the properties of episodic memory and that we are dealing with a case of severe impairment in episodic memory rather than its total absence (Squire & Zola, 1998). However, this possibility does not change the striking dissociation between episodic and other kinds of memory that the case of K.C. represents.

Why Is the Case of K.C. Relevant?

The case of K.C. is relevant in the context of the present essay for several reasons. First, unlike many other living beings who have no episodic memory (e.g., nonhuman animals and preverbal children), K.C. is capable of producing reasonably detailed introspective reports about his mental life. Thus he can do what these others cannot—provide direct first-person narrative evidence of the nature of the world of an otherwise normal person without episodic memory and autonoetic capability.

Second, K.C.'s introspective reports are valuable in drawing a connection between mental time travel into the past and mental time travel into the future. There is no simple way of directly comparing these two facets of time, and subjective time at that. Nevertheless, the fact that K.C.'s ability to think about his personal future seems to be as severely impaired as his ability to think about his personal past allows us to assume that mental time travel is a single neurocognitive capability, one whose domain of operations extends from the present in both possible temporal directions. Before his case, it would have been possible to imagine that the remembered time might be functionally different from the imagined future time, and the two might even be subserved by different neural substrates. The case of K.C. supports the idea of the continuity of subjective time, in this sense paralleling physical time.

Recently, an interesting and revealing case, of patient D.B., has been presented by Klein et al. (2002). It speaks rather directly to the issue of autonoetic mental time travel in both directions, the past and the future. As a result of hypoxic brain damage, D.B. suffers severe retrograde episodic amnesia. Like K.C., D.B. has a relatively well preserved general knowledge base, accumulated before the onset of his amnesia, but his ability to recollect premorbid personal experiences is severely impaired. The important new feature of the Klein et al. (2002) study was that they formally tested D.B.'s ability to imagine the future and his ability to anticipate future events. They found that this ability, like his retrograde memory, was fractured along the lines of "personal" versus "impersonal." D.B. has knowledge of the world's past and can intelligently express opinions about the world's probable future. But both his ability to recollect happenings from his own personal past and to imagine his own personal future are severely impaired. The case of D.B. thus formally illustrates a dissociation between semantic (noetic) and episodic (autonoetic) mental time travel.

Third, it is important to note that as long as K.C. continues to live in a stable world with which he is familiar, that is, with his parents in his home, he has no problem surviving, and surviving well. He is not dependent on others to tell him how to behave, what to do, or how to take care of himself. As long as somebody fills the refrigerator and pays the bills, and water flows from the taps and his bed is ready to be slept in in his bedroom, he manages without any difficulty. He probably also could, if necessary, walk to the supermarket, and (if he has written down what he needs, if he has not forgotten that he has the list in his pocket, and if he has not forgotten to take money with him), he could fill the basket and walk back home. The point is that in a stable environment there is no crying need for episodic memory to live a satisfying life. K.C.'s life may be abnormal and uninteresting by ordinary standards that people in our world are accustomed to, but because he himself is not aware of it, and his needs are taken care of, he has no complaints. When he is asked to rate the quality of his life on a five-point scale (5 "very good," 1 "very bad"), he judges it to be 4.

Fourth, K.C.'s case graphically illustrates the distinction between timeless and time-based self-awareness. As mentioned earlier, his knowledge of physical time is normal. He knows perfectly well what time is, and because he has no problems with thinking and reasoning, he also knows, and can articulate the fact, that he has lived in the past and is going to live in the future. But such knowledge does not translate into a felt time. He does not seem to possess what others do—an ever-present awareness of one's being existing in a subjective sea of time, always in transition from what is now becoming the past to what once was the future. K.C. possesses a noetic (knowing) self, but lacks an autonoetic (or projectable, or time-traveling or remembering self).

Autonoetic Memory in Children

The hypothesis that episodic memory is not present in animals receives support from the observation that episodic memory is also absent in young children. Young children can act upon their earlier experiences, and they can even verbally describe aspects of these experiences. The question is whether they also (autonoetically) remember these experiences. The proposed answer to the question is that young children do not remember personal experiences, and that the ability to remember events follows rather than precedes the development of the ability to become knowledgeable about the facts of the world (Wheeler, 2000).

The observations concerning the differentially delayed development of episodic memory are still somewhat controversial, and not all
developmentalists are willing to interpret them along the lines suggested here. The problem is rather similar to that in the interpretation
of learning in animals—many instances of learning can be (anthropomorphically) interpreted as revealing episodic memory, although they
need not, because nonepisodic forms of memory are sufficient. When
parents witness their 9-month-old daughter crawling to the spot
where she previously found her favorite toy, it is quite reasonable for
them to conclude that the child remembers the prior episode. Even
more convincing is a 3-year-old who verbally answers questions about
something that happened to him only a short time ago. It requires only
common sense and no specialized knowledge to attribute to the child
the ability to recollect the past. Surely an adult, answering the same
question, would rely on episodic retrieval, so why should the same
inference not apply to the child? The answer to this question is difficult to resolve conclusively, yet additional evidence now suggests that
even when young children are able to talk about the details of prior
events, it need not mean that they consciously recollect the events
(Lockhart, 1984; Nelson, 1993; Wheeler et al., 1997). It is also true, of
course, that just because an act of learning can be attributed to nonepisodic forms of memory, it cannot benefit from episodic memory.

The argument here is that children up to age of 4 years or so lack
the same kind of episodic memory and autonoetic consciousness that
seem to be missing in animals. The relevant findings have been provided by comparative studies of episodic and semantic memory in
children between the ages of 3 and 6 years. During these years, children are already highly verbal and very accomplished learners. They
can also recall novel events from their lives, sometimes across intervals on the order of months (Fivush, Hudson, & Nelson, 1984). Some
of these studies show striking dissociations between episodic and semantic memory. Many of the most relevant studies have examined
memory for context or for source. I provide examples below.

If one assumes, as I do, that the operations of episodic memory are
critically dependent on autonoetic consciousness, it follows that any
child who is incapable of this highest level of consciousness should be
unable to recollect the personal past. Therefore, assessing autonoetic
awareness in children should set boundary conditions on the presence
or absence of episodic memory (Wheeler, 2000).

One relevant piece of evidence comes from the behavior of infants
when they are placed in front of mirrors. Exposure to a mirror typically causes older children and adults to begin paying attention to
themselves, and it often stimulates them to begin reflecting on their
own mental states (Duval & Wicklund, 1973). Before the age of about
18 months, young children will pay attention to their mirror image

but do not realize that it represents their body, and they will not use the mirror as a tool to think about themselves (see Lewis and Brooks-Gunn, 1979, for an extensive discussion of children's behavior around mirrors).

It would be convenient to assume that the toddlers who recognize themselves in the mirror possess self-awareness. And if self-awareness were defined in terms of the mirror test, the statement would be true, by definition. However, passing the mirror test does not mean that the children have autonoetic consciousness, that they are aware of themselves as individuals with a past and a future. Autonoesis emerges only later, as an integral component of episodic memory.

Episodic memory matures gradually, and therefore it is difficult to pin down a particular age at which young children's episodic memory capabilities can be said to have become fully functional. But one magic number that is frequently used in the attempts to do so is 4 years (Nelson, 1992). It does not mean, of course, that episodic memory emerges suddenly around a child's fourth birthday. Nor does it mean that it becomes fully established shortly thereafter. What the number designates is the common finding that most 3-year-olds fail or do poorly on tasks that require them to bring back to mind their own personal experiences, whereas most 5-year-olds do very much better on the same tasks.

One of the most instructive examples of this generalization is provided by experiments reported by Gopnik and Graf (1988). They had 3-, 4-, and 5-year-olds learn about the contents of a drawer in one of three different ways. Some of the children were told about the contents without seeing them, others saw with their own eyes what was in the drawer, and a third group was given hints so they could infer what was there. Gopnik and Graf were interested in two things: (1) Do the children know what is in the drawer? (2) Do they know why they know—was it via seeing, hearing, or inferring? The first question has to do with acquired knowledge, and, over the studied age range, there were no age differences on this question, even on a delayed test when recall was far from perfect. As to the second question, the reasoning was that for the subjects to be able to answer it, they must be able to recollect how they found out about the contents of the drawer. While the 5-year-olds made very few mistakes on this second question, few of the 3-year-olds could respond at levels higher than chance. Thus, all children knew "what" (the contents of the drawer), but only the older ones knew why they knew (remembering the event of seeing what was in the drawer).

The general finding has been replicated in a number of different ways (Lindsay, Johnson, & Kwon, 1991; Wimmer, Hogrefe, & Perner, 1988). It appears that young children cannot, or do not, represent their knowledge as deriving from a particular time in the personal past (e.g., "I saw that there are crayons in the drawer"), but rather as detached, impersonal knowledge (e.g., "There are crayons in the drawer").

The studies just described may even overestimate children's abilities to understand how they learned information. The critical test questions used by Gopnik and Graf (1988) and others only asked children to differentiate between different intraexperimental sources of information (seeing, hearing, inferring). Many children cannot acknowledge the simple fact that a recently learned bit of information has been acquired recently. In one experiment (Taylor, Esbensen, & Bennett, 1994), 4- and 5-year-old children were taught unfamiliar color names (e.g., chartreuse, taupe). All the children learned the names easily, and after learning were able to select items from an array of colors according to the specified name. They were then questioned about when they had learned the new color names. Incredibly, a large majority of the 4-year-olds claimed to have "always" known these names, and only a few would admit that they had been taught the colors that day. The 5-year-olds performed markedly better in identifying the source of their knowledge, although a few of them consistently made this same source error. Across several experiments, the authors showed that young children typically are unaware of recent learning events and claim to have known recently acquired information for a long time. Thus, it looks as if children are better at making use of learned facts than they are of identifying the episode during which the facts were learned. One plausible reason for such failure is that because they lack fully fledged episodic memory, the children actually do not remember the learning episode. This suggestion is consistent with the idea that childhood amnesia reflects nothing more nor less than the absence of episodic memory in young children (Perner & Ruffman, 1995).

Children's ability to remember how and when and in what setting they learned a new fact can be assessed even more directly. When this is done, findings again suggest a magical number of 4 as the number of years needed to develop a nearly fully operational episodic memory system.

When young children are more directly assessed for the extent to which they suffer from source amnesia, the findings again point to a critical age around 4 years. Drummey and Newcombe (2002) used the paradigm like the one introduced by Schacter, Harbluk, and McLachlan (1984). Children were taught new facts in the laboratory setting (e.g., "giraffes are the only animals that cannot make a sound") and were later tested for (1) their knowledge of the learned facts and (2) their recollection of the learning episode. Children's retention of the learned facts showed steady improvement with age from 4 years to 8 years. At the same time, however, the 4-year-olds were very much worse than the older children in remembering where and how they had learned the facts that they now knew.

These lines of research show what young children can, and cannot, do. There is little question that children as young as 3 or 4 years can talk about events from their own lives. But an important limitation appears to be that the event must have been novel. It is a common finding that when young children are asked to talk about novel or interesting events that occurred several months ago, they are able to do so (Fivush et al., 1984). Yet if they are asked in the evening what happened at school that day, they do not know; they cannot remember. Children below the age of about 5 years can only talk about daily events if something unusual has happened.

For a period of at least a few years, children may have what Katherine Nelson (1984) has called a "general undifferentiated knowledge base," perhaps even at the age of 4 years. Information exists in the knowledge base in noetic form only. Even when a child can master semantic concepts like "time," "future," "yesterday," and "me," there is some considerable period of time, on the order of years, before there is a qualitative shift in thought, allowing the child to remember the past episodically.

One example of a test that probably cannot be used with young children is the remember/know task (Gardiner, 1988; Gardiner & Richardson-Klavehn, 2000; Rajaram & Roediger, 1997). If children are truly pre-episodic and have not yet developed the capacity to recollect the past autonoetically, then it will not make any sense to ask them to distinguish between remembering and knowing. Evidence that these terms are problematic for children was reported by Johnson and Wellman (1980). (It is edifying to note that this study appeared many years before the formally articulated distinction between remembering and knowing.) They found that 4-year-olds were not cognizant of differences between cases of remembering, knowing, and guessing, although in some cases they could distinguish their mental state from an externally perceived state. Five-year-olds showed some ability to differentiate these mental states, while 6-year-olds generally had a very solid command of the terms. The authors stress that this is not a simple vocabulary problem, as children of that age are fully capable of acquiring and using words and concepts that, to adults, are much more sophisticated than words like "know" or "guess." Difficulties likely stem from the inability to monitor one's own mental states.

Nelson and Fivush (2004; see also chapter 4, this volume) have recently proposed a major social-cultural theory of the development of autobiographical memory, which for them represents a subset of episodic memory (for a somewhat different idea on the relation between episodic and autobiographical memory, see Conway & Pleydell-

Pearce, 2000). Autobiographical memory is said to entail a "personal significance that characterizes specific memories that re-appear many times during one's life, often decades after the event." They are contrasted with "lesser episodic memories [which] tend to lead an ephemeral existence, leaving little trace in the future." Nelson and Fivush contend that autobiographical memory emerges following a number of changes developments in language, consciousness, and self-awareness. The developing system begins with a basic, functional declarative-like memory system that is able to retain information about events (routines and episodes) for weeks or, eventually, months. A critical addition, however, is the beginning of language comprehension and expression, especially the burgeoning capacity to provide labels to elaborate upon and retain information. Around the age of 18 months, young children begin to establish a cognitive self (see also Howe & Courage, 1993) which serves as a foundation for encoding and understanding ongoing events. For the first time, a child can begin to understand his own special place in the world (and his own idiosyncratic feelings), as distinct from others.

An additional necessary step occurs when parents and other adults begin to talk about past and future events in the presence of the child, especially when the adults describe such events narratively. Such conversations provide the support for the child's developing concept of time. It is between about the ages of 2 and 5 years that developing language and narrative skills allow children to represent and become aware of complex sequences of events, and to think about the events in terms of a personal past, present, and future.

In summary of this section, young children represent a prime example of a population that possesses some critical aspects of episodic memory but lacks others. As such, the discussion of children's memory may be useful as a way to understand our eventual interpretation of evidence from animal research. Children between the ages of 2 and 5 years can encode, store, and retrieve declarative-like information and learn new facts about the world, and they are fully capable of applying this learned information flexibly and confidently. Yet developmental limitations in their conscious awareness place boundary conditions upon their uses of memory. It is not until children can reflect upon subjective experiences in the past, present, and future that they can experience the past episodically. Evidence from multiple, diverse sources implies that, below the age of approximately 4 or 5 years, young children lack the linguistic, representational, and "self"-related skills to reflect upon the personal past. The developmental findings not only emphasize the role that a fully developed human brain plays in episodic memory; they also underscore the fact that episodic memory is not necessary in a world in which one's needs can be and are satisfied without remembering autonoetically what happened in the past.

ANALYSIS: EPISODIC MEMORY IN ANIMALS

We now return to the main point of this chapter and the question: Do animals other than humans possess episodic memory? Hundreds of articles have been written on the topic of mental capacities of animals, and to say that the topic is controversial is to greatly understate the vehemence with which the issue has been pursued. By restricting our analysis of the mental capacities to episodic memory, it is possible to expect closer agreement.

The answer to the question is multiply determined. It depends partly on what one means by episodic memory, partly on the kinds of evidence one considers, and partly on how one interprets the evidence. When episodic memory is defined loosely as "memory for (specific) past events," then the standard commonsense answer is that of course animals have it. Every owner of a pet dog or cat, every visitor to the monkey cages in the zoo, anyone who has ever watched Walt Disney cartoons knows that even if animals are not like people in every way, they are like people in many ways, and those many ways include their memory abilities. They may not have human language, may lack the capacity for abstract reasoning, and may fall short on some other esoteric human traits (the likes of musicality, religiosity, science, literature, and love of the arts), but surely they know what they are doing in their daily lives and they naturally remember it too. When one sees a dog bury a bone one day and next day make a beeline to the place, it is easy to imagine that on the first day the dog was completely aware of his purpose in burying the bone, and that on the second day he was completely aware of having done so the day before.

This kind of anthropomorphically driven thinking, which Charles Darwin put to scientific and practical use in his *Descent of Man* (Darwin, 1874/1998), and which George Romanes (1881) developed to high art, comes naturally to human minds. Despite Lloyd Morgan's (1894) early strictures against it, in the form of his famous canon, and continued urgings of caution by contemporary writers, it is very much alive today. It is quite possible that anthropomorphizing is an evolutionary adaptation, as suggested by Povinelli and Vonk (2003, p. 157) in their musings about why the chimpanzee mind seems so suspiciously human: "the human mind may have evolved a unique mental system that cannot help distorting the chimpanzee's mind, obligatorily recreating it in its own image. This idea should be taken seriously. After all, from change-blindness, to false memories, to cognitive dissonance, don't we already know the various ways in which the human mind systematically distorts its own workings?"

Many memory researchers have adopted the commonsense notion and have taken it for granted that animals have episodic memory. A good example is provided by the animal model of memory and amnesia proposed by Squire and Zola, and their associates (Alvarez, Zola-Morgan, & Squire, 1994; Squire, 1987; Squire & Zola, 1998). A central tenet of the model is that the hippocampal system plays a critical role in declarative memory. The hippocampal declarative memory system covers both memory for events (episodic memory) and memory for facts (semantic memory) and is the same in rats, monkeys, and human beings (Squire, 1992). If animals have declarative memory, and if declarative memory comprises both episodic and semantic memory, then, logically, animals must have episodic memory. Comparable views are held by Eichenbaum and his collaborators (Eichenbaum, 2000; Eichenbaum, Otto, & Cohen, 1996), although the critical neuroanatomy is seen somewhat differently from Squire and Zola.

The idea seems perfectly reasonable; otherwise its popularity would not have lasted. But what it demonstrates above all is how subtle important differences in brain and behavior can be, and how difficult to come to grips with. On closer reflection, there are several problems with it.

First, in common sense and theories based on it, the question of the existence of episodic memory in animals is "solved" by postulation instead of empirical inquiry. Memory for events and memory for facts are lumped together as one and not treated separately. The practice may serve for certain purposes—such as investigation of the neuroanatomical correlates of declarative (conjunction of episodic and semantic) memory—but it possibly cannot help to answer the question I am asking here.

Second, the kinds of tasks that have been used in evaluations of the hippocampal declarative memory system do not, and cannot, distinguish between memory for events and memory for facts. A great deal of laboratory research on animal memory is essentially concerned with perceptual (recognition) memory (Aggleton & Pearce, 2001; Wright, Santiago, Sands, Kendrick, & Cook, 1985), as is research done with preverbal human infants (Rovee-Collier & Hayne, 2000), and requires no declarative (semantic and episodic) memory. The widely used DNMS (delayed nonmatching to sample) and other kinds of object recognition tasks can be effectively executed by identifying the stimulus objects on the basis of their perceived novelty or familiarity. Moreover, there is increasing evidence that the execution of DNMS tasks does not even depend on the integrity of the hippocampus (Aggleton & Brown, 1999; Aggleton & Pearce 2001; Murray, 1996; Murray & Bussey, 2001; Mishkin, Vargha-Khadem, & Gadian, 1998). The ability of animals to perform the task, and the effects of experimentally induced lesions on the performance, therefore, have no bearing on the issue of whether animals have episodic memory. Even when we consider tasks that cannot be handled at the level of perceptual memory alone, it turns out that most of them require only semantic memory and not episodic. Young children can acquire knowledge about the world efficiently and rapidly long before they develop the ability to recollect specific happenings from their past (Nelson, 1993). Although not all amnesic patients are capable of doing so (Kopelman, 2002; Manns, Hopkins, & Squire, 2003), some amnesic patients, who have severely impaired or no functional episodic memory, can nevertheless acquire new semantic information (Guillery et al., 2001; Hamann & Squire, 1995; Hayman et al., 1993; Kitchener, Hodges, & McCarthy, 1998; McKenna & Gerhand, 2002; Rajaram & Coslett, 2000; Van der Linden et al., 2001; see also Verfaellie, Koseff, & Alexander, 2000).

Third, the kinds of tasks that have been typically used in laboratory studies usually test the subjects' knowledge of what they perceived or what they did at the time of study (training), and may also test the subjects' knowledge of the spatial coordinates of the to-be-remembered objects (where something was). However, they do not challenge the subjects' knowledge of the time of the occurrence (when) of the event in question (Griffiths et al., 1999). Thus, one key element of episodic memory, the temporal dimension of what is remembered, has been lacking in laboratory experiments on animal memory.

Clayton and Dickinson and their colleagues have remedied this shortcoming, and reported ingenious and convincing demonstrations of memory for time in scrub jays. Scrub jays are food-caching birds, and connoisseurs when it comes to choosing what they eat. When they have food they cannot eat, they hide the food and recover it later. Because some of the cached foods (such as wax worms and crickets) are preferred but perishable and must be consumed within a few days of caching, while other foods (such as seeds and nuts) are less preferred but do not perish easily, for efficient recovery the birds must recall not only cache locations (What did I hide where?) but also the time of caching (When did I do it?). Clayton and her colleagues made clever use of these facts in designing their laboratory experiments, whose outcomes clearly showed that, even days after caching, scrub jays knew not only what kind of food was where but also when they had cached it. Similar laboratory findings of these kinds have not yet been reported for rodents or nonhuman primates.

The Fourth Problem

The three problems I have mentioned—solving a theoretical issue by postulation rather than empirical inquiry, difficulty of distinguishing memory for events and memory for facts, and the absence, until recently, of evidence of memory for when an event occurred—are simple in comparison with the fourth. What I here call the fourth problem is the central one.

How do we know what kinds of mental experiences accompany memory-based activities in nonverbal organisms? How can we find out whether there is any evidence for episodic memory in its narrow (unique) definition in animals, given that animals do not talk, and that even rudiments of human-taught language, known from some very rare cases, cannot be used for the purpose? How can we find out whether animals autonoetically remember past experiences? That they are capable of mentally traveling in time? Do Clayton's clever scrub jays actually remember when they cached the wax worms and when they cashed the peanuts, or do they know, on some other basis, how to act at the time of the recovery of the food?

Scientists and others interested in the issue do not doubt that their fellow human beings, like they themselves, have the capacity to mentally travel in time and the capacity to distinguish the kind of conscious awareness that accompanies mental time travel from other forms of consciousness. Normal human beings can remember events such as a visit to Washington, DC; they know, without necessarily remembering any personal encounter, what the capitol in Washington looks like; and they can perform behavioral feats, without any conscious awareness that they are using their memory, such as unhesitatingly completing the word fragment C-P-T-L. These kinds of distinctions, between autonoetic, noetic, and anoetic consciousness (Tulving, 1985b) come to humans as naturally as the ability to tell the difference between seeing white and black, or hearing a ping and a thud, or feeling the difference between a sharp and a dull pain. The extensive human literature on the distinction between two kinds of conscious awareness, remembering and knowing (Gardiner, 1988; Gardiner & Richardson-Klavehn, 2000; Rajaram & Roediger, 1997), together with early findings of neural correlates of subjectively experienced states (Düzel, Vargha-Khadem, Heinze, & Mishkin, 2001; Eldridge, Knowlton, Furmanski, Bookheimer, & Engel, 2000) has helped do away with the fourth problem in the study of human memory. But as yet no one has come up with a comparable solution to the fourth problem in the study of animal memory.

The fourth problem as such looms large in the thinking of others who have thought about the time sense in animals, and who have arrived at conclusions similar to those I am arguing for here. An exceptionally thorough and lucid discussion of the topic is found in an article by Suddendorf and Corballis (1997); another is an equally detailed and scholarly treatment of the same theme by Roberts (2002; see also Roberts & Roberts, 2002).

In an article titled "Mental Time Travel and the Evolution of the Human Mind," Suddendorf and Corballis (1997), in much greater depth than I have been able to do here, have anticipated and laid bare the kinds of arguments I have been presenting. I very much agree with most of the things that they say, including their main point that "the ability to travel mentally in time constitutes a discontinuity between humans and other animals," their sober observation that "the importance of mental time travel as a prime mover in human cognitive evolution has not been adequately recognized," and their declaration that "the real importance of mental time travel applies to travel into the future rather than into the past." I am also in complete agreement with their assessment of the development of time sense in young children and with their idea that language, although greatly facilitating the use of the human capacity for mental time travel, is not necessary for it.

Suddendorf and Corballis (1997) have done a further good deed in bringing to the attention of Anglophone readers what they refer to as the Bischof-Köhler hypothesis. This hypothesis is "that animals other than humans cannot anticipate *future* needs or drive states, and are therefore bound to a present that is defined by their current motivational state." The thesis of this essay is clearly very similar to it, except perhaps in that it is a part of a broader theory of episodic memory, with all the ramifications that it entails. Because the original texts do not seem to be readily accessible, a more informed comparison has to wait for the future.

Roberts's (2002) article is titled "Are Animals Stuck in Time?" After a thorough review, and after appropriate caveats, he concludes that although the picture is not entirely clear, most of the evidence suggests that animals are indeed stuck in time. Even chimpanzees' ability to imagine their extended future is in doubt. Wolfgang Köhler (1917/1927), famous for his discovery of "insight" in chimpanzees, noted this kind of shortcoming in the mental makeup of his otherwise intelligent subjects: "The time in which the chimpanzee lives is limited in past and future" (p. 272). Roberts (2002) suggests that chimpanzees are able to "think future," in the sense of planning ahead to solve problems, only when (1) they are hungry, and (2) they can see the food reward they will receive for solving the problem. In other words, solving a complex goal-oriented task seems to depend on the anticipated satisfaction of a current need in the very near future.

I myself stumbled across the idea that mental time travel into the future may be more important than mental time travel into the past, in a quest for the answer to the question of biological utility of episodic memory. What is episodic memory good for? Given that there are relatively few obvious advantages of episodic memory over semantic memory—kind of "who really needs to know when or where a past event happened; the important thing is the lessons we can learn from the fact that it did happen"—it is easy to think of episodic memory as an evolutionary frill, as a Stephen Jay Gould kind of spandrel. When I first attempted to speculate about the adaptive utility of episodic memory, all I could offer was the thought that it provides knowledge in which one can be more confident than the knowledge that is frequently obtained second hand (Tulving, 1985b). It may have been plausible, but not convincing.

My more recent thought on the topic was that episodic memory's adaptive value lies in the autonoetic awareness of subjective time, and especially future time (Tulving, 2002a). The idea is that this kind of awareness may have been a critical driver of human cultural evolution. Culture is usually thought of as a behavior pattern of a community. I use the term, because of the lack of a better one, to signify the sum total of the differences between the world as it existed before humans changed it and as it exists now (or has existed at various times before the present). It includes changes in both of the two human realities, physical and mental.

The key notion behind human cultural evolution can be put simply: For anyone to take steps at one point in time that would make the unpredictable, frequently inhospitable natural environment more predictable at a future time, it is necessary to be able to be consciously aware of the existence of a future. An animal that cannot "think future"—cannot pre-experience possible happenings, as suggested by Atance and O'Neill (2001)—that is, cannot think about time that has not yet arrived, will not initiate and persist in carrying out activities whose beneficial consequences will become apparent only in the future, at a time that does not yet exist. For the human species, the masters of the awareness of the future, that nonexistent time has been and continues as a powerful determinant of higher-level behaviors, behaviors not motivated by the satisfaction of physiological needs. Awareness of the future has radically changed the humans' relationship with their environment. When one thinks about it, it becomes clear that a staggeringly large proportion of human behavior today— social, economic, political, religious, and otherwise—is governed, both directly and indirectly, by awareness of the future. At any rate, the point is that the ability to think about the future, as articulated by Suddendorf and Corballis (1997; see also Suddendorf, 1994), can be seen as all-important on a fundamentally broader scale of things.

RESOLUTION

It is commonly thought that the question of whether or not animals can and do travel mentally in time can never be answered. Language is necessary, the argument is, for the verification of phenomenal mental processes, such as autonoetic awareness of time. Because animals cannot talk, their mental processes will forever remain beyond the domain of objective science. This is why researchers such as Robert Hampton (chapter 11, this volume) suggest that we should limit our concerns regarding animal learning and memory to observable behavior and leave subjective experience out. Nicola Clayton and her colleagues (Clayton, Bussey, Emery, & Dickinson, 2003) have also proposed purely behavioral test criteria—content, structure, and flexibility—but these are for episodic-like memory rather than episodic memory, because they do not address the criterion of autonoesis.

Phenomenal Experience Without Language?

A minor obstacle to accepting the "behavioral resolution" of the problem of episodic memory in animals is that there exist people like myself. We are very much interested in objectively observable behavior—this is, after all, the mainstay of our science—but we also wish to reach beyond behavior and scientifically study the even more puzzling and fascinating domain of subjective reality. If we leave the phenomenal considerations out of the equation and limit ourselves to "mindless" behavior, we will automatically deny ourselves any hope of getting at concepts such as autonoesis. A major obstacle lies in the well-established fact that it is always possible to account for any form of behavior in a number of different ways. Some of these accounts may appear more reasonable or plausible than others, but their evaluation is usually highly subjective, determined as much by the characteristics of the observers as the characteristics of the observed behavior.

A useful criterion that can be applied in situations of this kind is Lloyd Morgan's (1894) canon. The canon does not solve the problem of disagreements among observers, but its application does impose constraints on the domain of possible interpretations of the observed behavior. A typical problem situation is one in which the animal behaves in a way that encourages a human observer to impute mental time travel to the animal but which also leaves open the possibility of accounting for the behavior without the need to invoke such a complex concept. Your pet dog burying the bone one day, and digging it up the next, is an excellent example of the situation. Human beings, lucky owners of autonoetic episodic memory, are intimately familiar with problems of finding their car in a huge parking lot, and equally familiar with the solution: You "just remember" where you left it. By analogy, it makes sense to imagine that the dog's ideas about the out-of-sight bone are based on the same kind of a just-remember internal mechanism. The possibility, the thesis of this essay, that just remembering is an unbelievably complicated and near-miraculous invention of nature, only available to healthy humans older than 4 years or so, does not occur to a casual observer. But it must be considered, because an alternative, and simpler, explanation is that the dog acts on its noetic knowledge, acquired during a particular episode but not stored in episodic memory, that the world is the kind of place where there's a bone buried in a particular place. The dog's knowledge-guided action is like that of any other intelligent organism who has no episodic memory. K.C. knows that the world is a place in which he, as an individual, owned a black Honda. He knows that there are fictional characters like James Bond who have aliases like 007. He also knows that "dogs confront bullfrogs," because he learned it in an experiment (Tulving et al., 1991). Therefore, when he is asked to complete the sentence frame "dog confronted . . . ?" he is happy to respond with the word "bullfrog," without remembering, and without any need to remember, that he himself saw the complete three-word phrase only 5 minutes ago. Similarly, the 4-year-old who has just learned the color name "chartreuse" and now displays the knowledge, without remembering the learning event that occurred 10 minutes earlier, is also doing nothing more than exhibiting her noetic skills.

Thus, the difficulty in demonstrating episodic memory in animals lies in the availability of simpler explanations of "episodic-looking" behavior, explanations that do not require evoking episodic memory. But if so, the logical solution to the problem is obvious. Arrange for the animal to engage in a kind of episodic-looking behavior for which no such simpler explanation is possible. Make the invoking of episodic memory necessary. In other words, set up a situation in which a nonlinguistic organism exhibits behavior that can be readily accounted for in terms of phenomenal ability such as autonoetic awareness but cannot be accounted for in terms of mindless behavior.

One straightforward suggestion of a test designed along these lines was proposed by Thomas Suddendorf in his MA thesis (Suddendorf, 1994), which provided the basis for the Suddendorf and Corballis (1997) article that I referred to earlier in this essay. As the thesis is available on the Internet, I leave it to the interested reader to get its details. What is important are the basic principles that should be generally agreed upon: It is necessary to reliably show that animals engage in an activity that (1) is not instigated and maintained by the animals' motivational states or the presence of discriminative stimuli in their internal or external environment, and (2) has no immediate relevance to satisfying present needs but has consequences that have value to the animal at a future time. Under these conditions, it becomes not only meaningful but necessary to argue that the observed behavior reflects awareness of and ability to think about one's personal future. This then would be evidence for mental time travel, and hence evidence for autonoetic episodic memory.

Suddendorf's suggestion means that, at least in principle, the possibility of proving the Bischof-Köhler hypothesis wrong is open already.

Given the expectation that creative experimenters in the future will come up with additional clever designs (Morris, 2001), the possibility of rejecting the central hypothesis of this essay becomes increasingly probable, and the challenge that it entails practically manageable.

Herein lies the challenge to comparative psychologists. In pursuing the challenge, they may find useful hints on how to proceed from studies of brain-damaged patients who lack the ability to mentally travel in time, as well as studies of young children who are extremely capable learners in the absence of episodic memory.

I am not convinced that the kind of surprise that Zentall, Clement, Bhatt, and Allen (2001) wrote about is necessary for the test—healthy humans benefit from their autonoetic consciousness in many life situations that are not unexpected. And I agree with Bennett Schwartz (chapter 9, this volume; see also Schwartz, Colon, Sanchez, Rodriguez, & Evans, 2002; and discussion of the issue by Morris, 2001) that the important feature of episodic memory, and hence of a test for it, need not be built around immediate, single-trial learning. Young children, long before they acquire episodic memory, learn not only to avoid hot stoves but also acquire scores upon scores of new words every day after a single exposure, in ways that still mystify developmental psychologists. In addition, there is no reason to doubt that a great deal of adults' acquisition of new knowledge of the world occurs on a single "trial." It is for these reasons that "fast encoding" is assigned to the category of properties that semantic and episodic memory systems have in common, shown on the left-hand side of table 1.1.

Here I would like to propose another version of a definitive test of autonoetic episodic memory that can be administered to nonlinguistic animals such primates. (Nonprimate versions require fine-tuning of some of the practical details.)

The Spoon Test

It is indeed difficult to see how one could differentiate between autonoetic remembering and noetic knowing in nonverbal organisms in situations where both the remembered events and acquired knowledge are derived from the past. But if one accepts the idea that autonoetic consciousness encompasses not only the past but also the future, the problem becomes tractable. The resolution of the fourth problem lies in autonoetic awareness of the future.

Here I propose a future-based test of autonoetic consciousness that does not rely on and need not be expressed through language. In order for us to be able to unambiguously refer to the kind of a test for autonoetic episodic memory that I have in mind, and that others would find convincing, let me refer to it as the spoon test. Because no other spoon test exists in the literature, the use of the term gets us immediately to the idea referred to.

In an Estonian children's story with a moral, a young girl dreams about going to a friend's birthday party where the guests are served delicious chocolate pudding, her favorite. Alas, all she can do is to watch other children eat it, because everybody has to have her own spoon, and she did not bring one. So the next evening, determined not to have the same disappointing experience again, she goes to bed clutching a spoon in her hand.

We do not know much about the heroine of the story. But we can surmise that she is intelligent, can learn from experience, is capable of reasoning, and can solve problems like that of the missing spoon: If they do not give you one, bring your own. At this point in the story in this essay, we also know that she can mentally travel in time, not only into the past but also into the future, that therefore she must possess autonoetic consciousness, and, furthermore, that she is probably more than 4 years old.

I would like to suggest the spoon test as a possible kind of test for the purpose of assessing the presence of autonoetic episodic memory in any species, or, indeed, in any individual member of a species. The test is independent of linguistic or other symbolic abilities of the tested species or individuals, and does not require any first-person testimony regarding phenomenally apprehended processes or states. Yet, if successful, it would provide evidence of the kind that could not be readily explained without the postulation of something like covert, neurocognitively grounded, autonoetic consciousness of one's existence in protracted time and the ability to make use of this consciousness. Therefore, if successful, the test would force the rejection of the hypothesis.

To pass the test, the individuals must act analogously to carrying their own spoon to a feast that is likely to come in another place and at another time. In practical terms, a chimpanzee or gorilla "spoon" could be a straw for drinking water that is not otherwise accessible. They can do so, the argument is, if and only if they possess the ability to mentally travel into (or foresee, preexperience, anticipate) the future. Lloyd Morgan's canon would not apply in this case, because it is difficult to imagine any simple explanation of the behavior in question that does not include a reference to a neurocognitive capacity like autonoesis.

The spoon test can be arranged in a number of specific ways, provided that three general requirements are observed. Its first, central requirement is that the test subject must deliberately engage in behavior that could not come about in the absence of mental time travel into the future. That means, as already discussed, the behavior in question must not be instigated by, and must not satisfy, a present need or be governed by current physiological states.

A second important requirement is that the execution of the critical behavior should not be triggered, evoked, or guided by specific environmental stimuli that were present in the original learning situation. This requirement has turned out to be the most difficult one to meet in past research on episodic memory in animals. Yet is critical because in its absence one cannot rule out the possibility that the behavior is governed by nonautonoetic associative learning and retrieval mechanisms. This means that the test subject must not be tested in the same environment in which the to-be-remembered information was encountered or the event witnessed.

A third requirement is that the critical behavior should turn out to satisfy a need that will be a part of the physical or psychological reality of the animal on an occasion that actually will arise in the future. Behavior serving to satisfy current needs, or triggered and maintained by a discriminative stimulus potentiated during an earlier learning episode, requires no mental time travel; it can occur, even if on a particular occasion it need not occur, independently of the current, perceptually present reminders of the learning episode. Behavior not serving any current needs but serving future needs does so.

The spoon test has implications for the possibility of observing future-oriented behavior in animals in their natural habitat. For example, it is not the making and using of tools that is critical, but rather storing them, or carrying them from one place to another, that points to mental awareness of the future. Goodall (1986) has reported such behavior in her chimpanzees of Gombe. If the observations could be repeatedly confirmed, under conditions where no physiological need for food and hence food-related behavior is present, they would constitute evidence against the thesis of this essay. Conversely, using the same line of argument, deliberate burial of the dead is a possible piece of evidence of future thinking in early hominids, but more convincing is the provision of the dead with grave goods.

Finally, note the requirement regarding a different place: The future intention should be directed at something that happens in a place other than one in which the present preparatory action is carried out. The spoon has to be picked up here and now, with a deliberate intention of putting it to use somewhere else at a future time. The major reason for the insistence on different place has to do with the minimization of the influence of the present situational cues on the spoon-carrying behavior. [Keeping in mind the Clever Hans story, the requirement for differences between original learning and present test should be extended to the experimenters, as indeed has been done in some of the well-controlled recent studies (Menzel, 1999; chapter 9, this volume; see also Schwartz et al., 2002).] In their research on "what, where, and when" of memory with scrub jays, Clayton and colleagues (Clayton et al., 2003; Clayton & Dickinson, 1998) tested the knowledge of the jays' spatial (where) component of an earlier event in the same environment in which the original learning took place. Thus their "where" component of the jays' knowledge was defined in terms of differences in local space, within one and the same visual environment. Testing episodic recollection of an event in a place other than the one in which the event took place would make for a more realistic analogue.

Is the Spoon Test Unfair?

Is the spoon test too difficult for nonhuman animals? Are we expecting and demanding too much? Are all the conditions that the nonhuman test subjects must meet to satisfy really necessary? In general, by repeatedly changing the rules of the game and setting the bar at increasingly high levels, are we being unfair to our fellow travelers on Spaceship Earth? Let me briefly note three points.

First, the spoon test is not difficult by human standards. Many, if not most, 5-year-old children would have no trouble passing it, and the rest of humankind takes the kind of abilities required to pass the test so much for granted that they have not even found it necessary to develop special terminology to discuss it objectively. Indeed, generations of humans have been taking thousands upon thousands of spoon tests over thousands upon thousands of years, even if they did not know they were doing so. And they have been passing them satisfactorily, at least some of the time, even if not always with flying colors. They have learned what the world is like from their experience and then, being armed with the extraordinary insight that the world in which they and their children will have to live will be there tomorrow, and again the day after, and even after the next dry season, or the next cold season, they have gone ahead to fashion it into a more hospitable place to live. The discovery that one need not always adapt to the world as it exists, and that one can change aspects of it for the better, has been made only by a few species, scattered here and there through the animal kingdom. In all cases other than humans, the ability to shape the world to better suit one's needs is limited in scope and requires no autonoetically guided learning. In the case of humans, the discovery that one can improve one's chances of survival by reshaping the world was based on the presumably gradual emergence of a wholesale awareness of a dimension of the world that does not exist as a component of the brain/mind in other species. Like the electric fish with their self-generated electromagnetic fields in which they can detect signals of which other creatures under the sea remain unaware, and like the migrating birds that are sensitive to the magnetic properties of the earth which exist for others only physically but not physiologically, human beings are blessed with a remarkable awareness of a dimension of the world that seems to have eluded the grasp of other nervous systems. The slow emergence of this special kind of awareness, autonoesis, in ways that we can only guess at, must have been one of the most momentous events in human evolution.

Second, as to the fairness of moving standards, think of the electric fish, or bats, or barn owls, and imagine them trying to test humans on the kinds of brain/mind achievements that they take very much for granted. If Dr. Doolittle asks them, would they admit being worried about the tests being fair for humans? I think not. If something is possible for one species, it is, in principle, obviously possible for another.

Third, it is regrettable, perhaps, that our ideas about the world, including ideas about the brain/mind and memory, do not stay put over time. Life would be simpler if they did. For example, Nicola Clayton's scrub jays would have been certified as full-fledged episodic creatures back in 1972. But whether we like or do not like the changes in our ideas about nature, there is no other way in science. Science lives and survives only as long as there is progress in its understanding of nature, and change is a necessary condition of progress. Those who seek and need the comfort of permanent certainty can find it in other scripts and books composed by great authorities.

SUMMARY

Many claims have been made about human uniqueness, that is, about human brain/mind capacities that other animals do not possess. The list of such capacities is long. It is reasonable to assume that no single item in the list alone is responsible for "making us what we are." What makes humans unique is a collection of capabilities that emerged in human evolution some time after what became the human line broke off from what became the chimpanzee line.

In this essay, I have discussed what I believe is a worthy candidate on the list of unique human traits, namely autonoetic episodic memory. Autonoetic episodic memory makes it possible for people to engage in a kind of conscious activity, mental time travel, that is beyond the reach of living creatures who do not possess episodic memory. Mental time travel takes the form of remembering personally experienced and thought-about events, occasions, and situations that occurred in the past, together with imagining (preexperiencing) personal happenings in the subjectively felt future.

Autonoetic episodic memory is a singular, even if underappreciated, achievement of biological evolution. Its separate existence was largely unknown until recently, and its relationship to other kinds of memory has not yet been thoroughly studied. We have good evidence of its existence only in humans, but even among humans the distribution and prevalence of (autonoetic) episodic memory is not yet well known. It is reasonable to assume that there are (large) individual differences among humans in autonoetic episodic memory, but the matter has not yet been studied. It is even possible to imagine that intelligent and cognitively capable human beings live in our world today who have no autonoetic episodic memory and who may not be even (fully) aware that they lack a kind of consciousness that others sometimes talk about. This issue seems to be worthy of careful study quite independently of the central thesis of this essay.

Episodic memory is unique to humans in the sense that no other animals have yet been reliably reported as being capable of behaviors that require episodic memory. Many kinds of complex behaviors of many kinds of animals can be, and have been, interpreted as manifesting episodic memory, and in many cases these behaviors do have many features in common with behaviors that are grounded in episodic memory. Practically invariably, however, the same behaviors can also be interpreted more parsimoniously, as manifestations of semantic or declarative memory, which do not provide for, and do not require postulation of, the apprehension of subjective past or subjective future time.

The hypothesis that episodic memory does not exist in nonhuman animals is part of, and follows from, a broader theory of episodic memory that is meant to be (1) internally consistent, or at least as consistent as possible at the present stage of our knowledge, and (2) not clearly contradicted by any empirical facts, at least as they are known to us today.

A central part of the theory is the assumption that episodic memory "grows out of but remains embedded within" other memory systems, in particular semantic memory (Tulving, 1984, p. 260). Semantic (or declarative) memory temporally precedes episodic memory both in phylogenetic evolution and in ontogenetic human development, and it provides a foundation for the operations of episodic memory in organisms that possess it. To accept the thesis of this essay, one must accept the idea of the precedence of semantic over episodic memory, along the lines indicated above, or in some improved form. This idea is one of the linchpins of the theory.

The hypothesis of the uniqueness of episodic memory in humans, like many other scientific hypotheses, is difficult to prove, for logical reasons. But it is amenable to evaluation by empirical data, and it can be proven false. I have suggested one scenario, dubbed the spoon test, whose empirical demonstration would be contrary to the uniqueness hypothesis. The test is independent of linguistic or other symbolic abilities of the tested species or individuals and does not require any first-person testimony regarding phenomenally apprehended processes or states. Yet, if successful, it would provide evidence of the kind that could not be readily explained without the postulation of covert, neurocognitively grounded, autonoetic consciousness of one's existence in protracted time and the ability to make use of this kind of conscious ability. That is, if successful, the outcome of the test would force the rejection of the hypothesis as currently formulated.

Finally, what about Darwin's differences in kind and in degree between humans and others? What about the rope of phylogenetic continuity with its two ends? How do the various claims for human uniqueness, including autonoetic episodic memory, fit into the picture?

There is no profound mystery here, and no need to create one. There are things that bees, birds, and humans all do. But there are also things that bees do but birds and humans do not. There are things that birds do that bees and birds do not. And there are also things that humans do but bees and birds do not. All living creatures are similar to one another in many ways, and they are also different from one another in many ways. The differences are neither in kind nor in degree; they are differences in light of similarities. Life is part of an endless matrix of sameness and diversity that is nature.

ACKNOWLEDGMENTS I greatly appreciate the invaluable help in writing this chapter provided by Mark A. Wheeler and fruitful discussions on the topic with Hans J. Markowitsch. My research is supported by a grant from the Natural Sciences and Engineering Research Council of Canada and by an endowment by Anne and Max Tanenbaum in support of research in cognitive neuroscience.

REFERENCES

Aggleton, J. P., & Brown, M. W. (1999). Episodic memory, amnesia and the hippocampal-anterior thalamic axis. *Behavioral and Brain Sciences, 22,* 425–444.

Aggleton, J. P., & Pearce, J. M. (2001). Neural systems underlying episodic memory: Insights from animal research. *Philosophical Transactions of the Royal Society, B356,* 1483–1491.

Alvarez, P., Zola-Morgan, S., & Squire, L. R. (1994). The animal-model of human amnesia—long-term-memory impaired and short-term-memory intact. *Proceedings of the National Academy of Sciences U.S.A., 91,* 5637–5641.

Atance, C. M., & O'Neill, D. K. (2001). Episodic future thinking. *Trends in Cognitive Sciences, 5,* 533–539.

Bergson, H. (1911). *Matter and memory.* London: Allen and Unwin.

Calabrese, P., Markowitsch, H. J., Durwen, H. F., Widlitzek, H., Haupts, M., Holinka, B., & Gehlen, W. (1996). Right temporofrontal cortex as critical locus for the ecphory of old episodic memories. *Journal of Neurology, Neurosurgery, and Psychiatry, 61,* 304–310.

Cermak, L. S., & O'Connor, M. (1983). The anterograde and retrograde retrieval ability of a patient with amnesia due to encephalitis. *Neuropsychologia, 21,* 213–234.

Chalmers, D. J. (1996). *The conscious mind: In search of a fundamental theory.* New York: Oxford University Press.

Clayton, N. S., Bussey, T. J., & Dickinson, A. (2003). Can animals recall the past and plan for the future? *Nature Reviews Neuroscience, 4,* 685–691.

Clayton, N. S., Bussey, T. J., Emery, N. J., & Dickinson, A. (2003). Prometheus to Proust: The case for the behavioral criteria for "mental time travel." *Trends in Cognitive Sciences, 7,* 436–437.

Clayton, N. S., & Dickinson, A. (1998). Episodic-like memory during cache recovery by scrub jays. *Nature, 395,* 272–274.

Cohen, N. J., Poldrack, R. A., & Eichenbaum, H. (1997). Memory for items and memory for relations in the procedural/declarative memory framework. *Memory, 5,* 131–178.

Conway, M. A., & Pleydell-Pearce, C. W. (2000). The construction of autobiographical memories in the self memory system. *Psychological Review, 107,* 261–288.

Dalla Barba, G. (2000). Memory, consciousness, and temporality: What is retrieved and who exactly is controlling retrieval? In E. Tulving (Ed.), *Memory, consciousness and the brain: The Tallinn Conference* (pp. 138–155). Philadelphia: Psychology Press.

Dalla Barba, G. (2001). Beyond the memory-trace paradox and the fallacy of the homunculus—A hypothesis concerning the relationship between memory, consciousness and temporality. *Journal of Consciousness Studies, 8,* 51–78.

Darwin, C. (1998). *Descent of man* (2nd ed.). Amherst, NY: Prometheus Books. (Original work published 1874)

Drummey, A. B., & Newcombe, N. S. (2002). Developmental changes in source memory. *Developmental Science, 5,* 502–513.

Duval, S., & Wicklund, R. A. (1973). Effects of objective self-awareness on attribution of causality. *Journal of Experimental Social Psychology, 9,* 17–31.

Düzel, E., Vargha-Khadem, F., Heinze, H. J., & Mishkin, M. (2001). Brain activity evidence for recognition without recollection after early hippocampal damage. *Proceedings of the National Academy of Sciences U.S.A., 98,* 8101–8106.

Eichenbaum, H. (1997). How does the brain organize memories? *Science, 277,* 330–332.

Eichenbaum, H. (2000). A cortical-hippocampal system for declarative memory. *Nature Reviews Neuroscience, 1,* 41–50.

Eichenbaum, H., Otto, T., & Cohen, N. J. (1996). The hippocampal system: Dissociating its functional components and recombining them in the service of declarative memory. *Behavioral and Brain Sciences, 19,* 772.

Eldridge, L. L., Knowlton, B. T., Furmanski, C. S., Bookheimer, S. Y., & Engel, S. A. (2000). Remembering episodes: A selective role for the hippocampus during retrieval. *Nature Neuroscience, 3,* 1149–1152.

Fivush, R., Hudson, J., & Nelson, K. (1984). Children's long-term memory for a novel event—an exploratory study. *Merrill-Palmer Quarterly Journal of Developmental Psychology, 30,* 303–310.

Gaffan, D. (2001). What is a memory system? Horel's *critique* revisited. *Behavioral Brain Research, 127,* 5–11.

Gardiner, J. M. (1988). Functional aspects of recollective experience. *Memory and Cognition, 16,* 309–313.

Gardiner, J. M., & Richardson-Klavehn, A. (2000). Remembering and knowing. In E. Tulving & F. I. M. Craik (Eds.), *The Oxford handbook of memory* (pp. 229–244). New York: Oxford University Press.

Giovagnoli, A. R., Erbetta, A., & Bugiani, O. (2001). Preserved semantic access in global amnesia and hippocampal damage. *Clinical Neuropsychologist, 15,* 508–515.

Goodall, J. (1986). *The chimpanzees of Gombe: Patterns of behavior.* Cambridge, MA: Harvard University Press.

Gopnik, A., & Graf, P. (1988). Knowing how you know: Young children's ability to identify and remember the sources of their beliefs. *Child Development, 59,* 98–110.

Griffiths, D. P., Dickinson, A., & Clayton, N. S. (1999). Declarative and episodic memory: What can animals remember about their past? *Trends in Cognitive Sciences, 3,* 74–80.

Guillery, B., Desgranges, B., Katis, S., de la Sayette, V., Viader, F., & Eustache, F. (2001). Semantic acquisition without memories: Evidence from transient global amnesia. *NeuroReport, 12,* 3865–3869.

Haith, M. M. (1997). The development of future thinking as essential for the emergence of skill in planning. In S. L. Friedman & E. Kofsky-Scholnick (Eds.), *The developmental psychology of planning: Why, how, and when do we plan?* (pp. 25–42). Hillsdale, NJ: Erlbaum.

Haith, M. M., Benson, J. B., Roberts, R. J., Jr., & Pennington, B. F. (1994). *The development of future-oriented processes.* Chicago: University of Chicago Press.

Hamann, S. B., & Squire, L. R. (1995). On the acquisition of new declarative knowledge in amnesia. *Behavioral Neuroscience, 109,* 1027–1044.

Hayman, C. A. G., Macdonald, C. A., & Tulving, E. (1993). The role of repetition and associative interference in new semantic learning in amnesia. *Journal of Cognitive Neuroscience, 5,* 375–389.

Howe, M. L., & Courage, M. L. (1993). On resolving the enigma of infantile amnesia. *Psychological Bulletin, 113,* 305–326.

Ingvar, D. H. (1985). "Memory of the future": An essay on the temporal organization of conscious awareness. *Human Neurobiology, 4,* 127–136.

James, W. (1890). *Principles of psychology.* Cambridge, MA: Harvard University Press.

Johnson, C. N., & Wellman, H. M. (1980). Children's developing understanding of mental verbs: Remember, know, and guess. *Child Development, 51,* 1095–1102.

Kapur, N. (1999). Syndromes of retrograde amnesia: A conceptual and empirical analysis. *Psychological Bulletin, 125,* 800–825.

Kircher, T. T. J., & Leube, D. T. (2003). Self-consciousness, self-agency, and schizophrenia. *Consciousness and Cognition, 12,* 656–669.

Kitchener, E. G., Hodges, J. R., & McCarthy, R. (1998). Acquisition of postmorbid vocabulary and semantic facts in the absence of episodic memory. *Brain, 121,* 1313–1327.

Klein, S. B., Loftus, J., & Kihlstrom, J. F. (1996). Self-knowledge of an amnesic patient: Toward a neuropsychology of personality and social psychology. *Journal of Experimental Psychology: General, 125,* 250–260.

Klein, S. B., Loftus, J., & Kihlstrom, J. F. (2002). Memory and temporal experience: The effects of episodic memory loss on an amnesic patient's ability to remember the past and imagine the future. *Social Cognition, 20,* 353–379.

Knowlton, B. J., & Squire, L. R. (1995). Remembering and knowing: Two different expressions of declarative memory. *Journal of Experimental Psychology: Learning, Memory and Cognition, 21,* 699–710.

Köhler, W. (1927). *The mentality of apes* (E. Winter, Trans.). London: Routledge and Kegan Paul. (Original work published 1917)

Kopelman, M. D. (2002). Disorders of memory. *Brain, 125,* 2152–2190.

Leahey, T. H. (1987). *A history of psychology* (2nd ed.). Englewood Cliffs, NJ: Prentice-Hall.

Levine, B., Black, S. E., Cabeza, R., Sinden, M., McIntosh, A. R., Toth, J. P., Tulving, E., & Stuss, D. T. (1998). Episodic memory and the self in a case of isolated retrograde amnesia. *Brain, 121,* 1951–1973.

Lewis, M., & Brooks-Gunn, J. (1979). *Social cognition and the acquisition of self.* New York: Plenum Press.

Lindsay, D. S., Johnson, M. K., & Kwon, P. (1991). Developmental changes in memory source monitoring. *Journal of Experimental Child Psychology, 52,* 297–318.

Lockhart, R. S. (1984). What do infants remember? In M. Moscovitch (Ed.), *Infant memory* (pp. 131–143). New York: Plenum.

Macphail, E. M. (1998). *The evolution of consciousness.* Oxford, UK: Oxford University Press.

Manns, J. R., Hopkins, R. O., & Squire, L. R. (2003). Semantic memory and the human hippocampus. *Neuron, 38,* 127–133.

Markowitsch, H. J., Calabrese, P., Liess, J., Haupts, M., Durwen, H. F., & Gehlen, W. (1993). Retrograde amnesia after traumatic injury of the frontotemporal cortex. *Journal of Neurology, Neurosurgery, and Psychiatry, 56,* 988–992.

McKenna, P., & Gerhand, S. (2002). Preserved semantic learning in an amnesic patient. *Cortex, 38,* 37–58.

Menzel, C. R. (1999). Unprompted recall and reporting of hidden objects by a chimpanzee (*Pan troglodytes*) after extended delays. *Journal of Comparative Psychology, 113,* 426–434.

Mishkin, M., Suzuki, W. A., Gadian, D. G., & Vargha-Khadem, F. (1997). Hierarchical organization of cognitive memory. *Philosophical Transactions of the Royal Society, B352,* 1461–1467.

Mishkin, M., Vargha-Khadem, F., & Gadian, D. G. (1998). Amnesia and organization of the hippocampal system. *Hippocampus, 8,* 212–216.

Morgan, C. L. (1894). *An introduction to comparative psychology.* London: Scott.

Morris, R. G. M. (2001). Episodic-like memory in animals: Psychological criteria, neural mechanisms and the value of episodic-like tasks to investigate animal models of neurodegenerative disease. *Philosophical Transactions of the Royal Society, B356,* 1483–1491.

Murray, E. A. (1996). What have ablation studies told us about the neural substrates of stimulus memory? *Seminars in Neuroscience, 8,* 13–22.

Murray, E. A., & Bussey, T. J. (2001). Consolidation and the medial temporal lobe revisited: Methodological considerations. *Hippocampus, 1,* 1–7.

Nadel, L. (1994). Multiple memory systems: What and why, an update. In D. L. Schacter & E. Tulving (Eds.), *Memory systems 1994* (pp. 39–63). Cambridge, MA: MIT Press.

Nelson, K. (1984). The transition from infant to child memory. In M. Moscovitch (Ed.), *Infant memory: Its relation to normal and pathological memory in humans and other animals* (pp. 103–130). New York: Plenum.

Nelson, K. (1992). Emergence of autobiographical memory at age 4. *Human Development, 35,* 172–177.

Nelson, K. (1993). The psychological and social origins of autobiographical memory. *Psychological Science, 4,* 7–13.

Nelson, K., & Fivush, R. (2004). The emergence of autobiographical memory: A social-cultural developmental theory. *Psychological Review, 111,* 486–511.

Noelle, D. C. (2001). Exorcising the homunculus: There is no one behind the curtain. *Free Inquiry Magazine, 21*(2).

Nyberg, L., Habib, R., Tulving, E., Cabeza, R., Houle, S., Persson, J., & McIntosh, A. R. (2000). Large scale neurocognitive networks underlying episodic memory. *Journal of Cognitive Neuroscience, 12,* 163–173.

Nyberg, L., & Tulving, E. (1997). Searching for memory systems. *European Journal of Cognitive Psychology, 9,* 121–125.

Olton, D. S. (1984). Comparative analysis of episodic memory. *Behavioral and Brain Sciences, 7,* 250–251.

Olton, D. S. (1985). Memory: Neuropsychological and ethopsychological approaches to its classification. In L.-G. Nilsson & T. Archer (Eds.), *Perspectives on learning and memory* (pp. 95–113). Hillsdale, NJ: Lawrence Erlbaum.

Olton, D. S., Becker, J. T., & Handelmann, G. E. (1979). Hippocampus, space, and memory. *Behavioral and Brain Sciences, 2,* 313–365.

Olton, D. S., Becker, J. T., & Handelmann, G. E. (1980). Hippocampal function: Working memory or cognitive mapping? *Physiological Psychology, 8,* 239–246.

Olton, D. S., & Pappas, B. C. (1979). Spatial memory and hippocampal function. *Neuropsychologia, 17,* 669–682.

Perner, J., & Ruffman, T. (1995). Episodic memory and autonoetic consciousness: Developmental evidence and a theory of childhood amnesia. *Journal of Experimental Child Psychology, 59,* 516–548.

Povinelli, D. J., Landau, K. R., & Perilloux, H. K. (1996). Self-recognition in young children using delayed versus live feedback: Evidence of a developmental asynchrony. *Child Development, 67,* 1540–1554.

Povinelli, D. J., & Vonk, J. (2003). Chimpanzee minds: Suspiciously human? *Trends in Cognitive Sciences, 7,* 157–160.

Rajaram, S., & Coslett, H. B. (2000). New conceptual associative learning in amnesia. *Memory and Language, 43,* 291–315.

Rajaram, S., & Roediger, H. L., III. (1997). Remembering and knowing as states of consciousness during recollection. In J. D. Cohen & J. W. Schooler (Eds.), *Scientific approaches to the question of consciousness* (pp. 213–240). Hillsdale, NJ: Erlbaum.

Roberts, W. A. (2002). Are animals stuck in time? *Psychological Bulletin, 128,* 473–489.

Roberts, W. A., & Roberts, S. (2002). Two tests of the stuck-in-time hypothesis. *Journal of General Psychology, 129,* 415–429.

Roediger, H. L., III, Marsh, E. J., & Lee, S. C. (2002). Kinds of memory. In H. Pashler & D. Medin (Eds.), *Stevens' handbook of experimental psychology: Vol. 2. Memory and cognitive processes* (3rd ed., pp. 1–41). New York: Wiley.

Romanes, G. J. (1881). *Animal intelligence.* London: Kegan Paul.

Rosenbaum, R. S., Kohler, S., Schacter, D. L., Moscovitch, M., Westmacott, R., Black, S. E., Gao, F., & Tulving, E. (in press). The case of K.C.: Contributions of a memory-impaired person to memory theory. *Neuropsychologia.*

Rousseaux, M., Godfrey, O., Cabaret, M., Bernati, T., & Pruvo, J. P. (1997). Retrograde memory after rupture of aneurysms of the anterior communicating artery. *Revue de Neurologie, 153,* 659–668.

Rovee-Collier, C., & Hayne, H. (2000). Memory in infancy and early childhood. In E. Tulving & F. I. M. Craik (Eds.), *The Oxford handbook of memory* (pp. 267–282). New York: Oxford University Press.

Schacter, D. L., Harbluk, J. L., & McLachlan, D. R. (1984). Retrieval without recollection: An experimental analysis of source amnesia. *Journal of Verbal Learning and Verbal Behavior, 23,* 593–611.

Schacter, D. L., & Tulving, E. (1994). What are the memory systems of 1994? In D. L. Schacter & E. Tulving (Eds.), *Memory systems 1994* (pp. 1–38). Cambridge, MA: MIT Press.

Schacter, D. L., Wagner, A. D., & Buckner, R. L. (2000). Memory systems of 1999. In E. Tulving & F. I. M. Craik (Eds.), *The Oxford handbook of memory* (pp. 627–643). New York: Oxford University Press.

Schwartz, B. L., Colon, M. R., Sanchez, I. C., Rodriguez, I. A., & Evans, S. (2002). Single-trial learning of "what" and "who" information in a gorilla (*Gorilla*): Implications for episodic memory. *Animal Cognition, 5,* 85–90.

Sherry, D. F., & Schacter, D. L. (1987). The evolution of multiple memory systems. *Psychological Review, 94,* 439–454.

Shettleworth, S. (1998). *Cognition, evolution, and behavior.* New York: Oxford University Press.

Squire, L. R. (1987). *Memory and brain.* New York: Oxford University Press.

Squire, L. R. (1992). Memory and the hippocampus: A synthesis from findings with rats, monkeys, and humans. *Psychological Review, 99,* 195–231.

Squire, L. R., & Kandel, E. R. (1999). *Memory: From mind to molecules.* New York: Scientific American Library.

Squire, L. R., & Zola, S. M. (1998). Episodic memory, semantic memory, and amnesia. *Hippocampus, 8,* 205–211.

Suddendorf, T. (1994). *Discovery of the fourth dimension: Mental time travel and human evolution.* Unpublished master's thesis, University of Waikato, New Zealand.

Suddendorf, T., & Corballis, M. C. (1997). Mental time travel and the evolution of the human mind. *Genetic and Social General Psychology Monographs, 123,* 133–167.

Taylor, M., Esbensen, B. M., & Bennett, R. T. (1994). Children's understanding of knowledge acquisition: The tendency for children to report that they have always known what they have just learned. *Child Development, 65,* 1581–1604.

Tulving, E. (1972). Episodic and semantic memory. In E. Tulving & W. Donaldson (Eds.), *Organization of memory* (pp. 381–403). New York: Academic Press.

Tulving, E. (1983). *Elements of episodic memory*. Oxford, UK: Clarendon Press.

Tulving, E. (1984). Relations among components and processes of memory. *Behavioral and Brain Sciences, 7*, 257–268.

Tulving, E. (1985a). How many memory systems are there? *American Psychologist, 40*, 385–398.

Tulving, E. (1985b). Memory and consciousness. *Canadian Psychology, 26*, 1–12.

Tulving, E. (1989a). Memory: Performance, knowledge, and experience. *European Journal of Cognitive Psychology, 1*, 3–26.

Tulving, E. (1989b). Remembering and knowing the past. *American Scientist, 77*, 361–367.

Tulving, E. (1993a). What is episodic memory? *Current Perspectives in Psychological Science, 2*, 67–70.

Tulving, E. (1993b). Self-knowledge of an amnesic individual is represented abstractly. In T. K. Srull & R. S. Wyer, Jr. (Eds.), *The mental representation of trait and autobiographical knowledge about the self* (pp. 147–156). Hillsdale, NJ: Erlbaum.

Tulving, E. (1993c). Varieties of consciousness and levels of awareness in memory. In A. Baddeley & L. Weiskrantz (Eds.), *Attention: Selection, awareness and control. A tribute to Donald Broadbent* (pp. 283–299). London: Oxford University Press.

Tulving, E. (1995). Organization of memory: Quo vadis? In M. S. Gazzaniga (Ed.), *The cognitive neurosciences* (pp. 839–847). Cambridge, MA: MIT Press.

Tulving, E. (1998). Study of memory: Processes and systems. In J. K. Foster & M. Jelicic (Eds.), *Memory: Systems, process, or function?* (pp. 11–30). Oxford, UK: Oxford University Press.

Tulving, E. (2000). Concepts of memory. In E.Tulving & F. I. M. Craik (Eds.), *The Oxford handbook of memory* (pp. 33–43). New York: Oxford University Press.

Tulving, E. (2001a). Episodic memory and common sense: How far apart? *Philosophical Transactions of the Royal Society B, 356*, 1505–1515.

Tulving, E. (2001b). The origin of autonoesis in episodic memory. In H. L. Roediger, J. S. Nairne, I. Neath, & A. M. Suprenant (Eds.), *The nature of remembering: Essays in honor of Robert G. Crowder* (pp. 17–34). Washington, DC: American Psychological Association.

Tulving, E. (2002a). Chronesthesia: Awareness of subjective time. In D. T. Stuss & R. C. Knight (Eds.), *Principles of frontal lobe functions* (pp. 311–325). New York: Oxford University Press.

Tulving, E. (2002b). Episodic memory: From mind to brain. *Annual Review of Psychology, 53*, 1–25.

Tulving, E., Hayman, C. A. G., & Macdonald, C. A. (1991). Long-lasting perceptual priming and semantic learning in amnesia: A case experiment. *Journal of Experimental Psychology: Learning, Memory and Cognition, 17*, 595–617.

Tulving, E., & Markowitsch, H. J. (1998). Episodic and declarative memory: Role of the hippocampus. *Hippocampus, 8*, 198–204.

Tulving, E., Schacter, D. L., McLachlan, D. R., & Moscovitch, M. (1988). Priming of semantic autobiographical knowledge: A case study of retrograde amnesia. *Brain and Cognition, 8,* 3–20.

Van der Linden, M., Brédart, S., Depoorter, N., & Coyette, F. (1996). Semantic memory and amnesia: A case study. *Cognitive Neuropsychology, 13,* 391–413.

Van der Linden, M., Cornil, V., Meulemans, T., Ivanoiu, A., Salmon, E., & Coyette, F. (2001). Acquisition of novel vocabulary in an amnesic patient. *Neurocase, 7,* 283–293.

Vargha-Khadem, F., Gadian, D. G., Watkins, K. E., Connelly, A., Van Paesschen, W., & Mishkin, M. (1997). Differential effects of early hippocampal pathology on episodic and semantic memory. *Science, 277,* 376–380.

Vargha-Khadem, F., Salmond, C. H., Watkins, K. E., Friston, K. J., Gadian, D. G., & Mishkin, M. (2003). Developmental amnesia: Effect of age at injury. *Proceedings of the National Academy of Sciences U.S.A., 100,* 10055–10060.

Verfaellie, M., Koseff, P., & Alexander, M. P. (2000). Acquisition of novel semantic information in lesion location. *Neuropsychologia, 38,* 484–492.

Viskontas, I. V., McAndrews, M. P., & Moscovitch, M. (2000). Remote episodic memory deficits in patients with unilateral temporal lobe epilepsy and excisions. *Journal of Neuroscience, 20,* 5853–5857.

Weiskrantz, L. (1985). *Animal intelligence.* Oxford, UK: Oxford University Press.

Westmacott, R., & Moscovitch, M. (2001). Names and words without meaning: Incidental postmorbid semantic learning in a person with extensive bilateral medial temporal damage. *Neuropsychology, 15,* 586–596.

Wheeler, M. A. (2000). Episodic memory and autonoetic awareness. In E. Tulving & F. I. M. Craik (Eds.), *The Oxford handbook of memory* (pp. 597–608). New York: Oxford University Press.

Wheeler, M. A., & McMillan, C. T. (2001). Focal retrograde amnesia and the episodic-semantic distinction. *Cognitive, Affective, and Behavioral Neuroscience, 1,* 22–37.

Wheeler, M. A., Stuss, D. T., & Tulving, E. (1997). Toward a theory of episodic memory: The frontal lobes and autonoetic consciousness. *Psychological Bulletin, 121,* 331–354.

Wimmer, H., Hogrefe, G.-J., & Perner, J. (1988). Children's understanding of informational access as source of knowledge. *Child Development, 59,* 386–396.

Wright, A. A., Santiago, H. C., Sands, S. F., Kendrick, D. F., & Cook, R. G. (1985). Memory processing of serial lists by pigeons, monkeys, and people. *Science, 229,* 287–289.

Zentall, T. R., Clement, T. S., Bhatt, R. S., & Allen, J. (2001). Episodic-like memory in pigeons. *Psychonomic Bulletin and Review, 8,* 685–690.

2

Self-Reflective Consciousness
and the Projectable Self

Janet Metcalfe & Hedy Kober

In 1619, while secluded in his poele, Descartes undertook to discover the indisputable source of all knowledge, the unshakable foundation upon which he could base his philosophy with certainty. Many years later, in his 1637 *Discourse on Method*, he reported that the one thing that he was unable to doubt, which became this foundation, is something that today we might dub self-reflective consciousness, metacognition, secondary representation, or autonoetic consciousness—the reflection of the self upon its own thoughts, memories, mental processes, and other possible worlds, including the ability to mentally project oneself outside the boundaries of one's immediate stimulus environment and thereby entertain counterfactuals. He affirmed that in order to have self-reflection of this sort, one must have a self (cf. Russell, 1945/1972). "But what then am I? A thing that thinks. What is that? A thing that doubts, understands, affirms, denies, wills, refuses, and that also imagines and senses" (p. 66). In this chapter, we refer to the kind of self-reflective consciousness so aptly captured in Descartes's meditations and discourse as the *projectable self*. It can, as Descartes noted, perceive the present and understand, affirm, and deny; but it can also be projected into the past to allow episodic memory (Tulving, 2002; Wheeler, Stuss, & Tulving, 1997; chapters 1 and 7, this volume). It can imagine the future and itself in it. It can imagine other possible perspectives, including, importantly, the points of view of other people, both physically and also, even more interestingly, mentally and emotionally. The potential to project oneself in outer and inner space and time allows capabilities familiar to people, but perhaps rare or unknown in other animals: reminiscence, planning and scheming, connection to other people through empathy and understanding, and manipulation of other people through lies and deception.

Descartes equated this self-reflective ability with the soul and argued, primarily on religious grounds (but with the uniqueness of language being his empirical evidence), that only humans have it. Without it, a creature is a "mere" mechanism, regardless of the complexity of the behavior. While taking no stand on the ineffability of the soul, we here argue that the projectable self is the singular evolutionary adaptation underpinning the most advanced achievements of humans including our culture—without doubt what Dennett (1991) would call a Good Trick.

Humphrey (2003) advanced that we humans have what he unashamedly called an inner eye. This inner eye could look down on more basic cognitions and interpret them in a user-friendly way, that is, as motivations, feelings, goals, hopes, intentions, fears, thoughts, memories, and so on (rather than as, say, p300s, serotonin imbalances, hippocampal activation, or reverberating Hebb nets). He was specific about noting that this self-reflective capability is an evolutionary advance (though he did not specify exactly at what point it came into being). He allayed concern about the problem of having to postulate a homunculus within a homunculus within a homunculus, saying: "The problem of self-observation producing an infinite regress is, I think, phony. No one would say that a person cannot use his own eyes to observe his own feet. No one would say, moreover, that he cannot use his own eyes, with the aid of a mirror, to observe his own eyes. Then why should anyone say a person cannot, at least in principle, use his own brain to observe his own brain?" (p. 11).

Humphrey (2003) noted that one could exhibit many skills without this kind of self-reflective consciousness, as in the top panel of figure 2.1. For example, one might well be able to drive, play the piano, protect one's young, or do many of the things that people have been shown to be able to do automatically without input from the inner eye. An issue that is investigated in much of this book is whether or not much highly complex behavior of nonhuman primates might be possible without this kind of consciousness and what behavior actually requires self-reflective consciousness. On the phenomenology— the transcendent or otherworldly qualities of this kind of consciousness—Humphrey demurs, alluding only to "one curious feature: the output of the inner eye is part of its own input. As I expect you know, a self-referential system of this sort may well have strange and paradoxical properties—not least that so-called 'truth functions' go awry" (p. 12).

So why would such an inner eye evolve? The answer given by Humphrey, much like that of Terrace, Nelson, Higgins, and others in this volume, is that people are intensely social, as a species. Having an inner eye—which gives a quick and accessible description of how one feels and thinks oneself, what one wants, plans, and fears—may

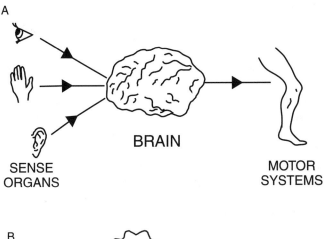

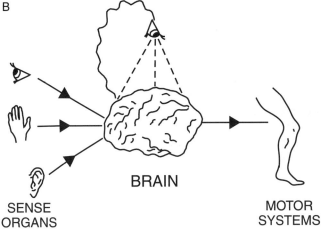

Figure 2.1 A. Diagrammatic representation of an entity lacking insight. B. Diagrammatic representation of an entity possessing insight.
Illustrations courtesy of N. Humphrey.

allow one to make similar attributions to other people, and quickly.
Facility at predicting the behavior of others, by getting inside their
minds, provides an enormous social advantage. A person with this
ability highly honed is attractive as a mate and formidable as a foe.
This social aspect of the projectable self has come to be known as
theory of mind, and some of the literature concerned with this specific
issue is reviewed below.

    A related just-so story about the evolution of the projectable self is
that "one can let one's hypotheses die instead of oneself." The ability

to imagine possible future situations with oneself in them in considerable detail, and to play out possibilities in the mental rather than the physical world, allows a person to consider disastrous alternatives without physical consequences, and hence to find new solutions that might otherwise be impossible. Thinking, in this sense of simulating events—both social and physical—has clear advantages for a species that can do it, and some explorations of this are given in chapter 8. Impulsiveness due to the lack of projecting the self in this way (i.e., acting without first thinking) in humans is considered a mental disorder.

Finally, the ability to look back on the details of one's personal past, to be able to revisit what happened to oneself in the past via episodic memory (rather than merely having one's semantic memory or automatic responses changed, without the possibility of reflection on the earlier events that caused the changes), also may enhance survival. For example, one could update current judgments and courses of action in the light of new information about the causes of events in the past. Such malleability seems highly adaptive and also entertaining. In the print shown in figure 2.2, by the Japanese master Hiroshige, a powerful samurai is seen in three panels: the past, the present, and the future. He is portrayed as looking fiercely into his own personal past (but gesturing toward and guarding his much-hoped-for future protectively). He contemplates the ghosts of his now-vanquished enemies, which are multistable figures—at one moment innocuous snow-laden trees, at the next fearsome skulls that come back to haunt him. This time travel into his past, and the flexibility of the interpretation of that past from different vantage points, as is characteristic of episodic memory, enhances the beauty of his imagined future, portrayed as the beyond-lovely courtesan housed in the exquisite palace in the right panel. Episodic memory (see Nelson, 2000; chapter 4, this volume) constitutes the foundation for one's personal self, with all three panels, as well as the narrative that joins them. Such time travel into one's own personal past, also, according to Tulving (chapter 1, this volume), provides the basis for all future planning and is the mental foundation of human culture.

Formally, the idea that people have an inner eye that can look at other cognitive functions and content is the same as the description, agreed upon by the field, given by Nelson and Narens (1994) for metacognition (and see chapter 12, this volume). They propose that there are at least two levels, one of which is considered to be basic cognition, and the other "meta"—at a higher level looking down upon and making judgments about the events happening at the basic level. When they are judgments about events in the world, of brightness or numerosity, say, rather than about entities of the mind, such as memories or beliefs, then they are not properly called metacognitions. To be

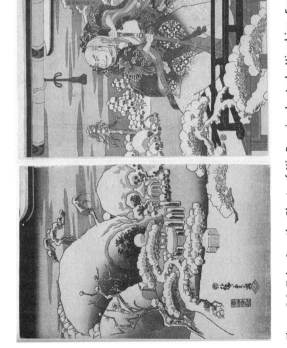

Figure 2.2 *Taira Sees the Ghosts of His Enemies*, by Ando Hiroshige. From the collection of J. Metcalfe. See color insert.

in a position to have metacognitions, an animal must first have cognitions (i.e., mental representations). But the issue at stake here is not whether other primates have cognitions (which we assume they do) but rather whether they can reflect upon them. In Nelson and Narens's scheme, there is a feedback loop whereby the metacognitive level can change or modulate what goes on at the basic level. This feedback allows the person to have control over basic-level thoughts.

Some kinds of metacognition need not require a full-blown projectable self. For instance, metacognitive judgments might be made about semantic knowledge (bona fide representations, but not personal ones). The inner eye could stay stationary, in space and time, to make such judgments. Metacognitions might also be made about events involving the self over time past and future, however, or involving what it is like to be another person, and such judgments would involve projection. Insofar as having an inner eye that looks at one's own cognitions is true self-reflection, investigation of metacognition, even in the nonprojective form, can be informative concerning the evolution of the projectable self. Presumably the ability to make even simple metacognitive judgments is a precursor to full-blown projective consciousness. It may, indeed, be this particular capability in nonhuman primates that provides the most incisive clues to the evolution of our human consciousness, since it may have been the first to manifest itself (see also chapters 3 and 12, this volume).

In this chapter, we propose that the emergence of the projectable self is the central evolutionary advance culminating in human consciousness. For this conjecture, we owe much to Tulving (2002; Wheeler et al., 1997), to Suddendorf and Corballis (1997) and Suddendorf and Whiten (2001), to Humphrey (2003), and to Donald (1991). This projectable self, full blown, is the capability that makes us unique, but it is a very new adaptation. We seek to find evidence of where, in the evolutionary tree, this capability originated. The word "consciousness" is very slippery, insofar as there are undoubtedly many kinds and levels of consciousness. While the projectable self indisputably involves consciousness at the very highest level, there are many other lower forms of consciousness sometimes referred to as awareness, phenomenology, noetic and anoetic consciousness, sentience (see especially chapters 1, 4, and 5, this volume). Beings that do not have a fully developed sense of self-reflective projectable consciousness may nevertheless have these other kinds of consciousness, and furthermore, these are sufficient to underlie much clever behavior and learning (see chapter 12, this volume, for an argument that they may, indeed, underlie metacognition itself). The central tenet of this chapter is that while there is considerable evidence for these other kinds of consciousness in nonhuman primates, there are also some indications of at least some characteristics of the projectable self. For example, there is now some suggestion that monkeys may have the beginnings of metacognition (see chapters 10, 11, and 12, this volume), though the flexibility of this capability is far from impressive. Chimps, bonobos, gorillas, and orangutans show greater metacognitive capabilities (see chapter 13, this volume). Glimmerings of episodic memory, it is asserted by some, may be within the range of chimps and gorillas (chapters 8 and 9, this volume;cf. chapter 1). At the human end of the scale, there is also an indication of the newness of this capability. Evidence from studies of autistic humans suggests that the fully articulated projectable self may have not yet fully saturated the human gene pool.

SELF-RECOGNITION

To have self-reflective consciousness, one must have a self. Thus, tasks that tap into a person's feeling of self, or self-recognition, provide an obvious empirical starting point. The most famous task of this ilk is the dye or rouge test, devised by Gallup (1970). Unbeknownst to the person or animal, a spot of dye or rouge is put on his or her face, in a location that cannot be seen without a mirror. Once the person or animal looks in a mirror, the question is, does he or she self-refer concerning the rouge? Gallup has argued that such self-reference indicates that the creature has a sense of self (though a number of other researchers, see Heyes 1994, 1998; Povinelli, 1993; Tomasello & Call, 1997, have suggested that self-awareness, in the Cartesian sense, might not be implied because the animal might simply be using the mirror to gain visual access to a part of the body previously perceived only tactually or proprioceptively, or it might be recognizing only its own behavior rather than its psychological or Cartesian self).

Humans

By the age of around 18 to 24 months (Amsterdam, 1972; Lewis & Brooks-Gunn, 1979), human babies pass the rouge test. Asendorpf, Warkentin, and Baudonniere (1996) note that at around the same time, and in synchrony, they show evidence of recognition of mind in others—showing empathy, communication through synchronic imitation, and cooperation. If this correspondence, and the implied cross-task dependence, turns out to be correct, then mirror self-recognition may indeed be a marker of a projectable self. Although young children without experience with mirrors showed some deficits in relating reflection to location in space, they showed no impairment in self-recognition (Priel & De Schonen, 1986).

Although most autistic children recognize themselves, some do not. Spiker and Ricks (1984) reported that only 36 of 52 autistics in their sample, between the ages of 4 and 12 years, showed evidence of self-recognition. Failure to self-recognize was predicted by language impairment and level of functioning. Another study (Neuman & Hill, 1978) found that 1 out of 7 autistics between the ages of 5.5 and 11 years failed to recognize themselves. Last, Ferrari and Matthews (1983) found that those autistics who did not clearly recognize themselves (46.7% of their sample) had the lowest mental age in the sample (22 months) and were rated by their teachers as significantly lower-functioning on behavioral observations of affect, attentional skills, language, and interpersonal skills.

Nonhuman Primates

There is considerable evidence that chimps, so long as they are given experience with mirrors, and so long as they are socially raised, can pass the rouge test (Gallup, 1970; Gallup, McClure, Hill, & Bundy, 1971; Tomasello & Call, 1997). In Gallup's (1970) seminal studies with chimps and macaques, the chimps initially displayed aggressive behavior toward their own mirror image—as if the reflection were another, and threatening, chimp. Within a few days, however, they started using the mirror in a self-directed way—to pick food out of their teeth, and so on. When the chimps were anesthetized and marked with dye on a spot that they could not see directly without the use of the mirror, they would touch the spot on their own face—much as young children do when they are surreptitiously marked with a trace of rouge on their face (figure 2.3). Chimps, then, pass this

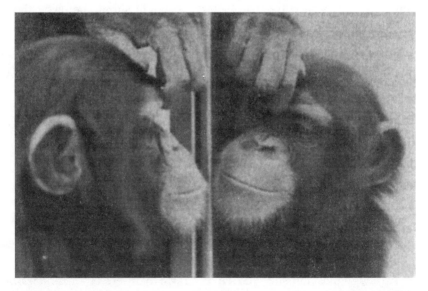

Figure 2.3 Megan looking in the mirror. Photo courtesy of the Cognitive Evolution Group, University of Louisiana at Lafayette.

test of self (see Tomasello & Call, 1997, for a review), as do orangutans (Suarez & Gallup, 1981), and some gorillas. Koko, for example, the famous human-reared gorilla (Patterson & Cohn, 1994), and King, the circus gorilla studied by Schwartz (chapter 9, this volume), both passed.

Despite extensive testing and extensive use of mirrors, there is still scant evidence for self-recognition in monkeys. An exception was reported for six cotton-topped tamarins (Hauser, Kralik, Botto, Garrett, & Oser, 1995), but the results did not replicate (Hauser, Miller, Liu, & Gupta, 2001). The fact that monkeys will look away rather than staring back at another monkey may qualify the results of mirror testing. Novak (1996, cited in Tomasello & Call, 1997) found that when monkeys were first trained to look at one another, they showed some evidence of mirror self-recognition. Overall, though, clear evidence for monkey self-recognition is lacking.

THEORY OF MIND

Gallup (1982) has argued that awareness of self implies awareness of other minds. The self, by this perspective, is an essentially social being who gains his or her definition from the social matrix (see also chapters 3, 4, and 6, this volume). However, one might imagine that a mind could exist in a solipsistic world, in which there is self-reflection, but no other-reflection. This may be an empirical question though, and, as mentioned above, self-recognition and empathy seem to develop at about the same time. Furthermore, Frith and Happe (1999) have shown an association between impairment on theory of mind tasks and an inability to introspect, reflect on one's own actions, or anticipate one's own actions. Even so, self-recognition typically develops earlier (it is usually in place by age 18 months) than does theory of mind (which is only entrenched by about 4 years). Insofar as an individual might have a mind, but not extend the attribution to other beings, a failure to show evidence of theory of mind does not necessarily rule out the possibility of self-reflective consciousness of some sort. But if a nonhuman primate showed evidence of having theory of mind, this in itself would be proof positive of self-reflective consciousness of a highly projectable form.

Humans

For most adult humans, theory of mind is a ubiquitous attribution to other people. It is often so overextended that we also attribute mind—intentions, goals, thoughts, memories, plans, emotions—to animals, indiscriminately, and even to inanimate objects. People will anthropomorphize even to moving abstract shapes, ascribing volitional mental states to them. For example, Adolphs (1999) reviewed a replication of a classic study by Heider and Simmel (1944) in which people viewed a short film of an open square and some triangles and circles moving in various directions. A typical description was, "And then the big triangle chased the little triangle around. Finally, he went in, got inside the box to go after the circle, and the circle was scared of him ... and they went off on their way, and the big triangle got upset and started breaking the box open" (p. 473). Contrast Klin's (2000, p. 840) transcription of an autistic's description of the same film: "The big triangle went into the rectangle. There were a small triangle and a circle. The big triangle went out. The shapes bounce off each other. The small circle went inside the rectangle. The big triangle was in the box with the circle." It is the rare person who can stick to the kind of strict operational description of the patterns of movement given by the autistic, stripped of intentional terminology. When they do so, they sound very odd indeed.

Wellman, Cross, and Watson (2001) concluded from a meta-analysis of experiments on theory of mind capabilities in human infants that the development of theory of mind begins at around 2 years of age, and continues until about 4 years of age (see also Nelson, 2000; Perner, 1991). Of course, insofar as social intelligence is highly related to theory of mind, the development of this capability may continue well into adolescence and beyond. There are some cases of patients, however, who apparently lack the ability.

Stuss, Gallup, and Alexander (2001) described a patient with lesions to the right frontal cortex (or with bifrontal lesions) who failed an inference-based theory of mind task. The patient was to indicate which of two graduate students (both of whom had previously demonstrated their trustworthiness) he wished to show where a prize, which was concealed from his own view by a barrier, was hidden. One student sat by the subject in front of the barrier as the experimenter hid the prize, while the other student sat next to the experimenter, behind the barrier, and could clearly see where the prize was hidden. When normal people, or patients with nonfrontal or left frontal lesions are asked, in this situation, they consistently choose the student who sat next to the experimenter, the one who could see where the prize was hidden. Presumably they choose this student because they imagine what they would see if they were him, and realize, effortlessly, that only the person behind the barrier could actually see where the prize was hidden. Without theory of mind, or the realization that another's experience is like their own, however, they might not make this inference. The right frontal patient chose at random between the two students.

In contrast to Stuss's finding, which implicates the right prefrontal cortex in theory of mind, Happe and colleagues (1996), in a positron emission tomography study using normals, found that a highly circumscribed region of the left medial prefrontal cortex was activated during story comprehension that involved taking another's perspective. This area was not activated in Asperger's autistics, however, who (as we shall review), have great difficulty with theory of mind tasks. Rowe, Bullock, Polkey, and Morris (2001) found theory of mind deficits in patient groups with either left or right unilateral frontal lesions, and Stone, Baron-Cohen, and Knight (1998) found deficits, similar to those of Asperger patients, in patients with bilateral orbitofrontal lesions.

It has been proposed (Baron-Cohen, Leslie, & Frith, 1985; Baron-Cohen, 1995) that the fundamental impairment in autism is a lack of theory of mind. Although numerous other idiosyncratic behaviors and perceptions are associated with autism (for example, stereotypy of movement, compulsions, extremely repetitious behavior, lack of appropriate voice modulation, heightened perceptions, pain tolerance, language deficits, etc.), the inability to understand another person's perspective is a theme that underlies much research (see, for example, Adolphs, Sears, & Piven, 2001; DeLong, 1992; Hobson, 1990; Hughes & Russell, 1993; Leslie, 1987; Ozonoff, Pennington, & Rogers, 1991, for other theories of the dysfunction). The lack of theory of mind would result in a social blindness that allows the highly developed Asperger's autistic to follow rules of behavior well, but without the sensitivity to nuance that we take for granted as part of a person's social skills. Such people often behave inappropriately without realizing it.

Two tasks, both with a number of variants, have come to be classic tests of theory of mind research. The first (Wimmer & Perner, 1983), often called the Sally-Anne task, is one in which a person (Sally), or sometimes a puppet, sees some kind of reward being hidden and then leaves the room. A second person (Anne) then changes the location of the reward. When Sally returns, the child being tested is asked where she will look. Normals typically say that she will search in the original location in which she left the reward, but autistic children (and normal children younger than age 4) typically say that she will look where the reward is actually currently located (Baron-Cohen et al., 1985). The second task is one in which a package that typically contains candy (i.e., M&M's) is opened and revealed to contain pencils. The child is asked what a new person will think is in the package. Normals say M&Ms, but autistic children frequently say pencils— revealing an inability to put themselves in the epistemic position of the other person (Perner, Frith, Leslie, & Leekam, 1989).

It would appear that, insofar as autism is a genetically predisposed condition, and insofar as the theory of mind hypothesis is correct, this very high level of self-reflective consciousness may not have yet fully saturated the human gene pool, or that it is, at the least, fragile.

Nonhuman Primates

The first exploration of theory of mind in nonhuman primates was done by Premack and Woodruff (1978), who gave their chimpanzee, Sarah, a series of problems to solve that they claimed involved inferences about the goals, wants, needs, desires, and knowledge of other people, that is, which implied theory of mind. For example, a videotape may have shown a human trying to get some inaccessible food, or trying to extricate himself from a locked cage, or shivering from a nonfunctioning, unplugged heater, or trying to play an unplugged record player. Sarah was then given a forced-choice test in which one of the alternatives was a solution to the human's problem. That she picked the correct choices most of the time suggested to the authors that she empathized with the human's problem, exhibiting theory of mind. Humans, in this situation, would solve the problem, essentially, by asking themselves what they would do if they were in the other person's shoes, and the claim was that Sarah did the same thing.

This interpretation, while intriguing, might be disputed. It is possible that the chimps simply gave the solution as a learned response, or remembered the correct sequence from having seen it before, rather than projecting themselves into the position of the other. The authors argued against mere familiarity as a possibility, since the chimps would have had the opportunity to view unplugged as well as plugged-in plugs, or burned wicks as well as new ones. They also argued for intentionality insofar as the responses varied depending upon whether Sarah liked the humans involved or not. Keith was Sarah's favorite keeper. When he was the actor in the problems, she solved them correctly eight out of eight times. However, when Bill, an acquaintance whom Sarah disliked, was the actor, she was right only two out of eight times.

The nature of the problems posed clouds a straightforward interpretation. These were not classic theory of mind problems, such as the Sally-Anne task or the M&M's task, but rather sequences that culminated in a solution. Notably, in the research on autism, three types of sequence problems are typically given: (1) mechanical, which are understood by all autistic participants; (2) behavioral, which can be done without reference to mental states; and (3) mentalistic, which require knowledge of the depicted person's state of belief, and which typically autistics cannot do. Only the third type provides information about theory of mind, though all three types seem to have been included in the Premack and Woodruff set. Thus, although Premack and Woodruff's contention is intriguing, their conclusions are not beyond dispute.

A second approach was taken by Povinelli and his group. A number of researchers have shown that chimps, like children, follow a person's gaze. When people do this, presumably it is because they are looking to see what the other person sees, and it implies theory of mind. However, based on a series of clever experiments, Povinelli (2000; Povinelli & Eddy, 1996a, 1996b, 1996c) argued that this interpretation does not necessarily follow with chimps, insofar as they do not distinguish between people who can see or cannot (because they either have a mask on or a bucket over their heads, say). They seem to respond, instead, to body orientation, and conform to what Povinelli thinks is a lower order rule rather than to a notion about what the other person or animal is perceiving. He concludes that gaze following does not necessarily imply theory of mind.

Interestingly enough, Premack and Premack (1983), years earlier, noted that Jessie was the only one of the four non-language-trained juvenile chimps who, in trying to get a trainer to move across the room to help her with a task, without hesitation and on the first trial, removed a blindfold from the eyes of the trainer—apparently realizing that a blindfold on the eyes impaired vision. Jessie did not remove the blindfold when it was over the mouth. It may be the rare chimp who actually understands the relation between eyes and seeing, and Povinelli may not have had such a rare chimp in his cohort. It is possible, though, that despite this lack of realization, chimps might still understand that another creature has a mental life similar to their own. Even so, gaze-following by chimpanzees can no longer be taken as unequivocal evidence that chimps have theory of mind.

A third approach was taken by Call and Tomasello (1999), who devised a nonverbal false belief (Sally-Anne) task. One adult human (the hider) hid a reward in one of two identical containers. Another adult (the communicator) attempted to help the subject by placing a sticker on the container that she believed to hold the reward. Both 4- and 5-year-old children and the apes (chimps and orangutans) were able to use the stickers to locate the rewards in the control trials. In the critical trials, though, the communicator left the room, and the hider switched the location of the reward. When the communicator came back, she marked the location at which she had last seen the reward. The hider then gave the child or the ape the chance to look for the reward. The question was whether the subject went for the container that had the sticker. The children tended to discount the sticker—revealing that they knew that the communicator did not know; but the apes went for it—revealing what appears to be a lack of appreciation of the communicator's knowledge, and a lack of theory of mind.

Although these results mitigate against chimps having theory of mind, more recently Tomasello, Call, and Hare (2003) have revised their negative conclusions, and demonstrated what may be a genuine case of chimpanzees having theory of mind. The mind that they have a theory of, though, has to be one they care about. Tomasello et al. used pairs of dominant and subordinate chimps, in competition for food. Some of the time, the subordinate chimp could see the food and could also see that the dominant could not see it, by virtue of a barrier. The subordinates took advantage of their knowledge of what the dominant did not know in a variety of flexible ways that suggested that they knew what he knew. In a second set of experiments, the subordinate watched a human hide the food and also observed whether or not the dominant also saw the hiding. The researchers found that when the subordinate had observed that the dominant had not observed the hiding, he behaved quite differently than when he knew that the dominant had seen the hiding. Povinelli and Vonk (2003) have criticized these experiments on the grounds that the chimps might have had past experience or innate wiring in such situations, and that, to test the notion of knowledge of mental states, one needs to use situations that could not possibly have innate or experiential precedents (which might allow "behavioral abstraction") for the subject chimps:

> Any experiments that rely upon a behavioral abstraction will be of little use, especially when this invariant is one the subject has previously witnessed, or that they are likely to have evolved to detect or exploit. Indeed, contrary to recent speculations, behavioral interactions that make the most ecological sense to the organism are precisely the ones that will be least diagnostic about whether the organism is reasoning about mental states and behavior or behavior alone. (p. 159)

But if, following Povinelli and Vonk, we grant that tests for theory of mind are valid only if the minds and situations have no importance or meaning (that could be generalized from any past experience or innate predispositions) or social importance to the person or animal being studied, it seems doubtful that anyone, including normal adult humans, would ever show positive results. Povinelli and Vonk (2003) concluded that "the idea that theory of mind is the 'holy grail' of comparative cognition needs to be abandoned" (p. 160). We are more inclined to agree with Tomasello et al.'s (2003) conclusion: "The stakes here are large. At issue is no less than the nature of human cognitive uniqueness" (p. 156).

In summary, then, there is no completely undisputed evidence that any nonhuman primate has theory of mind, though there is a suggestion that in some circumstances that are deeply social, chimps may have it. There is considerable evidence that some humans—those with autism—do not have theory of mind, or at least have deficits in this area. As mentioned above, however, this is an extreme form of projection. Not only does the individual have to have self-reflective consciousness, but he or she also has to be able to attribute it to others and to correctly make inferences from that attribution. Some kinds of self-reflective consciousness might well exist prior to this highly articulated form.

DECEPTION

Humans

The ability to deceive is an interesting one, from the perspective of the projectable mind, because the tactical deceiver—to be effective—must be able, at least to some extent, to second-guess the target of his or her deception, understanding the thoughts, feelings, and inferences that will be made. It implies a glimmering of theory of mind—though perhaps short of that required for the tasks detailed in the previous section. Without an ability to, at least partially, project oneself into the other person's mind, deception would be ineffective. Furthermore, the deception has to be subtle enough to be undetected, since a detected deception can be disastrous for the perpetrator (see Cosmides & Tooby, 1992, for evidence and arguments concerning the evolution of so-called cheater-detector mechanisms in humans). People are extremely good at deception, as well as at the detection of potential deception. Novels and histories revel in it.

However, as with the other indications of social understanding, autistics appear to have particular problems both in deceiving and in detecting deception. Frith (1989) noted that the profiles given of many of the hermit saints suggest autism. These saints are often known for their simplicity and lack of deceit. Their truthfulness has historically been taken as virtue, but this characterization seems altogether undeserved since, if Frith is correct, it results not from self-restraint and goodness under pressure from the dark side, but rather from of a simple lack of understanding of the other's point of view.

Several studies have investigated deception in autistic populations, and all have shown them to be guileless. For example, Russell, Maunthner, Sharpe, and Tidswell (1991) compared autistic subjects, children with Down's syndrome, and normal 3- and 4-year-olds. The children learned that it was in their interest to tell the experimenter to look into an empty box for a chocolate, rather than into the box that actually contained the chocolate. Both the 4-year-olds and the children with Down's syndrome used the deceptive strategy, but the autistic children and the 3-year-olds consistently went with the box that actually contained the chocolate, failing to inhibit the knowledge of their own epistemic state. Similarly, Yirmiya, Solomonica-Levi, and Shulman (1996), using a procedure in which a doll creates a false trail of footprints, showed that while the autistic children could use the deceptive method as well as mentally retarded children (but not nearly as well as normals), they did not realize that by so doing they manipulated the belief of the other person involved. Other researchers have shown deficits in deceptive tasks such as penny hiding (Baron-Cohen, 1992; Oswald & Ollendick, 1989) in autistic participants. Thus, deception, like other tasks requiring a projectable self, appears to show as a deficit in autism.

Nonhuman Primates

The literature on tactical deception in nonhuman primates is largely anecdotal. For example, de Waal (1992) cites a case in which a young female chimp was aggressively chased by an older female, but managed to escape. Ten minutes later, the older female made reconciliatory gestures, approaching the younger with an open hand and making soft panting noises (the usual chimp prelude to a kiss). However, when the younger chimp came close, the older one lunged and bit her fiercely, before she was able to free herself. Presumably, the sweet gestures were just a deceptive attempt to lure the foe in close enough for the bite. Many such tales of chimp subterfuge have been recorded by primatologists and tabulated, systematized, and categorized in an enormous study by Byrne and Whiten (1992; Whiten & Byrne, 1988) who requested all reports of observed tactical deception among primate researchers. The kinds of observations reported were like that of Coussi-Korbel (1994), in which a subordinate young male would move in an indirect route toward a food goal to mislead a dominant male (and thus get the food for himself), or in which monkeys would point to the wrong location for hidden food (Mitchell & Anderson, 1997), or in which females would use their charms to distract a male in order to get food. "One of the female baboons at Gilgil grew particularly fond of meat, although males do most hunting. A male, one who does not willingly share, caught an antelope. The female edged up to him and groomed him until he lolled back under her attentions. She then snatched the antelope carcass and ran" (Jolly, 1985, p. 412). A standardized request, which included a computation of hours of observation, species, and so on, resulted in 253 such records, which were then analyzed, categorized by deception type, and classified by species.

The most common reports of deception came from our nearest relatives, genus *Pan*—chimpanzees and bonobos, followed closely by baboons. Some primates—lemurs in particular—appear not to deceive at all, despite the fact that it would presumably be much to their advantage. Deception, among monkeys, was rare. Whiten and Byrne (1988) noted some caveats to their results. First, the species reported with such a high rate of deception is also one studied by researchers who have been vocally antibehaviorist. But even leaving aside the possibility that some researchers might see mind to a greater extent than others, and while acknowledging that a more experimental approach would be desirable, it is difficult not to be convinced (and amused) by the many anecdotes provided in this massive work. While formal tests of theory of mind in nonhuman primates are equivocal, insofar as that capacity is reflected in deceptive behavior, we humans do not appear to be the only ones who have it.

METACOGNITION

Humans

A large and rapidly developing literature is investigating the metacognitive capabilities of adults (see Metcalfe, 1996, 2000, for fairly recent reviews of data and theory). Judgments about what one knows are used to guide problem-solving behavior in humans (Metcalfe & Wiebe, 1987; Simon, 1979; Simon & Reed, 1976) and to indicate how close to the solution to a problem one is, or how near one is to remembering a forgotten memory (Metcalfe, 1986a). Such judgments serve as controls of problem-solving search processes and also of memory retrieval efforts (Miner & Reder, 1994). Adults are capable of highly refined judgments of confidence, both prospectively and retrospectively (Morris, 1990). People are even able to predict, with high accuracy, what they will be able to remember later, even though they cannot remember the answer at the time they make such "feeling-ofknowing" judgments (Blake, 1973; Butterfield, Nelson, & Peck, 1988; Costermans, Lories, & Ansay, 1992; Cultice, Somerville, & Wellman, 1983; Gruneberg & Monks, 1974; Hart, 1965, 1967; Hertzog & Dixon, 1994; Lachman, Lachman, & Thronesbury, 1979; Leonesio & Nelson, 1990; Metcalfe, 1986a, 1986b; Nelson, Leonesio, Shimamura, Landwehr, & Narens, 1982; Schacter, 1983). Adults are not perfect, however, in their metacognitions, and some of their inaccuracies about their own cognitive processes and capabilities have garnered a great deal of attention (e.g., Bjork, 1994; Nelson & Dunlosky, 1991). These biases and inaccuracies notwithstanding, however, it is safe to say that normal adult humans are able to make remarkably accurate judgments about what they currently know and what they will know, and they put those judgments to use, either implicitly or explicitly (Koriat & Goldsmith, 1996), in their behavior.

There is consensus in the field that the judgments are made by monitoring mental contents, in a manner that is consistent with Humphrey's (2003) inner eye. For example, in making judgments of learning, people are thought to attempt to retrieve whatever they can, given the retrieval cues available to them, then to mentally look at the content of what they retrieved, as well as at the characteristics of the process in which they just engaged during the retrieval (was it easy, fluent, and fast, or labored?). Then, based on the results of this inner looking, they give a judgment, numerical or otherwise, about how well they have learned the targeted item. In making feeling-of-knowing judgments, they look at the quantity and familiarity of all the information they have, including the cue and partial information about the target (Koriat, 1993; Metcalfe, 1993; Metcalfe, Schwartz, & Joaquim, 1993) and they assess this to make their judgment.

The monitoring and control involved in metacognition appears to be associated with the last-developed area of the brain, namely the frontal cortex. As with the frontal patient reported by Stuss et al. (2001) who showed deficits in theory of mind, deficits in metacognition are also associated with frontal damage (Janowsky, Shimamura, & Squire, 1989). Insofar as the frontal lobes mature late, it is not surprising that metacognitions also appear developmentally late.

There has been very little research on metacognition in autistics, so no firm conclusions can yet be reached. One study (Farrant, Boucher, & Blades, 1999) investigated whether children knew about strategies for doing things like enhancing their memory span, or whether or not retrieval cues or verbalization enhanced performance, and found no differences among autistic and other children. Another study (Farrant, Blades, & Boucher, 1999) showed some impairment in the correspondence between predictions and later performance between autistic and other children, but they may have stemmed from an underlying memory problem rather than from an inability of the autistics to predict what they should be able to remember. Clinical and self-reports of autistics, though, suggest that they may be able to make rather refined metacognitive judgments in some areas. They can, for example, understand others' behavior by constructing a theory based on their experience of contingencies (Frith, 1989; Sacks, 1995). Insofar as the same mechanisms might be used in some metacognitive judgments, and it is not necessary to mentally project to do the tasks, one might not expect deficits in autistics. Certain metacognitive tasks may thus be the simplest of tasks involving an inner eye, and may be possible where more complicated tasks that require not only an inner eye, but that the individual be able to project it in space and time, may be impossible.

Nonhuman Primates

There are now a number of indications that nonhuman primates, including even monkeys, may be capable of making some metacognitive judgments. Researchers (Shields, Smith, & Washburn, 1997; Smith, Shields, Allendoerfer, & Washburn, 1998; Smith, Shields, & Washburn, 2003; chapter 10, this volume) have shown that monkeys can make uncertainty judgments, although it is not generally agreed upon whether uncertainty judgments, in and of themselves, are metacognitive (Metcalfe, 2003). Hampton (2001; chapter 11, this volume) has given an impressive demonstration of metacognition, with judgments about the contents of working memory, in monkeys. Finally, Son and Kornell's data (chapter 12, this volume) also indicate that even rhesus monkeys are able to perform metacognitive tasks. Insofar as metacognitions, however simple, may be the germ of full-blown self-reflection and may be the first indication of an inner eye, the discovery of these capabilities in species other than ourselves may be the strongest primordial indication of self-reflective capability in other primates.

Call (chapter 13, this volume) documents a particularly advanced metacognitive/control capability in chimps and other primates. Not only do they appear to know what they do not know (see also Son & Metcalfe, 2004, for a similar capability in humans), but they also seek to remedy their lack of knowledge. Call shows that several species of primates (unlike lower animals such as dogs, say), in the face of uncertainty, will actively seek information in a effort to remedy their ignorance.

EPISODIC MEMORY

Tulving and his colleagues (Tulving, 2002; Wheeler, Stuss, & Tulving, 1997; chapter 1, this volume) have made a compelling case concerning the close relation between episodic memory and autonoetic consciousness. We claim that both are closely related to what we, in this chapter, refer to as the projectable self. It follows that the pattern seen for other markers of the projectable self, outlined above, should also be manifested with episodic memory tasks. Nelson (2000; chapter 4, this volume) provides an authoritative description of the development of episodic memory in early childhood and illustrates how it relates to the development of self-reflection, self-concept, consciousness, and infantile amnesia. The timing of the onset of episodic memory seems to correspond well with that of other projectable-self capabilities. Whether or not nonhuman primates show any signs of episodic memory is a topic of focal concern in other chapters (chapters 8 and 9, this volume; and see Schwartz & Evans, 2001). Since these chapters deal with this issue specifically, and there is much discussion throughout the book, we defer to them.

The one domain in the literature that bears on the relation between the projectable self and episodic memory that is not covered in other chapters in this volume—the missing piece to the puzzle—is the memory capability of autistics. As reviewed above, autistics have demonstrated deficits in self-recognition, in theory of mind, and in deception. If autistics lack a projectable self, then this should also be manifested by impairments in episodic memory.

The few studies that we have been able to find on this topic suggest, though with some equivocation, that autistics do indeed have difficulties with just this kind of memory, though not with all kinds of memory. For example, Boucher (1981a) reported that recall of recent events in autistic children was inferior to that of both normal children and ability-matched retarded control children. In a different study, she (Boucher, 1981b) reported similar overall free recall of word lists, but the autistic children relied more heavily on recalling the most recently presented items and reported fewer of the earlier words—perhaps suggesting less "time travel" to the earlier parts of the list. Tager-Flusberg (1991) found that autistic children were not different from mentally retarded and normal children in free recall of an unrelated list of words, or in their use of semantic or rhyme cues to retrieve unrecalled words from memory. However, they were impaired in their free recall of the semantically related list.

Boucher and Warrington (1976) compared autistic children to controls in a variety of tasks. Tasks that we would classify as implicating episodic memory, namely, recall tasks (in this case of pictures, written words, and spoken words), revealed memory deficits. In tasks that involved less of an autonoetic component because they were cued, the autistic children were not impaired. They were not impaired on cued recall tasks or a test of unrelated paired associates. Oddly, though, the autistic children were impaired on a forced-choice recognition task, a task that might presumably be done on the basis of familiarity, and that need not entail autonoetic involvement. Overall—though the data are not entirely consistent—it would seem that the memory tasks on which the autistic children were impaired were those that may require autonoetic consciousness. The authors of these studies suggested a parallel between autism and amnesia.

Similarly, Bennetto, Pennington, and Rogers (1996) found that autistics were impaired on source memory, temporal order memory, free recall, and working memory (though the last need not involve a projective self, and its impairment is also not a consistent finding in the autism literature). They were unimpaired on short- and long-term recognition, cued recall, and new learning ability. Boucher and Lewis (1989) have pointed out that autistic children have difficulties answering questions about their own past activities.

Finally, Klein, Chan, and Loftus (1999) conducted an interesting case study investigating semantic and episodic self-knowledge in a high-functioning autistic individual. At the time of the study, R.J. was a 21-year-old whose autistic symptoms dated back to about 8 months of age. His immediate memory span was normal, as was his verbal fluency in generating category exemplars (measuring a kind of semantic memory). Like other autistics, R.J.'s free recall of unrelated nouns was impaired. Interestingly, R.J. was found to have rather accurate knowledge of his own personality traits, as measured by both his own test-retest reliability and also by the concordance of his self-ratings with his mother's ratings of him. However, his accurate semantic assessment of himself was in stark contrast to his inability to retrieve autobiographical events from his own past, when given those traits as cues. Normal subjects were able to do this retrieval 10 out of 10 times, meeting all criteria of episodic scoring. R.J. attained a score of only 2 out of 10, and then only when the criterion for acceptance was extremely lenient. An example: "*Tester:* Can you remember a time when you acted friendly toward someone? *R.J.:* Mmm . . . when . . . when people were nice to me. *Tester:* Was this a particular person you remember being nice to you? *R.J.:* Anyone" (p. 422). As the authors put it, "Apparently, R.J. did not need to remember how he had behaved in the past to know what he was like" (p. 425).

In summary, then, autistic children appear to be selectively impaired on memory tasks that are episodic in nature and that would appear to involve autonoetic consciousness. These findings suggest that they may be unable to project themselves into their own pasts, as is required by such tasks. Both theory of mind tasks (requiring projection to another's point of view), and episodic memory tasks (requiring projection into one's own personal past) appear to be impaired in autism.

CONCLUSION

The conclusion that seems to be emerging, but which is debated and disputed more fully in the other chapters in this volume, is that there are some indications of self-reflective consciousness in some primates other than humans. There are indications of self-recognition in the great apes. There are suggestions of some fragmentary episodic (-like) memory in some of the great apes. Other primates, though hardly candidates for CEO of a major corporation, have the beginnings of an ability to deceive. The great apes, and even monkeys, appear to have some metacognitive capabilities. So far, the evidence that any primates other than humans have full-blown theory of mind is still under dispute, but then very little research has been conducted on this intriguing topic, and it may turn out that with further investigation, a consensus will emerge in favor of humans not being alone in this regard. Adult humans project their consciousness of themselves into their own past and future, and into the minds of others, with remarkable ease. Investigation of the emergence of these capabilities, in a primordial form in other primates, as well as the acknowledgment of their fragility, as shown in autistic and frontal lobe patients, provides insight into this most quintessentially human kind of knowledge—our consciousness of ourselves.

REFERENCES

Adolphs, R. (1999). Social cognition and the human brain. *Trends in Cognitive Sciences, 3,* 469–479.

Adolphs, R., Sears, L., & Piven, J. (2001). Abnormal processing of social information from faces in autism. *Journal of Cognitive Neuroscience, 13,* 232–240.

Amsterdam, B. K. (1972). Mirror self-image reactions before age two. *Developmental Psychobiology, 5,* 297–305.

Asendorpf, J. B., Warkentin, V., & Baudonniere, P. (1996). Self-awareness and other-awareness II: Mirror self-recognition, social contingency awareness, and synchronic imitation. *Developmental Psychology, 32,* 313–321.

Baron-Cohen, S. (1992). Out of sight or out of mind: Another look at deception in autism. *Journal of Child Psychology and Psychiatry, 33,* 1141–1155.

Baron-Cohen, S. (1995). *Mindblindness: An essay on autism and theory of mind.* Cambridge, MA: MIT Press.

Baron-Cohen, S., Leslie, A. M., & Frith, U. (1985). Does the autistic child have a "theory of mind"? *Cognition, 21,* 37–46.

Bennetto, L., Pennington, B. F., & Rogers, S. J. (1996). Intact and impaired memory functions in autism. *Child Development, 67,* 1816–1835.

Bjork, R. A. (1994). Memory and metamemory considerations in the training of human beings. In J. Metcalfe & A. P. Shimamura (Eds.), *Metacognition: Knowing about knowing* (pp. 185–206). Cambridge, MA: MIT Press.

Blake, M. (1973). Prediction of recognition when recall fails: Exploring the feeling-of-knowing phenomenon. *Journal of Verbal Learning and Verbal Behavior, 12,* 311–319.

Boucher, J. (1981a). Memory for recent events in autistic children. *Journal of Autism and Developmental Disorders, 11,* 293–301.

Boucher, J. (1981b). Immediate free recall in early childhood autism: Another point of behavioural similarity with the amnesic syndrome. *British Journal of Psychology, 72,* 211–215.

Boucher, J., & Lewis, V. (1989). Memory impairments and communication in relatively able autistic children. *Journal of Child Psychology and Psychiatry, 30,* 99–122.

Boucher, J., & Warrington, E. K. (1976). Memory deficits in early infantile autism: Some similarities to the amnesic syndrome. *British Journal of Psychology, 67,* 73–87.

Butterfield, E. C., Nelson, T. O., & Peck, V. (1988). Developmental aspects of the feeling of knowing. *Developmental Psychology, 24,* 654–663.

Byrne, R. W., & Whiten, A. (1992). Cognitive evolution in primates: Evidence from tactical deception. *Man, 27,* 609–627.

Call, J., & Tomasello, T. (1999). A nonverbal false belief task: The performance of children and great apes. *Child Development, 70,* 381–395.

Cosmides, L., & Tooby, J. (1992). Cognitive adaptation for social exchange. In J. H. Barkow, L. Cosmides, & J. Tooby (Eds.), *The adapted mind* (pp. 163–228). New York: Oxford University Press.

Costermans, J., Lories, G., & Ansay, C. (1992). Confidence level and feeling of knowing in question answering: The weight of inferential processes. *Journal of Experimental Psychology: Learning, Memory and Cognition, 18,* 142–150.

Coussi-Korbel, S. (1994). Learning to outwit a competitor in mangabeys. *Journal of Comparative Psychology, 108,* 164–171.

Cultice, J. C., Somerville, S. C., & Wellman, H. M. (1983). Preschoolers memory monitoring: Feeling of knowing judgments. *Child Development, 54,* 1480–1486.

DeLong, G. R. (1992). Autism, amnesia, hippocampus, and learning. *Neuroscience and Biobehavioral Reviews, 16,* 63–70.

Dennett, D. C. (1991). *Consciousness explained.* Toronto, Canada: Little, Brown.

Descartes, R. (1999). *Discourse on method.* London: Penguin Books. (Original work published 1637)

de Waal, F. B. M. (1992). Intentional deception in primates. *Evolutionary Anthropology, 1,* 86–92.

Donald, M. (1991). *Origins of the modern mind.* Cambridge, MA: Harvard University Press.

Farrant, A., Blades, M., & Boucher, J. (1999). Recall readiness in children with autism. *Journal of Autism and Developmental Disorders, 29,* 359–366.

Farrant, A., Boucher, J., & Blades, M. (1999). Metamemory in children with autism. *Child Development, 70,* 107–131.

Ferrari, M., & Matthews, W. S. (1983). Self-recognition deficits in autism: Syndrome-specific or general developmental delay? *Journal of Autism and Developmental Disorders, 13,* 317–324.

Frith, U. (1989). *Autism: Explaining the enigma.* Cambridge, MA: Basil Blackwell.

Frith, U., & Happe, F. (1999). Theory of mind and self-consciousness: What is it like to be autistic? *Mind and Language, 14,* 1–22.

Gallup, G. G. (1970). Chimpanzees: Self-recognition. *Science, 167,* 86–87.

Gallup, G. G. (1982). Self-awareness and the emergence of mind in primates. *American Journal of Primatology, 2,* 237–248.

Gallup, G. G., McClure, M. K., Hill, S. D., & Bundy, R. A. (1971). Capacity for self-recognition in differentially reared chimpanzees. *Psychological Record, 21,* 69–74.

Gruneberg, M. M., & Monks, J. (1974). "Feeling of knowing" and cued recall. *Acta Psychologica, 38,* 257–265.

Hampton, R. R. (2001). Rhesus monkeys know when they remember. *Proceedings of the National Academy of Sciences U.S.A., 98,* 5359–5362.

Happe, F., Ehlers, S., Fletcher, P., Frith, U., Johansson, M., Gillberg, C., Dolan, R., Frackowiak, R., & Frith, C. (1996). "Theory of mind" in the brain: Evidence from a PET scan study of Asperger syndrome. *NeuroReport, 8,* 197–201.

Hart, J. T. (1965). Memory and the feeling-of-knowing experience. *Journal of Educational Psychology, 56,* 208–216.

Hart, J. T. (1967). Memory and the memory-monitoring process. *Journal of Verbal Learning and Verbal Behavior, 6,* 685–691.

Hauser, M. D., Kralik, J., Botto, C., Garrett, M., & Oser, J. (1995). Self recognition in primates: Phylogeny and the salience of species-typical traits. *Proceedings of the National Academy of Sciences U.S.A., 92,* 10811–10814.

Hauser, M. D., Miller, T. C., Liu, K., & Gupta, R. (2001). Cotton-top tamarins (*Saguinus oedipus*) fail to show mirror-guided self-exploration. *American Journal of Primatology, 53,* 131–137.

Heider, F., & Simmel, M. (1944). An experimental study in apparent behavior. *American Journal of Psychology, 57,* 243–259.

Hertzog, C., & Dixon, R. A. (1994). Metacognitive development in adulthood and old age. In J. Metcalfe & A. P. Shimamura (Eds.), *Metacognition: Knowing about knowing* (pp. 227–252). Cambridge, MA: MIT Press.

Heyes, C. M. (1994). Reflection on self-recognition in primates. *Animal Behavior, 47,* 909–919.

Heyes, C. M. (1998). Theory of mind in nonhuman primates. *Behavioral and Brain Sciences, 21,* 101–134.

Hobson, P. R. (1990). On acquiring knowledge about people and the capacity to pretend. *Psychological Review, 97,* 114–121.

Hughes, C., & Russell, J. (1993). Autistic children's difficulty with mental disengagement from an object: Its implications for theories of autism. *Developmental Psychology, 29,* 498–510.

Humphrey, N. K. (2003). The uses of consciousness. In N. Humphrey (Ed.), *The mind made flesh: Essays from the frontiers of psychology and evolution* (pp. 65–85). New York: Oxford University Press.

Janowsky, J. S., Shimamura, A. P., & Squire, L. R. (1989). Memory and metamemory: Comparisons between patients with frontal lobe lesions and amnesic patients. *Psychobiology, 17,* 3–11.

Jolly, A. (1985). *The evolution of primate behavior* (2nd ed.). New York: Macmillan.

Klein, S. B., Chan, R. L., & Loftus, J. (1999). Independence of episodic and semantic self-knowledge: The case from autism. *Social Cognition, 17,* 413–436.

Klin, A. (2000). Attributing social meaning to ambiguous visual stimuli in higher-functioning autism and Asperger syndrome: The social attribution task. *Journal of Child Psychology and Psychiatry, 7,* 831–846.

Koriat, A. (1993). How do we know that we know? The accessibility model of the feeling of knowing. *Psychological Review, 100,* 609–639.

Koriat, A., & Goldsmith, M. (1996). Monitoring and control processes in the strategic regulation of memory accuracy. *Psychological Review, 103,* 490–517.

Lachman, J. L., Lachman, R., & Thronesbury, C. (1979). Metamemory through the adult life span. *Developmental Psychology, 15,* 543–551.

Leonesio, R. J., & Nelson, T. O. (1990). Do different metamemory judgments tap the same underlying aspects of memory. *Journal of Experimental Psychology: Learning, Memory, and Cognition, 16,* 464–470.

Leslie, A. M. (1987). Pretense and representation: Origins of "theory of mind." *Psychological Review, 94,* 412–426.

Lewis, M., & Brooks-Gunn, J. (1979). *Social cognition and the acquisition of self.* New York: Plenum Press.

Metcalfe, J. (1986a). Feeling of knowing in memory and problem solving. *Journal of Experimental Psychology: Learning, Memory, and Cognition, 12,* 288–294.

Metcalfe, J. (1986b). Premonitions of insight predict impending error. *Journal of Experimental Psychology: Learning, Memory, and Cognition, 12,* 623–634.

Metcalfe, J. (1993). Novelty monitoring, metacognition, and a control in a composite holographic associative recall model: Implications for Korsakoff amnesia. *Psychological Reviews, 100,* 3–22.

Metcalfe, J. (1996). Metacognitive processes. In E. L. Bjork & R. A. Bjork (Eds.), *Memory: Handbook of perception and cognition* (pp. 381–407). San Diego, CA: Academic Press.

Metcalfe, J. (2000). Metamemory: Theory and data. In E. Tulving & F. I. M. Craik (Eds.), *The Oxford handbook of memory* (pp. 197–211). New York: Oxford University Press.

Metcalfe, J. (2003). Drawing the line on metacognition. *Behavioral and Brain Sciences, 26,* 350–351.

Metcalfe, J., Schwartz, B. L., & Joaquim, S. G. (1993). The cue-familiarity heuristic in metacognition. *Journal of Experimental Psychology: Learning, Memory, and Cognition, 19,* 851–864.

Metcalfe, J., & Wiebe, D. (1987). Intuition in insight and non-insight problem solving. *Memory and Cognition, 15,* 238–246.

Miner, A. C., & Reder, L. M. (1994). A new look at feeling of knowing: Its metacognitive role in regulating question answering. In J. Metcalfe & A. P. Shimamura (Eds.), *Metacognition: Knowing about knowing* (pp. 47–70). Cambridge, MA: MIT Press.

Mitchell, R. W., & Anderson, J. R. (1997). Pointing, withholding information, and deception in capucin monkeys (*Cebus apella*). *Journal of Comparative Psychology, 111,* 351–361.

Morris, C. C. (1990). Retrieval processes underlying confidence in comprehension judgments. *Journal of Experimental Psychology: Learning, Memory, and Cognition, 16,* 223–232.

Nelson, K. (2000). Memory and belief in development. In D. Schacter & E. Scarry (Eds.), *Memory, brain, and belief* (pp. 259–289). Cambridge, MA: Harvard University Press.

Nelson, T. O., & Dunlosky, J. (1991). When people's judgments of learning (JOLs) are extremely accurate at predicting subsequent recall: The "delayed-JOL-effect." *Psychological Science, 2,* 267–270.

Nelson, T. O., Leonesio, R. J., Shimamura, A. P., Landwehr, R. S., & Narens, L. (1982). Overlearning and the feeling of knowing. *Journal of Experimental Psychology: Learning, Memory, and Cognition, 8,* 279–288.

Nelson, T. O., & Narens, L. (1994). Why investigate metacognition?. In J. Metcalfe & A. P. Shimamura (Eds.), *Metacognition: Knowing about knowing* (pp. 1–25). Cambridge, MA: MIT Press.

Neuman, C. J., & Hill, S. D. (1978). Self-recognition and stimulus preference in autistic children. *Developmental Psychobiology, 11,* 571–578.

Oswald, D. P., & Ollendick, T. H. (1989). Role taking and social competence in autism and mental retardation. *Journal of Autism and Developmental Disorders, 19,* 119–127.

Ozonoff, S., Pennington, B. F., & Rogers, S. (1991). Executive function deficits in high-functioning autistic individuals: Relationship to theory of mind. *Journal of Child Psychology and Psychiatry, 32,* 1081–1105.

Patterson, F. G. P., & Cohn, R. H. (1994). Self-recognition and self-awareness in lowland gorillas. In S. Taylor Parker, R. W. Mitchell, & M. L. Boccia (Eds.), *Self-awareness in animals and humans: Developmental perspectives* (pp. 273–290). Cambridge, MA: Cambridge University Press.

Perner, J. (1991). *Understanding the representational mind.* Cambridge, MA: MIT Press.

Perner, J., Frith, U., Leslie, A., & Leekam, S. (1989). Exploration of the autistic child's theory of mind: Knowledge, belief, and communication. *Child Development, 60,* 689–700.

Povinelli, D. J. (1993). Reconstructing the evolution of mind. *American Psychologist, 48,* 493–509.

Povinelli, D. J. (2000). *Folk physics for apes.* New York: Oxford University Press.

Povinelli, D. J., & Eddy, T. J. (1996a). Chimpanzees: Joint visual attention. *Psychological Science, 7,* 129–135.

Povinelli, D. J., & Eddy, T. J. (1996b). Factors influencing young chimpanzees' recognition of "attention." *Journal of Comparative Psychology, 110,* 336–345.

Povinelli, D. J., & Eddy, T. J. (1996c). What young chimpanzees know about seeing. *Monographs of the Society for Research in Child Development, 61,* record #247.

Povinelli, D. J., & Vonk, J. (2003). Chimpanzee minds: Suspiciously human? *Trends in Cognitive Sciences, 7,* 157–160.

Premack, D., & Premack, A. J. (1983). *The mind of an ape.* New York: Norton.

Premack, D., & Woodruff, G. (1978). Does the chimpanzee have a theory of mind?. *Behavioral and Brain Sciences, 4,* 515–526.

Priel, B., & De Schonen, S. (1986). Self-recognition: A study of a population without mirrors. *Journal of Experimental Child Psychology, 41,* 237–250.

Rowe, A. D., Bullock, P. R., Polkey, C. E., & Morris, R. G. (2001). "Theory of mind" impairments and their relationship to executive functioning following frontal lobe excisions. *Brain, 124,* 600–616.

Russell, B. (1972). *A history of western philosophy.* New York: Simon and Schuster. (Original work published 1945)

Russell, J., Mauthner, N., Sharpe, S., & Tidswell, T. (1991). The "window task" as a measure of strategic deception in preschoolers and autistic subjects. *British Journal of Developmental Psychology, 9,* 331–349.

Sacks, O. W. (1995). *An anthropologist on Mars: Seven paradoxical tales.* New York: Knopf.

Schacter, D. L. (1983). Feeling of knowing in episodic memory. *Journal of Experimental Psychology: Learning, Memory, and Cognition, 9,* 39–54.

Schwartz, B. L., & Evans, S. (2001). Episodic memory in primates. *American Journal of Primatology, 55,* 71–85.

Shields, W. E., Smith, J. D., & Washburn, D. A. (1997). Uncertain responses by humans and rhesus monkeys (*Macaca mulatta*) in a psychophysical same-different task. *Journal of Experimental Psychology: General, 126,* 147–164.

Simon, H. A. (1979). Information processing models of cognition. *Annual Review of Psychology, 30,* 363–396.

Simon, H. A., & Reed, S. K. (1976). Modeling strategy shifts in a problem-solving task. *Cognitive Psychology, 8,* 86–97.

Smith, J. D., Shields, W. E., Allendoerfer, K. R., & Washburn, D. A. (1998). Memory monitoring by animals and humans. *Journal of Experimental Psychology: General, 127,* 227–250.

Smith, D. J., Shields, W. E., & Washburn, D. A. (2003). The comparative psychology of uncertainty monitoring and metacognition. *Behavioral and Brain Sciences, 26,* 317–339.

Son, L. K., & Metcalfe, J. (2004). *Judgments of learning: Evidence for a two-stage process.* Manuscript submitted for publication.

Spiker, D., & Ricks, M. (1984). Visual self-recognition in autistic children: Developmental relationships. *Child Development, 55*, 214–225.

Stone, V. E., Baron-Cohen, S., & Knight, R. T. (1998). Frontal lobe contribution to theory of mind. *Journal of Cognitive Neuroscience, 10*, 640–656.

Stuss, D. T., Gallup, G. G., & Alexander, M. P. (2001). The frontal lobes are necessary for theory of mind. *Brain, 124*, 276–286.

Suarez, S. D., & Gallup, G. G. (1981). Self-recognition in chimpanzees and orangutans, but not gorillas. *Journal of Human Evolution, 10*, 175–188.

Suddendorf, T., & Corballis, M. C. (1997). Mental time travel and the evolution of the human mind. *Genetic, Social, and General Psychology Monographs, 123*, 133–167.

Suddendorf, T., & Whiten, A. (2001). Mental evolution and development: Evidence for secondary representation in children, great apes, and other animals. *Psychological Bulletin, 127*, 629–650.

Tager-Flusberg, H. (1991). Semantic processing in the free recall of autistic children: Further evidence for a cognitive deficit. *British Journal of Developmental Psychology, 9*, 417–430.

Tomasello, M., & Call, J. (1997). *Primate cognition.* New York: Oxford University Press.

Tomasello, M., Call, J., & Hare, B. (2003). Chimpanzees understand psychological states—the question is which ones and to what extent. *Trends in Cognitive Sciences, 7*, 153–156.

Tulving, E. (2002). Episodic memory: From mind to brain. *Annual Review of Psychology, 53*, 1–25.

Wellman, H. M., Cross, D., & Watson, J. (2001). Meta-analysis of theory-of-mind development: The truth about false belief. *Child Development, 72*, 655–684.

Wheeler, M. A., Stuss, D. T., & Tulving, E. (1997). Toward a theory of episodic memory, the frontal lobes, and autonoetic consciousness. *Psychological Bulletin, 121*, 331–354.

Whiten, A., & Byrne, R. W. (1988). Tactical deception in primates. *Behavioral and Brain Sciences, 11*, 233–273.

Wimmer, H., & Perner, J. (1983). Beliefs about beliefs: Representation and constraining function of wrong beliefs in young children's understanding of deception. *Cognition, 13*, 103–128.

Yirmiya, N., Solomonica-Levi, D., & Shulman, C. (1996). The ability to manipulate behavior and to understand manipulation of beliefs: A comparison of individuals with autism, mental retardation, and normal development. *Developmental Psychology, 32*, 62–69.

3

Metacognition and the Evolution of Language

Herbert S. Terrace

Psychology is the only life science that has yet to assimilate the theory of evolution. Language provides a clear example. A child's vocabulary increases dramatically from approximately 18 months to 4 years, from a few words to thousands, reaching a rate that has been estimated to be one new word per hour. Equally impressive is a child's mastery of complex grammatical rules without any formal instruction. These facts, which have been confirmed in all human cultures, suggested to Chomsky (1965) that children are born with a language acquisition device (LAD), an innate structure of the brain that contains the abstract rules of a universal grammar.

Chomsky and other linguists have asked, quite reasonably, how could so major a structural change have evolved by natural selection during the approximately 6 million years that have elapsed since humans and chimpanzees split from a common ancestor? To be sure, the point of Chomsky's question is not whether language evolved but how natural selection could account for the sudden appearance (as measured in evolutionary time) of the most complex form of natural communication known to man (Chomsky, 1986). Was there a stage at which grammar was a quarter evolved, two thirds evolved, and so on? If there was, what kind of grammar would that be?

Because language is so radically different from other forms of communication, Chomsky argued that the LAD is an exaptation of a structure that evolved by natural selection for some other function, such as navigation (Hauser, Chomsky, & Fitch, 2002). In this view, the LAD does not owe its existence to natural selection because it was already in place when the need to generate and comprehend grammatical utterances arose. A number of biologists, citing Darwin's concept of "pre-adaptation" (Gould, 1977; Gould & Vrba, 1982; Williams, 1966), have argued that many structures first appeared as exaptations. Wings, for example, are considered to be exaptations of structures whose original functions were predation and/or thermoregulation. It is important to recognize, however, that exapted structures are just as susceptible to environmental pressures as structures that evolved by natural selection. Primitive wings, for example, which could propel birds in flight for only very short distances, were modified by natural selection for long-distance flying.

In this chapter, I show how natural selection can provide a plausible explanation of the necessary conditions for the origin of language. My explanation is constrained by known facts about the development of language in children and about differences in the cognitive abilities of human infants and nonhuman primates. It also explains how language evolved as rapidly as it did by building upon a prelinguistic developmental stage that is also uniquely human.

The rapid onset of language in human infants appears to differ radically from other developmental processes only if one ignores the social skills from which language emerges. Prominent among those skills is the ability to "read" another person's mind, that is, to detect similarities and differences between another person's perception of the world and one's own. That ability is an example of metacognition, the central concept of this book. The simplest forms of metacognition, which appear during the first year of life, do not require language.

In agreement with Chomsky, I argue that language is uniquely human and that its grammatical structure distinguishes it from all other forms of animal communication. However, I also argue that the fundamental divergence between human and nonhuman minds resulted from selection for metacognitive skills. Indeed, it seems inconceivable that language could have evolved without the ability to perceive that other individuals think as well as act.

The plan of this chapter is as follows. To highlight the importance of social skills in the evolution of language, I contrast two types of research that investigate cognitive precursors of language in nonhuman primates. The traditional approach has been to determine the complexity of cognitive processes that can be trained in individual laboratory-housed subjects, for example, problems administered on a Wisconsin General Test Apparatus, tool use, list-learning, and so on. The success of this approach, in particular Skinner's imaginative applications of the principles of operant conditioning (Skinner, 1953), fostered a climate in which it seemed possible to teach an animal to master any skill, including language. It was in that Zeitgeist that projects were begun whose goal was to provide evidence that an ape could learn the rudimentary features of language.

A more recent approach focuses on social intelligence, in particular, the ability of nonhuman primates to infer what their conspecifics can and cannot perceive in a particular situation (Povinelli, 2001; Povinelli

& Prince, 1999; Povinelli, Rulf, & Bierschwale, 1994; Tomasello, 1999; Tomasello, Hare, & Fogleman, 2001). Although there have been far fewer experiments on the social intelligence of nonhuman primates than on the intelligence of individual subjects, it appears that our understanding of the social intelligence of our nearest relatives will prove to be at least as important as our understanding of an animal's ability to master complex skills that can be trained individually.

As I hope to make clear in the remainder of this chapter, research on the cognitive abilities of individual subjects can provide interesting information about the comparative psychology of problem solving, but even the most complex problem-solving skills are not sufficient for learning a language. What is also needed is a comparative psychology of social intelligence. Instead of viewing language as an extension of the ability to understand and produce complex sequences of arbitrary symbols, it is also necessary to understand the social contexts in which symbols can, and cannot, be used by nonhuman primates. In this regard, it is encouraging that questions about the social functions of language have begun to supersede more narrowly based questions about the linguistic abilities of apes. A similar shift of emphasis can be seen in research on the development of language in children. In addition to measuring vocabulary size and the ability to use particular grammatical rules, researchers have begun to focus on social skills that emerge before a child learns to speak (Bruner, 1983; Scaife & Bruner, 1975).

THE EVOLUTION OF PROBLEM-SOLVING SKILLS

An unintended consequence of the cognitive revolution was its positive influence on the study of animal cognition. In particular, the contrast between Chomsky and Skinner's views of language generated interest in the acquisition of language and whether it was uniquely human. During the late 1960s, two independent projects sought to demonstrate that chimpanzees could acquire the rudiments of human language, grammar in particular (Gardner & Gardner, 1969, 1975a, 1975b; Premack, 1970, 1971). Though differing in details of methodology, both projects attempted to reverse earlier failures to teach chimpanzees to communicate with spoken words (Hayes, 1951; Hayes & Hayes, 1951; Kellogg & Kellogg, 1933/1967; Ladygina-Kohts, 2002) by shifting from a vocal to a visual medium of communication. At the time, it seemed reasonable to attribute previous failures to significant differences in the human and chimpanzee vocal apparatus, the position of the larynx in particular, that made it impossible for a chimpanzee to articulate human phones (Lieberman, 1968, 1975).[1]

The Gardners endeavored to teach an infant female chimpanzee named Washoe to use American Sign Language (ASL), a natural language used by thousands of deaf Americans (Gardner & Gardner,

1969). Washoe was trained in a home environment in which the predominant medium of communication was ASL. Premack trained the principal subject of his study, a juvenile female chimpanzee named Sarah, to use an artificial visual language consisting of plastic chips of different colors and shapes (Premack, 1970). Rather than wait for language to emerge spontaneously, as one might with a child or with a home-reared chimpanzee, Premack devised specific training procedures for teaching Sarah various "atomic" components of language.

In an early diary report, the Gardners noted that Washoe used "two or more signs . . . in 29 different two sign combinations and four different combinations of three signs" (quoted in Brown, 1970, p. 211). That report prompted Brown, an eminent psycholinguist, to comment, "It was rather as if a seismometer left on the moon had started to tap out 'S-O-S'" (p. 211). Indeed, Brown compared Washoe's sequences of signs to the early sentences of a child and noted similarities in the structural meanings of Washoe's and children's utterances (agent-action, agent-object, action-object, and so on).

Other projects reported similar combinations of two or more symbols. Sarah produced strings of plastic chips such as *Mary give Sarah apple* (Premack, 1976). Lana, a juvenile female chimpanzee, was trained to use an artificial visual language of "lexigrams." Each lexigram, a combination of a particular geometric configuration and a particular colored background, was presented on the keys of a computer console or on a large visual display. After learning to use individual lexigrams, Lana learned to produce sequences of lexigrams such as *Please machine give M&M* (Rumbaugh, Gill, & von Glasersfield, 1973). Two young gorillas (Koko and Michael) and a young male orangutan (Chantek) were trained to use signs by Patterson (1978; Patterson & Linden, 1981) and Miles (1983), respectively. Both investigators reported that their subjects produced many combinations containing two or more signs. By the late 1970s, a considerable amount of evidence suggested that apes could create new meanings by combining words according to grammatical rules.

That claim was challenged by two independent analyses of purported grammatical sequences. One was based on data collected on Project Nim (Terrace, 1979b) a replication of the Gardners' project involving Washoe. The goal of Project Nim was to obtain nonanecdotal evidence of the grammatical structure of sequences of signs produced by a chimpanzee. Nim Chimpsky was a young male chimpanzee that, like Washoe, had been reared by his human surrogate parents in an environment in which ASL was the major medium of communication. Over the course of 4 years, Nim's teachers recorded more than 20,000 combinations of two or more signs. Superficially, many of Nim's combinations appeared to be generated by simple finite-state grammatical rules (e.g., *more + x; transitive verb + me* or *Nim*). Many of Nim's multi-sign utterances resembled a child's initial multiword utterances (cf. Braine, 1976; Bretherton, McNew, Snyder, & Bates, 1983; Nelson, 1981). All told, the corpus of Nim's utterances provided the strongest evidence to date of an ape's ability to create sentences.

As clear as the combinatorial evidence seemed, closer inspection showed otherwise. A frame-by-frame analysis of videotapes of Nim's signing revealed that his signs were nothing more than elaborate requests for rewards that he could not otherwise obtain and that there was no basis for interpreting the various sequences of signs he produced as sentences (Terrace, 1979b; Terrace, Petitto, Sanders, & Bever, 1979). The vast majority of Nim's signs, both in his single- and multi-sign utterances, occurred when his teachers withheld rewards until he signed. They were also full or partial imitations of signs that his teachers used to prompt Nim to sign. Virtually none of Nim's sequences were spontaneous. When, for example, Nim wanted to play with a cat his teacher was holding, he might sign *Nim cat, me cat, hug cat, Nim hug cat* before his teacher handed him the cat. Even then, videotape analyses showed that the teacher prompted Nim continuously as he was signing, for instance, *Who that?* or *Nim want cat?* (see figure 3.1).

In hindsight, the meanings of Nim's signs were projections of his teachers, who directed all of their attention to capturing what they thought he was saying. So focused were they on Nim's signs that they were unaware of their nonspontaneous and imitative nature. It is, of course, true that young children imitate many of their parents' utterances. But the relative frequency of a child's imitated utterances is substantially lower than that of a chimpanzee. Further, although the imitative phase in children is transitory, Nim never moved beyond that phase (Terrace et al., 1979). Unlike a child's speech at the end of Stage I of language acquisition (cf. Bloom, Rocissano, & Hood, 1976; Brown, 1973), Nim's signing remained predominantly nonspontaneous and imitative. Analyses of available films of other signing apes revealed similar patterns of nonspontaneous and imitative discourse (e.g., Washoe signing with the Gardners (Gardner & Gardner, 1973) and her other teachers, and Koko signing with Patterson (Schroeder, 1977). Miles (1983) performed a discourse analysis of videotapes of the orangutan Chantek's signing with his teachers and reported, "there is no evidence . . . that Chantek's multi-sign combinations . . . are sentences" (p. 53). My conclusions that the signs uttered by an ape are imitative of the trainer's signs and that their sole function is to request rewards (Terrace, 1985a) has yet to be challenged by evidence to the contrary, in particular by unedited videotapes or films of an ape signing.

Different considerations led to a rejection of the view that Lana's and Sarah's sequences were sentences. Thompson and Church (1980) analyzed a corpus of approximately 14,000 of Lana's combinations that were collected by a computer. They concluded that the vast ma-

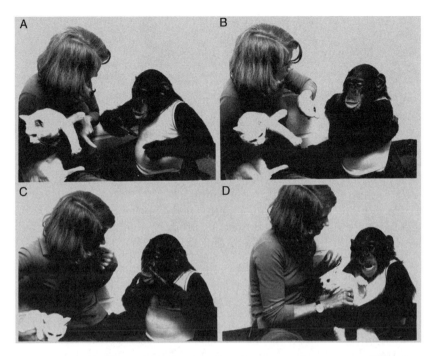

Figure 3.1 Nim signing *me hug cat*. In panel A, Nim signs *me* in response to his teacher signing *you*; in panel B, Nim signs *hug* in response to his teacher beginning the sign for *Nim*; in panel C, Nim signs *cat* in response to his teacher signing *who?* Nim's signing would have been of greater interest had his teacher not signed to him while he was signing *me hug cat*. Photo by H. Terrace.

jority of those combinations resulted from paired-associate and conditional discrimination learning. First, Lana learned that particular lexigrams were associated with particular incentives (e.g., lexigram$_{apple}$ → apple). She then learned conditional discrimination rules that specified which of six stock sequences she should produce. For example, if the incentive was in view, the stock sequence was, *Please machine give piece of X.* (*X* refers to the symbolic member of the paired associate, e.g., the lexigrams *apple, music, banana,* and *chocolate.*) Similarly, if there were no incentive in view, the stock sequence was, *Please put into machine X.* The symbol for the incentive was typically inserted in the last position of the stock sentence. Although Lana clearly understood the meanings of those lexigrams (in the sense that she could use lexigrams contrastively to request particular rewards), there is no evidence that she understood the meanings of the other lexigrams she used to assemble stock sentences (e.g., *Please, machine, give, put,* and *piece of*). Similar arguments have been made about the plastic symbols that Sarah used to produce her sequences (Terrace, 1979b).

Like the sequences produced by apes that were trained to sign, the sole function of the sequences reported by Rumbaugh and Premack was to obtain rewards. Consider, for example, the sequence glossed as *Please machine give food*. That sequence could just as well been described as a sequence composed of four arbitrarily selected letters, say, X → N → F → G. That a nonhuman primate could be taught to touch symbols that its trainer glossed as *please, machine, give,* and *food* is of interest not because of the purported meanings of those symbols, but because it raises an important evolutionary question about cognitive precursors of language. How does a nonhuman primate memorize arbitrary sequences without language, in particular, without understanding the meaning of each symbol?

To explore that question, I performed experiments in which pigeons and monkeys were trained to produce rote sequences (Straub & Terrace, 1981; Swartz, Chen, & Terrace, 1991). The sequences in question were lists of arbitrarily selected photographs. Although there are fundamental differences in the manner in which pigeons and monkeys represent an arbitrary sequence (Terrace, 1993), there is no reason to assume that either species required linguistic ability of any kind to learn those sequences. In the following section, I summarize the remarkable ability of monkeys to develop expertise at learning arbitrary lists (Terrace, Son, & Brannon, 2003). Although the lists on which the monkeys were trained were longer by a considerable margin than any list mastered in previous experiments by a nonhuman primate, including sequences learned by "linguistic apes," they were as meaningless as a list of nonsense syllables of the type used in experiments on human memory.

Simultaneous Chains

The lists on which the monkeys were trained differed radically from traditional tasks that have been used to train animals to learn an arbitrary task (e.g., running through a maze). To navigate a maze, a subject must learn how to respond at successive choice points. For example, to find one's way while driving through a strange town, one must remember to turn left at the library, right at the bank, right at the gas station, and so on—in short, a series of stimulus-response associations. Because the choice points of a maze are experienced in isolation from one another, there is no need to represent one's position in the sequence while navigating the maze. It is sufficient to recognize each choice point as a particular stimulus of a successive chain and to then respond appropriately.

Instead of training monkeys to learn successive chains, we trained them to learn simultaneous chains, a much more difficult serial task. In contrast to a successive chain, all of the choice points that comprise a simultaneous chain are displayed at the same time, typically on a touch-sensitive video monitor (Terrace, 1984). Another important feature of a simultaneous chain is that the configuration of the choice points can be changed randomly from trial to trial. These features of a simultaneous chain force a subject to maintain a representation of its position in the sequence before making each response. The following thought experiment, based on the seven-item simultaneous chains on which the monkeys were trained, shows why.

Imagine trying to enter your seven-digit personal identification number (PIN) at a cash machine, say 9-2-1-5-8-4-7, on which the positions of the numbers were changed each time you tried to obtain cash. You could not enter your PIN by executing a sequence of distinctive motor movements, that is, first pressing the button in the lower right corner of the number pad to enter 9, then the button in the upper middle position to enter 2, and so on. Instead, you would have to search for each number and keep track mentally of your position in the sequence as you pressed different buttons. As difficult as this task may seem, it would be far more difficult if you did not know your PIN and you had to discover it by trial and error. Any error ended that trial and resulted in a new trial on which the digits were displayed in a different configuration. Thus, to determine your PIN, you would have to recall the consequences of any of the 21 types of logical errors you could make while attempting to produce the required sequence. Further, you would have to determine the first six digits without getting as much as a penny from the cash machine. This is precisely the type of problem the monkeys had to solve at the start of training on each 7-item list. Instead of numerals, the monkeys had to respond to photographs. Instead of cash, they were given banana pellets.

Figure 3.2 illustrates the trial structure of the seven-item lists on which the monkeys were trained. Each list was composed of different photographs that were selected arbitrarily from a library of more than 2,500 photographs of natural or artificial objects. The monkey's task was to respond to each item in a particular order (figure 3.2A), regardless of its spatial position (figure 3.2B). The simultaneous display of all of the items ensured that the monkey's task was at least as difficult as the paradigms used by Premack and Rumbaugh. In those paradigms, all of the symbols the apes had to manipulate or touch were available at the same time, but their positions were fixed.

The monkeys had to learn each list by trial and error. As shown in figure 3.2C, any error terminated the trial and produced a brief time-out during which the computer monitor was dark. All correct responses allowed the trial to continue and also produced brief auditory and visual feedback. A food reward, in the form of small banana-flavored pellets, was provided only after the subject completed the entire sequence correctly. Thus, to learn the ordinal positions of the first $n - 1$ items of each list, subjects had to rely exclusively on second-

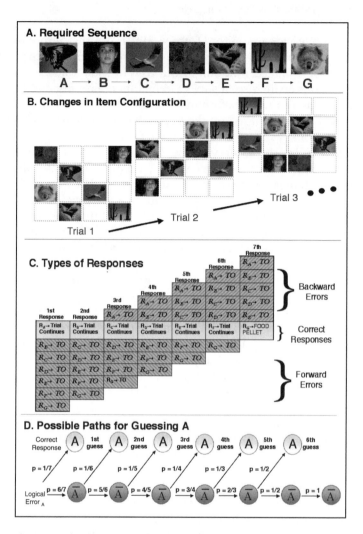

Figure 3.2 Simultaneous chaining paradigm. A. Example of a seven-item list. Subjects are required to respond to each color photograph in a prescribed order (A → B → C → D → E → F → G). B. Variation of the configuration of list items. List items were presented on a touch-sensitive video monitor in randomly configured displays. The task was to touch the items in the prescribed order irrespective of their position on the monitor. Prior to each trial, a new configuration was selected at random from the more than 5.8 million configurations that could be generated by presenting seven items in any of 16 positions. C. Types of forward and backward errors. The shaded boxes show the types of logical errors that could occur before a subject discovers the correct sequence. See text for additional details. D. Determining the ordinal position of a list item. The probability of guessing A by making logical errors to eliminate the A⁻ items. See text for additional details. See color insert.

ary reinforcement (the positive or negative feedback that followed their responses to each of the first $n - 1$ items).

The bottom half of figure 3.2C shows the different types of logical error a subject can make while determining the ordinal position of each item at the start of training on a new seven-item list. A logical error is the first incorrect guess a subject makes to a particular item at a given position of the list (e.g., responding to G at the second position). By definition, each type of logical error can occur only once. Although logical errors are necessary for discovering the ordinal position of an item, repetitions of the same error are not. Logical errors are made to obtain information by virtue of their consequences; for example, G cannot be the second item because the trial was terminated. Repetitive errors occur because the subject has forgotten the consequences of an earlier logical error.

The subjects of this experiment were trained to memorize 7 three-item lists, 11 four-item lists, and 4 seven-item lists. The goal of three- and four-item training was based on Harlow's (1949) classic study of learning sets. Instead of achieving a high level of proficiency on each list, the goal was to have the monkeys learn a trial-and-error strategy for determining the order of items from a new list. Thus, on three- and four-item lists, subjects were given a maximum of 3 days of training and then moved onto a new list. If they responded at better than chance levels of accuracy before 3 days, a new list was introduced at the start of the next session. On seven-item lists, subjects were trained to a stringent criterion of completing at least 65% of the trials correctly during a 60-trial session.

Learning New Lists

Subjects made progressively fewer errors during the course of learning new three- and four-item lists. However, the most dramatic evidence of expertise at acquiring new lists was subjects' performance on seven-item lists. The likelihood of guessing the correct order in which to respond to the items of a novel seven-item list (.0005) was less than 1/1000th the likelihood of guessing the correct order on a novel four-item list (.04). Each monkey nevertheless needed progressively fewer sessions to satisfy the high accuracy criterion on these lists (65% correctly completed trials in one session). As can be seen in figure 3.3, subjects needed on average 31.5, 17.5, 13, and 12.25 sessions to master seven-item lists 1, 2, 3, and 4, respectively (ranges: 21–55, 11–25, 11–19, and 7–17, respectively).

Knowledge of the Ordinal Position of List Items

Monkeys are not only adept at learning new lists but can also apply their knowledge of each list to solve new problems. Consider the following example. You are given the name of two baseball players from

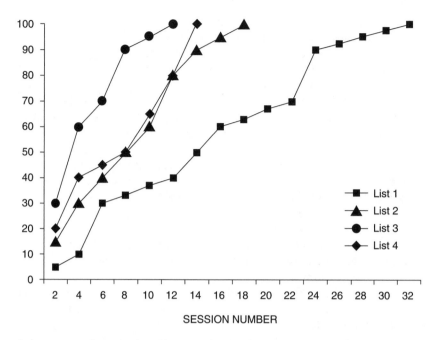

Figure 3.3 Learning seven-item lists. Each function shows the mean accuracy of responding on each seven-item list during even-numbered sessions. The probability of executing a new seven-item list correctly by chance is $1/7! = 1/5{,}040$ (assuming no backward errors).

your local team and asked which one bats first, Smith or Jones. You solve that problem by recalling each player's position in the batting order. Since Jones bats fourth and Smith seventh, you answer that Jones bats first. You're then asked the same question about players from different teams: Thompson, the fourth batter from Team B, or Armstrong, the second batter from Team C. Using the same rule of choosing the batter whose position is lowest in the batting order, you answer Armstrong. Suppose, however, that, like monkeys, you never learned numbers. To come up with the correct answer, you would have to go through each team's batting order mentally and stop when you came to one of the players.

Surprisingly, monkeys excelled on a similar test based on the seven-item lists they learned without the benefit of any knowledge of numbers or names. The monkeys were presented with all of the two-item subsets that could be derived from the 28 items used to compose those lists: 84 within-list subsets and 252 between-list subsets. Within-list subsets were composed of items from a particular list (e.g., the subsets A_3B_3, A_3C_3 ... A_3G_3; B_3C_3, B_3D_3 ... F_3G_3, from List 3). Between-list subsets were composed of items drawn from different lists (e.g., the subsets A_2B_4 from Lists 2 and 4, C_3F_5 from Lists 3 and 5, E_1G_3 from Lists 1 and 3, and so on). Within- and between-list pairs were interspersed randomly throughout the subset test. Subjects were rewarded if they responded in the order specified by their ordinal positions on the original list. For example, subjects were rewarded for responding to items C and F, in that order, whether or not they came from the same or different lists (e.g., C_3F_3 or C_2F_6). Excluded from the subset test were the 21 pairs that could be composed of items occupying the same ordinal positions on the 4 seven-item lists (e.g., the subsets A_1A_2, A_1A_3 ... G_3G_4).

Subjects' accuracy to the first item of both within- and between-list subsets was almost perfect on the first presentation of each subset type. On average, subjects responded correctly on 94% of the trials on the first occasion on which a particular token of a within-list subset was presented, and on 91% of the trials on the first occasion on which a particular token of a between-list subset was presented. These data are significant because they show that each monkey represented, in long-term memory, the ordinal position of the items of each seven-item list and that they were able to compare, in working memory, the ordinal positions of any two items drawn from those lists.

Representation of the Ordinal Position of List Items

How might a monkey compare the ordinal positions of subset items from the same or from different lists without the benefit of numerical tags such as first, second, and so on? An analysis of subjects' reaction times (RTs) to the first item of each subset suggested that they represented each item's ordinal position spatially along a linear continuum and then used the distance from the beginning of the list to decide which item came first. For this analysis, subsets were assigned to one of six categories that were defined by the distance between their ordinal positions on the original lists (e.g., pairs of items separated by a distance of 1: the subsets A_1B_1, B_2C_2 ... A_1B_2; B_2C_3, C_3D_4 ... F_3G_4; a distance of 2: A_1C_1, B_2D_2 ... A_1C_2; B_2D_3, C_3E_4 ... E_3G_4; a distance of 6: A_1G_1, A_2G_1 ... A_2G_1, A_2G_2, A_2G_3 ... A_4G_4). As can be seen in figure 3.4, reaction time to the first item of a subset decreased linearly as distance increased. At a distance of 1, reaction time increased linearly as the ordinal position of the first item increased. This was true for both within- and between-list subsets.

The functions shown in figure 3.4 suggest that subjects represented the ordinal position of each item in working memory and that they then compared those positions on a linear scale to see which item was closer to the beginning of the list. The more advanced the first item on the original list, the longer it took to determine its position. Similarly, the greater the distance between the two ordinal positions, the less time it took to discriminate their ordinal positions. Analogous

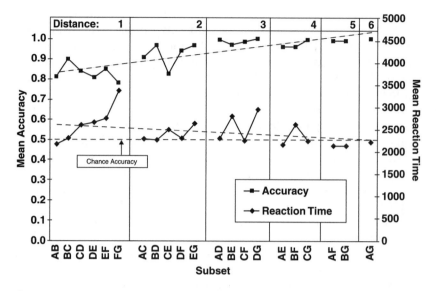

Figure 3.4 Accuracy and reaction times on subset test. The upper functions show mean accuracy to each type of within- and between-list subsets at distances 1–6. The entries on the abscissa are generic in that they refer to the types of within- and between-list subsets that are represented at each position. For example, AB refers to A_1B_1, A_2B_2, A_3B_3, A_4B_4 in the case of within-list subsets and to A_1B_2, A_1B_3, . . . A_4B_1 subsets in the case of between-list subsets. The lower functions show mean RTs to each type of within- and between-list subsets.

reaction time functions have been obtained from human subjects in experiments in which they were asked to discriminate pairs of letters whose position in the alphabet varied from trial to trial (e.g., G vs. B, M vs. R, C vs. J; Hamilton & Sanford, 1978) or between adjectives (Potts, 1974).

Serial Expertise Without Language

The lists trained in this study are by far the most difficult lists mastered by a nonhuman primate. These include the production of symbolic and numerical lists (Matsuzawa, 1985; Premack, 1976; Rumbaugh, 1977) and arbitrary lists (Colombo, Eickhoff, & Gross, 1993) and the recognition of the ordinal position of items on arbitrary lists (Carpenter, Georgopolous, & Pellizzer, 1999; Orlov, Yakovlev, Hochstein, & Zohary, 2000). It is doubtful, however, that the sequential skills observed in this study reflect the upper limit of a monkey's serial expertise. The ease with which monkeys learned seven-item lists and the steady decrease in the number of sessions they needed to master new lists suggests that they could learn such lists more rapidly and that they could also master longer lists. Subjects were also able to instantly apply their knowledge of seven-item lists to determine the correct order in which to respond to novel pairs of items that were selected at random from four different lists.

The Gap Between Serial Expertise and Language

The serial expertise of monkeys undermines claims that the sequences of symbols produced by language-trained apes are meaningful or grammatical. It also serves as a reminder that serial expertise per se is not a sufficient condition for language. Just as the ability of a human savant who can tell you instantly the day of the week on which September 3 fell in 1445 does not generalize to mathematical ability, the ability to memorize arbitrary sequences quickly does not generalize to grammatical ability. Serial skills are crucial for grammatical ability, and grammatical skills are necessary to use language. It does not follow, however, that our ancestors' first linguistic utterances were sequential or grammatical.

The suggestion that language did not start out with grammatical structure is not to deny that grammar is the sine qua non of language, at least as we know it. The point is that language could only have evolved from ancestors who had already been selected for their ability to share and exchange knowledge nonverbally. Although it seems uncontroversial that the social function of language antedated its semantic and grammatical functions, it has been argued that there can be no serious discussion of the order in which different aspects of language emerged in the absence of physical (paleological) evidence of the evolution of language (Chomsky, 1986).

If physical evidence of language use by our ancestors is a requirement for theorizing about the evolution of language, a glorious moment of human history will remain forever shrouded in mystery. It is not clear, however, why psychologists cannot emulate other sciences that have overcome similar problems. Astrophysics provides a clear example. Although astrophysicists lack physical evidence as to just when and how the universe was created, their hypotheses are constrained by empirical knowledge about the current state of the universe.

Recent research on the verbal and nonverbal cognitive abilities of human infants and apes suggest analogous constraints with respect to language. Below, I consider two important examples of such constraints; one centered on the issue of ape "language" I discussed earlier, and the other on the ability of human infants to share attention toward a particular object with another person. Both examples illustrate why language presupposes metacognition.

APE LANGUAGE PROJECTS

The goals of recent ape language projects were defined by the Chomskian Zeitgeist in which grammar was regarded as the essential feature of language. As noted earlier, claims that apes can produce grammatical sequences (Gardner & Gardner, 1975b; Premack, 1976; Rumbaugh, 1977) have been widely criticized (Pinker, 1994; Terrace et al., 1979). It was, however, generally assumed that apes can acquire sizeable vocabularies (Gardner & Gardner, 1973; Patterson & Linden, 1981; Premack, 1976; Rumbaugh, 1977). Because that assumption seems less controversial, the vocabularies attributed to various apes have undergone less scrutiny than claims about grammar. It is easy to show, however, that the contents of ape vocabularies have been greatly exaggerated. There is no evidence that apes used any of the symbols they learned to *refer* to objects or events or that those symbols had any function other than to request whatever food or drink its trainer could provide (e.g., *please, me, more*, etc.). This was true even of the symbols that apes used to obtain particular rewards (e.g., *apple, Coke, banana*, etc.).

To see why, it is important to recognize a fundamental limitation of association theory as an explanation of vocabulary development (e.g., Mowrer, 1954; Winitz, 1969). Such explanations have been justified on the grounds that words are learned individually (unlike sentences) and that a child's use of words can be characterized as associations between particular conditioned stimuli and particular conditioned responses. Skinner (1957), for example, distinguished between two kinds of conditioned verbal responses. Requests for primary reinforcers, called *mands,* are reinforced in whatever context they occur (e.g., requests for food, comfort, a smile, etc.). Skinner referred to verbal behavior that is rewarded in a specific context and followed by a secondary reinforcer as a *tact.* For example, a child might say *look,* or *a butterfly* in the presence of a butterfly, after which a parent might respond, *good, I see it too,* and so on.

Mands are egocentric. An infant mands whether or not his or her caretaker is paying attention. As illustrated in the following diagram, mands are composed of two events: the child's utterance and a primary reinforcer. Tacts, which require the listener's attention and are only reinforced in particular contexts, consist of three events: the context, the child's utterance, and a secondary reinforcer.

$R_{mand} \rightarrow$ primary reinforcer (e.g., food)

Specific context: $R_{tact} \rightarrow$ secondary reinforcer (e.g., verbal acknowledgement)

Tacts are metacognitive in the sense that the speaker expects the listener to attend to the referent of the speaker's tact. For example, when a child says *blue jay,* and then points to a blue jay, a listener might acknowledge what the child said with verbal praise, such as *Yes! It is a blue jay*, or with some nonverbal acknowledgment that the child's message was received (e.g., a smile, nodding the head, etc.). Tacts are not followed by primary reinforcement. Their sole function is to share knowledge with another person for its own sake.

It is clear that apes can learn to mand. There is, however, no evidence that they can learn to tact. Examples of mands include spontaneous requests for a reward, for example, a chimp signing *eat, drink, tickle*, and so on, or touching the lexigrams *eat, drink, chase, tickle*, and so forth, on a computer keyboard. Chimpanzees can also learn to request food by using a particular symbol in response to a stimulus presented by their trainer (e.g., the sign for *dog* in American Sign Language in response to a picture of a dog). It should be clear, however, that the function of the utterance *dog* is to obtain some reward and not to initiate a conversation with the trainer about the presence of a dog. To think otherwise is sheer projection. Conceptually, the chimpanzee's response *dog* is a mand that occurs in a particular context:

Picture of a dog: $R_{dog} \rightarrow$ primary reinforcer (e.g., food)

Chimpanzees can be trained to produce mands in a wide variety of contexts. Consider, for example, the kinds of tests that Premack (1976) administered to Sarah, the main subject of his project. When tested on her knowledge of names and colors, Sarah might be asked *what color?* in the presence of an apple. If Sarah selected the symbol glossed as *red* (as opposed to the symbol for some other color), her trainer gave her a small morsel of food. If Sarah were asked *what name?*, she was rewarded for selecting the symbol glossed as *apple* (as opposed to the symbol for some other object).

To solve these problems, Sarah simply had to learn to attend to the color of an object on trials on which the symbol glossed as color was presented, and to the type of object on trials on which the symbol glossed as name was presented (Terrace, 1979a). If the same test were given to a child, the child would expect verbal praise and not a candy or some similar reward for her answers. But, unlike a child, Sarah would stop answering questions if her trainer stopped supplying the tidbits of food and drink to which she had become accustomed.

Do Bonobo Chimpanzees Have the Capacity to Learn Language?

In a more recent study, Savage-Rumbaugh described the remarkable ability of Kanzi, a young male bonobo chimpanzee (*Pan paniscus*), to learn lexigrams by observational learning (Savage-Rumbaugh, 1994). The ease with which Kanzi added new lexigrams to his vocabulary surpassed, by a considerable margin, that observed in other studies of ape language. Kanzi's model for using lexigrams was his foster mother Mutata. Like other chimpanzees trained by Savage-Rumbaugh, Mutata learned, by trial and error, to press particular lexigrams to obtain a particular reward. Solely by observing Mutata, Kanzi learned to use lexigrams in a similar manner. Without any formal training, his vocabulary increased so rapidly that it exceeded the number of lexigrams that the computer could accommodate at a particular time (256 lexigrams).

Kanzi was also encouraged to explore a 50-acre forest (with his caretakers) containing 16 food sites. Each site, which was designated by a particular lexigram, contained a particular food item (e.g., strawberries, M&M's, kiwis, etc.). Thus, it was not unusual for Kanzi to select both the lexigram for a particular site (e.g., the A-frame house) and the food that could always be found there (e.g., strawberries) when he asked a trainer to take him on a trip.

Most surprising was Kanzi's ability to respond to spoken English. For example, he could carry out the appropriate actions in response to a command to perform a novel act, such as *put the collar in the water, pour the lemonade in the Coke, get the balloon that's in the microwave,* and so on. On a test of his English comprehension, he responded correctly to 445 out of 660 different sentences, each containing three to five words. On the basis of the size of Kanzi's vocabulary and his ability to carry out multiword commands in English, Savage-Rumbaugh concluded that "Kanzi could understand language at least as well as a child of two to three years old" (Savage-Rumbaugh, Shanker, & Taylor, 1998, p. 67).

There is no evidence that other animals, or 2- to 3-year-old children for that matter, could solve problems as complex as those that Kanzi solved. It does not follow, however, that Kanzi's performance qualifies as language. All of the problems presented to Kanzi, which are undeniably difficult, can be construed as conditional discrimination problems whose solution is devoid of any intentional meaning (Terrace, 1979a, 1985b, 2002). Consider, for example, the command *put the collar in the water.* This command was part of a series of commands in which Kanzi was instructed to perform some action with an object, either by having that object do something to another object or by having that object interact with some agent. On each trial, the object and any potential agents were in plain view. Kanzi's task was simply to understand the meanings of any of the symbols that were associated with an object, an action, or an agent, and to then follow a simple rule such as "the first object acts on the second object," "retrieve object that Kanzi has recently put away," and so on.

The absence of intentional meaning in an ape's use of symbols is especially evident in various double-blind tests of vocabulary that have been administered to rule out covert cues from the trainer. Consider, for example, a widely cited "vocabulary" test given to Washoe, the first chimpanzee trained to use signs of American Sign Language

(Gardner & Gardner, 1974). Trainer 1 showed Washoe a photograph of a familiar object. Washoe's signed answers were evaluated by Trainer 2, who could not see the photographs. Throughout the test, Trainer 2 sat impassively and gave Washoe a small piece of food whenever Washoe's sign matched the sign that appeared on her answer sheet. Even though Washoe responded at high levels of accuracy, it should be clear that she was not attempting to converse with Trainer about the test items.

After more than 30 years of research on ape language, it is clear that apes are remarkably astute at learning symbols that are related to various rewards but that they do not use those symbols to share information. Evidence of symbol use for the purpose of having a conversation with a trainer (or with another ape) is glaringly absent from *any* report of language use by apes. By contrast, there are abundant examples of the remarkably intelligent ways in which chimpanzees learn to use symbols to solicit rewards. This killjoy interpretation of an ape's use of symbols can be easily tested. Suppose that the considerable range of foods, drinks, and physical games that function as rewards for a chimp's use of symbols were eliminated (or reduced to the low level at which they are given to children during the normal course of a day). I predict that symbol use would gradually disappear under those conditions.

THE EVOLUTION OF VOCABULARY AND GRAMMAR

The ability of apes to use arbitrary symbols to solve conditional discrimination problems and to learn arbitrary lists of symbols is an impressive intellectual achievement, especially because it is not mediated by language. But questions about an ape's grammatical ability are premature if, as all of the available evidence suggests, they do not use symbols referentially. The same can be said of theories of the evolution of language that rely exclusively on grammatical ability as a criterion for distinguishing between communication by human and nonhuman primates.

Paradoxically, the hard question about the evolution of language is not at the level of syntax or serial expertise, but at the level of meaningful words. A grammar provides speakers with a mechanism for creating particular meanings by arranging meaningful symbols into particular sequences. Grammar also provides listeners with a mechanism for comprehending the meaning of those sequences (Chomsky, 1957, 1965).

Like grammatical ability, referential ability is uniquely human. It is important to recognize, however, that those abilities emerged at different times during the evolutionary progression from apes to humans. Grammatical ability is the end point of a long process of cognitive development that was set in motion when some ancestral group of primates began to communicate in a manner that differed radically from the ritualized calls they made to one another while foraging, grooming, mating, sensing danger, and so forth. At some critical point, particular utterances acquired an intentional function in the sense that one individual sought to influence another individual's mental state, rather than behavior.

The addition of intentional communication to apes' already extensive repertoire of social skills set the stage for an explosive expansion of their considerable cognitive abilities. Most likely, intentional communication began modestly in small groups of our ancestors, whose intentional vocabularies were initially limited. From such ordinary beginnings, however, it is easy to see how intentional communication took root and how it could escalate. For the first time, it was possible for primates to share their thoughts, perceptions, and desires and to comment about events and individuals of mutual interest, such as feeling happy, a particular patch of fruit, someone who broke a rule, and so on. It was also possible to maintain small cultures, engage in simple pedagogy, plan trips, and so forth (Donald, 1991). Each of these examples has obvious adaptive value. In combination, there would be strong selective pressure for larger and larger vocabularies of intentional utterances.

Empirical Evidence of the Development of Intentional Skills

Although less complex than grammatical ability, the origins of even the simplest forms of intentional communication pose questions that are similar to those raised by the origins of grammatical ability. What types of evidence are needed to attribute intentional communication to a nonhuman primate? Is intentional communication an innate ability? What were its immediate precursors?

Unlike questions about the origins of grammatical ability, questions about the origins of intentional communication are more amenable to research, both with human and nonhuman subjects. One important line of research was inspired by Premack and Woodruff's (1978) influential article on a chimpanzee's "theory of mind" (TOM), specifically, a chimpanzee's ability to "impute mental states to [one]self and to others" (p. 515). To provide evidence for a TOM, Premack and Woodruff designed a paradigm in which Sarah (their star subject) was shown a videotape of an actor in a stressful situation. Sarah was then asked to report the actor's state of mind by choosing one of two photographs. One depicted an appropriate course of action, the other an inappropriate alternative, such as a picture of a key on a trial on which the actor was shown trying to open a door, as opposed to a photograph of the actor eating, sleeping, or some such. Because Sarah reliably chose the photograph showing the appropriate course of action, Premack and Woodruff concluded that she could infer the actor's state of mind.

Premack and Woodruff's article on TOM attracted much attention from psychologists and philosophers (Carruthers & Smith, 1996; Heyes, 1993; Hobson, 1991). Some commentators questioned the validity of Premack's evidence that Sarah had a TOM on the grounds that it took many trials to learn to perform a TOM task (Povinelli, 1998). That would provide ample time for her to respond correctly by learning particular associations (e.g., door-key). It was also suggested that Sarah could have based her answers on the solution to problems she mastered in earlier experiments.

Objections to Premack and Woodruff's conclusions inspired a variety of new paradigms, many of which have been used in experiments on human infants, children, and nonhuman primates (Moore & Dunham, 1995; Tomasello & Call, 1997). But, methodological problems aside, Premack and Woodruff's article exerted a revolutionary influence on cognitive research. Of greatest significance is the foundation TOM provided for comparing the intentional states of chimpanzees (our closest living relative) with those of human infants. In particular, the concept of a TOM calls attention to two preverbal stages of metacognitive cognitive development: the ability to perceive another individual's intentional state and the ability to communicate about that state.

Although psychologists disagree as to what constitutes a proper test of TOM, and how the results of such tests should be interpreted, their differences center on evidence for TOM in children aged 2 to 5 years, who are well on their way toward mastering language. Those and related issues concerning TOM have been discussed in a number of excellent reviews (Baron-Cohen, Tager-Flusberg, & Cohen, 2000; Byrne, 2000; Dunbar, 1998; Gopnik, 2002). In the remainder of this chapter, I focus exclusively on some experiments on the perception of intentional states in human infants younger than 2 years and by nonhuman primates. I then use that evidence to support my claim that the perception of intentional states plays a crucial role in the transition from nonintentional to intentional communication and, ultimately, language.

JOINT ATTENTION

At about the same time that Premack introduced the concept of TOM, Bruner independently introduced the concept of joint attention as an example of nonverbal intentional communication between an infant and her caregiver (Bruner, 1975, 1983). Bruner regarded joint attention as an essential component of what he referred to as the language acquisition support system (LASS), a cognitive system that had to be in place before the LAD proposed by Chomsky could start operating. Joint attention is an offshoot of two unremarkable and common behaviors: attending to a particular object and learning an instrumental act to recruit another individual's help in obtaining that object. An infant, for example, might cry repeatedly and look at a toy she desired until the caretaker moved it within reach. This type of behavior, which has been referred to as "protoimperative," also occurs in many nonhuman species (Bates, 1976).

Between the ages of 6 and 9 months, a new type of behavior emerges, but only in human infants. The infant again tries to get a caretaker to attend to some object, often by crying, looking back and forth between the object and the caretaker, or simply by pointing at it. The infant's only discernible goal is to announce that she has perceived an object and that she wants her caretaker to perceive it. When she succeeds, she stops crying and smiles, to acknowledge the caretaker's attention. This type of behavior, which has been referred to as "protodeclarative," has not been observed in nonhuman primates.[2]

The transition from protoimperatives to protodeclaratives is a remarkable cognitive leap, one that appears to be uniquely human. Protodeclaratives are guided solely by an infant's wish to share his knowledge of the world with another person. As the infant gets older, his protodeclaratives become shorter and less variable. He might simply point to an object or hold it up for an adult to see, or offer it to the adult with nothing more than the expectation that it will be returned. If the relevant object is not in sight, the infant might try to lead the adult to a place where it can be seen.

By definition, protodeclaratives presuppose the ability to perceive the caregiver as a social agent, an agent whose perception of the world may or may not be the same as the infant's. Once an infant can engage an adult's attention with a protodeclarative, it is but a small step to use a particular word instead of a gesture. As the child gets older, she learns more and more words that function as protodeclaratives. As her vocabulary expands, she will eventually need rules for combining words in a consistently meaningful manner. Only then, Bruner argued, is the infant's LAD activated.

Aside from a few anecdotal observations, there is no evidence that nonhuman primates use protodeclaratives in their natural environment. There is, however, evidence that chimpanzees that have been socialized in a human environment will point to an object, on occasions on which they do not appear to be interested in actually gaining possession of it. This degree of overlap is to be expected. Like all new behaviors, protodeclaratives did not evolve suddenly. It is therefore not surprising to see precursors of protodeclaratives in our nearest living relative. Indeed, similar behaviors have been identified in recent experiments on TOM in laboratory-housed chimpanzees.

Experiments on TOM in Nonhuman Primates

The current literature on TOM in nonhuman primates is too large (and contentious) to summarize in this chapter. Leading investigators who had initially interpreted various behaviors as evidence of a TOM have since adopted a more skeptical view of that evidence (Povinelli, 2000; Premack, 1988). In this section, I describe an experiment that illustrates the difficulties of investigating TOM in a nonhuman primate and the elaborate control conditions that are needed to rule out simpler interpretations of their behavior.

There is little question that a nonhuman primate can follow eye gaze. Less clear is what it sees. Imagine, for example, two chimpanzees, both of which hear an unfamiliar sound that evokes an orienting response. Chimpanzee 1 has a direct line of sight to the source of the sound. Chimpanzee 2 does not, but Chimpanzee 2 can observe the direction of Chimpanzee 1's orienting response. How should we interpret Chimpanzee 2's state of mind? Does Chimpanzee 2 try to imagine what Chimpanzee 1 observed? Or does Chimpanzee 2 simply interpret Chimpanzee 1's orienting reflex as a discriminative stimulus for vigilance?

In an ingeniously simple experiment, Povinelli and Eddy (1996) investigated the relationship between eye gaze and seeing. Chimpanzees were first trained to reach through a hole in a Plexiglas wall to solicit, from their trainer, food that was too far away to reach on their own. The trainer was seated on the other side of the wall. The subjects were then given a choice of soliciting food from either of two trainers, only one of whom could see the food that the chimpanzee was seeking (Trainer 1). As shown in figure 3.5, Trainer 2 was prevented from seeing the food by a variety of obstacles, some obvious, others more subtle. In Figure 3.5A, Trainer 2's head is covered with a bucket; in figure 3.5B, Trainer 2 covers her eyes with her hands; in figure 3.5C, with a blindfold. In figure 3.5D, Trainer 2 simply sits with her back to the chimpanzee.

Povinelli and Eddy asked what, at first glance, appears to be a trivial question: would a chimpanzee solicit food from Trainer 1, who could see the food, or would it choose randomly between Trainer 1 and Trainer 2? Intuitively, we would guess that the chimpanzee would choose Trainer 1 on the grounds that only Trainer 1 could know what the chimpanzee was requesting and why. Surprisingly, the opposite was true, with but one exception. In the conditions shown in figure 3.5A–C, the chimpanzee directed its requests for food to both trainers at random. The one exception was the condition in which Trainer 2 had her back to the subject (figure 3.5D).

To give their subjects the benefit of the doubt, Povinelli and Eddy hypothesized that chimpanzees used either of the following simple rules to obtain food: respond to the trainer who faces forward; do not

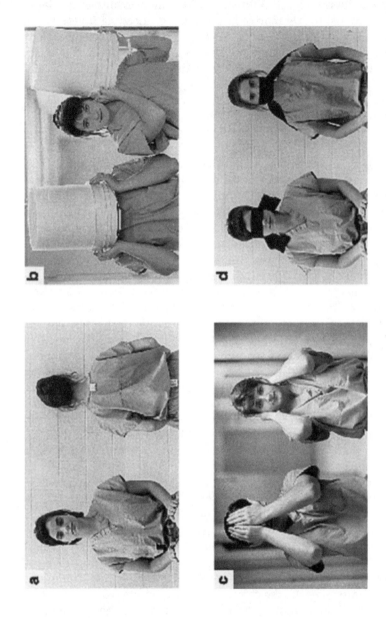

Figure 3.5 Conditions presented to the chimpanzee in the original seeing/not-seeing experiment, where the chimpanzee decides from which trainer to solicit food. Sight may be blocked by A, having the back turned; B, bucket; C, hands over eyes; and D, blindfolds (adapted from Povinelli & Eddy, 1996).

respond to a trainer who presents her back. However, further variations of the procedure for preventing Trainer 2 from seeing the food revealed the shortcomings of those rules. For example, when one of the trainers sat with her back to the subject and, at the same time, looked over her shoulder (figure 3.6A), subjects reverted to the practice of randomly asking either trainer for food. Similar results were obtained when Trainer 2 simply placed an opaque screen in front of her face (figure 3.6B) or looked off to the side (figure 3.6C).

Being the intelligent creatures they are, these chimpanzees eventually learned to respond correctly on all of the tests. Again, Povinelli and Eddy sought to rationalize their subjects' failure to perceive immediately what Trainer 1 and Trainer 2 could see by assuming that they simply needed a few examples to learn the concept "ask the trainer who can see the food." That explanation also failed as the chimpanzees reverted to random responding on each new occasion on which they encountered a new condition that prevented Trainer 2 from seeing the food, for example, Trainer 1 facing the chimpanzee with her eyes closed and Trainer 2 holding a mask in front of her face with her eyes open (figure 3.7A), or when both trainers held masks in front of their faces: Trainer 1 with her eyes open; Trainer 2 with her eyes shut (figure 3.7B). Additional evidence that the chimpanzees had not really learned the concept "solicit food only from the trainer who can see the food" came from trials on which a previously trained condition was repeated, for example, when Trainer 2 had a bucket over her head. On those trials, the chimpanzees reverted to a trial-and-error strategy of determining which trainer could provide food. Overall, the results of this experiment suggest that chimpanzees are unable to infer what the trainer could see and, instead, based their requests on external cues that they had to learn one by one.

Interestingly, Povinelli and Eddy obtained diametrically opposite results when they tested children with the same paradigm. Even the youngest subjects, of a group of 2½- to 3-year-olds, responded correctly on most (and in, some instances, all) of the conditions, from the very first trial under each condition. The contrast between the results obtained from chimpanzees and children illustrate how difficult it is to imagine how a child and a chimpanzee could look at the same stimulus, have the same incentive to make the correct response, and yet behave so differently. The child was able to respond to all variations of the experimental conditions on the basis of his sense of what each trainer could perceive. The chimpanzees were able to succeed only by identifying specific features of each situation.

"Natural" Environments for Inferring Intentionality?

In the Povinelli and Eddy experiment, the chimpanzees may have failed to infer what the trainer perceived because the conditions on

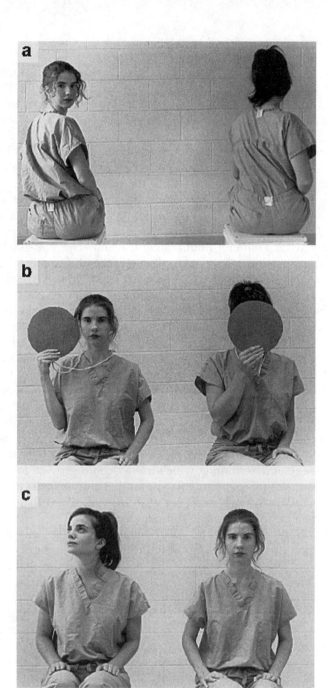

Figure 3.6 Conditions used to confirm results of experiment shown in figure 3.5. A. Looking-over-the-shoulder condition. B. Screen-versus-no-screen condition. C. Attending-versus-distracted condition (adapted from Povinelli & Eddy, 1996).

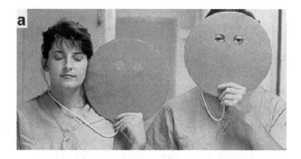

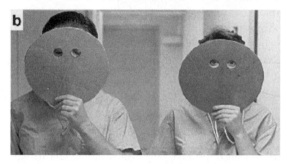

Figure 3.7 Conditions used to distinguish the relative importance of the eyes versus the face in the appreciation of "seeing." A. Eyes closed, face revealed versus eyes open, face masked. B. Face masked, eyes closed versus eyes open (adapted from Povinelli & Eddy, 1996).

which they were tested were unnatural. When foraging for food, chimpanzees do not normally encounter other members of their group who are blindfolded. Nor do they have to depend on a trainer to pass them food from inaccessible sources. To avoid those and similar problems, Hare and colleagues (Hare, Call, Agnetta, & Tomasello, 2000; Hare, Call, & Tomasello, 2001) designed an experiment that, prima facie, seemed to simulate natural feeding situations.

When foraging for food, a dominant chimpanzee has the perogative to begin eating before a subordinate does. Hare et al. reasoned that a subordinate chimpanzee would track the extent to which a dominant chimpanzee could perceive items of food that were attractive to both chimpanzees. If the food were in plain view of both chimpanzees, the subordinate chimpanzee would defer to the dominant chimpanzee. But if the subordinate chimpanzee sensed that the dominant chimpanzee was unable to see the food, it might go after the food before the dominant chimpanzee could react.

In Hare et al.'s (2001) experiment, a pair of chimpanzees were housed in separate rooms; the dominant in one room, the subordinate in the other. The experimenters placed tidbits of food in a third room that was situated between the rooms in which the chimpanzees were housed and observed the interactions between the dominant and subordinate chimpanzees under three conditions: (1) the dominant chimpanzee could (or could not) see where the food was hidden in the third room, (2) the subordinate chimpanzee was (or was not) given an opportunity to track what the dominant chimpanzee could see of the third room, and (3) the dominant chimpanzee did (or did not) have access to the third room. Without any prior training on these conditions, the subordinate chimpanzee responded appropriately under all three conditions from the very first trial. That is, the subordinate chimpanzee only went after food when it was clear that the dominant chimpanzee could not see where it was hidden or when the subordinate chimpanzee could perceive that the path of the dominant chimpanzee was blocked. As in other experiments on primate cognition, the results of this experiment suggest that the paradigm used to investigate a particular ability is crucial to the outcome.

BECOMING HUMAN: WHY TWO MINDS ARE BETTER THAN ONE

Since Descartes, language has been the main basis for distinguishing between human and nonhuman animals. Language may be the most obvious difference but, as I have tried to show in this chapter, the cognitive leap from chimpanzees, our nearest living ancestor, to *Homo sapiens* required at least one other major change. Before language evolved, our ancestors had to develop nonverbal skills for reading another individual's mind. By taking those skills into account, the problem of the evolution of language is reduced to a more manageable scale. In particular, it draws attention away from formal models of grammar (an undeniable universal of language) to metacognitive precursors of language that can be investigated in apes and human infants. Even metacognition is too complex a metacognitive skill to have emerged full-blown in one of our ancestors. Metacognition as we know it is undoubtedly a blend of many precursors. Whether we can identify all of those precursors and the order in which they evolved is a question that cannot at present be answered. We can, however, try to examine nonverbal examples of the metacognitive skills of infants and apes. The fruitfulness of that approach has been confirmed in experiments on joint eye gaze and joint attention in children and apes, and on the ability of a subordinate chimpanzee to sense whether the coast is clear to grab some food behind the dominant chimpanzee's back.

The results of those experiments allow us to frame the broad question of when and how language evolved as a narrower and more manageable question of when and how nonverbal sharing of information evolved. The narrower question suggests an era in human evolution during which the benefits of having a nonverbal means of sharing information within a social group could establish an advantage over groups lacking that ability. Adding the spark of language to those exchanges would lead to the explosion of cognitive skills that we take for granted in human adults.

NOTES

1. A study by Nishimura, Mikami, Suzuki, and Matsuzawa (2003) showed that the larynx of an infant chimpanzee and a human infant were morphologically similar. Thus, the inability of a chimpanzee to produce humanlike sounds cannot be attributed to anatomical differences of the articulatory apparatus.

2. Protoimperatives and protodeclaratives are conceptually similar to the categories of mands and tacts, respectively, described earlier.

REFERENCES

Baron-Cohen, S., Tager-Flusberg, H., & Cohen, D. H. (Eds.). (2000). *Understanding other minds: Perspectives from developmental cognitive neuroscience.* New York: Oxford University Press.

Bates, E. (1976). *Language and context: The acquisition of pragmatics.* New York: Academic Press.

Bloom, L. M., Rocissano, L., & Hood, L. (1976). Adult-child discourse: Developmental interaction between information processing and linguistic knowledge. *Cognitive Psychology, 8,* 521–552.

Braine, M. D. S. (1976). Children's first word combinations. *Monographs of the Society for Research in Child Development, 41,* 1–96.

Bretherton, I., McNew, S., Snyder, L., & Bates, E. (1983). Individual differences at 20 months: Analytic and holistic strategies in language acquistition. *Journal of Child Language, 10,* 293–320.

Brown, R. (1970). *Psycholinguistics: Selected papers by Roger Brown.* New York: Free Press.

Brown, R. (1973). *A first language: The early stage.* Cambridge, MA: Harvard University Press.

Bruner, J. S. (1975). From communication to language: A psychological perspective. *Cognition, 3,* 255–287.

Bruner, J. S. (1983). *Child's talk: Learning to use language.* New York: Norton.

Byrne, R. W. (2000). Evolution of primate cognition. *Cognitive Science, 24,* 543–570.

Carpenter, A. F., Georgopolous, A. P., & Pellizzer, G. (1999). Motor control encoding of serial position in a context-recall task. *Science, 283,* 1752–1757.

Carruthers, P., & Smith, P. K. (Eds.). (1996). *Theories of theory of mind.* Cambridge, UK: Cambridge University Press.

Chomsky, N. (1957). *Syntactic structures.* The Hague: Mouton Publishers.

Chomsky, N. (1965). *Aspects of the theory of syntax.* Cambridge, MA: MIT Press.

Chomsky, N. (1986). *Knowledge of language.* Wesport, CT: Praeger.

Colombo, M., Eickhoff, A. E., & Gross, C. G. (1993). The effects of inferior temporal and dorsolateral frontal lesions on serial-order behavior and visual imagery in monkeys. *Cognitive Brain Research, 1*, 211–217.

Donald, M. (1991). *Origins of the modern mind.* Cambridge, MA: Harvard University Press.

Dunbar, R. (1998). Theory of mind and the evolution of language. In J. R. Hurford, M. Studdert-Kennedy, & C. Knight (Eds.), *Approaches to the evolution of language* (pp. 92–110). New York: Cambridge University Press.

Gardner, B. T., & Gardner, R. A. (1969). Teaching sign language to a chimpanzee. *Science, 162*, 664–672.

Gardner, B. T., & Gardner, R. A. (1973). *Teaching sign language to the chimpanzee: Washoe.* University Park, PA: The Psychological Cinema Register.

Gardner, B. T., & Gardner, R. A. (1974). Comparing the early utterances of child and chimpanzee. In A. Pick (Ed.), *Minnesota symposia on child psychology* (pp. 3–23). Minneapolis: University of Minnesota Press.

Gardner, B. T., & Gardner, R. A. (1975a). Early signs of language in child and chimpanzee. *Science, 187*, 752–753.

Gardner, B. T., & Gardner, R. A. (1975b). Evidence for sentence constituents in the early utterances of child chimpanzees. *Journal of Experimental Psychology, 104*, 244–267.

Gopnik, A. (2002). *Theory of mind.* Retrieved September 12, 2002, from cognet.-mit.edu/library/erefs/mitecs/gopnik.html.

Gould, S. J. (1977). *Ontogeny and phylogeny.* Cambridge, MA: Harvard University Press.

Gould, S. J., & Vrba, E. S. (1982). Exaptation: A missing term in the science of form. *Paleobiology, 8*, 4–15.

Hamilton, J. M. E., & Sanford, A. J. (1978). The symbolic distance effect for alphabetic order judgements: A subjective report and reaction time analysis. *Quarterly Journal of Experimental Psychology, 30*, 33–43.

Hare, B., Call, J., Agnetta, B., & Tomasello, M. (2000). Chimpanzees know what conspecifics do and do not see. *Animal Behaviour, 59*, 771–785.

Hare, B., Call, J., & Tomasello, M. (2001). Do chimpanzees know what conspecifics know? *Animal Behavior, 61*, 139–151.

Harlow, H. F. (1949). The formation of learning sets. *Psychological Review, 56*, 51–65.

Hauser, M., Chomsky, N., & Fitch, W. T. (2002). The faculty of language: What is it, who has it, and how did it evolve? *Science, 298*, 1569–1579.

Hayes, C. (1951). *The ape in our house.* New York: Harper.

Hayes, C., & Hayes, K. (1951). The intellectual development of a home-raised chimpanzee. *Proceedings of the American Philosophical Society, 95*, 105–109.

Heyes, C. (1993). Anecdotes, training, trapping, and triangulating: Do animals attribute mental states? *Animal Behavior, 46*, 177–188.

Hobson, R. P. (1991). Against the theory of "theory of mind." *British Journal of Developmental Psychology, 9*, 33–51.

Kellogg, L. A., & Kellogg, W. N. (1967). *The ape and the child: A study of environmental influence and its behavior.* New York: McGraw-Hill. (Original work published 1933)

Ladygina-Kohts, N. N. (2002). *Infant chimpanzee and the human child: A classic*

1935 comparative study of ape emotions and intelligence. Oxford, UK: Oxford University Press.

Lieberman, P. (1968). Primate vocalizations and human linguistic ability. *Journal of the Acoustical Society of America, 44,* 1574–1584.

Lieberman, P. (1975). The evolution of speech and language. In J. F. Kavanagh & J. E. Cutting (Eds.), *The role of speech in language* (pp. 83–106). Cambridge, MA: MIT Press.

Matsuzawa, T. (1985). Use of numbers by a chimpanzee. *Nature, 315,* 57–59.

Miles, H. L. (1983). Apes and language: The search for communicative competence. In J. de Luce & H. T. Wilder (Eds.), *Language in primates: Perspectives and implications* (pp. 43–61). New York: Springer-Verlag.

Moore, C., & Dunham, P. J. (Eds.). (1995). *Joint attention: Its origins and role and development.* Hillsdale, NJ: Lawrence Erlbaum.

Mowrer, O. M. (1954). The psychologist looks at language. *American Psychologist, 9,* 660–694.Nelson, K. (1981). Individual differences in language development: Implications for development and language. *Development of Psychology, 17,* 170–187.

Nishimura, T., Mikami, A., Suzuki, J., & Matsuzawa, T. (2003). Descent of the larynx in chimpanzee infants. *Proceedings of the National Academy of Sciences U.S.A., 100,* 6930–6933.

Orlov, T., Yakovlev, B., Hochstein, S., & Zohary, E. (2000). Macaque monkeys categorize images by their ordinal number. *Nature, 404,* 77–80.

Patterson, F., & Linden, E. (1981). *The education of Koko.* New York: Holt, Rinehart, and Winston.

Patterson, F. G. (1978). The gestures of a gorilla: Language acquisition by another pongid. *Brain and Language, 12,* 72–97.

Pinker, S. (1994). *The language instinct.* New York: William Morrow.

Potts, G. R. (1974). Storing and retrieving information about ordered relationships. *Journal of Experimental Psychology, 103,* 431–439.

Povinelli, D. J. (1998). Can animals empathize? Maybe not. *Scientific American, 9*(4), 72–75.

Povinelli, D. J. (2000). *Folk physics for apes: The chimpanzee's theory of how the world works.* New York: Oxford University Press.

Povinelli, D. J., & Eddy, T. J. (1996). What young chimpanzees know about seeing. *Monographs of the Society for Research in Child Development, 61*(3).

Povinelli, D. J., & Prince, C. G. (1999). When self met other. In M. Ferrari & R. J. Sternberg (Eds.), *Self-awareness: Its nature and development* (pp. 37–107). New York: Guilford.

Povinelli, D. J., Rulf, A. B., & Bierschwale, D. T. (1994). Absence of knowledge attribution and self-recognition in young chimpanzees (*Pan troglodytes*). *Journal of Comparative Psychology, 108,* 74–80.

Povinelli, D. M. (2001). On the possibilities of detecting intentions prior to understanding them. In B. F. Malle, L. J. Moses, & D. A. Baldwin (Eds.), *Intentions and intentionality: Foundations of social cognition* (pp. 225–248). Cambridge, MA: MIT Press.

Premack, D. (1970). A functional analysis of language. *Journal of the Experimental Analysis of Behavior, 4,* 107–125.

Premack, D. (1971). Language in a chimpanzee? *Science, 172,* 808–822.

Premack, D. (1976). *Intelligence in ape and man*. Hillsdale, NJ: Lawrence Erlbaum.

Premack, D. (1988). "Does the chimpanzee have a theory of mind?" revisited. In R. Byrne & A. Whiten (Eds.), *Machiavellian intelligence* (pp. 160–179). Oxford, UK: Oxford University Press.

Premack, D., & Woodruff, G. (1978). Does the chimpanzee have a theory of mind? *Behavioral and Brain Sciences, 1*, 515–526.

Rumbaugh, D. M. (1977). *Language learning by a chimpanzee: The Lana project*. New York: Academic Press.

Rumbaugh, D. M., Gill, T. V., & von Glasersfeld, E. C. (1973). Reading and sentence completion by a chimpanzee. *Science, 182*, 731–733.

Savage-Rumbaugh, E. S. (1994). *Kanzi: The ape at the brink of the human mind*. New York: Wiley.

Savage-Rumbaugh, S., Shanker, S. G., & Taylor, T. J. (1998). *Apes, language, and the human mind*. New York: Oxford University Press.

Scaife, M., & Bruner, J. (1975). The capacity for joint visual attention in the infant. *Nature, 253*, 265–266.

Schroeder, B. (Producer) (1977). *Koko: The talking gorilla*. Home Vision.

Skinner, B. F. (1953). *Science and human behavior*. New York: Macmillan.

Skinner, B. F. (1957). *Verbal behavior*. New York: Appleton-Century-Crofts.

Straub, R. O., & Terrace, H. S. (1981). Generalization of serial learning in the pigeon. *Animal Learning and Behavior, 9*, 454–468.

Swartz, K. B., Chen, S., & Terrace, H. S. (1991). Serial learning by rhesus monkeys. I: Acquisition and retention of multiple four-item lists. *Journal of Experimental Psychology: Animal Behavior Processes, 17*, 396–410.

Terrace, H. S. (1979a). Is problem solving language? A review of Premack's *Intelligence in Apes and Man*. *Journal of the Experimental Analysis of Behavior, 31*, 161–175.

Terrace, H. S. (1979b). *Nim*. New York: Knopf.

Terrace, H. S. (1984). Simultaneous chaining: The problem it poses for traditional chaining theory. In M. L. Commons, R. J. Herrnstein, & A. R. Wagner (Eds.), *Quantitative analyses of behavior: Discrimination processes* (pp. 115–138). Cambridge, MA: Ballinger.

Terrace, H. S. (1985a). In the beginning was the name. *American Psychologist, 40*, 1011–1028.

Terrace, H. S. (1985b). On the nature of animal thinking. *Neuroscience and Biobehavioral Reviews, 9*, 643–652.

Terrace, H. S. (1993). The phylogeny and ontogeny of serial momory: List learning by pigeons and monkeys. *Psychological Science, 4*, 162–169.

Terrace, H. S. (2002). Serial expertise and the evolution of language. In J. H. A. Wray & F. J. Newmeyer (Eds.), *The transition to language* (pp. 64–90). New York: Oxford University Press.

Terrace, H. S., Petitto, L. A., Sanders, R. J., & Bever, T. G. (1979). Can an ape create a sentence? *Science, 206*, 891–902.

Terrace, H. S., Son, L., & Brannon, E. (2003). The development of serial expertise by rhesus macaques. *Psychological Science, 14*, 66–73

Thompson, C. R., & Church, R. M. (1980). An explanation of the language of a chimpanzee. *Science, 208*, 313–314.

Tomasello, M. (1999). Having intentions, understanding intentions, and understanding communicative intentions. In J. W. Astington, D. R. Olson, & P. D. Zelazo (Eds.), *Developing theories of intention: Social understanding and self-control* (pp. 63–76). Mahwah, NJ: Lawrence Erlbaum.

Tomasello, M., & Call, J. (1997). *Primate cognition.* New York: Oxford University Press.

Tomasello, M., Hare, B., & Fogleman, T. (2001). The ontogeny of gaze following in chimpanzees, *Pan troglodytes,* and rhesus macaques, *Macaca mulatta. Animal Behavior, 61,* 335–343.

Williams, G. C. (1966). *Adaptation and natural selection.* Princeton, NJ: Princeton University Press.

Winitz, H. (1969). *Articulatory acquisition and behavior.* New York: Appleton-Century-Crofts.

4

Emerging Levels of Consciousness in Early Human Development

Katherine Nelson

In this chapter, I am concerned with tracing the emergence during ontogenesis of a specifically human kind of consciousness from a more primitive awareness. This view of emergent levels of consciousness builds on recent work in the evolution of human cognition, particularly that of Merlin Donald (1991, 2001). What I propose here is, first, that consciousness is not unitary but that we can discern levels of consciousness from simple awareness of feelings and perceptions to complex extended states of consciousness (Damasio, 1999). A distinction can therefore be made between consciousness in animals and humans, and particularly between evidence of very simple kinds of metacognition and full self-knowing consciousness. Tulving (1983) made the distinction between semantic (noetic) and episodic (autonoetic) memory, which brought the issue of a specifically human self-knowing memory into focus in cognitive psychology, and raised important issues for research on memory development as well. In this light, I propose that full human consciousness can be understood only in terms of both its evolutionary and developmental history. Thus, before turning to the proposed levels of development and evidence for them in the developmental literature, I provide some background on the developmental and evolutionary perspectives.

DEVELOPMENTAL PERSPECTIVE

A developmental perspective necessarily concerns dynamic change in processes as they occur over time. For this reason, many developmental theorists have adopted the perspective of dynamic systems analysis, conceptualizing human development as a self-organizing system involving brain, body, and mind functioning together in interaction with both the internal and external environment, and arising from this process successive periods of organization. In a larger perspective, the individual (brain, body, mind) and the social world form an interdependent transactional system that is in a constant process of organization. We can consider the "elements" of the system separately at any point in time, but only with the caveat that they are not in fact separable, that the context, especially the social context, is always part of the process to be traced.

From this developmental perspective, it is misleading to hunt for origins or for a missing link, which implies a search for one specific point where something is added such that the system takes on a new form and subsequently takes off in a trajectory that results in human adult competence. Admittedly, many developmental psychologists take exactly this stance, so it is not surprising that the general field of cognitive science does as well. The problem is that the search for the missing link, in development or in evolution, is likely to fail because the particular capacity we are looking for will not be found in a recognizable form, whether we call it metacognition or reflective consciousness or something else. Rather, because complex systems are constituted of many different subcomponents that may recombine in different ways, self-reflective knowing may initially appear as a small kernel of something else that eventually finds itself coopted as a function in a system that takes on new powers (Fischer & Bidell, 1991). Under these conditions, we need to study the development of the system on its own terms, recognizing transformations and the emergence of new capacities from the combinations and recombinations of old forms and functions. Just such a process is now recognized as an essential part of phylogenetic evolution (DePew & Weber, 1999). Thus, instead of proposing a theory of origins, my proposal here is in terms of development from a less complex to a more complex organization that functions effectively for the individual in a social environment at a particular moment in time, and that in turn also leads to new levels of organized function.

As part of a developing functional system, it is obvious that what is relevant to the experiencing individual changes over time with changes in capacities, needs, and external supports. In consequence, the child's capacity for experiencing the complexity of the world and making sense of it changes, not only with brain development but also with body development and the potentials these offer for experiencing in new ways. These considerations make it imperative to take an experiential perspective on the course of development. Experience is conscious, the source of memory, knowledge, and belief, both present and past experience, and serves to guide and support action in both familiar and unfamiliar situations.

Like consciousness, everyone's experience is uniquely personal and unavailable to objective observation. As adults, we use speech and writing to convey aspects of personal experience and mediated knowledge to one another, as well as to construct aspects of knowledge that exist only in the abstractions of language (e.g., in academic discussions). But for the infant and young child, experience is not only personal but private in an extreme sense: the child cannot share her thoughts with others. This condition is, I believe, central to understanding the development of consciousness. It also requires us to imagine what it is like to be an infant or child in the same sense that we need to imagine what it is like to be a bat (Nagel, 1974) or like a chimpanzee. I will take up this challenge in the section on the development of consciousness. I first consider some general characteristics of human development that differ in important ways from other animals studied, including nonhuman primates.

The first point is that for each human infant the world is unique and unpredictable in all but the most basic ways, because each infant is born into a unique cultural arrangement. This is not a claim of radical cultural difference, but rather of unpredictability from the point of view of any knowledge that evolution might have provided through genetic or more general prenatal developmental mechanisms. (This point deserves to be especially emphasized, but limitations of space prevent dwelling on it here at length.)

The second point to be noted is the rapid change of perceptual and motor capacities over the course of infancy and early childhood. Unlike other primates, human infants are born in a fetal state, that is, a state of development that most other mammals complete prior to birth. They are uniquely helpless, totally dependent upon caregivers. Most of the first few months are spent in a prone or supine position, unless propped or held in a more upright state. Thus the view of the world is highly restricted; even parts of the self, such as hands or feet, await further motor development before they can be seen and examined. So also, the view of others is at the disposal of those others to make themselves seen in particular perspectives. By the midpoint of the first year, however, the infant has learned to sit up and usually to move about by creeping or crawling. Thus, some control over what can be seen and handled has been gained. When the infant pulls herself up to standing position and begins to cruise along the edge of a piece of furniture, a new viewpoint is gained, and when that is succeeded by independent walking around toward the end of the first year, the sequence of motor development and its accompanying broadening of perspectives and experience of the surroundings is almost complete (Campos, Bertenthal, & Kermoian, 1992).

The third point complements these developments: the infant and young child is always in and dependent upon the social world, defined by the cultural choices that particular social others have made in terms of dwellings, furnishings, foods, friends, toys, activities, and myriad other things. Although the infant's experience from the beginning thus depends totally upon the social arrangements of the cultural world, the social world and its choices also change with the child's own development, both guiding experience and leading the way, sometimes blocking particular pathways as well. Thus the child's experience in the world is almost completely at the disposal of the social others in the early years, primarily of course parents and other family members, but in different cultures and social arrangements a variety of people may serve in important roles as guides and caretakers. In sum, the child's experience is at once both utterly private and totally social, while constantly changing within a stable background.

EMERGENCE OF CONSCIOUSNESS IN EVOLUTION AND DEVELOPMENT

Gould (1977) cautioned against the idea of the recapitulation in ontogeny of a phylogenetic sequence in evolution for a number of reasons, among them its basis in the mistaken assumption that there is in fact a sequence from lower to higher animals culminating in the human species, rather than a contingent process of organism-environment adaptation leading to an infinite number of possible solutions.[1] But acceptance of this caution does not rule out the recognition of similarities in developmental and evolutionary problems and processes. The particular issue in focus here, the origins of self-knowing consciousness, is a case in point. The "origins" may escape our grasp for the very reasons that Gould warned about, namely that two species from different phylogenetic branches might exhibit different aspects of cognition that in a third unrelated species might appear to be combined into a "higher" level of cognitive functioning, yet this level in turn might be unrelated to our own branch of the phylogenetic bush. Even looking backward through our primate roots faces us with the dilemma that our closest relatives, the chimpanzee, bonobo, and gorilla, display similar cognitive skills in infancy appearing in different developmental sequences (Tomasello & Call, 1997). When we look backward from the adult human to the human infant or to earlier species in the hominid or primate line, we are always looking for the earliest appearance of some component skill or capacity that the adult person displays. But the capacity or skill in question may be the product of the organization of some components that in isolation bear no functional relation to the finished product.

Studies of children's theory of mind are instructive here. Work on the development of theory of mind in children actually began in response to Premack and Woodruff's (1978) questioning of whether the chimpanzee had a theory of mind. (Their answer was yes, but Premack has since retreated from this conclusion; see Premack, 1988.) For many years, studies were carried out within a few experimental paradigms to establish when children might be said to have a theory of mind, according to the logical requirement that understanding others' minds involves understanding that they may hold beliefs that are false with respect to states of the world (for lack of access to relevant information, for example; see Astington, Harris, & Olson, 1988, for an early compendium of this work).

Some attempts to explain the origins of this capacity searched for the beginnings of a theory and eventually settled on the idea that children begin with a built-in theory and then subject the theory to successive revisions as disconfirming data are encountered (Gopnik, Capps, & Meltzoff, 2000; Gopnik & Wellman, 1994). Another effort presumed that the capacity involved a brain module that must have evolved in humans for this purpose (Leslie, 1987, 1991) and thus was present at birth and evident in behavior by 1 year but depended on additional cognitive skills to become fully operative at about 4 years. Both of these efforts were hampered by the assumption that the capacity they were viewing at 4 years would be visible in the same form at some earlier point in development. It is notable that both ran into the same dead end, namely the conclusion that the capacity must be built into the human brain/mind to begin with. By similar reasoning, virtually all of the child's and adult's cognitive capacities must be innately given. This is a position that is quite in accord with Chomsky's (1965) claims about language and Fodor's (1975) claims about the language of thought, but not one congenial to the developmental point of view.

However, this route is not inevitable. Other theorists have looked for the roots of theory of mind in earlier social relations and skills. For example, Harris (1992) found evidence in children's empathy for others and in their pretense for a simulation account of theory of mind development. Tomasello (1999a, 1999b) focused on the establishment of joint attention with a caretaker toward the end of the first year as the seed from which theory of mind later emerged, after due nurturing through further interaction, both linguistic and nonlinguistic. Both of these accounts reflect a developmental perspective. In addition, they shed light on the difference in theory of mind between humans (at least by 4 years) and other primates by virtue of their focus on specifically human social conditions of development, rather than on the cognitive givens.

Most of the great apes (chimpanzees, gorillas, bonobos) live in social groups and display social intelligence, so that many theorists now propose that the necessity of solving social problems (e.g., of competition for mates) led to the increase in cognitive power displayed by these creatures in comparison with other animals.[2] However, the social conditions of human infancy differ from those of other primates in terms of the intimate caretaking and social involvement of parents, particularly mothers, over an extended period of time—for 3 to 7 years or more (Hrdy, 1999). It is within this intimate caretaking circle that joint attention (not evident in the same way in other primates) becomes established and soon thereafter supports the beginnings of language in first word learning.

This approach to development—examining development in situ—focuses on tracing what conditions and experiences obtain and how they enter into new relations and skills and become transformed over time. The often convoluted pathways that lead toward emerging new skills are the target of discovery, recognizing that many components may be recombined to produce a new level of functioning.

Evolution of Consciousness

Some of the difference between the other primates and humans is evident in the comparison of brain size and particularly in the expansion of tertiary cortex. But such physical changes in themselves do not explain how and why cognitive differences in functioning occurred and what the critical changes in hominid evolution were. Donald (1991) proposed a model of the "hybrid" modern mind that involved three major transitions beyond a general primate brain/mind such as the modern great apes exhibit.

The first major transition that Donald identified was from a strictly episodic mind to mimetic functioning. In his conception, the episodic mind—the general primate model—is confined to the here and now in the sense that memory is evoked in relevant circumstances but is not accessible to voluntary recall. Both past and future are confined to concerns of the present situation (where "present" may occupy a reasonably extended episodic period of time). Thus social life flourishes, organized around ongoing needs and actions, but culture as such does not. Planning (as for a hunt or an attack) is short-lived; memory is instrumental, not reflective. Although Donald named this level of cognitive functioning "episodic," this should not be confused with Tulving's use of the term to distinguish among kinds of memory. It is unlikely that Tulving's sense of episodic memory could exist at this level; rather, memory could be either procedural or semantic in the terms of his system.[3]

Mimesis emerged, according to Donald (1991), during the period of *Homo erectus* about 2 million years ago, evident in the appearance of deliberately constructed flaked stone tools and the use of fire. More recent evidence suggests a more complex cultural mix during the period before *Homo sapiens* (Donald, 2001). The cultural advances of this level seem to signify a new capacity for planning and the practice of skills, such as those involved in tool making. But for Donald, these capacities reach much farther, in terms of reflective cognition, and are based in a new use of precise imitation, of both social models and self-repetitions. The former allow deliberate teaching; the latter enable practice and reflection on actions outside of their practical application. A common example is that of a young boy practicing the throwing of stones, the only aim of which is to improve that particular skill, based on an internalized ideal throw. Other primates have not been observed to practice skills in this way; rather, when practice—and the limited form of imitation or emulation—exists, it is always in the interest of obtaining some goal, such as food or a mate. Mimesis, moreover, enabled new forms of gestural communication (and perhaps verbal communication as well) and the creation of communally shared rituals, dance, and other group practices, supporting a new level of cultural organization. A summary of these potentials includes the capacity for reenactment, imitation, skill development, and whole-body gesture. Each of these, Donald points out, involves the direction of attention from the world to the self, to consciously monitor one's own actions toward the accurate achievement of an internal model, derived from action in the world, one's own or another's. However, important as this transition was, it was also limited.

Little change in cultural practices or anatomical form, including brain size, was observed for over 2 million years before the appearance of *Homo sapiens* about 500,000 years ago. Dramatic changes are evident from the arrival of humans in modern anatomical form about 125,000 years ago, particularly with the invention of complex spoken language.[4] There followed a rapid expansion of culture, quickly eclipsing that of the earlier mimetic period. Donald calls this transition "mythic" to emphasize the critical role of language in constructing oral cultural narratives that provide a common history and a common cultural understanding. That is to say that in Donald's terms the move to language was in the service of communication and culture, drawing people into communities of understanding. The cognitive foundation for the emergence of language must have been established through mimesis, but symbolic language itself was a product of cultural communication within "communities of mind," and in turn it enabled cultures to take off in ways that were not possible without it. "Language emerges only at the group level and is a cultural product, distributed across many minds" (Donald, 2001, pp. 11–12). From this perspective, "cultural mind sharing" is the unique contribution of human life, the by-products of which are communally shared systems such as mathematics, athletics, music, and literacy. In turn, the nature of the individual human mind was changed as symbolic capability became part of its structure and function.

The third transition, to external memory representations, is now traced by Donald (2001) to its beginnings about 40,000 years ago (e.g., in paintings, stone markings, emblems, and the like), although its most extraordinary effects have emerged in more recent historical time, after the invention of written language about 4,000 to 5,000 years ago, and the subsequent spread of literacy through print, as recently as 500 years ago. Donald's conception of how this changed the function of individual memory is important, involving, as he put it, the transferring of memory from mind to external forms of print, graphics, and so on.

This entire evolutionary/historical sequence challenges "naturalistic" and universalist conceptions of modern adult cognitive functioning and also provides an important perspective on the development of cognition in human childhood. In his most recent book, Donald (2001) extended his analysis to the consideration of the evolution of human consciousness. He argued there that human conscious capacity "provides the biological basis for the generation of culture, including symbolic thought and language." He posited a process of "brain-culture symbiosis" termed "deep enculturation," such that in human evolution, "our brains coevolved with culture and are specifically adapted for living in culture" (p. 11). Perhaps the most provocative claim that Donald makes, and the one with the most resonance for a developmental perspective on consciousness, is the following: "The ultimate irony of human existence is that we are supreme individualists, whose individualism depends almost entirely on culture for its realization. It came at the price of giving up the isolationism, or cognitive solipsism, of all other species and entering into a collectivity of mind" (p. 12). The challenge I am taking up here is in part how to track this exchange in the ontogenetic process.

DEVELOPMENT OF CONSCIOUSNESS

What emerges from Donald's work is a view of consciousness that is active in directing attention and activity, in keeping track over time, holding multiple ends in view, and in other ways augmenting and directing cognitive functions (see also Damasio, 1999). But consciousness is not in this view a unitary state; rather, it expands in both evolution and development, where levels of consciousness emerge over time, but where earlier levels continue to function as subcomponents or alternative modes to more recently developed levels. The development of levels of consciousness has been proposed as well by Lewis and Ramsay (1999) and by Zelazo (1999), and the scheme described here shares some features with these others. The present proposal was worked out in light of Donald's theory and in relation to the emergence of self-understanding revealed in children's use of narrative and the beginnings of autonoetic memory (Nelson, 2001, 2003). Thus I begin with a brief overview of early memory development, specifically concerned with the emergence of autobiographical memory.

Research on memory in infants and young children is a surprisingly recent enterprise, with few serious efforts undertaken prior to the 1970s. Experimental work in this period typically revealed impoverished memory through the preschool period (Flavell, Friedrichs, & Hoyt, 1970). Renewed interest in the memory of children during the preschool period came from a number of researchers who worked with children in natural everyday settings in the home or in preschools (Perlmutter, 1980). My research at that time focused on children's memory for everyday events, in particular their scripts for familiar routines (Nelson & Gruendel, 1981; Nelson & Ross, 1980). We were intrigued to find that when 3-year-old children were asked to tell what had happened at dinner the night before, or last week at a birthday party, they responded with a general script for the event rather than with a specific episodic account. For example, when asked to tell what happened at dinner, they replied as though asked what happens at dinner: "You eat and then you go to bed." These children were representing a whole event, and they typically reported the correct sequence of actions, but they represented it as a semantic schema, generalized knowledge without particular details or personal reactions. Of special interest was the finding that these young children used the objective "you" form rather than the subjective "I" and the generalized present tense of the verbs rather than the specific past, suggesting that this knowledge form was neither personal nor temporally located in the past.

On the basis of these findings, we initially hypothesized that young children had general semantic but not specific episodic memory. This conclusion seemed to provide a satisfying explanation for the phenomenon of infantile amnesia, the inability of adults to recall episodes from their childhood before the age of about 3 years (Nelson, 1988). Subsequent research has revealed complexities that have obscured the clarity of this original hypothesis. We now know that children do have some memories of specific episodes from the age of 2 or 3 years, including memory fragments that seem to involve the self in a reflective sense. Such fragments have appeared in the context of "memory talk" with parents, which has been studied extensively by researchers over the past 20 years (Nelson & Fivush, 2000, 2004), where the fragments may be incorporated by the parent into whole narratives about the remembered event, which the child is not yet able to organize. It is interesting that young children's fragments appear similar to many reports from this period of childhood by adults who remember a scene or a bit of action but cannot recall the entire episode (Pillemer & White, 1989).

The implication of this line of memory research is that children learn to talk about memories, both as present events are happening and in reflecting on past events and on future happenings, beginning at around 2 years of age (in our society). Evidence for this is that the amount and kind of memory talk at 4 years is correlated with the amount and specificity of children's episodic memories 2 years later (Reese, Haden, & Fivush, 1993). It is important to note that significant cross-cultural differences have been found in each of these factors, with Asian (Chinese, Japanese, and Korean) adults having fewer and later early childhood memories than American adults, Asian mothers engaging in less memory talk than American mothers, and Asian children reporting fewer and less detailed episodic memories (Han, Leichtman, & Wang, 1998; Mullen, 1994, Mullen & Yi, 1995). Cultural differences of this kind support the conclusion that conversational experience contributes to episodic memory development, with different cultural practices resulting in different developmental trajectories.

This brief summary of the work on memory in early childhood provides only a glimpse of what has become an extremely active research domain, with some of the most provocative questions emerging around the issues of explaining the phenomenon of infantile amnesia and the appearance of episodic memory during childhood. Each of these questions is also clearly related to the topics covered in this volume in terms of self-knowing consciousness, metacognition, and autonoetic memory processes. The social-cultural approach to these issues that Robyn Fivush and I have elaborated (Nelson & Fivush, 2000, 2004) supports the proposal that consciousness of self in time emerges through autobiographical (autonoetic) memory and is fostered through the same kinds of social conversational experiences that influence the development of the 4-year-old's theory of mind. Emergence of levels of consciousness based on this approach is detailed in what follows.

I propose that six levels of consciousness emerge during the first years of life, with implications for self, social, and cognitive functioning. These levels are schematized in table 4.1 and described in more detail in the following sections. To a large extent, the levels of consciousness outlined here reflect those that Donald laid out as stages in human evolution; however, the process envisioned in development is somewhat different. The process of emergence in development depends on the interaction of the self and the social world. As the child functions at one level, social experiences made possible at that level enable movement to the next. Thus, what is envisioned here with regard to emerging consciousness is consistent with social theories of the development of self (e.g., Mead, 1934).

Conciousness Levels in Infancy

As pointed out earlier, to track the experience of consciousness in infancy requires imagining the perspective of the infant beginning in the first encounter with the world. The neonate seeing the world for the first time is undergoing a truly unique experience. Although William James (1890/1950) thought the experience must be of a "booming

Table 4.1 Levels of Consciousness

Level of Consciousness	Onset Age	Memory	Self-Other Contrast	Self-World Contrast
Physical	Postnatal	Perceptual	Physical boundary	Physical boundary
Social	6–12 mo.	People, schemas	Social sharing, communication	Routines, object kinds, words
Cognitive	18–24 mo.	Events, routines, categories, words	I-you perspective	Conscious self/objective self
Representational/ Reflective	2–4 years	Episodes shared with others	My self-experience/ other self-experience	Social and physical causality
Narrative	3–6 years	Episodic, autobiographical memory	Stories of me/stories of others, autonoesis	Past-future, real and imaginary worlds
Cultural	5–10 years	External representations, textual	Cultural roles	Cultural knowledge, institutions

buzzing confusion," psychologists now know that it is quite organized, although slowly unfolding as visual acuity increases and shapes come into sharper focus. Recent research on infant perception shows that infants either come into the world with highly organized expectations about the nature of three-dimensional objects, human faces, and voices, or very quickly gain information about the structure of these basic features of the world. We should not have been surprised by these findings, Piaget to the contrary notwithstanding. After all, human infants are descended from a long line of mammals, including the higher primates, most of which very soon after birth become independently mobile and thus would be extremely vulnerable to fatal accidents if they were not equipped by evolution with the ability to negotiate their way in the world of objects and animate creatures, and to recognize conspecifics by sight and sound.

What is of most interest to human infants throughout the first year are the sights, sounds, touch, and movement of people. Over this period, the infant's consciousness grows rapidly from fleeting levels of awareness interspersed with long periods of sleep to sustained periods of engagement with the physical and social world. The first level of experiential awareness is that of a physical self that distinguishes the boundary between self and other. Over the first few months, infants attend to many different aspects of the world that are changing around them; shifts in attention, in fact, are the basis for much of the experimental research on infant cognition, using the paradigms of habituation and preference for novelty. We can assume that much experiential organization is taking place during this period, although the phenomenology of that experience is difficult to fathom. The mental content of this period seems to concern primarily emotional attachment to the important social figures in the infant's world.

Beginning midway in the first year, a new level of consciousness emerges, as almost all students of infant development agree. The physical boundary between self and other, and self and object, is now extended to a three-way relation between self, other, and object, where self and other share attention to the same object. Thus a new consciousness of self and other comes into play, where the tracking of the other's attention (that is, attention to attention) is of interest. It may be that prior to this point, the infant implicitly assumed that she was the sole object of the other's attention; now a new realization that the other may attend to some other point of interest (another person, another object) may bring on a crisis of confidence in the other, manifested through such new behaviors as fear of strangers, looking to the other for clues to how to react in new situations, and generally following closely the behavioral clues of the other.

But this crisis also provides the incentive for new organizations of experience. Tracking attention merges into tracking intentions, of both self and other. Sharing attention to objects leads to drawing the other's attention to objects through pointing and other means of gestural communication. Expressing one's own wants and needs, for example, by raising arms to indicate a desire to be picked up, becomes part of the repertoire. A newly emerging ability to use imitation as a learning tool, as well as an enjoyable activity, comes into play. Tracking the sequence of routines, games, and caretaking experiences such as a bath or a feeding provides the basis for predicting and reacting to change, as well as providing the basis for taking reciprocal roles in the activity. This capacity also indicates an expanding working memory that is capable of extending over a sequence of actions and interactions, keeping track of where the point of action is at present and what is to come next.

All of these well-documented developments make it clear that a revolution in consciousness takes place in the last six months of the first year, culminating in the possibility of responding to and reproducing the sounds of language in ways consistent with the acquisition of actual words, an achievement transitional to the next level. The onset of the following period is initiated as the contrast between the social possibilities of the nonsymbolic, nonlinguistic exchanges and the linguistic world that is being carried on around the infant (but without her participation) becomes apparent, motivating the development of "cognitive consciousness."

Cognitive Consciousness

As suggested in table 4.1, cognitive consciousness is the first level at which the child begins to take an objective view of the self in relation to others and the world. This level has been recognized as a significant advance by many theorists (e.g., Lewis & Ramsey, 1999; Neisser, 1997) and has been seen as the beginning of the autobiographical self by the neuropsychologist Damasio (1999) and the developmental psychologists Howe and Courage (1993). The onset of this level of consciousness is gradual (and variable among infants), becoming apparent over the course of the second year. It is coincident with the acquisition of language, specifically the learning of first words and the construction of simple sentences. In conjunction with that advance in communication, one can observe related moves on the cognitive level, recognized by Piaget (1962) as the emergence of the semiotic function.

By late in the second year, children provide good evidence of recognizing the self and differentiating the perspective of self and other. The mirror test devised originally for gorillas and chimpanzees has been used to test self-recognition in young children as well. In this test, a mark is surreptitiously placed on the child's forehead while he or she is otherwise engaged, and then the child is allowed to view himself or herself in a mirror. The question is whether children recognize that the mirror image reflects themselves, or whether it is treated simply as that of a child. The critical observation is whether they point to the mark on their own forehead and perhaps try to rub it off, or point to the mark on the mirrored forehead, or ignore the mark. Touching one's own forehead is taken as evidence for recognizing the "objective" self in the mirror. Children pass this test usually sometime between 16 and 24 months (about the same time that they typically acquire a first 50-word vocabulary).

The capacity for delayed imitation, that is, the imitation of an action or gesture observed but not imitated on a prior occasion, comes into play toward the end of the first year and has been used in recent research on children's developing memory during this period. Bauer and others have found that children's memory for an original experience may be retained over weeks and up to 6 months by 13-month-olds, with longer extensions typical of older toddlers (Bauer, Wenner, Dropik, & Wewerka, 2000; Fivush, 1994). Other studies have revealed the abilities of toddlers (1–2-year-olds) to organize sequential knowledge of familiar events in terms of causal relations (Bauer & Mandler,

1989a) and, using a form of sorting, to construct well-organized categories of objects (Bauer & Mandler, 1989b; Gopnik & Choi, 1990; Gopnik & Meltzoff, 1986).

Evidence from language use during this period indicates that children are capable of distinguishing the perspective of the other from their own, although one would not want to say that they are capable of taking another's perspective, a later achievement. One good clue is that they usually quite easily acquire the pronouns "I" and "you" and use them distinctively in conversation. Children often begin by labeling themselves with their own name or by using "me" or "mine" for first-person address (Budwig, 1995; Nelson, 1989). Careful analysis of these uses suggests that children are struggling with the varied perspectives on person (agent, actor, experiencer, object, possessor) that are embedded in the language uses that they are in the process of acquiring. That understanding the objective status of the self is deeply interconnected to that of others is revealed in the evidence of a new self-consciousness, embarrassment, and sense of shame or guilt that becomes evident at around 2 years of age (Kagan, 1991; Lewis, 1997). This interconnectedness reflects the social dependence of the process of self-knowing described by Mead (1934).

All of these cognitive and interpersonal developments add up to a substantial advance from infancy into early childhood, and in the terms in which we are interested here, in self-knowing consciousness. Most of these transformations can be seen as resulting from the new awareness that emerged at the prior level of social consciousness compounded by the new contrasts made possible through the medium of words as they come into use by the self and understanding of the uses by others. As Gopnik and her colleagues have argued, using words advances cognition in this period in a number of ways (Gopnik & Meltzoff, 1986). They make explicit concepts that have begun to emerge through experience, but they also can guide the distinctions among concepts and categories that were not previously recognized. As Bauer's work (Bauer & Wewerka, 1997) has shown, memory for events does not depend upon language, but the ability to use language in reference to the objects or actions in an event leads to retention of the memory for a longer period of time (see also Simcock & Hayne, 2002). Thus, early language and the advances of this period appear to be interconnected, but it is not clear that one is necessary to or sufficient for the other. Rather, it appears that the social, cognitive, and linguistic abilities mutually support each other.

Is this, then, the dawn of self-knowing consciousness? Is it the missing link we are looking for? Is it the point of origin of autonoesis? Considering the latter, I believe that the answer is no. Clearly, the child of 2 years has advanced, as documented, toward a new understanding of self and other. Moreover, language is becoming a useful tool for both communication and cognition. However, despite the claims made by Howe and Courage (1993) and others, there is no evidence in all of these new skills and capabilities that children at 2 years have a sense of self in the past of the kind that Tulving refers to. Indeed, as I have argued (Nelson, 1988, 1989, 2001), the child at this age has no conception of the past or future; in Donald's sense, she is living in an episodic present. It is true that retention of memory for an event may last for many months, but there is no evidence that such memory is anything but noetic; that is, it is a representation of knowledge about this kind of event. As I noted previously, the evidence from 3-year-old children's reports on their experience of events (e.g., a birthday party) tend to be very general and are reported in the present tense. This evidence is not definitive, of course, because children might have a sense of self in the past but not be able to express it. However, I believe that the bulk of the evidence indicates that 1- or 2-year-old children are not yet tuned in to the significance of the specific past or the possible future and have no sense of themselves in past experience.

This is not to say that children at this age are confined to the present moment. Referring to Donald's concept of mimesis, it seems appropriate to think of the 2-year-old as a mimetic child, capable of replaying in consciousness, as well as in external play with toys or substitute objects, the actions of herself and others. Thus, a certain degree of reflection on states of self and other can be achieved through the imagination, either in thought or in play. But this is play with what is and what can be, not with what was and what may yet be. It is not using objects in play to stand for real things, or to symbolize the self in another place or time (Nelson, in press).

Reflective Consciousness

The cognitive consciousness of the previous level, I argued, does not imply a level of self-reflective consciousness, but it leads toward that level, through the potentials it opens up in the cognitive contents and social interactions involved. One of the most significant of those potentials is engagement in conversations made possible by the acquisition of beginning language skills, which at the same time contributes to the advancement of those skills. What conversations involve is *representational language*, the use of symbolic communication to represent a thought, a state of the world from the past or the future, an explanation, a description, a hypothesis or prediction, an invitation to engage in pretense, and so on. These possibilities are not available without the considerable resources of language, not just words for objects and actions, but the complexity of the symbolic systems that people create to make such communications feasible. Both Merlin Donald and I have talked about this potential of language in similar ways as "communities of mind" (Donald, 2001) or as "entering a community of mind" (Nelson, in press; Nelson, Henseler, & Plesa, 1999; Nelson et al., 2003).

Researchers have found that 3-year-olds are aware of how others feel, of their visual perspectives on a visual scene, of how others' wants and tastes may differ from their own. Such contrasts may be evident in nonverbal social situations, but expressing them in linguistic form makes them more explicit. My colleagues and I were able to observe the process involved in coming into this level in detail in the study of a single child (Emily) over the course of the crucial age from 2 to 3 years, because her practice of talking to herself at bedtime provided a unique perspective on the emerging thought of the young child (Nelson, 1989). These monologues were supplemented by recordings of dialogues between father and daughter prior to his leaving the room at bedtime. The conversations included much talk about what would happen in the coming day or days, talk that Emily was highly attuned to and often attempted to replicate in a subsequent monologue.

Several observations derived from this study are notable. First, at the beginning of the third year, the focus of her talk was almost entirely on how the events of her life were organized, for example, the morning routine, the day care routine, the afternoon play, the trips to the store, and so on. She began to focus on singular events during this time period, but at first with an emphasis on their organization, not their "meaning" or place in relation to herself. In the latter half of the year, she showed a new focus on self, and on people's reactions to herself, as well as her own reactions to events. Moreover, she began to use talk as a means of imagining different storylike possibilities. Previously, she had used her monologues as a means of raising questions and problems, such as what was likely to happen at the doctor's or who would bring a book to day care the next day. These questions focus on the organization of not quite familiar events or open slots within events. New questions—"why" questions—opened up toward the end of the year. One notable question revolved around why her father could not run in a race, notable both for the question of cause and for its focus on another person. Although there was always talk about what she wanted or did not want at bedtime, Emily's discussion of her own feelings or of others' reactions to her emerged only toward the end of this third year. Overall, for this child the questions of desires and emotions seemed less in focus in the talk around bedtime than questions of what, how, and why.

These observations add concrete details to the general description of notable advances in reflective consciousness between 2 and 5 years. I have labeled this level of consciousness "reflective" because verbally interacting with others in discussions about feelings, thoughts, and experiences evokes reflection on these aspects, as well as on current activities. As our evidence from Emily's monologues indicated, the capacity for using language in talk to oneself enables the same kind of individual reflection through private speech. This invokes the process that Vygotsky (1986) proposed as involving the internalization of what is first experienced on an intermental level through verbal interaction. His account of verbal thought, a beginning of which we were observing in Emily's bedtime talk, posited the move from social speech to private speech and finally to inner speech or internalized verbal thought. Emily's monologues suggest that many children may take on the intrapersonal reflective role much earlier than implied in Vygotsky's discussion of the emergence of inner speech (or verbal thought) from private speech, but that the process is likely the same as he proposed.

Observational studies of young children have long noted the onset of "why" questions early in this period, when a child suddenly appears to shift from a focus on "what" to why things are the way they are. It appears that after a long period during which children have focused only on understanding how things are arranged in the world (and on keeping them in that particular arrangement), they suddenly open up to the possibility that things might be some other way, but happen to be the way they are, so the question that emerges is why? A recent diary study of children's why questions found that psychological and physical causation questions were asked by preschoolers about equally often (Callanan & Oakes, 1992).

It is also during this period that parents and children begin engaging in talk about the past and the future. As previously noted, this talk has been extensively studied, and the gradual development of the child's role from listener to contributor of fragments and fuller sequences of action up to full narratives has been documented. The influence of parental framing and scaffolding has also been documented in important longitudinal research by Reese (2002) and her colleagues. They found that children's cognitive sense of self in the toddler period and parental talk about the past during the 2- to 3-year-old period both contribute independently but interactively to the child's interest in and ability to engage in autobiographical memory discussions at 3 to 4 years.

Yet despite the good evidence that 3-year-olds in general have begun to understand a "continuing me"—a sense of self that extends from the past to the future—there is also convincing evidence that this is a transitional stage, that they do not yet have a well-defined distinction between the experience of the self and the experience of others. This evidence comes from their vulnerability to false suggestions about what happened (Ceci & Bruck, 1993), source errors, and intriguing evidence of the appropriation of others' memories (Miller,

Potts, Fung, Hoogstra, & Mintz, 1990). This evidence suggests that when it first becomes accessible to the child, representational language appears to become part of the general noetic knowledge system, joined with experientially based knowledge gained from direct experience in the world. Thus, no fine distinctions are made between the child's own memory/knowledge and that of another. There are no noetic/autonoetic and no mine/yours distinctions in memory at this time.

The conversations that parents have with children about episodes from their past or what they can expect in the future, or how they feel about happenings in their lives, what they like and what others like—these may all incorporate distinctions between the child's experience and others' way of experiencing the same thing. An important part of the present proposal is the claim that conversational interactions that involve the child in reflection on self, the past, feelings, and thoughts provide the context for the representational and reflective use of language by the child, either through external private speech, or internal verbalization that makes such reflection possible. The assumption here is that verbal representing invokes a cognitive object that is accessible to cognitive reflection. In some sense, a thought, a feeling, an experience from the past becomes "visible" for examination by the thinking child when it is represented in verbal form. This becomes possible when it is externalized in verbal form, first by the parent, then by the child, and eventually when the function is internalized. The process is similar to that involved in using language to remember some part of an activity sequence that is not evident in the present context—the word holds its place in memory. A relevant question to be addressed is this: to what extent is this kind of "off-track" reflection possible without language or some other symbolic system? Can nonhuman primates reflect on past events or past feelings?

In any case, what takes place during the transitional period of the reflective level of consciousness is an introduction to the uses of verbal communication and thought as both representational and reflective mediums. To the extent that children take up the representational and reflective functions, they are led further into the mysteries of the mental world through the potentials unleashed by narrative thought.

Narrative Consciousness

In this scheme, narrative consciousness is the center of the action, just as Donald (1991, 2001) proposes that mythic culture is the initial flowering of all modern human cultural and cognitive advances. Adults surround children with stories and narratives, mythic and experiential, from the beginnings of their lives, but it is only as children become competent at verbal representations (both receptive and productive) that they are able to participate in narrative making and narrative comprehension. As I have long argued, children are very good at remembering event representations for familiar events and also at retaining the sequence of short novel events. However, narrative is not simply a presentation of events. It involves personal perspectives, motivations, temporal and spatial locations, evaluations—all of the aspects that Bruner (1990) calls "the landscape of consciousness" that together with "the landscape of action" constitute a narrative. Children's play may come to invoke aspects of this landscape as children begin to collaborate on imaginative play scenarios, but play also begins as the simple playing out of everyday events.

Between age 3 and 5 years, children come to contribute more to the construction of accounts of past experience and to participate in the making of narratives about their own lives. They also begin to listen with understanding and to follow the story line from storybooks, videos, television, and other media. Out of these experiences come a plethora of transformations in the child's consciousness, among them the following (for details see Nelson, 2001):

- An explicit awareness of the contrast between other people's stories and one's own experiential story, as well as "made-up" stories, although the understanding of the difference between a real and a fictional story may be long in coming (Applebee, 1979; Fontaine, 2002)
- Past, present, and future contrasts with an explicit concept of the location of events at past times and temporal locational language such as "yesterday" and "tomorrow"
- A sense of the "continuing me"—the idea that the self existed in the past as a baby and will continue to exist in the future as an adult
- The contrast between other people's minds and one's own mental states—a theory of mind

This level thus realizes the potential inherent in the transitional reflective level and goes beyond it. Most notable is the newly emerging sense of self that is situated in time. These two constructs—self and time—go together and are undoubtedly specifically human and made specifically possible through the symbolic capacities of human language used communicatively and cognitively. It is at this level that true autobiographical memory begins and infantile amnesia is overcome. The new sense of self is reflected in the autonoesis of episodic memory, which is the basis for the development of autobiographical memory. In this theory narrative, autobiographical memory (stories of the self) and self-concept are interdependent in development.

It hardly needs to be stressed that the achievement of this level of consciousness is a true landmark, one that no other animal could reach, as it depends not only on the capacity for acquiring symbols, but on the surround of stories produced by members of the culture, including the child herself. It is of interest that toward the end of her third year, Emily began producing made-up stories in her monologue, a creative move that signifies a distinctive sense of "otherness" and "other experience" to be explored through linguistic means.

In what sense is this a new level of cognitive consciousness beyond the reflective/representational level? Phil Zelazo (1999), who has focused on cognitive tasks that require switching between different classifications of the same stimulus cards (e.g., between color and identity), emphasizes the move to a new level of executive function during this age period. Could maturation of the brain areas that subserve executive control functions explain the developments at this level? Certainly the capacity to keep different perspectives in mind, to switch between story lines while keeping a whole narrative in mind, may be seen as an advanced executive skill. But note also that these skills can only be exercised through symbolic means. Thus in some sense, executive control and language are intertwined (a point that Zelazo recognizes).

The more important aspect of the transition at this level is, I believe, that signaled in Donald's conception that human minds are cultural constructions. It is at the level of the narrative mind, which is able to take in a whole story about a piece of the world that has never been experienced, that the self is truly opened to "cultural programming" for better or worse. Prior to this level, children may know how to do things in the world, but they are ignorant about the complexities and proliferation of "possible worlds," of cultural roles that people play, thoughts that people may have, true and false, and of their own possible futures. It is at this level that children finally emerge from their private mind state and become part of the community of minds. Is there more? Of course, the view from within the cultural community includes all of the possibilities that lie ahead, including most immediately the possibility of school, literacy, and its rewards. Obviously, the extension of consciousness does not stop at the preschool level.

Cultural Consciousness

The level of cultural consciousness takes us far beyond the achievement of metacognitive thinking or autonoesis, but I would maintain that it is a legitimate extension of consciousness to a new level, as implied in Donald's conception of the "theoretical" transition in human history. At the beginning, this move reveals to the child (at about school age) the existence and significance of cultural roles and of cultural rules invoked by institutions, moral, ethical, legal, or simply administrative. The beginnings of cultural identity—national, religious, ethnic—are established at this level. And of course, the acquisition of cultural knowledge systems—literary, mathematical scientific, philosophic, artistic—becomes possible as literacy consciousness is established and nurtured. This level is where mature human minds dwell much of the time, although of course all the previous levels of consciousness are in play as well.

SUMMARY AND CONCLUSION: LANGUAGE, SELF, AND CONSCIOUSNESS

This excursion into the development of human consciousness has obviously taken us far beyond the questions of whether some or any animals display metacognitive awareness. One may question whether the term "consciousness" is being misused when it extends so far. However, part of my point here is that there is no firm line to be drawn and no point of origin when we examine consciousness in its human developmental path. Rather, what we find is a continuous enlargement and extension, taking awareness to new levels both vertically (categorical dimension) and horizontally (temporal dimension).

In human development, social interaction is crucial to this enlargement, and language practices provide the grounds on which children find their way into human ways of knowing self and others within cultural groups. Developments in infancy awaken the initial sense of self, but its further development at the reflective and narrative levels are constrained by the use of symbolic representations among social groups. Reflective consciousness relies on the kind of social interactions made possible by simple language and gesture or mime. These in turn lead in normal development in natural language-using environments to more complex language and abstract symbolic social interactions that construct concepts like mind and shared representations of past and future as well as facts and fiction.

Because these language-based levels are unique to humans, we should look to the earlier levels—perhaps to cognitive consciousness—for the closest relation to our own experience among nonhuman animals, including nonhuman primates. Self-awareness in episodic memory—autonoesis—does not appear at this level for children, and it seems likely that it does not appear for any other animal. Thus, Tulving (1983) was correct when he stated that humans are the only creatures who can travel backward in time to relive their own prior experiences. Some reflective consciousness might be achieved by "language learning" enculturated primates, but not narrative consciousness; no evidence of understanding anything like a story or even an account of the past has been reported from the studies of these primates.

However, I would also note again that human infancy is also unique in its social dimensions, which set up the achievements of the cognitive consciousness of the 1- to 2-year-old. Thus, this level of consciousness may also be unique to humans. But the conclusion should not be to rule out anything except basic awareness for other animals (on the level of the newborn infant). Rather, the evolutionary lesson is that other animals may evolve their own different levels of conscious awareness, including levels of metacognition, which the chapters in this volume appear to document for some species but not for others.

NOTES

1. Gould also wanted to destroy the idea of successive stages of phylogenesis as an adding-on process, emphasizing instead different developmental timing changes, for example, the possibility of neoteny.

2. This thesis has its flaws (see Nelson et al., 2000), but that is not the issue here.

3. The terminology used by both Tulving and Donald is unnecessarily confusing. "Semantic" was originally chosen presumably because of the assumption that general knowledge existed in some semantic form, where the term implies a relation to language. This made sense in 1972, when all of the literature being reviewed was verbal, and when "episodic" referred to learning lists of words. The attempt to relate these terms to nonhuman or infant learning and memory encounters the infelicity of both. The use of "noetic" and "autonoetic" would avoid this, but these terms are not generally familiar to readers.

4. See Donald (1991) for a defense of the proposition that language as we know it arrived late as a human cultural invention.

REFERENCES

Applebee, A. N. (1978). *The child's concept of story*. Chicago: University of Chicago Press.

Astington, J. W., Harris, P. L., & Olson, D. (Eds.). (1988). *Developing theories of mind*. Cambridge, UK: Cambridge University Press.

Bauer, P. J., & Mandler, J. M. (1989a). One thing follows another: Effects of temporal structure on one- to two-year-olds' recall of events. *Developmental Psychology, 25*, 197–206.

Bauer, P. J., & Mandler, J. M. (1989b). Taxonomies and triads: Conceptual organization in one- to two-year-olds. *Cognitive Psychology, 21*, 156–184.

Bauer, P. J., Wenner, J. A., Dropik, P. L., & Wewerka, S. S. (2000). Parameters of remembering and forgetting in the transition from infancy to early childhood. *Monographs of the Society for Research in Child Development, 65*(4, Serial No. 263).

Bauer, P. J., & Wewerka, S. S. (1997). Saying is revealing: Verbal expression of event memory in the transition from infancy to early childhood. In P. W. van den Broek, P. J. Bauer, & T. Bourg (Eds.), *Developmental spans in event comprehension and representation* (pp. 139–168). Mahwah, NJ: Lawrence Erlbaum.

Bruner, J. S. (1990). *Acts of meaning*. Cambridge, MA: Harvard University Press.

Budwig, N. (1995). *A developmental-functionalist approach to child language*. Mahwah, NJ: Lawrence Erlbaum.

Callanan, M. A., & Oakes, L. M. (1992). Preschoolers' questions and parents' explanations: Causal thinking in everyday activity. *Cognitive Development, 7*, 213–233.

Campos, J. J., Bertenthal, B. I., & Kermoian, R. (1992). Early experience and emotional development: The emergence of wariness of heights. *Psychological Science, 3*, 61–64.

Ceci, S. J., & Bruck, M. (1993). Suggestibility of the child witness: A historical review and synthesis. *Psychological Bulletin, 113*, 403–439.

Chomsky, N. (1965). *Aspects of a theory of syntax*. Cambridge MA: MIT Press.

Damasio, A. (1999). *The feeling of what happens: Body and emotion in the making of consciousness*. New York: Harcourt.

Depew, D. J., & Weber, B. H. (1995). *Darwinism evolving: Systems dynamics and the genealogy of natural selection*. Cambridge MA: MIT Press.

Donald, M. (1991). *Origins of the modern mind*. Cambridge MA: Harvard University Press.

Donald, M. (2001). *A mind so rare: The evolution of human consciousness*. New York: Norton.

Fischer, K. W., & Bidell, T. (1991). Constraining nativist inferences about cognitive capacities. In S. Carey & R. Gelman (Eds.), *The epigenesis of mind: Essays on biology and cognition* (pp. 199–236). Hillsdale, NJ: Lawrence Erlbaum.

Fivush, R. (Ed.). (1994). Long-term retention of infant memories [Special issue]. *Memory, 2*, 353–382.

Flavell, J. H., Friedrichs, A. G., & Hoyt, J. D. (1970). Developmental changes in memorization processes. *Cognitive Psychology, 1*, 324–340.

Fodor, J. A. (1975). *The language of thought*. New York: Crowell.

Fontaine, R. G. (2002). *Preschoolers' understanding of story books: The influence of story genre, affect, and language*. Unpublished PhD dissertation, City University of New York, New York.

Gopnik, A., Capps, L., & Meltzoff, A. N. (2000). Early theories of mind: What the theory theory can tell us about autism. In S. Baron-Cohen, H. Tager-Flusberg, & D. J. Cohen (Eds.), *Understanding other minds: Perspectives from developmental cognitive neuroscience* (pp. 50–72). Oxford, UK: Oxford University Press.

Gopnik, A., & Choi, S. (1990). Language and cognition. *First Language, 10*, 199–216.

Gopnik, A., & Meltzoff, A. (1986). Words, plans, and things: Interactions between semantic and cognitive development in the one-word stage. In S. Kuczaj & M. Barrett (Eds.), *The development of word meaning* (pp. 199–223). New York: Springer-Verlag.

Gopnik, A., & Wellman, H. (1994). The theory theory. In L. A. Hirschfeld & S. A. Gelman (Eds.), *Mapping the mind* (pp. 257–293). New York: Cambridge University Press.

Gould, S. J. (1977). *Ontogeny and phylogeny*. Cambridge, MA: Harvard University Press.

Han, J. J., Leichtman, M. D., & Wang, Q. (1998). Autobiographical memory in Korean, Chinese, and American children. *Developmental Psychology, 34*, 701–713.

Harris, P. L. (1992). From simulation to folk psychology: The case for development. *Mind and Language, 7*, 120–144.

Howe, M. L., & Courage, M. L. (1993). On resolving the enigma of infantile amnesia. *Psychological Bulletin, 113*, 305–326.

Hrdy, S. B. (1999). *Mother Nature: A history of mothers, infants, and natural selection.* New York: Pantheon.

James, W. (1950). *The principles of psychology.* New York: Dover. (Original work published 1890)

Kagan, J. (1991). The theoretical utility of constructs for self. *Developmental Review, 11*, 244–250.

Leslie, A. M. (1987). Pretense and representation: The origins of "theory of mind." *Psychological Review, 94*, 412–426.

Leslie, A. M. (1991). The theory of mind impairment in autism: Evidence for a modular mechanism of development? In A. Whiten (Ed.), *Natural theories of mind* (pp. 63–78). Oxford, UK: Basil Blackwell.

Lewis, M. (1997). The self in self-conscious emotions. In J. G. Snodgrass & R. L. Thompson (Eds.), *The self across psychology* (pp. 119–142). New York: New York Academy of Sciences.

Lewis, M., & Ramsey, D. (1999). Intentions, consciousness, and pretend play. In P. D. Zelazo, J. W. Astington, & D. R. Olson (Eds.), *Developing theories of intention: Social understanding and self-control* (pp. 77–94). Mahwah, NJ: Lawrence Erlbaum.

Mead, G. H. (1934). *Mind, self, and society.* Chicago: University of Chicago Press.

Miller, P. J., Potts, R., Fung, H., Hoogstra, L., & Mintz, J. (1990). Narrative practices and the social construction of self in childhood. *American Ethnologist, 17*, 292–311.

Mullen, M. K. (1994). Earliest recollections of childhood: A demographic analysis. *Cognition, 52*, 55–79.

Mullen, M. K., & Yi, S. (1995). The cultural context of talk about the past: Implications for the development of autobiographical memory. *Cognitive Development, 10*, 407–419.

Nagel, T. (1974). What is it like to be a bat? *Philosophical Review, 83*, 435–450.

Neisser, U. (1997). The roots of self-knowledge: Perceiving self, it, and thou. In J. G. Snodgrass & R. L. Thompson (Eds.), *The self across psychology: Self-recognition, self-awareness, and the self concept* (pp. 19–33). New York: New York Academy of Sciences.

Nelson, K. (1988). The ontogeny of memory for real events. In U. Neisser & E. Winograd (Eds.), *Remembering reconsidered: Ecological and traditional approaches to the study of memory* (pp. 244–276). New York: Cambridge University Press.

Nelson, K. (1989). Monologue as the linguistic construction of self in time. In K. Nelson (Ed.), *Narratives from the crib* (pp. 284–308). Cambridge MA: Harvard University Press.

Nelson, K. (2001). From the experiencing I to the continuing me. In C. Moore & K. Skene (Eds.), *The self in time: Developmental issues* (pp. 15–34). Mahwah, NJ: Lawrence Erlbaum.

Nelson, K. (2003). Making sense in a world of symbols. In A. Toomela (Ed.),

Cultural guidance in the development of the human mind (pp. 139–162). West-
port, CT: Greenwood.

Nelson, K. (in press). Language pathways to the community of minds. In
J. W. Astington & J. Baird (Eds.), *Why language matters to theory of mind.*
New York: Oxford University Press.

Nelson, K., & Fivush, R. (2000). Socialization of memory. In E. Tulving & F.
Craik (Eds.), *Handbook of memory* (pp. 283–295). New York: Oxford University Press.

Nelson, K., & Fivush, R. (2004). Emergence of autobiographical memory: A
social-cultural theory. *Psychological Review, 111,* 486–511.

Nelson, K., & Gruendel, J. (1981). Generalized event representations: Basic
building blocks of cognitive development. In M. Lamb & A. Brown (Eds.),
Advances in developmental psychology (Vol. 1, pp. 131–158). Hillsdale, NJ:
Lawrence Erlbaum.

Nelson, K., Henseler, S., & Plesa, D. (2000). Entering a community of minds:
Feminist perspective on theory of mind development. In P. Miller & E.
Scholnick (Eds.), *Toward a feminist developmental psychology* (pp. 61–84).
New York: Routledge.

Nelson, K., Plesa, D., Goldman, S., Henseler, S., Presler, N., & Walkenfeld,
F. F. (2003). Entering a community of minds: An experiential approach to
theory of minds. *Human Development, 46,* 24–46.

Nelson, K., & Ross, G. (1980). The generalities and specifics of long term memory in infants and young children. In M. Perlmutter (Ed.), *Children's memory: New directions for child development* (Vol. 10, pp. 87–101). San Francisco:
Jossey-Bass.

Perlmutter, M. (Ed.). (1980). *Children's memory.* (Vol. 10). San Francisco: Jossey-Bass.

Piaget, J. (1962). *Play, dreams, and imitation in childhood.* New York: Norton.

Pillemer, D. B., & White, S. H. (1989). Childhood events recalled by children
and adults. In H. W. Reese (Ed.), *Advances in child development and behavior*
(Vol. 21, pp. 297–340). New York: Academic Press.

Premack, D. (1988). "Does the chimpanzee have a theory of mind?" revisited.
In R. Byrne & A. Whiten (Eds.), *Machiavellian intelligence* (pp. 160–179).
Oxford, UK: Oxford University Press.

Premack, D., & Woodruff, G. (1978). Does the chimpanzee have a theory of
mind? *Behavioral and Brain Sciences, 1,* 515–526.

Reese, E. (2002). A model of the origins of autobiographical memory. In J. W.
Fagen & H. Hayne (Eds.), *Progress in infancy research* (Vol. 2, pp. 215–260).
Mahwah, NJ: Lawrence Erlbaum.

Reese, E., Haden, C. A., & Fivush, R. (1993). Mother-child conversations about
the past: Relationships of style and memory over time. *Cognitive Development, 8,* 403–430.

Simcock, G., & Hayne, H. (2002). Breaking the barrier? Children fail to translate their preverbal memories into language. *Psychological Science, 13,* 225–
231.

Tomasello, M. (1999a). *The cultural origins of human cognition.* Cambridge, MA:
Harvard University Press.

Tomasello, M. (1999b). Having intentions, understanding intentions, and understanding communicative intentions. In P. D. Zelazo, J. W. Astington, &

D. R. Olson (Eds.), *Developing theories of intention: Social understanding and self-control* (pp. 63–76). Mahwah, NJ: Lawrence Erlbaum.

Tomasello, M., & Call, J. (1997). *Primate cognition.* New York: Oxford University Press.

Tulving, E. (1983). *Elements of episodic memory.* New York: Oxford University Press.

Vygotsky, L. (1986). *Thought and language.* Cambridge, MA: MIT Press.

Zelazo, P. D. (1999). Language, levels of consciousness and the development of intentional action. In P. D. Zelazo, J. W. Astington, & D. R. Olson (Eds.), *Developing theories of intention: Social understanding and self-control* (pp. 95–118). Mahwah, NJ: Lawrence Erlbaum.

5

A Continuum of Self-Consciousness That Emerges in Phylogeny and Ontogeny

Marcel Kinsbourne

> The beast does but know, but the man knows that he knows.
> John Donne, sermon, 1628

IS SELF-CONSCIOUSNESS A MATTER OF DEGREE?

Are only humans capable of self-reflection? Descartes and his follow-ers, as well as Tulving (chapter 1, this volume) are among those who subscribe to this "discontinuity" theory. Or did our highly developed facility for self-reflection emerge from humbler origins in less behav-iorally sophisticated creatures, as Hampton (chapter 11) and Terrace (chapter 3) propose? The argument for discontinuity echoes that for language, which is considered barely to exist in nonhuman animals. That proposition is still widely contested. However, it is not known whether language is essential for self-reflection, or merely puts into words what the brain has already accomplished preverbally or even preconsciously. My discussion does not purport to resolve this sweep-ing issue, any more than previous discussions have. Rather, I use the premise of continuity theory to present some critical ideas about test-ing for self-awareness in animals and also in human infants, and about how conscious and self-conscious processes may be instantiated in the brain.

I favor the continuity assumption because it offers a better fit with our current understanding of the evolution of species and also with the functional anatomy of the brain. I offer alternative explanations for why animals and human infants frequently fail on tests that are designed to probe the ability to self-reflect. I take as my premise the view that consciousness is the subjective aspect of the patterned acti-vation of the forebrain. If so, self-awareness may reflect the ability to maintain multiple representations in the network at the same time.

Self-awareness would then be one of many abilities that a highly differentiated brain can master. It need not be regarded as the specialized product of a uniquely constituted neural module. Self-awareness may be unique to humans without being modular. However, arguments for human uniqueness are often presented in terms of modularity. I take a module to refer to a uniquely specialized part of the brain, regardless of whether its components are concentrated within a discrete area or distributed as a system.

THE MODULARITY ASSUMPTION

Chomsky's concept of a "language acquisition device," which humans have and other animals do not, exemplifies a modular conception of brain organization. An engineering notion, modularity is a gloss on the exquisite degree of regional specialization that has long been known to characterize the human cerebral cortical mantle. It implies discontinuity, even the ultimate discontinuity, that hypothetical extra module that makes us human. However, the functional neuroanatomy of the human cerebral cortex, though highly differentiated, does not feature discontinuity between modules. The cerebral neural network is completely continuous, with only a few degrees of synaptic separation between any neuron and any other (Braitenberg & Schuz, 1992). Overused as an explanatory concept, modularity has fueled "neurologizing," instant explanations for why any focal lesion might disable a complex set of mental operations. "It takes something that clearly is a very complex consequence of underlying mechanisms, and simply plugs it in as an explicit structure, bypassing the question of what these underlying mechanisms might be" (Hofstadter, 1985, p. 642). Complex activities emerge from the coordination of multiple underlying component processes, and these are unlikely to be dedicated exclusively to any single purpose. It has long been taken for granted in neuropsychology that one has to determine whether a disabled mental operation actually is impaired due to a more general, basic underlying cognitive deficit before one can conclude that its constituent mental operations are uniquely dedicated to a single purpose. This presumption motivates a search for the component skills that interact to enable the performance under scrutiny. Is the neural basis of self-reflective behavior a network of component operations that are also involved in other complex cognitions, some of which are plausibly available to other animals also?

SHARP INEQUALITIES IN COGNITIVE SKILLS ARE COMPATIBLE WITH CONTINUITY THEORY

The term "missing link," with which this book is titled, has an intriguing implication. It suggests continuity but expresses surprise about the size of disparities between species. I argue that even in the face of enormous disparity, a continuity interpretation is viable. There need not be a missing link.

It is uncontroversial that the cognitive differences between our species and nonhuman primates are enormous. A behavioral parameter, customarily referred to as the "ascent to man," is graphically represented along an upward sloping linear gradient, the coordinate expressing complexity and the abscissa representing time. On it, various creatures, all facing rightward and looking wistfully upward, are arranged left to right from the lower to the upper end, in order of their apparent behavioral sophistication, the human at the right upper end. On this linearly conceived time scale, chimpanzees crowd in rather closely behind us—after all, they are supposedly our cousins. The implication is that any differences between nonhuman primates and humans are rather limited. However, continuity does not imply linearity, and this linear presumption is not supportable. The straight line is an artifact of human invention. In nature, the values of variables rise and fall nonlinearly: exponentially or even hyperbolically. I am not aware of any adaptive characteristic that varies linearly across species, nor can I imagine one. The gradient of ascent in behavioral sophistication may be sharply positively accelerated, originating at a minimal level of the aptitude of interest. At the origin, the gradient may be so gradual that it is indeterminate at what point back in phylogenesis the cognitive ability originated. At the endpoint, where the positive acceleration is extreme, disparities between neighboring species can be enormous, without the existence of a missing link. Self-awareness could have evolved along a sharp curve.

It is tantalizing to note how similar our genomes are to those of the other primates, barely differing by 1% or 2%. However, it is simplistic to compare genomes arithmetically. Genes are not created equal. For instance, consider that genes control how many times neurons divide; when they stop dividing, the species' full complement of brain cells is present. Now imagine a single mutation that relaxes the control on cell division to the extent that the neurons divide one more time before they rest. One mutation could create a forebrain twice as large, with twice the computing space within which to be smart. Pertinent to this claim is a gene called ASPM that is involved in regulating brain size. Null mutations of this gene lead to a 70% decrease in brain volume (Evans et al., 2004). The claim that the genomes of humans and chimpanzees are closely similar is an intuition pump, in Hofstadter and Dennett's (1981) sense. It sounds like it should mean something, even though it does not. In nature, differences may be great and yet reside on a continuum.

FALSE NEGATIVE DEMONSTRATIONS OF METACOGNITIVE SKILLS

Unbridgeable gaps in behavioral potential between humans and other animals may exist due to insurmountable constraints in animals' nervous systems, or because animals lack the type of socialization that Terrace (chapter 3, this volume) posits as being essential for metacognitive functioning. But when animals fail on tests that are designed to elicit self-awareness, this may not prove that they lack self-awareness. Task-irrelevant features that contaminate the test situation can mask cognitive competence.

Escape From Stimulus Control

Extraexperimental salient stimuli can mask potentially successful performance. Self-awareness calls for the ability to escape external stimulus control, so that attention is released and can shift internally to representations about the self, its history, attributes and experiences, that is, to the "self-archive." Metcalfe and Kober's (chapter 2, this volume) "projectable self" cannot project unless the individual can disengage his attention from the external here and now, and access his self-archive by introspection. A similar constraint limits episodic remembering. While nonhuman primates no doubt lack the extreme flexibility with which people can disengage their attention from the here and now, if the situation enables them to disengage from ambient stimulus control, they may be able to admit aspects of past experiences to the present moment to some extent.

Episodic memory calls for the ability to disengage attention from the salient stimulus field, so as to permit recollected associates of the cue to replace external stimuli in the phenomenal present. In "time travel," it is the past that travels into the present. There it is updated automatically and outside awareness before it becomes conscious. When the memory of the event is next retrieved, it is the updated version that is recollected, updated yet again. So a superseded external reality is replaced by a present but internalized reality.

Problem solving also calls for disengagement. In this instance, the problem solver has to disengage from his own previous thoughts as well as from the outside world. He has to be able to disengage from a superficial but incorrect solution, to clear the way for a less obvious but perhaps more apt alternative to rise into awareness. If the problem is complex, several successive disengagements from several failed solutions may be necessary before it is solved.

Disengaging from salient appearances is necessary for success on tests of conservation and tests for theory of mind, which implies an awareness of the self as distinct from other selves. These constructs both require the subject to qualify her percepts by factoring in an event in the past. If the child cannot disengage from the immediate percept, she will respond as though she cannot conserve, or as though she lacks theory of mind. Yet, operating outside her boundary conditions, she may have failed to mobilize knowledge that she could have expressed under different conditions, because it was overridden by salient appearances. Escaping stimulus control is difficult for young children. It becomes easier as they mature. However, even the adult human brain does not always reconcile contradictory beliefs or impressions but may let the currently more immediately applicable belief overshadow its less salient contradictory counterpart.

In Piaget's nonconservation demonstrations, the child views two equivalent quantities—mass, number, and so on. One display is then manipulated, so that its quantity (volume, number, extent, etc.) now looks greater to the child than that of the other. The child indicates that this display is indeed greater, although she had seen these two displays looking equal a moment earlier, and all that had happened was that one had been displaced (spread out, poured into a differently shaped container, etc.). Does the child not realize that manipulating an array, for instance a row of tokens, cannot make its constituents fewer or more? Perhaps she does in principle, but she may not have taken the antecedent maneuver and the conservation principle into account when she made the judgment that reflects "nonconservation." In general, past events and impressions are less salient than ongoing ones. How things look in the present outweighs how they might be expected to look, in view of what happened just before. Salience obscures the less attention-grabbing memory of a prior manipulation and overshadows the fact that an appearance conflicts with a rule.

Manipulating the salience of stimuli can unmask an unsuspected ability in a relatively simple nervous system. I draw an example from my own work. Lashley (1938) opined that rats could not tell oppositely inclined obliques apart, because when tested in a jumping stand, they could not perform the discrimination. Kinsbourne (1967) made the direction of slope of the stimulus stripes salient. He outfitted a Y-maze with a vivid array of alternating black and white oblique stripes, all sloping in the same direction, along the two walls of one arm, and stripes inclined in opposite directions along each of the two walls of the other arm. The rats learned to discriminate the direction of slope with ease. As in the previous studies, the perceptual problem was to discriminate obliques. But the difference between directions of slope had been rendered salient, and therefore was now discriminated.

Conversely, an abnormal shift of attention away from task-relevant cues may render them less salient. Autistic children (though not adolescents or adults) typically fail the false belief test. Consequently, they are held not to appreciate that other people have minds or points of view, and it is assumed that they relate to people as though they were machines. But if autistic children equate people with machines, why do they actively avert gaze from people but not from machines? Perhaps the opposite is the case. Autistic children are only too aware that people have minds of their own, and therefore may do something unpredictable any time. This threatens to infringe autistic children's intense need for sameness. They may be so averse to social interaction that they won't even adopt an internalized perspective on behalf of someone else. Similarly, gaze avoidance may be why some autistic children do not recognize themselves in a mirror (chapter 2, this volume). Given the powerfully inward bent of autistic attention, does the child even orient to his reflection in the glass?

Working Memory Constraints

An individual manages to safeguard information held in or recycled through working memory from habituating, by continually refocusing attention on it, and inhibiting orienting responses to salient but task-irrelevant distracting stimuli (Estes, 1972). If certain animals, or children at a young age, fail on tests that require self-awareness, their working memory may not have been up to the demands of the particular tasks given. According to Case (1974), only by age 3 years can a child hold two representations in mind at a time, and an additional one every 2 years up to about seven representations. So if a younger child is given a task that calls for comparing two representations, he is likely to fail, regardless of whether self-reflection or an unrelated ability is being tested. In effect, the growing child perfects the ability to keep unrelated or conflicting representations simultaneously in mind, or hold one in check while letting the other control behavior. Inhibitory surrounds presumably save them from collapsing into each other.

The ability to suppress one representation so as to attend to another can generalize to enabling episodic remembering. The child inhibits the influence of the salient here and now, whereupon cued memory surfaces into recollection as episodic remembering by vector completion. From a selection of episodic memories, the individual constructs the parameters of a self-concept. Neither episodic remembering nor self-concept is necessarily a modular acquisition, perhaps unique to humans. Such mental activity may be available to any brain that has sufficient inhibitory and working memory capacity. In other words, episodic remembering and self-concept may be constrained by the power of general-purpose cognitive processes rather than lack of special-purpose mechanisms.

Boundary Conditions

Although it is usually couched in yes/no format, the question "Are nonhuman animals capable of episodic remembering?" does not necessarily call for a yes or no answer. The ability might be available, but only be accessible within restricted boundary conditions.

That an individual is able to apply a form of reasoning or computation in a given instance is no guarantee that he or she can apply it to every performance that would benefit from the same approach. Indeed, the opposite extreme is familiar in the term "expert system." This is a special-purpose mechanism that applies logic that the animal or device is unable to mobilize for any other purpose. The general purpose/special purpose distinction should not be considered a dichotomy but a continuum, or matter of degree. "The hallmark of the evolution of intelligence . . . is that a capacity first appears in a narrow context and later becomes extended into other domains. This seems to be quite a reasonable interpretation of cognitive development" (Rozin, 1975, p. 262).

As I write, I see through the window a seagull raise a clamshell high in the air, to let it fall against a rock and crack open (Beck, 1976). How did the seagull know to do this, and can it also solve similar problems that do not occur in its ecology? A more elaborate example of restricted boundary conditions is offered by the following tale about little fishes and the big one that feeds on them (Les Kaufmann, 2001, personal communication). The little fishes live in the mud in shallow waters, in holes that are too small for the big one to enter. Therefore the big fish can eat the little ones only when they issue forth from their hideouts to feed. But while he eats one, the others would scuttle back to safety. The big fish comes up with what, among humans, would pass for an ingenious solution. He seals the openings to the holes by flattening the mud. Then he can pick off fish after fish at his pleasure. He has planning capability (the tactic), impulse control (not diving for the first fish that swims into range), and theory of mind (inferring what the prey would do under given circumstances). Regrettably, this maneuver exhausts his tactical repertoire. He can apply his demonstrated problem-solving skills to no other situation.

Wooldridge (cited in Hofstadter, 1985) has described a dramatic instance of apparently intentional behavior that turns out to be due to a special-purpose mechanism. The wasp *Sphex* paralyzes a cricket with its sting and drags it into a burrow, to leave beside her eggs. The hatched wasp grubs later feed on the cricket. Before the wasp drags the cricket in, she enters the burrow and inspects it for intruders. Then she drags the cricket in. However, if when she reemerges, she finds the cricket displaced a few inches from the opening, she reiterates the dragging and the inspection. This continues as often as the experimenter chooses to displace the cricket. The wasp never deduces from her recent inspections that it is safe to pull the cricket right in. The expert system is rigid and does not profit from experience. It is not equipped to self-monitor. The wasp represents one end of a continuum. Clayton and Dickinson's (1998) demonstration that scrub jays have episodic memory for where food was buried may represent an expert system. Call (chapter 13, this volume) compares the ability of several mammalian species to override rigid rule-governed behavior and arrive at novel solutions.

CONSCIOUSNESS AND ZOMBIES

I use "consciousness" and "awareness" interchangeably. Terrace (chapter 3, this volume) draws a distinction between global awareness and a more structured consciousness of the perceptual field. This distinction may not be categorical. It could refer to different points on a continuum of complexity of the brain states that the neural network can generate.

Self-reference calls for the ability to monitor one's own brain states. Internal monitoring, the essence of metacognition, requires that the individual escapes from external stimulus control and is able to hold multiple representations concurrently in mind. Can some animals do this? Any attempt to prove that they can is restricted to demonstrating that the animal is capable of retrieving information about itself as a decision maker or experiencer in ways that in humans are attended by self-awareness. The proof can never be conclusive, since we are not, and cannot be, privy to the animal's subjective mental state. Researchers have therefore been reticent in ascribing subjectivity to animals that appear to display metacognitive behaviors (e.g., Hampton, 2001; Smith, Shields, Allendoerfer, & Washburn, 1998). By the same logic, they could call into question what we prefer to take for granted, that animals are conscious at all, let alone self-conscious.

The impasse is premised on a residue of the dualistic fallacy of the Cartesian theater (Dennett & Kinsbourne, 1992). This is that awareness is somehow separate and separable from the brain state that instantiates the experience. Prominent contemporary philosophers of mind harbor the notion that an organism may be observed to behave exactly like a conscious person and lack only the element of consciousness. In effect, the organism is a zombie.

So even if the animal, infant, or robot acts as though conscious, how can we know that she really is conscious? We do assume that other people are conscious, because they not only act as though they were but say so. We have to give them the benefit of the doubt. Should we extend this benefit of the doubt to any animal? Hampton (chapter 11, this volume) points out that the "hardened skeptic" is unlikely to do so. He would then be making a dualistic distinction between what the brain does and what it is like for the brain to do it.

If awareness is an aspect of certain brain states and has no independent existence, the question can be reformulated and the impasse avoided: Does the animal, infant, or device, when generating quasi-conscious behavior, instantiate it in neural networks more or less like ours, albeit less elaborate and specialized?

When measuring up the human against the animal mind, one typically tries to show that an animal can succeed on a problem that bears a family resemblance to one that a person can master only after reflecting on it. When nonhumans act like a human would under the circumstance, are they thinking like humans? Kohler (1927), describing insight in chimpanzees, wrote: "Chimpanzees . . . show by their careful looking around that they really begin with something very like an inventory of the situation" (p. 190). Dennett (1981) has called this pragmatically useful attitude the "intentional stance." So, if a nonhuman primate thumps his chest in a courtship display, we might well suppose that he is intentionally trying to attract the female's attention to himself and his assets. He appears to be capable of self-reference. But this behavior could have been naturally selected for adaptive reasons, without the animal having any introspection about what he is doing. The question is, could the animal generalize this behavior to other novel situations in which it would be adaptively advantageous?

HOW DOES CONSCIOUSNESS ARISE IN THE BRAIN?

According to the integrated cortical field model (Kinsbourne, 1988), consciousness is neither a product of brain activity nor epiphenomenal. Consciousness is not a product, because it has no known independent physical existence and is not separable from the functioning brain. It is not an epiphenomenon either, like exhaust gases are to the moving automobile, or the whistling sound is to the approaching missile. It is not a waste product of brain activity or any sort of product. It is an attribute that is inherent in the functioning of the neural network itself. The neural network has subjective access to some of its own states, and at any moment it has maximal access to the most activated circuitry. Accordingly, consciousness would not be something a brain needs to have to perform certain mental operations. Rather, one is conscious when, and because, one's brain is functioning. Of what one is conscious reflects what the brain is currently doing. For instance, the end product of an act of episodic remembering is a conscious experience. However, it is not "consciousness" that enables one to remember an episode. Rather, the attractor state that results from the act of memory retrieval persists long enough to linger into consciousness, that is, to be subjectively accessible.

THE MODEL: DOMINANT CONFIGURATION MODEL OF CONSCIOUSNESS

Is the neural basis of consciousness centered in a specific brain area or network, or is it "uncentered" and distributed across the cerebrum and its connections? The model treats unconscious, conscious, and self-conscious states not as discrete but as differing only in degree on a continuum of differentiation of the neural activation pattern of the forebrain.

I regard consciousness as uncentered in the brain. Integrated cerebral network and dominant configuration theory (Kinsbourne, 1988, 1996) assumes that there exists at any time a pattern of activation in the forebrain that outranks its competitors in amplitude and duration, and thereby controls the response processes of the moment. The relatively most activated areas supply most of the contents of consciousness. A brain that is capable only of simple mental operations (infant or animal) would be no less conscious than one that is more complex. The dominant configuration may represent sophisticated processing but also simple processing. A simple brain, animal or infant, will still have a dominant configuration, and this configuration will lend a subjective aspect to the mental functioning of the moment. Processing power does not determine whether one is conscious, but it does determine the range of experiences of which one can become conscious.

Any human or animal brain can potentially gain subjective access to those of its states that are dominant. Whether that access includes states that reflect self-awareness or episodic remembering depends on whether the animal's neural network is rich enough in excitatory and inhibitory neurons to instantiate more than one distinct brain state at a time within the cerebral manifold, without the states collapsing into one another, so as to generate a simpler, albeit more stable, state. Since only one state predominates at a time, this calls for working memory capability to alternate the two representations, keeping them sufficiently active so that they can be matched one against the other, or associated with each other. Whether animals have this capacity is ultimately an empirical issue, species by species.

Nelson (chapter 4, this volume) states that "consciousness expands in both evolution and development, where levels of consciousness emerge over time." I refer this expansion to the expansion of the neural network of behaviorally sophisticated species. Its increasingly intricate and nuanced functioning is reflected in an enriched sequence of subjective states. The consciousness per se does nothing.

Relatively enduring states involved in controlled processes, deployed under conditions of uncertainty (Shiffrin & Schneider, 1977), would typically be represented in dominant configurations. Rapidly shifting states that comprise the sequential phases of automatic sequential processes typically would not. The cognitive processing of the moment is that of the activated portions of the network, and the subjectivity of the moment is that of states which are prominent in that cognitive processing. The processing and its subjectivity are aspects of those same neural events and cannot be considered sepa-

rately. Consciousness is integral to the processing. The same processing, if it loses the competition for dominant configuration, would not
be conscious but could still proceed implicitly. As circumstances
change, the subdominant pattern may take the place of the dominant
configuration, or some of its elements may infiltrate the dominant pattern. In the living brain, the subjective field is constantly and endlessly
reinvented.

The pattern of cortical activation takes some time to lock into a
stable (attractor) state through reentrant feedback. Temporary end
states in cognition become conscious. By the time that happens, the
next dominant configuration is already being formed. Consciousness
is always a step behind the action. It reflects, rather than informs or
controls, what the brain is doing (e.g., Kinsbourne, 1988, 1996). The
processing, that is, the settling into attractor states, is preconscious.

Smith (chapter 10, this volume) refers to instances that "inherently
elicit higher level and even conscious modes of cognition and decision
making." From the perspective of dominant configuration theory,
what is an animal doing while hesitating? Is the animal generating an
impression or point of view, or more explicitly arriving at an opinion
(implying that it knows others might disagree)? A deliberate judgment might be beyond animals that lack language. But a belief can be
derived from any of the above. More likely than any of these, the
animal is forming a sentiment, which arises from an emotional response or feeling. In other words, it is in response conflict and is for-
mulating or selecting an action plan that feels better than the rest
(without necessarily introspecting about why it feels better). Hesitation reflects relatively enduring states, which are therefore good candidates for contributing their representations to consciousness. The
nature of the brain state suffices to explain why it is represented in
consciousness. There is no need to credit "consciousness" with providing help.

Do animals act automatically, and therefore remain unaware of
what they are doing? Humans are only unaware of their automatic
actions when their attention is focused elsewhere, and the same
should be true of other animals. Also, behaviors do not automatize
instantly, but only as an end point of practice while dealing with relationships that are not yet fully understood. During practice, the individual is very aware of what she is doing. Only later does the range
of cue utilization narrow to the point that little cortical territory is
implicated and attention is free to move elsewhere.

SELF-AWARENESS

Instead of being self-aware because conscious, the individual is conscious because he is engaged in being self-aware, which his brain does

by forming the corresponding dominant configuration. Instead of being a unique category of mental function, which an animal either has at its disposal or does not, self-awareness becomes an accomplishment of flexible and differentiated representing. It demands the ability to disengage some of the neural network from stimulus control and to shape its pattern of functioning so as to abstract from the remembered experiences, the continuity of the invariant experiencer. The invariant presence of one's background body sensation may be a minimal organizing principle (Kinsbourne, 1995). Phenomenal self-awareness does not make these operations possible. The reverse is the case. When the mental operations are performed, they are attended by subjective self-awareness.

I understand self-awareness to refer to an awareness of one's person as an independent experiencer and agent. This characterization, however, is spuriously definite. Self-awareness is a matter of degree. Its most explicit and crystallized state should be considered an end point of a continuum that emerges from infant and animal experience. Self-reflection appraises one's attributes, in the context of environmental opportunities, requirements, and threats. The metacognitive abilities that allegedly are predicated on the presence of self-awareness, such as predicting one's ability to perform a task and recollecting an event from the past, do not necessarily call for more than minimal explicit self-awareness. An unstructured sense of oneself as a presence or an agent may be enough, if not more than enough.

I have suggested that self-awareness originates in the invariant perceived presence of the body as somatosensory background to the infant's every experience and action (Kinsbourne, 1995, 2002). With continuing human development, this diffuse feeling of continuity is gradually elaborated into the adult's flexible and critical self-awareness, capable of being abstracted from the physical person. In animals, self-awareness might only exist in the rudimentary body-centered form. What is required? Sufficient computing power, that is, a sufficiently extensive neural network with enough inhibitory capacity to prevent the incipient self-construct from collapsing into undifferentiated merging with the experience of the moment. Of course, at those times when the relevant brain states are overshadowed by other ongoing mental representational work, our self-consciousness will give way to an intense engagement in the action at hand. But when we are disengaged from interaction with the world, we can reflect on ourselves. When we do so, the neural states that instantiate these representations are likely to be sufficiently activated long enough to make them viable candidates for contributing to ongoing consciousness.

The same applies to time estimation. When attention is fully engaged in a task, the representations on which one relies to estimate elapsed time are displaced from consciousness. As a result, durations that are filled with effortful activity are underestimated (Hicks, Miller, & Kinsbourne, 1976). We can attend interactively to the world, or intra-actively to our own states. To achieve the latter, we need only detach from the former. The thoughts, images, and fancies then come unbidden. Similarly, episodic memories, though sometimes evoked deliberately and with effort, at other times seem to drift into awareness spontaneously.

When animals behave as a human would when she is self-aware, would the animals also be self-aware (chapter 10, this volume), or could they be behaving in the same way but with the use of implicit processes (chapter 12, this volume)? If one regards consciousness as a separate modular acquisition, then the question is reasonable, though probably unanswerable. But based on the model of consciousness that I have explained, there is no reason why the animal could not be self-aware to some extent. The dominant configuration of neural processes, that is, the one that outdoes its rivals in amplitude and duration, is ipso facto conscious. That applies whether the task is hard or easy in an absolute sense, and whether the brain is large and complex or smaller and simple. In this view, if the animal is using controlled processes that in humans are conscious, then they are conscious in the animal. Similarly, when animals retrieve information based on unique events over long-term retention intervals (cf. chapter 9, this volume), are they subjectively remembering these events as we human adults would? If one dichotomizes between recollecting that requires consciousness and learning that does not, then one can deny the former to any species at will. If one regards episodic remembering as reinstating, in part, a previous brain state, then there is no reason to suppose that this is exclusive to humans. Consciousness as such does nothing. It is a result of the brain state, not its cause. So these animals might well remember consciously, as we do. Like us, by remembering they have demonstrated that they have the representational power to detach ("decenter") their attention from the current stimulus situation and reactivate elements of a brain state from the past. Since they were presumably conscious when they had the experience, why would they not consciously recollect it later? They recollect by generating "dominant configurations" that have awareness as an inherent and automatic attribute. In this view, consciousness is not a critical condition for, but integral to, episodic remembering.

In the uncentered brain model, there is no need to dichotomize creatures into those that own an autonoetic module and perhaps therefore an episodic memory module and those who do not. Animals' varieties of self-awareness are no doubt not as explicit and finely differentiated as those of mature humans. What they can accomplish in these domains must vary enormously between species and among ontogenetic levels within species. However, nonhuman animals could even become aware of the passing of time when it is adaptively relevant. The tiger lurks at the watering hole. The prey happens to be otherwise engaged. Finally the tiger picks up and retires for the night. Does her mental state reflect that a long time has passed (other than through the dimming of the light or the growling of her stomach)? Not in terms of "how many hours" and "how boring" perhaps, but at a simple level, why not?

SUMMARY

I have advocated a continuity approach to interspecies differences in self-awareness, which I have related to an uncentered model of consciousness. This model permits representational content anywhere in the brain to become conscious, by participating in a dominant configuration of the cerebral activation manifold. Awareness, consciousness, and self-consciousness differ only in degree, and the concept of a special-purpose module that implements self-awareness is superfluous. Metacognition requires escape from stimulus control, adequate working memory, and operating within appropriate boundary conditions. Any individual, human adult, child, animal, who can hold multiple representations in working memory can be self-conscious. Contrary to Donne's faith-based conviction about what the "beast" knows or does not know, for all we know, some beasts know that they know.

REFERENCES

Beck, B. (1976, June). *Predatory shell dropping by herring gulls.* Paper presented to the Animal Behavior Society, Boulder, Colorado.

Braitenberg, V., & Schuz, A. (1992). Basic features of cortical connectivity and some considerations on language. In J. Wind, B. Chiarelli, B. H. Bichakjian, A. Nocentini, & A. Jonker (Eds.), *Language origins: A multidisciplinary approach* (pp. 89–102). Dordrecht: Kluwer.

Case, R. (1974). Structures and strictures: Some functional limitations on the course of cognitive growth. *Cognitive Psychology, 6,* 544–573.

Clayton, N. S., & Dickinson, A. (1998). Episodic-like memory during cache recovery by scrub jays. *Nature, 395,* 272–274.

Dennett, D. (1981). *Brainstorms.* New York: Basic Books.

Dennett, D., & Kinsbourne, M. (1992). Time and the observer: The where and when of consciousness in the brain. *Behavioral and Brain Sciences, 15,* 183–247.

Estes, W. K. (1972). An associative basis for coding and organization in memory. In A. W. Melton & E. Martin (Eds.), *Coding processes in human memory* (pp. 161–190). Washington, DC: Winston.

Evans, P. D., Anderson, J. R., Vallender, E. J., Gilbert, S. L., Malcolm, C. M., Dorus, S., & Lahn, B. T. (2004). Adaptive evolution of ASPM, a major determinant of cerebral cortical size in humans. *Human Molecular Genetics, 13,* 489–494.

Hampton, R. R. (2001). Rhesus monkeys know when they remember. *Proceedings of the National Academy of Sciences U.S.A., 98*, 5369–5372.

Hicks, R. E., Miller, G. W., & Kinsbourne, M. (1976). Prospective and retrospective judgments of time as a function of amount of information processed. *American Journal of Psychology, 89*, 719–730.

Hofstadter, D. R. (1985). *Metamagical themas*. Toronto: Bantam.

Hofstadter, D. R., & Dennett, D. C. (1981). *The mind's I*. Cambridge, MA: MIT Press.

Kinsbourne, M. (1967). Sameness-difference judgments and the discrimination of obliques in the rat. *Psychonomic Science, 7*, 183–184.

Kinsbourne, M. (1988). Integrated cortical field model of consciousness. In A. J. Marcel & E. Bisiach (Eds.), *The concept of consciousness in contemporary science* (pp. 239–256). London: Oxford University Press.

Kinsbourne, M. (1995). Awareness of one's body: A neuropsychological hypothesis. In J. Bermudez, A. J. Marcel, & N. Eilan (Eds.), *The body and the self* (pp. 205–223). Cambridge, MA: MIT Press.

Kinsbourne, M. (1996). What qualifies a representation for a role in consciousness? In J. D. Cohen & J. W. Schooler (Eds.), *Scientific approaches to consciousness* (pp. 335–356). Hillsdale, NJ: Lawrence Erlbaum.

Kinsbourne, M. (2002). The brain and body awareness. In T. Pruzinsky & T. Cash (Eds.), *Body images: A handbook of theory, research and clinical practice* (pp. 22–29). New York: Guilford.

Kohler, W. (1927). *The mentality of apes*. New York: Harcourt Brace.

Lashley, K. S. (1938). The mechanism of vision: XV. Preliminary studies of the rat's capacity for detail vision. *Journal of General Psychology, 18*, 123–193.

Rozin, P. (1975). The evolution of intelligence and access to the cognitive unconscious. *Progress in Psychobiology and Physiological Psychology, 6*, 245–280.

Shiffrin, R. M., & Schneider, W. (1977). Controlled and automatic human information processing: II. Perceptual learning, automatic attending and a general theory. *Psychological Review, 84*, 127–190.

Smith, J. D., Shields, W. E., Allendoerfer, K. R., & Washburn, D. A. (1998). Memory monitoring by animals and humans. *Journal of Experimental Psychology, General, 127*, 227–250.

6

Humans as Applied Motivation Scientists: Self-Consciousness From "Shared Reality" and "Becoming"

E. Tory Higgins

How did self-knowing consciousness begin? One version of this question is: What caused self-knowing consciousness to appear in the first place? Like other evolutions, it is possible that it was simply an accident. Whatever the answer to this version of the question, what I want to consider is the following: Once self-knowing consciousness did appear, why did it remain? What were the functional pressures on its further development? In brief, I believe that self-consciousness has significant advantages for goal attainment and need satisfaction in human society. Self-consciousness is a basic motivational tool for getting along with others.

A key characteristic of humans is that they are highly dependent on conspecifics for survival. More than any other animal, human children need adults to provide them with nurturance and security for many years. Even as adults, humans as individuals are relatively helpless and survive by working together with other humans. This dependency means that humans must get along with others to survive. To a large extent, personal agency is social agency. A human needs to predict and influence what others do. This can be done more effectively by understanding how one fits into one's social world. Self-consciousness is a necessary ingredient for such understanding.

This chapter takes a motivational perspective on self-consciousness. I propose that self-consciousness has remained and developed among humans because it serves basic self-regulatory functions. I propose that *humans are applied motivation scientists.* I emphasize two functions in this chapter—*shared reality* and *becoming.* In brief, self-regulation in a social context involves understanding what significant others hope for and expect of you (shared reality), and understanding where you are now, have been, and plan to be in relation to these hopes and expectations (becoming). Both shared reality and becoming are central features of human self-regulation, and it is self-consciousness that makes them possible. The "self digest" model of self-regulation (see Higgins, 1996a; Higgins & May, 2001) forms the underpinnings of my motivational perspective on self-consciousness. I begin, then, with a review of this model.

THE SELF DIGEST

The self-regulatory perspective taken here shares the common assumption that human survival requires adaptation to the surrounding environment, especially the surrounding social environment. In order for children to obtain the nurturance and security they need to survive, they must establish and maintain relationships with caretakers who fulfill these needs (see Bowlby, 1969, 1973). To establish and maintain such relationships, children must learn how their appearance and behaviors influence caretakers' responses to them as objects in the world. Children must learn to regulate their appearance and behaviors in line with these interpersonal contingencies to increase the likelihood that caretakers will provide them the nurturance and security they need (cf. Bowlby, 1969; Cooley, 1902/1964; Mead, 1934; Sullivan, 1953).

To survive and adapt to their environment, people must also learn about their personal capabilities and, more generally, about their own strengths and weaknesses as one kind of object in the world. Children need to learn, for example, that certain activities, such as flying like a bird, are beyond their capabilities and to attempt such activities is dangerous. They must learn their limits, such as how long they can hold their breath underwater or stay outside in freezing weather. When choosing between alternative means to the same goal, it is adaptive to know which means best suit one's capabilities. When working to attain a goal, it is adaptive to know how much effort or personal resources should be expended, given one's capabilities, to attain the goal without wasting resources. Thus children must also learn to regulate their activity engagement to fit their personal attributes.

In previous works, I have introduced the notion of a *self digest* (Higgins, 1996a; Higgins & May, 2001). A digest summarizes a body of information, especially contingency rules and conclusions. A digest serves regulatory functions. The notion of a self digest is meant to capture the idea that self-knowledge summarizes information about oneself as an object in the world in order to serve self-regulatory functions. A self digest, then, is intended to highlight a new conceptualization of the nature of self-knowledge—*a summary of what the world is like in relation to oneself.*

It is proposed that what a person stores about himself or herself as a distinct object in the world depends on what information is useful for self-regulation. It was noted earlier, for example, that survival depends on learning about those attributes of oneself in relation to the world that produce beneficial interpersonal interactions and activity engagements. The self digest represents knowledge about oneself as an object in the world because, and to the extent that, such knowledge facilitates adaptation to one's environment. The self digest is a tool for survival. It summarizes a person's relations to the world and the personal consequences of these relations. It increases the likelihood of effective and efficient self-regulation in the service of survival. It is a handy sourcebook for people about their person-environment fit that helps them to fulfill their needs when interacting with their world.

The conceptualization of self-knowledge as a self digest involves no claim that the cognitive properties of self-knowledge are different from stored knowledge about other kinds of objects in the world. In addition, there is no claim that only self-knowledge contains functional information about the world. On the other hand, only knowledge about oneself as an object in the world is essential to represent because self-knowledge concerns the only object in the world that a person must continually regulate in order to survive. Thus, self-knowledge has a unique functional status among our stored knowledge of objects in the world. Conceptualizing self-knowledge as a self digest is meant to capture this unique functional status of self-knowledge. In addition, the notion of a self digest is intended to emphasize the self-regulatory nature of self-knowledge rather than the self-descriptive nature of self-knowledge that has been emphasized in the previous literature.

The actual self as one's own beliefs about one's stable properties as a distinct object in the world has received more attention than any form of the actual self in classic theories of the self (e.g., Epstein, 1973; Lecky, 1945; Rogers, 1951; Sarbin, 1952; Snygg & Combs, 1949). The philosopher Ryle (1949) suggested that people acquire self-knowledge about their own personal characteristics, what they think they are, through self-observation and inference. Bem (1967) and Andersen (1987) have made similar suggestions (see also Markus, 1980). Self-knowledge as self-description answers the question, "Who am I?" Indeed, this kind of self-knowledge is explicitly elicited with "Who are you?" and "Describe yourself" measures, such as McGuire's "Tell me about yourself" measure (e.g., McGuire & Padawer-Singer, 1976). In contrast, self-knowledge as self digest answers the question, "What is the world like in relation to me?"

Self-knowledge as self digest would contain quite different kinds of information than self-knowledge as self-description. For example, information about how others respond to you when you fail to be the kind of person they want you to be would not be part of self-knowledge as self-description but would be part of self-knowledge as self digest. On the other hand, information that described oneself, such as some physical characteristic, would be included as part of self-knowledge as self-description but would not be included in self-knowledge as self digest unless it was useful for self-regulation. In addition, self-knowledge as self-description involves representations of decontextualized "facts" about oneself in isolation, whereas self-knowledge as self digest involves representations of oneself in relation to other persons and activities in the world and the consequences of these relations.

The novel proposal of the self digest is that there is not a single actual self involving a descriptive representation of personal attributes but, rather, there are three different actual self-representations serving three distinct self-regulatory functions—an *instrumental self*, a *monitored self*, and an *expectant self*. Each of these self-regulatory functions occurs in a social context and requires taking into account other people's judgments, hopes, and wishes for oneself. It requires developing a shared reality with others, which in turn requires the development of different levels of self-consciousness. Let us now consider the nature of this development.

SHARED REALITY AND SELF-CONSCIOUSNESS

A fundamental characteristic of people is that they derive meanings from the events in their lives and then respond to those meanings. This insight into the nature of people was clearly developed at the turn of the twentieth century in the work of Weber, Durkheim, Freud, James, Cooley, and others. It is nicely captured in Thomas and Thomas's (1928) statement, "If men define situations as real, they are real in their consequences." In social psychology as well, Asch (1952), Lewin (1935), and Mead (1934) early on emphasized the importance of the psychological situation in determining people's motivations and actions. But what is the source of these psychological situations? Where do the meanings assigned to life events come from? Is there a source of meaning assignment that can account systematically for why people from different families and different cultures respond so differently to similar events in their lives?

A major source of psychological situations, and one that produces systematic variation in meaning assignment, is our sense of how the world works that social interactions provide. The ways that others respond to us communicate about the world around us and our place in it—messages about our person-environment fit. By accepting these messages about who we are in the world, we create a shared reality with the people in our lives (see Hardin & Higgins, 1996; Higgins, 1996b).

Almost a century ago, the eminent social scientist Max Weber (1967, pp. 156–157) stated, "In 'action' is included all human behavior when and in so far as the acting individual attaches a subjective meaning to it. . . . Action is social in so far as, by virtue of the subjective meaning attached to by the acting individual (or individuals), it takes account of the behavior of others and is thereby oriented in its course." Thus, action is "social" when its meaning and orientation takes account of other people. Self-regulation develops from social regulation, from children learning to take other people into account. From this perspective, *self-regulatory responses are social actions.*

Socialization involves individuals adopting the values and beliefs of their group, and when it is effective, people end up wanting to behave as others want and expect them to behave. As Jones and Gerard (1967, p. 77) point out, the "fascination stems from the fact that most of society's codes and values become part of the very fabric of an individual's personality during the process of socialization." This is, indeed, a fascinating issue, and it has been central to the work of Freud, Lewin, Murray, Vygotsky, Mead, and other founders of social-motivational science in psychology.

How does it all begin? To discuss the changes in self-regulation that develop a shared reality with others and increasing self-consciousness, I rely on the classic developmental literature that has described general shifts in children's ability to get along in the social world (e.g., Case, 1985; Damon & Hart, 1986; Fischer, 1980; Selman, 1980; see also Higgins, 1989, 1991; chapter 4, this volume).

Six to Twelve Months

By the end of the first year of life, children can represent the relation between two events, such as the relation between two successive responses their mother produces or the relation between a response that they produce and their mother's response to them (see Case, 1985). Children can produce and interpret communicative signals and anticipate the occurrence of some event and, thus, are capable of the preliminary form of role taking that Mead (1934) described—the ability to anticipate the responses of a significant other with whom one is interacting.

During this initial period, children begin to acquire the *instrumental self.* Actual self-knowledge serving an instrumental function represents one's self-attributes in relation to the responses they elicit from other people:

Something about me → How others respond to me

This is the first step in acquiring interpersonal contingencies that will become increasingly complex. This preliminary instrumental function is not unique to humans. Certainly chimpanzees, for example, learn observable behavioral contingencies concerning their behavior and the responses of others to them (see Povinelli, 2000). What is unique to human children during this period is social referencing or "shared attention," in which a child and an interaction partner will point out to each other some interesting object or event in the immediate environment and together pay attention to it (see Tomasello, 1999).

This joint attentional interaction provides an early example of the distinctive human motive for shared reality. Other animals will behave in ways that get others to do something they want, which includes getting their attention. Such behaviors are in the service of agency. But the joint attentional interaction of human children and their partners is in the service of understanding. It is this *sharing of an understanding* that is unique to humans. It is reflected in the unique way in which human adults actively instruct children about how the world works, which is the basis for cultural evolution (see Tomasello, 1999). It permits a kind of imitative learning that is unique to humans in that the child and adult are both motivated to have a common understanding of how to do something. It is not copying or mimicking an observed behavior for the purpose of agency. It is collaborating in order to share an understanding of how the world works and how to get along in it (see also Pittman & Higgins, 2002).

Sixteen Months to Two Years

During the second half of children's second year, there is a major shift in children's ability to represent events, which has been traditionally associated with the emergence of symbolic representation (e.g., Bruner, 1964; Case, 1985; Fischer, 1980; Piaget, 1951; Werner & Kaplan, 1963). Children can now represent the bidirectional relationship between themselves and another person as an interrelation between two distinct mental objects, self-as-object and other-as-object (see Bertenthal & Fischer, 1978; Harter, 1983; Lewis & Brooks-Gunn, 1979). Their ability to represent themselves and other persons as distinct objects in the world is reflected in their use of the pronouns "I" and "you." Children can now represent the relation between two relations: (a) the relation between a feature of themselves (e.g., their action, response, physical appearance) and a particular response by another person, and (b) the relation between a particular response by another person and a particular state that they will experience. Children, for example, can represent the relation between their making a mess at mealtime and their mother's frowning, yelling, or leaving, and the relation between their mother's frowning, yelling, or leaving and their experiencing a negative state.

This higher level of perspective taking that appears by 2 years of age is critical for what sociologists call *symbolic interaction*—the ability to anticipate the responses of others to their actions and the personal consequences of these social responses (see Stryker & Statham, 1985). Children's significant others link them to the larger society by providing the shared reality or social meaning of the child's features (i.e., societal responses to the child's features), as well as the importance of the child's features (i.e., the state produced in the child by these societal responses). In this way, children learn the interpersonal significance of their self-features.

The level of self-consciousness that children possess by 2 years of age can be used by children in a more sophisticated instrumental means-end fashion to regulate their actions, responses, or appearance. By representing the *interpersonal significance* of their self-features and using this information to plan their actions, children are better able to delay gratification, to control their momentary impulses, and to free themselves from the demands and forces of the immediate situation (see Miller & Green, 1985; Mischel & Moore, 1980; Mischel & Patterson, 1978).

Three to Six Years

From a motivational perspective, probably the most dramatic shift occurs between 3 and 6 years of age, the classic change from "egocentric" to "non-egocentric" thought (see Feffer, 1970; Flavell, Botkin, Fry, Wright, & Jarvis, 1968; Piaget, 1965; Selman & Byrne, 1974; Werner, 1957). Children can now coordinate two separate systems of interrelations, such as coordinating observable responses with unobservable responses (see Case, 1985), which underlies inferences about the thoughts, expectations, motives, and intentions of others (see Shantz, 1983).

Children now understand that other people have different attitudes about different types of responses, that they prefer some types of responses over others. They understand that performing the types of responses preferred by others is related to others' positive responses to them, and thus they are motivated to learn the types of responses that are preferred by their significant others. In addition to learning about a significant other's preferences from his or her personal reactions to them, children also learn by observing the significant other react to others (i.e., observational learning; see Bandura, 1977, 1986). For example, children can observe how their mother reacts to their sibling's responses and thereby infer which types of responses their mother prefers (see Bandura, 1986; Bandura & Walters, 1963).

The critical development during this period is that children learn that the relation between one of their self-features and another person's response to it depends on the other person's viewpoint or standpoint on this feature. A *standpoint* on the self is defined as a point of view from which a person can be judged that reflects a set of attitudes, opinions, or values (see Turner, 1956). For example, they can now represent the fact that it is the discrepancy between their behavior and the behavior that their mother prefers that underlies the association between their behavior and their mother's response to it (see Higgins, 1989). That is, children now understand that *social regulation of them is mediated by others' standpoints on them.*

This is a discovery of shattering importance. Children at this age are still totally dependent on older conspecifics for survival. It is clear to them that these older people are different from them, especially in their possession of *essential resources* that the children want to be *used for them and not against them.* Their highest priority is to figure out what determines how these resource-rich persons allocate their resources. Children want to tame these powerful animals called Mommy and Daddy by learning what motivates them.

The social-cognitive literature (in both developmental and social psychology) for decades has emphasized people's motivation to explain the behaviors of others ("why" questions), such as dispositional versus situational explanations. Although explaining others' actions is important, I believe that the major concern of both children and adults is to figure out what resources a target person has and whether they are likely to be used for or against them. These resources extend well beyond the typical traits that have been studied in the classic literature. They include the observable status and power of a person that is reflected in how family members and visitors treat that person. Rather than causal explanations for others' behaviors, children are trying to understand the *who, what, and where of resource allocation.*[1] Who makes the final decisions? Whose word is law? Does this vary by activity? For those things I want to happen, such as getting a new toy, who is in charge of what? For things I don't want to happen, such as getting punished, who is in charge of what? For things I enjoy doing, such as playing, who is a good playmate for which activity? For those things I don't enjoy doing, such as going to bed early, who allows me not to do which activity? I need to figure out who has which resources and then figure out what motivates them to use these resources for me rather than against me.

By the age of 6, children are much more masters of their universe than before. They have figured out that other people have wishes, hopes, expectancies, and demands of them. Other people like and dislike different things than they do. By *taking others' motivational orientations into account*—a new and critical kind of shared reality—children can plan their actions to increase the likelihood that others will use their resources for them and not against them. This increasing ability to take others' motivational orientations into account is also demonstrated in children's increasing ability to cooperate and collaborate with one another in a way that is not found in other animals, including primates (see Povinelli, 2000; Tomasello, 1999).

By taking into account others' standpoints on them, children develop a new kind of self-consciousness and a new kind of actual self-function. These standpoints become standards of self-evaluation—self-guides (see Higgins, 1989, 1991). Children now use self-guides as a basis for self-evaluation by assessing the amount of congruency or discrepancy between their current self-state and the end state that a significant other desires or demands of them (e.g., "How am I doing in relation to what father wants or demands of me?"). They can then respond to any perceived discrepancy by taking action to reduce it. They can also plan action by taking potential discrepancies into account, thereby using prospective self-evaluation in the service of self-regulation (see also Bandura, 1986; Carver & Scheier, 1990).

This self-evaluative process creates a new actual self-function—the *monitored self*. The monitored self is an actual self-representation that provides self-regulatory information regarding one's current state in relation to some desired end state, which together provide feedback about how well one is doing in meeting standards and pursuing desired goals:

Something about me → How well am I doing?

For young children, the desired end state is typically a shared reality with a significant other about what the child will hopefully accomplish (ideals) or what are the child's duties and responsibilities (oughts).

Eight to Ten Years

Between 8 and 10 years of age, children become capable of coordinating values along two distinct dimensions (see Case, 1985; Fischer, 1980; Piaget, 1970). When comparing their performance to that of another child, for example, children can now consider simultaneously the difference in actors' outcomes and the difference in actors' effort, thus making ability inferences possible (see Ruble, 1983). To be good at something now means to be better than others at something that is worthwhile, something that matters, as defined by a represented standard of value. Now the value of a target of comparison, such as performance on some task, depends on its relation to a represented goal or self-guide. Being "bad" or "good" at something thus acquires new significance.

The social comparison processes that develop during this period are a new way in which children take into account other people in their self-regulation. Through social comparison, children learn what is distinctive about themselves in relation to the world around them.

They learn what to expect about their own reactions to the world that need not be the same as other people's reactions. When doing certain things, not everyone has the same experience. By comparing their experience of an activity to the experience of other children, a child learns what the world is like for them in particular. The *expectant self* represents this relation between self-attributes and activity experiences:

Something about me → How I experience the world

Whereas the instrumental actual self answers the question "How does the world respond to me?," the expectant actual self answers the question "How do I respond to the world?" The expectant self includes personal preferences as well as personal skills or talents. The expectant self also develops from a shared reality. Significant others, both adults and peers, contribute to the construction of the expectant self by pointing out to children what is special and distinctive about them. Those distinctive self-attributes that are positive, such as talents, are perceived as resources by children's significant others. The significant others support (or pressure) the children to develop their talents further, such as spending hours on some artistic or athletic activity.

The actual self-representations during this period also develop into more global forms that refer to being a general type of person rather than a particular kind of behavior—being an "honest person" rather than just behaving honestly, being a "dancer" rather than just dancing. Children not only can evaluate a particular action they just performed by considering another person's likely response to it; they can also evaluate how the general traits they believe they possess relate to the general traits that significant others desire or expect them to possess. That is, they can now evaluate their success or failure at being the "type of person" that others desire or expect them to be.

Thirteen to Fifteen Years

From a motivational perspective, a major development that occurs between 13 and 15 years of age is that children can now simultaneously interrelate different perspectives on themselves as objects, including conflicting perspectives on themselves (Case, 1985; Fischer, 1980; Fischer & Lamborn, 1989; Inhelder & Piaget, 1958; Selman & Byrne, 1974). For the first time, two distinct systems of self-guides, such as one system involving a peer standpoint and another system involving a parental standpoint, can themselves be interrelated.

A related development during this period is that children become capable of constructing their *own* standpoint, distinct from the standpoint of others, which can function as the integrated solution to the complex array of alternative standpoints on them. Being conscious of having your own standpoint on yourself that is distinct from others' standpoint on you is another level of self-consciousness. With the development of a personal "own" standpoint, children can experience some personal self-guides that are shared with their parents' standpoint on them (a high level of identification), other personal self-guides that are not shared with their parents' standpoint (independent self-guides), and parental standpoints that are not shared with the children's own self-guides (introjects or the "felt presence of others"; see Moretti & Higgins, 1999).

In sum, there are progressive shifts from birth to adolescence in how children take other people into account in order to get along in their social world. With each shift in shared reality, a new level of self-consciousness appears. The instrumental self, monitored self, and expectant self components of the self digest are formed from these developments in shared reality and self-consciousness. Each of these components of the self digest provides children with an essential motivational tool for adapting to their enviroment. These motivational functions support, indeed press for, the maintenance and development of different levels of self-consciousness. The next section discusses another motivational support for (or pressure on) developing self-consciousness—"becoming."

BECOMING AND SELF-CONSCIOUSNESS

Imagine the following scenario. A young animal is rewarded for performing a certain behavior. But after a while, the young animal is no longer rewarded for performing that behavior. In classic terms, one would say that the animal now experiences a period of extinction trials for that behavior. When the young animal performs a behavior that takes more effort or greater skill than the earlier behavior, it is that behavior which is now rewarded. But after a while, that new behavior is also no longer rewarded. For most young animals, this would be very confusing. Indeed, it is not clear whether any animal could figure out the reinforcement contingency, with one key exception—human children.

To my knowledge, this kind of "improvement" or "progress" reinforcement contingency has not been explicitly investigated with either human children or young animals. Exactly when human children are able to figure out this kind of reinforcement contingency has not been studied. What is clear is that the development of a monitored self described earlier, which occurs between 3 and 6 years of age, typically involves such contingencies. As described earlier, during this period children figure out that parents (and others) have wishes, hopes, expectancies, and demands of them. But often what parents hope and expect of children is that they progressively become something that the parents have in mind for them. The parents want their child to improve, to make progress. The parents respond to children depending on whether they are or are not successful in "becoming," over time, what the parents have in mind. Thus, in order to control parental responses, children need to discover how the "becoming" contingency works. And, indeed, they do! They demonstrate (show off?) to parents what they can do now that they could not do earlier.

The monitored self provides feedback on how well one is doing in meeting the goals and standards (self-guides) held by significant others. The discovery of "becoming" contingencies creates a new level of self-consciousness for the monitored self. Children need to be conscious of where they are now, have been, and plan to be in relation to these self-guides or desired end states. They now evaluate themselves in terms of their success or failure in becoming. The positivity of the current self does not depend simply on whether it is congruent or discrepant from a self-guide but also on whether it is an improvement or progress from the past self (see Carver & Scheier, 1990). But if children want in the future to have a current self that is an improvement from their past self, then they have to plan in the present to have a future self that is better than their current self.

Contingencies of becoming, therefore, create motivational demands on children's self-consciousness to interrelate the past, present, and future. Contrary to what is necessary for most self-regulation, self-regulating improvement or progress requires not simply knowing in the present what you are like now but knowing how you were in the past and how you want to be in the future. To compare the current self with the past self requires having specific memories of what you were like in the past. It is no coincidence, then, that the developmental literature reports that it is during this age 3 to 6 period that children develop narrative self-consciousness and episodic memory (see chapter 4, this volume; Tulving, 1983).

Self-consciousness of becoming is also involved in young children's social modeling. Children at this age are fascinated with other children who are older than them, but not too much older. If children were simply interested in observing advanced skills, they would be as interested or more interested in watching adults than older children. But they are not. Their interest in older children is because they are fascinated with where they are going. They understand that they have improved from the past and watch somewhat older children to predict where they are going in the future.

Like self-consciousness in general, self-consciousness of becoming also develops further over time. As discussed earlier, between 8 and 10 years of age children become capable of coordinating values along two distinct dimensions, such as considering simultaneously the difference in actors' outcomes and the difference in actors' effort to make ability inferences possible. Such coordination along distinct dimensions can also be used by children in social comparison processes to evaluate personal skills. Then they can compare their becoming with the becoming of another child. "How am I doing?" becomes relative to other peers. "Am I improving on this skill faster or slower than other kids?" This level of self-consciousness contributes to the expectant self because personal talent (or deficit) is defined less by what you can do than by how quickly you improve relative to others.

In sum, along with the role of shared reality in providing a motivational push for developing self-consciousness, children's use of becoming in their self-regulation provides an additional push. This push involves children becoming self-conscious of others' wanting them to improve and make progress, which in turn requires interrelating their present self with both their past and future selves.

CONCLUSION

Self-consciousness is a motivational tool. For children to self-regulate in a social context, they need to understand what significant others hope for and expect of them (shared reality) and understand where they are now, have been, and plan to be in relation to these hopes and expectations (becoming). Shared reality and becoming are essential features of human self-regulation, and they both require the development of advanced forms of self-consciousness.

Like all fundamental psychological principles, shared reality and becoming have costs as well as benefits for humans. When individuals share reality with multiple significant others and these significant others have conflicting hopes or expectancies, the individuals suffer from feeling confused, uncertain, and unsure of themselves (see Van Hook & Higgins, 1988). When individuals have a significant other who shares only some of their beliefs about who they are, they suffer from alienation and loneliness (see Higgins, 1996b). Sharing reality with their audience through message tuning causes communicators to misremember their past to be more like what they said than what they saw (see Higgins, 1992). Controlling for the current magnitude of discrepancy with their hopes and aspirations (ideals), individuals who believe that they are no closer to attaining their ideals now than they were in the past suffer from depression-like symptoms (Strauman & Higgins, 1993).

These and other costs need to be weighed against the obvious benefits of shared reality and becoming. Without shared reality and becoming, there would be no human civilization. There would be no language, no social roles and identities, no education, and no governments.

Perhaps what is unique about humans is not so much their use of language or tools or instruction per se, but rather their motivation to share reality with others about the past, present, and future. Perhaps this motivation can account not only for the development of self-consciousness, but also for humans' use of language, tools, instruction, and so on. I began this chapter by stating that self-consciousness is a basic motivational tool for getting along with others. The others need not even be human. Humans are unique in trying to understand the feelings and desires of other animals and in responding to them in ways that cause them to be the resource humans want, whether as vehicles, machines, weapons, food producers, or pets. This taming of other animals to serve as resources has made a major contribution to the development of human civilization.

During the twentieth century, the study of human motivation was dominated by the notion that, motivationally, humans were fundamentally like other animals even though they had special cognitive skills. But humans are not like other animals motivationally. They are unique in being applied motivation scientists, constantly trying to shape the behaviors of others by figuring out their hopes and expectations. To understand human self-consciousness and human cognition more generally, we need to study the myriad implications of the fact that humans, motivationally, are fundamentally different from other animals.

ACKNOWLEDGMENTS The research reported in this chapter was supported by National Institute of Mental Health Grant MH39429 to E. Tory Higgins.

NOTE

1. Even when children and adults do make dispositional inferences, it is often in order to predict resource allocation rather than to predict behavior per se. Some attributes, such as intelligence, allow inferences about the power of a person as a resource (strength). Other attributes, such as the classic warm versus cold, allow inferences about the valence of a person as a resource, that is, whether the person is generally a positive (for) or negative (against) resource (direction). Still other attributes, such as honesty, allow inferences about the certainty or consistency of a person as a resource (stability).

REFERENCES

Andersen, S. M. (1987). The role of cultural assumptions in self-concept development. In K. Yardley & T. Honess (Eds.), Self and identity: Psychosocial perspectives (pp. 231–246). New York: Wiley.
Asch, S. E. (1952). Social psychology. Englewood Cliffs, NJ: Prentice-Hall.
Bandura, A. (1977). Social learning theory. Englewood Cliffs, NJ: Prentice-Hall.

Bandura, A. (1986). *Social foundations of thought and action: A social cognitive theory.* Englewood Cliffs, NJ: Prentice-Hall.

Bandura, A. L., & Walters, R. H. (1963). *Social learning and personality development.* New York: Holt, Rinehart and Winston.

Bem, D. J. (1967). Self-perception: An alternative interpretation of cognitive dissonance phenomena. *Psychological Review, 74,* 183–200.

Bertenthal, B. I., & Fischer, K. W. (1978). Development of self-recognition in the infant. *Developmental Psychology, 14,* 44–50.

Bowlby, J. (1969). *Attachment and loss: Vol. 1. Attachment.* New York: Basic Books.

Bowlby, J. (1973). *Attachment and loss: Vol. 2. Separation: Anxiety and anger.* New York: Basic Books.

Bruner, J. S. (1964). The course of cognitive growth. *American Psychologist, 19,* 1–15.

Carver, C. S., & Scheier, M. F. (1990). Origins and functions of positive and negative affect: A control-process view. *Psychological Review, 97,* 19–35.

Case, R. (1985). *Intellectual development: Birth to adulthood.* New York: Academic Press.

Cooley, C. H. (1964). *Human nature and the social order.* New York: Schocken Books. (Original work published 1902)

Damon, W., & Hart, D. (1986). Stability and change in children's self-understanding. *Social Cognition, 4,* 102–118.

Epstein, S. (1973). The self-concept revisited: Or a theory of a theory. *American Psychologist, 28,* 404–416.

Feffer, M. (1970). Developmental analysis of interpersonal behavior. *Psychological Review, 77,* 197–214.

Fischer, K. W. (1980). A theory of cognitive development: The control and construction of hierarchies of skills. *Psychological Review, 87,* 477–531.

Fischer, K. W., & Lamborn, S. D. (1989). Sources of variation in developmental levels: Cognitive and emotional transitions during adolescence. In A. de Ribaupierre, K. Scherer, & P. Mounod (Eds.), *Transition mechanisms in child development: The longitudinal perspective.* Paris: European Science Foundation.

Flavell, J. H., Botkin, P. T., Fry, C. L., Wright, J. W., & Jarvis, P. E. (1968). *The development of role-taking and communication skills in children.* New York: Wiley.

Hardin, C., & Higgins, E. T. (1996). Shared reality: How social verification makes the subjective objective. In R. M. Sorrentino & E. T. Higgins (Eds.), *Handbook of motivation and cognition: Vol. 3. The interpersonal context* (pp. 28–84). New York: Guilford.

Harter, S. (1983). Developmental perspectives on the self-system. In P. H. Mussen (Ed.), *Handbook of child psychology: Vol. 4. Socialization, personality, and social development* (pp. 275–385). New York: Wiley.

Higgins, E. T. (1989). Continuities and discontinuities in self-regulatory and self-evaluative processes: A developmental theory relating self and affect. *Journal of Personality, 57,* 407–444.

Higgins, E. T. (1991). Development of self-regulatory and self-evaluative processes: Costs, benefits, and tradeoffs. In M. R. Gunnar & L. A. Sroufe

(Eds.), *Self processes and development: The Minnesota symposia on child psychology* (Vol. 23, pp. 125–165). Hillsdale, NJ: Lawrence Erlbaum.

Higgins, E. T. (1992). Achieving "shared reality" in the communication game: A social action that creates meaning. *Journal of Language and Social Psychology, 11,* 107–131.

Higgins, E. T. (1996a). The "self digest": Self-knowledge serving self-regulatory functions. *Journal of Personality and Social Psychology, 71,* 1062–1083.

Higgins, E. T. (1996b). Shared reality in the self-system: The social nature of self-regulation. *European Review of Social Psychology, 7,* 1–29.

Higgins, E. T., & May, D. (2001). Individual self-regulatory functions: It's not "we" regulation, but it's still social. In C. Sedikides & M. B. Brewer (Eds.), *Individual self, relational self, collective self* (pp. 47–67). Philadelphia: Psychology Press.

Inhelder, B., & Piaget, J. (1958). *The growth of logical thinking from childhood to adolescence.* New York: Basic Books.

Jones, E. E., & Gerard, H. B. (1967). *Foundations of social psychology.* New York: Wiley.

Lecky, P. (1945). *Self-consistency: A theory of personality.* New York: Island Press.

Lewin, K. (1935). *A dynamic theory of personality.* New York: McGraw-Hill.

Lewis, M., & Brooks-Gunn, J. (1979). *Social cognition and the acquisition of self.* New York: Plenum.

Markus, H. (1980). The self in thought in memory. In D. M. Wegner & R. R. Vallacher (Eds.), *The self in social psychology* (pp. 102–130). New York: Oxford University Press.

McGuire, W. J., & Padawer-Singer, A. (1976). Trait salience in the spontaneous self-concept. *Journal of Personality and Social Psychology, 33,* 743–754.

Mead, G. H. (1934). *Mind, self, and society.* Chicago: University of Chicago Press.

Miller, S. M., & Green, M. L. (1985). Coping with stress and frustration: Origins, nature, and development. In M. Lewis & C. Saarri (Eds.), *The socialization of emotions* (pp. 263–314). New York: Plenum.

Mischel, W., & Moore, B. (1980). The role of ideation in voluntary delay for symbolically presented rewards. *Cognitive Therapy and Research, 4,* 211–221.

Mischel, W., & Patterson, C. J. (1978). In W. A. Collins (Ed.), *Minnesota symposia on child psychology* (Vol. 11, pp.199–230). Hillsdale, NJ: Lawrence Erlbaum.

Moretti, M. M., & Higgins, E. T. (1990). Relating self-discrepancy to self-esteem: The contribution of discrepancy beyond actual-self ratings. *Journal of Experimental Social Psychology, 26,* 108–123.

Moretti, M. M., & Higgins, E. T. (1999). Own versus other standpoints in self-regulation: Developmental antecedents and functional consequences. *Review of General Psychology, 3*(3), 188–223.

Piaget, J. (1951). *Play, dreams and imitation in childhood.* New York: Norton.

Piaget, J. (1965). *The moral judgment of the child.* New York: Free Press. (Original translation published 1932)

Piaget, J. (1970). Piaget's theory. In P. H. Mussen (Ed.), *Carmichael's manual of child psychology* (Vol. 1, 3rd ed., pp. 703–732). New York: Wiley.

Pittman, T. S., & Higgins, E. T. (2002). *The human nature of agency and understanding.* Unpublished manuscript, Princeton University.

Povinelli, D. J. (2000). *Folk physics for apes: The chimpanzee's theory of how the world works.* Oxford, UK: Oxford University Press.

Rogers, C. R. (1951). *Client-centered therapy: Its current practice, implications, and theory.* Boston: Houghton Mifflin.

Ruble, D. N. (1983). The development of social comparison processes and their role in achievement-related self-socialization. In E. T. Higgins, D. N. Ruble, & W. W. Hartup (Eds.), *Social cognition and social development: A socio-cultural perspective* (pp. 134–157). New York: Cambridge University Press.

Ryle, G. (1949). *The concept of mind.* London: Hutchinson.

Sarbin, T. R. (1952). A preface to a psychological analysis of the self. *Psychological Review, 59,* 11–22.

Selman, R. L. (1980). *The growth of interpersonal understanding: Developmental and clinical analyses.* New York: Academic Press.

Selman, R. L., & Byrne, D. F. (1974). A structural-developmental analysis of levels of role-taking in middle childhood. *Child Development, 45,* 803–806.

Shantz, C. U. (1983). Social cognition. In J. H. Flavell & E. M. Markman (Eds.), *Cognitive development,* Vol. 3 in P. H. Mussen (Ed.), *Carmichael's manual of child psychology* (4th ed., pp. 495–555). New York: Wiley.

Snygg, D., & Combs, A. W. (1949). *Individual behavior.* New York: Harper and Row.

Strauman, T. J., & Higgins, E. T. (1993). The self construct in social cognition: Past, present, and future. In Z. V. Segal & S. J. Blatt (Eds.), *The self in emotional distress: Cognitive and psychodynamic perspectives* (pp. 3–40). New York: Guilford.

Stryker, S., & Statham, A. (1985). Symbolic interaction and role theory. In G. Lindzey & E. Aronson (Eds.), *Handbook of social psychology* (Vol. 1, pp. 311–378). New York: Random House.

Sullivan, H. S. (1953). *The collected works of Harry Stack Sullivan: Vol. 1. The interpersonal theory of psychiatry* (H. S. Perry & M. L. Gawel, Eds.). New York: Norton.

Thomas, W. I., & Thomas, D. S. (1928). *The child in America.* New York: Knopf.

Tomasello, M. (1999). *The cultural origins of human cognition.* Cambridge, MA: Harvard University Press.

Tulving, E. (1983). *Elements of episodic memory.* New York: Oxford University Press.

Turner, R. H. (1956). Role-taking, role standpoint, and reference-group behavior. *American Journal of Sociology, 61,* 316–328.

Van Hook, E., & Higgins, E. T. (1988). Self-related problems beyond the self-concept: The motivational consequences of discrepant self-guides. *Journal of Personality and Social Psychology, 55,* 625–633.

Weber, M. (1967). Subjective meaning in the social situation. In G. B. Levitas (Ed.), *Culture and consciousness: Perspectives in the social sciences* (pp. 156–169). New York: Braziller.

Werner, H. (1957). *Comparative psychology of mental development.* New York: International Universities Press.

Werner, H., & Kaplan, B. (1963). *Symbol formation.* New York: Wiley.

7

Two Normative Roles
for Self-Consciousness

Patricia Kitcher

Modern philosophers regarded self-consciousness (or capacities that presupposed self-consciousness) as marking the fundamental divide between humans and other animals; our project in this book is to look for missing links between mere or first-order animal consciousness and full-blown human self-consciousness. Seemingly, arguments for links would be either analogical or compositional. Animals of Kind A possess something like some aspect of human self-consciousness; animals of Kind B possess one or more of the capacities required for some aspect of human self-consciousness. Both types of argument are likely to encounter similar lines of rebuttal: the "self-consciousness" of A animals is not very like human self-consciousness; even if it is implicated in human self-consciousness, the capacity of B animals does not enable them to have anything like human self-consciousness.

Much light would be shed on the ensuing debate by a theory describing what some or several aspects of human self-consciousness are like. I do not offer such a theory, but consider instead why self-consciousness was regarded as so important—so quintessentially human—by modern philosophers. The hope is that if we have some understanding of the important functions that self-consciousness performs in human life, then we can appeal to those functions to provide principled answers to questions about animal self-consciousness. Does the capacity that has been proposed as a variety of animal self-consciousness perform an analogous function in animal life? Of course, modern philosophy may have been seriously in error about the roles of human self-consciousness. Nevertheless, since the notion of self-consciousness arose in the modern period, having a better understanding of what the moderns took the functions of self-consciousness to be should illuminate debates about "missing links" to human self-consciousness—even if some or many of the modern views turn out to be incorrect. What we would learn in that case is not whether some animal capacities are very like human self-consciousness, but whether they are like what human self-consciousness has traditionally been taken to be. Further, when examining the motivations behind the traditional notion of self-consciousness points to a hypothesis that is now known to be wrong in the human case, that will also clarify the debate about animal self-consciousness. For if an alleged feature of human self-consciousness is rejected, then it can be ignored in debates about the aptness of an analogy between human and animal self-consciousness.

The notion of self-consciousness had many sources in the modern period, but I am going to focus on two central roles that it was thought to play, one moral and one epistemological. As indicated in my title, both roles are normative. This may seem to stack the deck, since normativity itself is often regarded as uniquely human. I hope the virtues of this approach will be evident in the remainder of the chapter, but I offer three quick justifications now. First, even if full-blown normativity only occurs among *Homo sapiens*, researchers are also looking for animal links to moral behavior in human beings, so a normative approach hardly forecloses the question of linkages. Second, as the reader will see below, modern discussions of self-consciousness were suffused with concerns about normativity. Under these circumstances, a strategy of trying to find animal links to aspects of human self-consciousness that have no normative dimension (if there are any) is very likely to prompt the criticism that the analogy is weak, because something essential to human self-consciousness has been left out. Finally, at least since Nicholas Humphrey's (1988) seminal paper, psychologists, anthropologists, and primatologists have been giving serious consideration to the hypothesis that the main function of intelligence in humans and animals is to navigate the complexities of the social world. Thus the modern view that one aspect of intelligence—the capacity to be self-conscious—enabled people to participate in normative social contexts comports well with current directions in research. The two roles I am going to consider, memory in moral responsibility and awareness of subjective limitations in what might be termed "epistemic responsibility,"[1] are fairly complex, and I have space to consider only a few aspects of each here. Both my discussions begin with Locke's seminal treatments of the issues.

CONSCIOUSNESS OF A PERSONAL PAST

In *An Essay Concerning Human Understanding*, Locke (1690/1959) famously claimed that since consciousness always accompanies thinking, and it is that which makes every one to be what he calls self, and thereby distinguishes himself from all other thinking things, in this alone consists personal identity ... and as far as this consciousness can be extended backwards to any past action or thought, so far reaches the identity of that person; it is the same self now it was then; and it is by the same self with this present one that now reflects on it, that that action was done. (2.27.11)[2]

Although Locke's understanding of "consciousness" has raised interpretive controversies, the standard reading of this passage is that it puts forward a memory criterion for personal identity: you are the same person as someone who perpetrated a deed if and only if you can remember doing the deed. Locke's immediate successors objected to both halves of this claim: memory was neither sufficient nor necessary for sameness of person.

Locke was explicit about why perfect recall was essential. On Judgment Day

everyone shall "receive according to his doings, the secrets of all hearts shall be laid open." The sentence shall be justified by the consciousness all persons shall have, that *they themselves,* in what bodies soever they appear, or what substances soever that consciousness adheres to, are the *same* that committed those actions, and deserve that punishment for them. (2.27.26)

This may seem unpromising. One function of consciousness of past deeds and thoughts is to bear witness to divine justice. Even those subject to the torture of "every sense of the flesh and every faculty of the soul" by fires fed by a brimstone "specially designed to burn for ever and for ever with unspeakable fury"[3] must at least admit that they committed the offenses for which they are being punished. But Locke also noted that "person" was a "forensic" term (2.27.26), so the focus of concern is not just divine fairness, but the fairness of human practices and attitudes. Society may fairly punish only where the person's own consciousness accuses him. And this forensic function of self-consciousness persists to the present day. In 1992, then Governor Clinton was criticized for not staying the execution of a man who had so injured himself after sentencing that his lawyers claimed he could not understand the connection between his crime and his punishment—even though he had been mentally competent during his trial.

At first glance, Locke's theory of extending consciousness backward may seem to be a forerunner of Tulving's hypothesis of "autonoetic" consciousness. Even the metaphors seem eerily similar: where Tulving (chapter 1, this volume) writes of autonoetic consciousness involving "time travel," Locke (1690/1959) described consciousness as being able to extend itself backward to past thoughts and deeds. He also tried to clarify the idea of the temporal extent of a person by an analogy with spatial extent. A person's sense of himself stretches over his whole body, in particular, to any part of whose good or harm he can be conscious: "the limbs of his body are to every one a part of himself; he sympathizes and is concerned for them" (2.27.11).[4] So too would a person's sense of himself stretch back to any previous "temporal part" of himself—say himself as a teenager—whose remembered deeds were a source of sympathy or concern to present consciousness (see 2.27.14, 16).

Still, there are at least two important differences between their views. The simpler is that, as far as I can tell, Locke had no inkling of the distinction between semantic and episodic memory that is central to Tulving's account. Locke thought of consciousness as extending backward to episodes, but he regarded "memory" as covering both experiences and facts. Where Tulving and his colleagues have elicited interesting differences in the way subjects use "know" and "remember" (Knowlton & Squire, 1995; Rajaram & Roediger, 1997; Tulving, 1985), Locke (1690/1959) divided up the territory differently. For him, memory was contrasted with current perception; memory was the capacity to revive previous perceptions "with this additional perception annexed to them, that *it has had them before*" (2.10.2). But he made no distinction between remembering, say, voting for Clinton and remembering that Clinton was elected. On the issue that is most important for the question of animal self-consciousness, however, they agree: Human beings have the capacity to remember episodes, the doings of past deeds.

The second difference is both harder to state and of direct relevance to the question of animal self-consciousness. As we have seen, Locke maintained that consciousness of a past thought or deed was a necessary and sufficient condition for the individual who had that consciousness to be identical with the person who had had the thought or done the deed. His readers thought his view was confused. In presenting memory as sufficient, Locke seemed to suggest that memory was what *made* the rememberer the same person as the doer of the remembered deed. But this could not be correct. Memory was only a means of *discovering* that someone existing now is the same person as someone who existed in the past. Derek Parfit (1984, p. 210) has introduced terminology that may make this distinction clearer. In the opinion of Locke's critics (and in Parfit's terminology), memory was revelatory of a "further fact," a fact in addition to the memory itself, namely, the fact that the rememberer and the doer of the past deed were the same person. In Locke's view, there was no further fact, but just one fact that could be described in two different ways: "Individual A today remembers doing something done by an individual in March 1993"; "A is the same person as someone who did that deed in that month and year."

Locke's position can seem vaguely crazy and his motivations completely irrelevant to contemporary concerns. On one level, the motivations were clear: As an empiricist, he was deeply suspicious of the notion of "substances" that endured through time but seemed to have no properties that were available to the senses. In the Scholastic view, substances were understood as the propertyless bearers of properties that endured through changes in properties. Locke wanted to offer an account of personal identity that did not depend on the (doubly) obscure notion of a "spiritual substance" that endured through time carrying identity with it. So he offered memory or "extended consciousness" as the basis of personal identity, and he persevered with that view in the face of seemingly compelling counterexamples. Surely we do not remember all our thoughts and deeds, yet are they any less ours? What about the law that punishes drunkards for their actions even in the face of plausible claims that they cannot remember what they did?

As Edwin McCann (1999) has argued, Locke's reply to the second problem is particularly telling.[5] In a letter to William Molyneux, he elaborated the brief discussion of the *Essay*. No, Locke (1690/1959) would not like to avail himself of a standard explanation for how the law deals with drunkards: Since the person was responsible for the drinking, he is held responsible for what ensues. To do so would be to abandon his theory that personal identity and the appropriateness of punishment was a matter of extended consciousness, for, ex hypothesi, the drunk did not remember (2.27.22, note). Locke's solution was quite different and consistent with his view. The laws punish "suitable to *their* way of knowledge" and "and in these cases they cannot distinguish certainly what is real, what counterfeit" (2.27.22). Since the fact can be proved against the person, but his want of memory cannot be proved for him, he is punished. That is, Locke resists the counterexample not by weakening his theory but by claiming that, as a practical matter, our legal punishments can be just even when there is a danger that they err. Presumably if an infallible test for memory failure could be developed, Locke would acquit a certain number of drunkards of the crimes of which they were accused.

Beyond his general suspicion of the notion of "substance," Locke seemed to have a special motivation for clinging to his understanding of personal identity, whatever its apparent problems. As noted, with extended consciousness, a person's own consciousness accuses her. Were personal identity to be a matter of something other than consciousness—call it factor X—then a present person could feel justly punished or rewarded for a past deed only by appreciating that factor X made her the same person as the perpetrator of the deed and, perhaps, that her present memory was an infallible test for the presence of X. Quite apart from worries about spiritual substances, Locke believed that we had no idea about the operation of whatever it is that enables us to think and to be persons. In which case, we would have no idea about what factor X might be.

From Locke's perspective, his opponents were adding an idle and incomprehensible piece to the mechanism. The practice of punishing and rewarding past actions seemed fair to people—and so functioned successfully—because they were held accountable for the deeds about which their own consciousnesses pained them. By the view he opposed, there would be an additional loop: A person's consciousness informed her about a past deed, thereby informing her that factor X was present between her and the perpetrator of the deed and, if she knew what factor X was and so what its presence implied, she would then know that she should be concerned about the remembered deed and so act or react accordingly. But she did not have that crucial bit of knowledge, so the concern she felt and the actions and attitudes that concern engendered could only come along with the memory itself. Thus, for Locke, the consciousness that made someone the person she was, was only a matter of the ability to extend something like a "consciousness with concern" back to past deeds. No other considerations were relevant.

Tulving's "autonoetic consciousness" seems more complex. Autonoetic consciousness involves an "autonoetic self" that is both psychologically real and that accounts for the fact of memory:

> When it comes to re-experiencing (remembering) of an earlier experience, an agent must exist that relates one to the other, that connects the two events. This agent is [the] autonoetic self. Episodic remembering can occur only if the self that does the re-experiencing of an event is the same self that did the experiencing originally. (Tulving, 2003, p. 7)

I take it that this is not meant to be a metaphysical claim, since the obvious counter would be that episodic memory may require nothing more than a memory trace and some means of conscious access to that trace. (So, for example, if time-lag mental telepathy were possible, I could access your past experiences and so "remember" them.) Rather, I assume that this account is offered as a description or analysis of the psychological reality of the autonoetic self: In a case of autonoetic consciousness, the subject not only recalls having a particular experience but implicitly recognizes that the memory is possible only if he is the same as the self who had the original experience. This may be correct for the human case. Perhaps whenever we have a sense of remembering a thought or deed, we tacitly review whether that episode can be fitted into our continuing mental lives as we represent them. So for example, a person might have a putative memory of seeing the Mardi Gras parade, but then realize that she had never been to New Orleans and so could not have seen it. But even a simple version of the ability to construct a coherent narrative of the course of your life seems far too complex to find in animals. It is not that all animals lack the ability to recall at least relative times and places of events—the results with scrub jays reported by Schwartz (chapter 9, this volume) demonstrate such an ability. What is missing is a sufficiently complex "theory of mind" to appreciate how mental states should relate to each other over time in the life of an individual, with, for example, memories following and not preceding experiences and beliefs following and not preceding perceptions.

By contrast, the extended consciousness that Locke thought crucial to the practice of punishment and reward might find analogues in animals. All that would be required is the ability of an animal's present consciousness to extend itself backward to a past deed in such a way that it acts appropriately to make amends for the deed or reacts appropriately to current chastisement for it. Nor does it seem very difficult to envision the kinds of evidence that might go some way toward establishing this consciousness. Some is already available. Frans de Waal (1996, p. 76) reports "thousands" of records of acts of reconciliation following spats, if not actual transgressions. Since these acts are much more frequent after difficulties than in times of harmony, they suggest that sufficient affect is connected to the past behavior to motivate present action—even if we might not want to go so far as describing that affect as "concern."

We might also be able to demonstrate that animals extend something like concerned consciousness back to past misdeeds experimentally. Do animals respond differently when they are punished for past misdeeds and when they receive the same treatment for neutral or positive behavior? In particular, what do animals do when they have committed no infraction and yet are punished? This would not be easy to set up, since we lack "stooge" animals to carry out the inappropriate responses. Still, it might be possible for trainers to punish the "innocent" and see whether this elicits a response that is different from that to noxious forms of treatment unconnected with punishments for past deeds. That certainly was what Locke thought happened in the human case: Unmerited punishment caused a special kind of pain in addition to whatever the punishment itself inflicted.

As noted, Locke's immediate successors also disagreed with his view that memory was necessary for establishing sameness of person. In his *New Essays on Human Understanding*, Leibniz (1704/1982) provided a different route:

> To discover one's moral identity unaided, it is sufficient that between one state and a neighbouring (or just a nearby) state there be a mediating bond of consciousness, even if this has a jump or forgotten interval mixed into it. Thus, if . . . I did not know how I had arrived at my present state even though I could remember things further back, the testimony of others

> could fill in the gap in my recollection. I could even be punished on this
> testimony.... And if I forgot my whole past ... I could still learn from
> others about my life during my preceding state.... All this is enough to
> maintain the moral identity which makes us the same person. It is true
> that if the others conspired to deceive me ... then the appearance would
> be false; but sometimes we can be morally certain of the truth on the credit
> of others' reports. (p. 236)

Although Leibniz appears to diverge significantly from Locke's position, I take the points of agreement to be more significant than the differences. Both agree that what is central in personal identity, and so in
the continuity made possible through self-consciousness, is moral identity. Further, they agree that personal, and so moral, identity is stan-
dardly disclosed through memory or consciousness of one's past deeds.
Leibniz also implicitly agreed that punishment and reward were justified only when the individual was morally certain (i.e., certain enough
to act) that he had perpetrated the deed. He simply suggested an alternative mechanism to such certainty via the testimony—and so memories—of others. In a sense, Leibniz merely offered a collective version
of Locke's memory criterion. Deeds can be imputed (and so fairly punished or rewarded) on the basis of the individual's memory of his past
or on the basis of other people's memories of his past.

If a person accepts the greater reliability of collective memory, then
her own consciousness, if not memory, would accuse her of the deed
and she would be more accepting of punishment. It might be possible
to observe something like collective memory producing self-consciousness among animals, though eliminating confounding factors would be
difficult. If an animal were more willing to engage in acts of reconciliation or to accept chastisement if it were collectively "accused"—treated
in the manner of a transgressor by many—then we might suspect that
collective memory can be a mechanism for self-consciousness, in the
sense of concern for past infractions, in animals as well as people.

Self-consciousness was important to modern philosophers in large
part because it was the capacity that underlay the ability of human
societies to be morally just. Through self-consciousness, someone's
own consciousness accused him of the misdeed and recognized the
appropriateness of some ensuing decrement to his happiness (though
possibly not the size of the decrement envisioned by the church fathers).
Given this background, if some species of animals can be shown to be
sensitive to the connection between reward or punishment and past
boon or misdeed, and/or inclined to ameliorate their present situations by "canceling out" a previous misdeed, then I think there would
be a strong argument that they possess some aspects of "self-consciousness," as that expression has traditionally been understood.

On the other hand, Locke and others also fastened on self-consciousness as the capacity that enabled one to behave well—or at least

against one's immediate interests—in the first place. Locke was very clear that self-consciousness involved not just a concern extending back to past deeds but also forward to future happiness or misery. Of course, there is no mystery about why he thought this. He believed that divine and human morality could function only when individuals were worried about the rewards and punishments that their actions might bring. Insofar as animals have no appreciation of the future, it might seem that no real analogue of the self-consciousness connected to rewards and punishments is possible. In fact, I think that the animal case suggests that modern philosophers may have been incorrect in the prima facie plausible assumption that since the human practices of punishing and rewarding involved both backward-looking and forward-looking projections of the self, then a single mechanism of self-consciousness underlay both. Being concerned about past action sufficiently to try to make amends or to acquiesce in retaliatory attacks might prevent a breakdown of the community even in the absence of an ability to project into the future that would have enabled one to foresee punishing and so not to transgress. Indeed, this kind of mechanism could be a link to a more symmetric type of self-consciousness that underlies the human practices of punishing and rewarding.

CONSCIOUSNESS OF SUBJECTIVE LIMITATIONS

Locke tempered his empiricism with what might uncharitably be described as "rationalism in empiricist clothing." In addition to the external senses, (i.e., the senses as normally understood), he hypothesized that we also had another source of ideas:

> the other fountain is,—the perception of the operations of our own mind within us, as it is employed about the ideas it has got;—which operations, when the soul comes to reflect on and consider, do furnish the understanding with another set of ideas, which could not be had from things without. And such are *perception, thinking, doubting, believing, reasoning, knowing, willing,* and all the different actings of our own minds;—which we being conscious of, and observing in ourselves do from these receive into our understanding as distinct ideas as we do from bodies affecting our senses. This source . . . though it be not sense, as having nothing to do with external objects is, yet is very like it, and might properly enough be called *internal sense.* (Locke, 1690/1959, 2.1.4)

Locke's claim that we can be self-consciousness in the sense of being conscious of our own mental "actings" is, to say the least, controversial. Karl Lashley (1958) denied it wholesale: "No activity of mind is ever conscious" (p. 4). More recently, Nisbett and Wilson (1977) have reviewed a large body of literature suggesting that subjects lack privileged access to their own higher and lower mental processes. It is tempting to think that Locke and his contemporaries erred by taking

Figure 2.2 *Taira Sees the Ghosts of His Enemies*, by Ando Hiroshige. From the collection of J. Metcalfe.

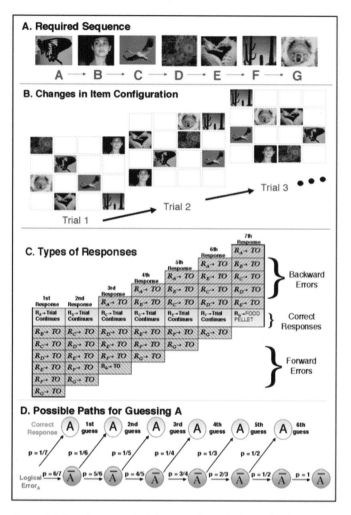

Figure 3.2 Simultaneous chaining paradigm. A. Example of a seven-item list. Subjects are required to respond to each color photograph in a prescribed order (A → B → C → D → E → F → G). B. Variation of the configuration of list items. List items were presented on a touch-sensitive video monitor in randomly configured displays. The task was to touch the items in the prescribed order irrespective of their position on the monitor. Prior to each trial, a new configuration was selected at random from the more than 5.8 million configurations that could be generated by presenting seven items in any of 16 positions. C. Types of forward and backward errors. The shaded boxes show the types of logical errors that could occur before a subject discovers the correct sequence. See text for additional details. D. Determining the ordinal position of a list item. The probability of guessing A by making logical errors to eliminate the A⁻ items. See text for additional details.

Figure 8.1 After touching the lexigram on her keyboard (visible in background) corresponding to the type of object hidden, Panzee points toward the location of the object. Photo by Charles R. Menzel.

Figure 9.1 King knuckle-walking in his outdoor area. He has .6 hectares of Florida hammock forest.

FACING PAGE

Figure 10.2 A. Frequency discrimination performance by a bottlenosed dolphin (*Tursiops truncatus*) in the procedure of Smith et al. (1995). The horizontal axis indicates the frequency (Hz) of the tone. The response *high* was correct for tones at exactly 2100 Hz, and these trials are represented by the rightmost data point for each curve. All lower tones deserved the response *low*. The percentages of trials ending with the *high* response (dashed line) or *low* response (dotted line) are shown. B. The dolphin's performance in the same auditory discrimination when he was also given the response *uncertain*. The solid line represents the percentage of trials receiving the uncertainty response at each difficulty level. The error bars show the lower 95% confidence limits. C. The intensity of the dolphin's incidental hesitation and wavering behaviors for tones of different frequencies (Hz).

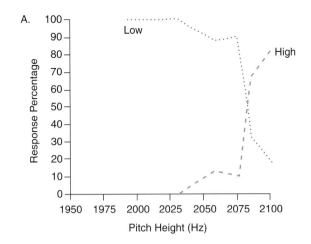

A.

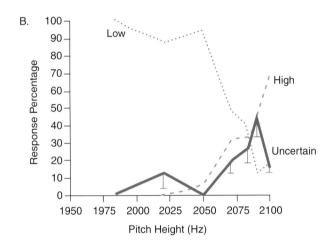

B.

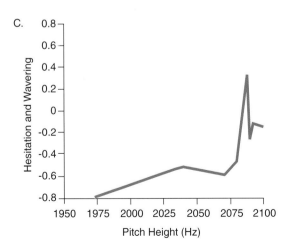

C.

A. Trial Screen

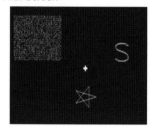

B. Monkey Abel

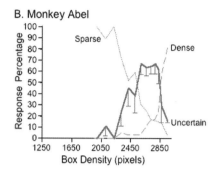

C. Monkey Baker

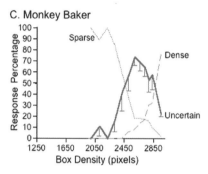

D. Humans

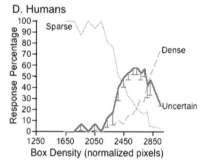

Figure 10.3 A. The screen from a trial in the dense-sparse discrimination of Smith et al. (1997). B. The performance of monkey Abel in the dense-sparse task. The response *dense* was correct for boxes with exactly 2,950 pixels—these trials are represented by the right-most data point for each curve. All other boxes deserved the response *sparse*. The horizontal axis indicates the pixel density of the box. The solid line represents the percentage of trials receiving the uncertainty response at each density level. The error bars show the lower 95% confidence limits. The percentages of trials ending with the *dense* response (dashed line) or *sparse* response (dotted line) are also shown. C. The performance of monkey Baker in the dense-sparse discrimination depicted in the same way. D. The performance of seven humans in the dense-sparse discrimination. To equate discrimination performance across participants, the data have been normalized to place each participant's discrimination crossover at a pixel density of about 2,700. The horizontal axis indicates the normalized pixel density of the box.

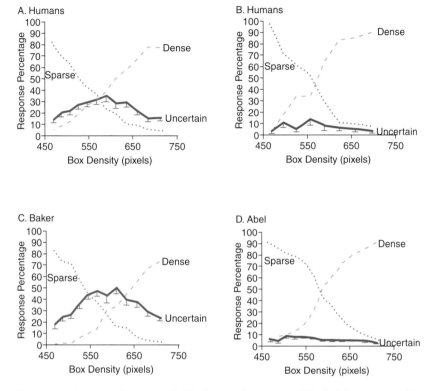

Figure 10.4 A. The performance of eight humans in the second kind of dense-sparse discrimination used by Smith et al. (1997). The lower and upper half of a range of densities deserved the *sparse* and *dense* response, respectively. The percentage of trials receiving the uncertainty response at each density are shown by the solid line. The error bars show the lower 95% confidence limits. The percentages of trials ending with the *dense* response (dashed line) or *sparse* response (dotted line) are also shown. B. The performance of one human in the same dense-sparse discrimination. C. The performance of monkey Baker in this discrimination. D. The performance of monkey Abel in this discrimination.

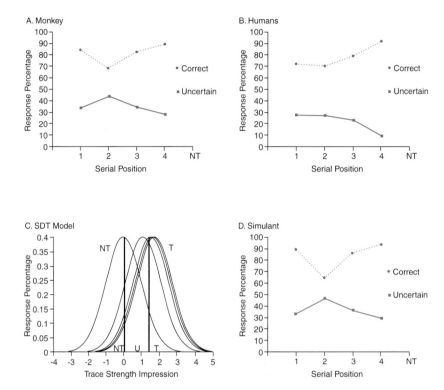

Figure 10.6 A. Serial probe recognition (SPR) performance by monkey Baker in the task of Smith et al. (1998). NT denotes *not there* trials. The serial position (1–4) of the probe in the list of pictures is also given along the x-axis for the probes on *there* trials. The percentage of trials of each type that received the uncertainty response is shown (bold line). The percentage correct (of the trials on which the memory test was attempted) is also shown (dotted line). B. Performance by 10 humans in a similar SPR task used by Smith et al. C. A signal detection theory (SDT) portrayal of monkey Baker's decisional strategy in the SPR task of Smith et al. (1998). Unit-normal trace-impression distributions are centered at the locations along the trace-strength continuum corresponding to the animals *d* for probes of the four serial positions in the memory lists (*there*, T), and at 0.0 for the NT probes. These normal curves are overlain by the decision criteria that define the animal's three response regions (from left to right, NT, *uncertain* [U], and T). D. Performance by the SDT simulant that fit best monkey Baker's performance.

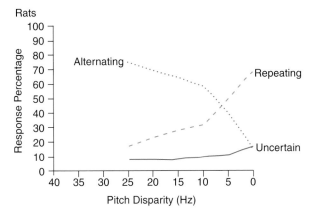

Figure 10.8 Performance by six rats in the frequency discrimination used by Smith and Schull (1989). The horizontal axis indicates the frequency difference between the alternating pitches on a trial. The repeating response was correct for trials with a frequency difference of 0, and these trials are represented by the rightmost data point for each curve. All other trials deserved the alternating response. The solid line represents the percentage of trials receiving the uncertainty response at each pitch disparity. The percentages of trials ending with the repeating response (dashed line) or alternating response (dotted line) are also shown.

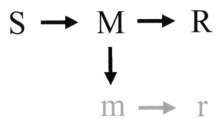

Figure 11.1 Measuring memory awareness behaviorally. Viewing an object (S) causes the formation of a mental representation, or memory, of the object (M) that persists in the brain even when the object is removed from view. The memory later guides the response (R) to the remembered object in a memory test. In the same way that M is about the object in the world, m is a secondary mental representation that is about the memory M. A secondary response (r) is required to infer the presence of m. A procedure for doing so is shown in figure 11.2.

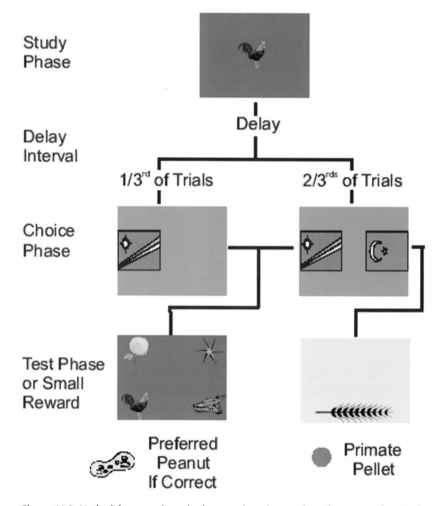

Figure 11.2 Method for assessing whether monkeys know when they remember. Each colored panel represents what monkeys saw on a touch-sensitive computer monitor at a given stage in a trial. At the start of each trial, subjects studied a randomly selected image. A delay period followed, during which monkeys often forgot the studied image. On two thirds of trials, animals chose between taking a memory test (right panel, left-hand stimulus) and declining the test (right panel, right-hand stimulus). On one third of trials, monkeys were forced to take the test (left panel). Better accuracy on chosen memory tests than on forced tests indicates that monkeys know when they remember and decline tests when they have forgotten, if given the option.

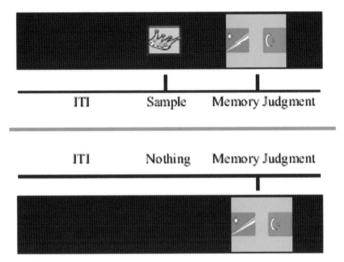

Figure 11.4 Schematic of a normal trial (upper panel) and a no-sample probe trial (lower panel). The white lines represent the passage of time. During the intertrial interval (ITI), the screen was black. On normal trials, a sample appeared and the monkeys had to touch it to advance the trial. After a delay, the monkeys could choose to either take or decline the memory test. Probe trials were identical, with the exception that no sample appeared, and the monkey did not have to touch the screen to advance the trial.

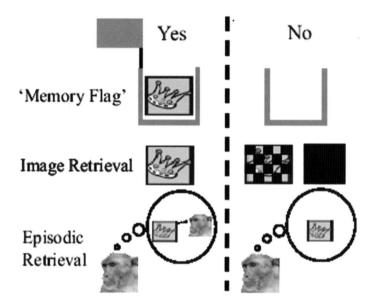

Figure 11.7 Cartoons of candidate processes underlying memory awareness. The left column represents the contents of cognitive processing during trials on which monkeys choose to take the memory test. The right column depicts the same on trials on which the test is declined. The memory flag hypothesis posits an indicator for the presence of memory. Monkeys can respond on the basis of the indicator but are not aware of the memory itself. In the case of the other two hypothetical mechanisms, the decision to take the memory test is based on the richness of the memory retrieved. See text for more details.

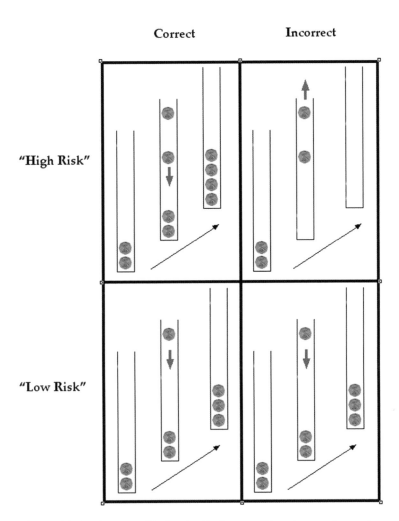

Figure 12.2 Contingency table showing the four possible outcomes of correct or incorrect response to the line task and high- and low-risk bets, starting with two tokens already present in the reservoir. When high risk was pressed, two tokens fell into the reservoir after correct responses, but flew out of the reservoir after incorrect responses. When low risk was pressed, one token fell into the reservoir regardless of whether the line response was correct or incorrect. Note that in Experiment 2, choosing high risk resulted in a grain or loss of three, rather than two, tokens.

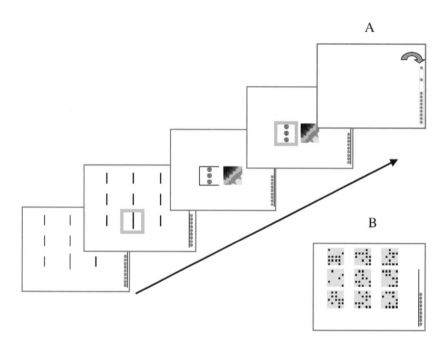

Figure 12.3 A. A sample trial for Experiment 1. In the first phase, nine lines appeared on the screen. A token reservoir appeared in the bottom right-hand corner of the screen, set at nine at the beginning of each session. The monkey's task was to press the longest line. For each touch, a green border appeared around the pressed item. Then the lines disappeared, and two risk icons appeared. The monkey's task was to report his confidence by betting either low or high risk. Once he made his bet, the token reservoir changed accordingly. In this sample trial, the monkey has bet high risk, and was correct on the line task. Thus, two tokens were added to the reservoir. B. Sample numerical stimuli for Experiment 2. The task was to press the stimulus with the most (Lashley) or the least (Ebbinghaus) items in them. Otherwise, the general methods remain the same as those in Experiment 1.

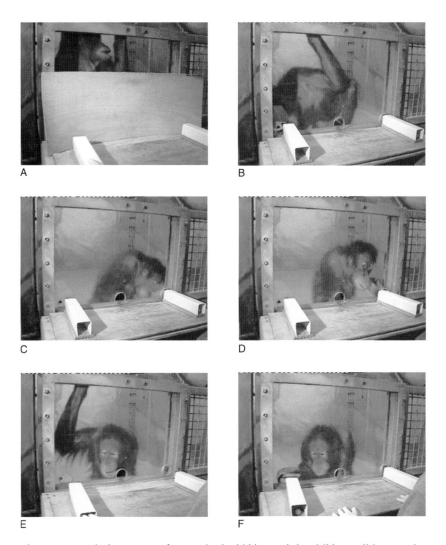

Figure 13.2 Typical sequence of events in the hidden and the visible conditions. In the hidden condition, the reward is hidden inside one of the tubes behind a screen (A), the orangutan looks inside the empty tube (B), then the baited tube (C), and makes a choice (D). In the visible condition, the reward is placed inside one of the tubes in full view of the subject (E), and the subject chooses (F). Note the absence of looking behavior in the visible condition compared to the hidden condition.

their metacognitive awareness that they were perceiving to be a perception of themselves perceiving. So this aspect of the modern theory of self-consciousness might well be rejected for the case of people, thus taking it out of any possible analogy with animals.

Although Locke introduced the notion of an "internal sense" as an awareness of mental actions, what he and his successors thought it explained was our ability to scrutinize our own thoughts. In particular, the internal sense enabled cognizers to see the relations among their ideas. To borrow one of Locke's examples, the internal sense told human beings that their idea of "murder" "contained" the idea of "man" and not the idea of "sheep" (3.5.6). Despite their empiricist credentials, both Locke (2.2.1) and Hume (1739/1978, p. 70) thought that we could obtain knowledge by considering the relations among our own ideas. As we can know that snow is white by observation through our external senses, we can know—indeed know with complete certainty—that triangles are three sided, murder involves killing humans, and bachelors are unmarried through observing our own ideas through the internal sense. In this case as well, later theorists have cast serious doubts on Locke's claim that we can be conscious of our own ideas in anything like this sense. Beyond Quine's (1953) well-known denial of any principled distinction between claims whose truth rests on empirical evidence and claims that are true by virtue of the relations among our ideas, it now seems fairly clear that insofar as we are able to determine what an idea or concept means to us, we do so by considering how we are prone to use the concept and not by engaging in some mysterious internal inspection. Still, even if Locke was wrong about the mechanism by which we are able to scrutinize our concepts, the ability to do so might still be thought of as a variety of self-consciousness, and one not to be found in animals lacking language.

Modern philosophers thought that self-consciousness of one's own ideas was important—was the hallmark of men as opposed to beasts—because it permitted something that they took to be unique to human beings, the capacity for epistemic self-improvement. Through being conscious of their ideas, human beings could discard confused ideas and clarify or patch up others. And they should. Modern philosophers regarded epistemology as a normative discipline not just because it was supposed to uncover standards for knowledge, but because those standards provided what has sometimes been described as an "ethics of belief." Although people had the right to believe whatever they chose, they had an obligation to do what they could to be epistemically responsible members of a mutually dependent society. From Kant's (1790/1987) perspective, this involved adhering to three fundamental epistemic maxims: "think for yourself," "think from the standpoint of others," and think "in accord with yourself" (p. 294). That is, try to ensure that your thinking was not a matter of prejudice, was broad-minded, and was consistent.

If one normative role for self-consciousness was to enable the epistemic self-improvement required for epistemic responsibility, what are the prospects for finding animal analogues of self-consciousness? Since Kant was giving voice (more or less) to Enlightenment bromides about the routes to epistemic self-improvement, we can consider the three processes captured in his maxims. The first and third look like nonstarters for animals. How can an animal test its representations for signs of prejudice or inconsistency without language? The second process is often mediated by language as well. We follow the advice "to think from the standpoint of others" in most circumstances by asking others what they think. I should note that, for Kant, two different norms were served by thinking from the standpoint of others: In this way, one both showed respect for others and also lived up to one's obligation to make one's beliefs as accurate as possible, by gaining more information. Even in the absence of language, it might be possible to observe rudimentary forms of both norms in animals, although I consider only the second. We seem to see something like this in cases where animals recognize the limitations of their own epistemic perspective in comparison with others and try to improve it by borrowing information from others rather than acting (precipitously) on their own limited information.

Josep Call's very interesting experiment (chapter 13, this volume) seems to offer some evidence that species of the great apes can both recognize the epistemic limitation of their situation and borrow information from others. So when food is placed in one of two tubes so that they cannot see which has the food, they will rely on the indications of trainers whom they recognize to have a clear view of the placements. Still, interpretation is a difficult problem. How can we distinguish cases where an animal is self-conscious of the limitations of its information from cases where it looks for more information simply because it has not got enough to proceed? The same difficulty seems to attend the results with monkeys that Call reported. When given the opportunity to opt out of a choice—when opting out provides a better reward than answering incorrectly—rhesus monkeys will avail themselves of that alternative, thereby significantly raising their percentage of correct choices. This implies that they choose only when they know; but it does not show that they do so because they recognize that they know or do not know rather than simply opting out when their information is weak. As David Premack (1988) noted, what is really needed is unequivocal evidence in nonhuman species that the animals "do not act directly on the information given them, but sometimes 'call to question' the information itself" (p. 173). And that sort of evidence is hard to find.

Seyfarth and Cheney have observed that some monkeys (the vervets) are able to ignore false information from conspecifics. They do not always react to juveniles' cries and, in an experiment, came to ignore the alarms of a "boy who cried wolf" (reported by Dennett, 1987, p. 270). Here, too, there are interpretive problems, however. Did they recognize that the information they had from immature members of the troop might be false, or is it just an innate response to juvenile informants? Did they come to question the unreliable alarm sounder or simply extinguish an unrewarded response? To get a good parallel to the human case, as the moderns envisioned it, one would like to see them punish a giver of false alarms, at least in the adult case.

Nevertheless, if we focus on the other aspect of the ability to improve one's epistemic situation—not the recognition of the limitations of one's information, but the ability to borrow information from appropriately placed other cognizers—then we can see a precursor not of self-consciousness itself, but of one of the capacities that self-consciousness enhances. When the ability to borrow information from others is available, then it would be useful to have a mechanism that makes one pause and evaluate one's own information. Further, the "disengage" mechanism, the mechanism that stops an animal from acting when it lacks information, would seem to be an essential component of the human ability to question our own information. Even philosophers cannot afford to reflect on each of their beliefs without quickly succumbing to starvation. So mechanisms must exist in the human case that lead us to consider the quality of our information in some cases rather than others. One obvious mechanism is the simple insufficiency of information for action.

Since it is not easy to say what human self-consciousness is, I have tried instead to consider what it does or, more precisely, what the modern philosophers who introduced the notion of self-consciousness thought it did. It seems to me that the central normative tasks assigned to self-consciousness by the moderns have either analogues with animal capacities or components in common with animal capacities. This is quite a surprising result. For, as noted at the outset, modern philosophers believed that in self-consciousness they had finally found the key to human uniqueness, that quality which, in Kant's (1978/1798) words, "elevated man *infinitely* above all other creatures that lived on earth" (p. 127, my emphasis).

NOTES

1. I discuss epistemic responsibility at greater length below.

2. The references to Locke (1690/1959) provide book, chapter, and section numbers, rather than page numbers, since these are common to different editions.

3. Here I borrow Joyce's (1976, pp. 130–131) borrowed description of hell in

Portrait. Joyce takes the description from Pinamoti's *Hell Open to Christians, to Causing them from Entering into it* (1688), which itself borrowed from Suarez, Aquinas, Loyola, and others.

4. The standard edition of the essay, A. C. Fraser's, has a numbering problem. There are two sections 2.27.10 and 2.27.11. This citation is to the second 2.27.11.

5. My discussion here is much indebted to McCann (1999).

REFERENCES

Dennett, D. (1987). *The intentional stance.* Cambridge, MA: MIT Press.

de Waal, F. (1996). *Good natured: The origins of right and wrong in humans and other animals.* Cambridge, MA: Harvard University Press.

Hume, D. (1978). *A treatise of human nature* (P. H. Nidditch, Ed.). Oxford, UK: Oxford University Press. (Original work published 1739)

Humphrey, N. K. (1988). The social function of the intellect. In R. Byrne & A. Witen (Eds.), *Machiavellian intelligence: Social expertise in the evolution of intellect in monkeys, apes, and humans* (pp. 13–26). Oxford, UK: Clarendon Press.

Joyce, J. (1976). *Portrait of the artist as a young man.* New York: Penguin.

Kant, I. (1987). *Critique of judgment* (W. Pluhar, Ed. & Trans.). Indianapolis, IN: Hackett. (Original work published 1790)

Kant, I. (1978). *Anthropology from a pragmatic point of view* (V. L. Dowdell, Trans.). Carbondale: Southern Illinois University Press. (Original work published 1798)

Knowlton, B. J., & Squire, L. R. (1995). Remembering and knowing: Two different expressions of declarative memory. *Journal of Experimental Psychology: Learning, Memory, and Cognition, 21,* 699–710.

Lashley, K. S. (1958). Cerebral organization and behavior. In H. C. Solomon & S. Cobb (Eds.), *Proceedings of the Association for Research in Nervous and Mental Disease: Vol. 36. The brain and human behavior* (p. 4). Baltimore, MD: W. Penfield.

Leibniz, G. (1982). *New essays on human understanding* (Abridged ed., P. Remnant & J. Bennett, Ed. & Trans.). Cambridge, UK: Cambridge University Press. (Original work published 1704)

Locke, J. (1959). *An essay concerning human understanding* (A. C. Fraser, Ed.). New York: Dover. (Original work published 1690)

McCann, E. (1999). Locke on identity: Matter, life, and consciousness. In M. Atherton (Ed.), *The empiricists: Critical essays* (pp. 63–88). New York: Rowman and Littlefield.

Nisbett, R. E., & Wilson, T. D. (1977). Telling more than we can know: Verbal reports on mental processes. *Psychological Review, 84,* 231–259.

Parfit, D. (1984). *Reasons and persons.* Oxford, UK: Clarendon Press.

Premack, D. (1988). "Does the chimpanzee have a theory of mind?" revisited. In R. Byrne & A. Whiten (Eds.), *Machiavellian intelligence: Social expertise and the evolution of the intellect in monkeys, apes, and humans* (pp. 160–179). Oxford, UK: Oxford Science Publications.

Quine, W. V. (1953). Two dogmas of empiricism. *From a logical point of view* (pp. 20–46). Cambridge, MA: Harvard University Press.

Rajaram, S., & Roediger, H. L., III (1997). Remembering and knowing as states of consciousness during recollection. In J. D. Cohen & J. W. Schooler (Eds.),

Scientific approaches to the question of consciousness (pp. 213–240). Hillsdale, NJ: Erlbaum.

Tulving, E. (1985). Memory and consciousness. *Canadian Psychology, 26,* 1–12.

Tulving, E. (2003). *Episodic memory and autonoesis: Uniquely human?* Unpublished manuscript.

8

Progress in the Study of Chimpanzee Recall and Episodic Memory

Charles Menzel

One of the central questions raised by this volume is whether nonhuman animals have self-reflective consciousness. Tulving's (chapter 1, this volume) opinion is that "no essential progress has been made toward resolving the issues involved for more than a hundred years." He recommends that we focus on the following questions: "What exactly makes some people believe that nonhuman primates do have the same kind of (autonoetic, self-knowing) consciousness that humans do, and why do some others believe that they do not?" and that we carefully examine the points of agreement and disagreement.

The idea that there is something fundamentally different about human and nonhuman memory dates back at least to the time of Aristotle (1990), who wrote:

> many also of the other animals [as well as man] have memory, but, of all that we are acquainted with, none, we venture to say, except man, shares in the faculty of recollection. The cause of this is that recollection is . . . a mode of inference. For he who endeavors to recollect *infers* that he formerly saw, or heard, or had some such experience, and the process [by which he succeeds in recollecting] is . . . a sort of investigation. But to investigate in this way belongs naturally to those animals alone which are also endowed with the faculty of deliberation. (p. 695)

The idea that human memory and nonhuman memory are different is also shared by numerous philosophers throughout written history as well as many current biologists and psychologists. The idea is based not simply on received wisdom but also on the conspicuous differences in what humans and nonhumans do. For example, only humans have locked themselves away in a room for years at a time to write their confessions and autobiographies. The classic explorations of memory by St. Augustine and Proust are outstanding examples. Equally important, only humans have created libraries, museums, and archives devoted exclusively to the preservation of writings, photographs, speeches, and other media documenting events and discoveries from the past.

Ruggiero and Flagg (1976), in discussing the history of the claim that animals do not have memory in the same sense as humans do, wrote, "Since the time of Aristotle, man has been regarded as different from animals because he possesses a reasoning ability, based on a spoken language. . . . Such thinking reflects the view that, man, by virtue of his verbal ability, is capable of actively recalling the past (i.e., generating information about a past event in the absence of the original event), whereas nonverbal organisms are capable of recognition at best" (p. 1). Ruggiero and Flagg argue that monkeys, apes, and other animals do possess representational, organized memory, but they point out, "If the term 'memory' is restricted to instances of active recall, we can begin to understand the . . . claim that animals do not have memory" (pp. 1–2). Indeed, in everyday life we normally accept a person's recounting (via written and verbal descriptions, maps, gestures, and so forth) of what he or she saw, heard, and felt on a previous occasion as prima facie evidence that he or she can recall the event. The number of independent details about past events that a normal adult human can recall and report exceeds by a wide margin that demonstrated to date for any nonhuman. Until recently, however, almost no data have been available on recall capabilities in nonhuman animals to take the issue further.

William James's (1890) definition of human "memory proper" also provides a contrast with most conceptions of nonhuman memory. James distinguished sharply between memory proper and the mere recurrence of behaviors or images, or their dependence on past experience, and went on to say:

> Memory proper . . . is the knowledge of a former state of mind after it has already once dropped from consciousness; or rather *it is the knowledge of an event, or fact,* of which meantime we have not been thinking, *with the additional consciousness that we have thought or experienced it before.* . . . Memory requires more than mere dating of a fact in the past. It must be dated in *my* past. In other words, I must think that I directly experienced its occurrence. It must have that "warmth and intimacy" which were so often spoken of in the chapter on the Self, as characterizing all experiences "appropriated" by the thinker as his own. A general feeling of the past direction in time, . . . a particular date conceived as lying along that direction, and defined by its name or phenomenal contents, an event imagined as located therein, and owned as part of my experience. (p. 288, italics in original)

James's definition "implies that the memory is conscious and that the subject has language and a formal concept of time and of Self" (E. Menzel, 1984, p. 511). The implication that the subject has a sense of personal agency during recall ties in closely with Tulving's view of episodic memory, discussed later. Although there have been hundreds of impressive demonstrations of memory in nonhuman animals (e.g., food-storing birds: Balda & Kamil, 1992; Sherry, 1984; Shettleworth, 1995; nonprimate mammals: Olton, 1978; Vander Wall, 1991; chimpanzees: E. Menzel, 1973a; Tinklepaugh, 1932; other primates: Garber, 1989; Janson, 1998; C. Menzel, 1991; E. Menzel & Juno, 1985; review, Tomasello & Call, 1997; bees: R. Menzel et al., 1996; other animals: Gallistel, 1990; Vander Wall, 1990), few if any of them could be said to involve memory proper in James's sense (Donald, 1993; Roberts, 1996; Schacter & Tulving, 1994).

Another influential statement regarding the contrast between humans and nonhumans was Köhler's (1925) proposal that the time in which nonhumans live is far more limited, both in the past and in the future. Many current investigators have echoed or extended this theme (e.g., Bickerton, 1995; Bischof, 1978; Roberts, 2002; Suddendorf & Corballis, 1997). For example, Tulving (1983) distinguishes between memory of facts ("semantic memory") and memory of particular events that an individual has experienced personally ("episodic memory"). An organism might retain a fact about the environment (e.g., Object X is there) without possessing information that would enable it to reconstruct an event (e.g., Self saw Person Y put out Object X). Tulving (1984) acknowledges that there is much evidence that animals can rely on information from the past, but he questions whether animals can "mentally travel back in time to recollect and reminisce the way humans do" (p. 258). An important part of Tulving's concept is that humans can perform recall in different situations and in different forms; they have a well-developed ability to "experience again now, in a different situation and perhaps in a different form, happenings from the past, and know that the experience refers to an event that occurred in another time and in another place" (Tulving, 1983, p. 1). The part of Tulving's definition emphasizing the ability to perform recall in different ways and from different situations than the situation in which the event originally occurred is often overlooked in recent discussions of "episodic-like" memory in animals.

Tulving and Markowitsch (1998) go on to say:

> Episodic remembering (mental time travel) is accompanied by a special kind of "autonoetic" conscious awareness that is clearly different from the kind of conscious awareness ("noetic" awareness) that accompanies retrieval of declarative information. . . . A normal individual can distinguish between recollecting a personal experience and recalling an impersonal fact as readily as she can distinguish between, say, perceiving and imaging. . . . Many animals other than humans . . . possess well developed knowledge-of-the-world (declarative memory) systems, and are capable of acquiring vast amounts of flexibly expressible information. But there is no

evidence that they have the ability to autonoetically remember past events in the way that humans do. (p. 202)

To date, few if any studies of animal memory could be said to "prove" episodic memory as Tulving and Markowitsch (1998) fully define it for humans, to everyone's satisfaction. Shettleworth (1998, p. 238), Clayton, Griffiths, Emery, and Dickinson (2002), and several contributors to this volume argue in particular that it is nearly impossible to test for "conscious recollection" in nonverbal animals. Authors such as Tulving and Markowitsch (1998) and Suddendorf and Corballis (1997) definitely have a point when they say that when it comes to the topics of "memory proper" or "true episodic memory," most of animal memory research is equivocal. I disagree, however, with the opinion that animal researchers have made no essential progress on the above topics in the past 100 years, or that no progress will be likely in the future. Vast improvements in methods, concepts, and the amount and quality of data have been made since the time of Thorndike (1898) in the study of animal memory (Kawai & Matsuzawa, 2001), self-recognition (Gallup, 1970; E. Menzel, Savage-Rumbaugh, & Lawson, 1985), spatial cognition (Kuhlmeier, Boysen, & Mukobi, 1999; E. Menzel, 1973a; Tinklepaugh, 1932), and communication (Savage-Rumbaugh et al., 1993), and there is always more to learn regarding what is and what is not essential. Further improvements in methods in the study of memory seem likely. To take one example, a current limitation in the study of nonhuman memory is that there are almost no data on recall capabilities. Shettleworth (1998) points out:

> With humans, either *recognition* or *recall* of past input can be tested. That is, a person can be presented with a stimulus and asked "Have you experienced this before?" (recognition) or simply instructed to "Tell me what you remember" (recall). Performance on recognition tasks is typically better than on comparable recall tasks. . . . Most tests of animal memory are tests of recognition [rather than recall]. (p. 238, italics in original)

If recall in animals is currently a fuzzy, underresearched topic, then, by comparison, self-reflective, conscious recollection in animals is many times as fuzzy. If we have not achieved general agreement about the existence and form of recall capabilities in animals, then we are unlikely to be able to agree about self-reflective, conscious recollection. On the other hand, if we can identify clear signs of recall capabilities in some of the everyday activities of animals, and if we can develop methods to investigate these activities in detail, then we can make an indirect approach to topics that are more difficult and inferential. These new methods should address the following two questions: What are the specific differences and similarities between human and nonhuman memory? And what is it that animals actually do?

Determining which features nonhuman animals do actually retain about trial-unique events, and the extent to which their memory involves recall as opposed to recognition, should help to clarify the similarities and differences between animal and human memory systems (Gaffan, 1994; Hampton, 2001; Kawai & Matsuzawa, 2001; Olton, 1984; Parkinson, Murray, & Mishkin, 1988; Roberts, 1996; Schacter & Tulving, 1994; Squire, 1992; Tulving, 1984, p. 258). The features of an event that a nonhuman animal retains might, in principle, include objective, impersonal details, such as "what," "where," "when" (Clayton & Dickinson, 1998, 1999a, 1999b), "size," "numerousness" (Beran & Beran, 2004), "surroundings," and "mobility" (living versus nonliving). The animal also might, in principle, retain more personalized details, such as "who was involved" (C. Menzel, 1999; Schwartz, Colon, Sanchez, Rodriguez, & Evans, 2002; Schwartz & Evans, 2001) and "why," and possibly "emotional impact." Specific questions arise: How much information about an event does an animal retain in long-term memory (Mishkin, Suzuki, Gadian, & Vargha-Khadem, 1997)? How much of this information can the organism access and transmit from outside the situation in which the event originally occurred (C. Menzel, 1999)? Can the organism use indirect cues to access the information (Bayley & Squire, 2002)? I emphasize that research on recall memory in chimpanzees is at a preliminary stage, and it is likely that we have underestimated the upper limits of ability.

In the remainder of this chapter, I review several prior studies of chimpanzee memory, with a focus on research that has used variations on delayed-response methods. I then describe my ongoing studies of memory in symbol-competent chimpanzees (genus *Pan*). I will argue that at least one chimpanzee's memory is, to a significant extent, organized independently of stimulation from the immediate environment in question and constitutes recall as opposed to recognition. Finally, I return to the broad themes of this book.

REMEMBERING VERSUS RECOGNITION AND REPRODUCTION

Köhler (1925) made the following statement while discussing the limits of his experimental findings:

> though one can prove some effects of recognition and reproduction after considerable lapses of time—as is actually the case in anthropoids—this is not the same as "life for a longer space of time." A great many years spent with chimpanzees lead me to venture the opinion that, besides in the lack of speech, it is in the extremely narrow limits in *this* direction that the chief difference is to be found between anthropoids and even the most primitive human beings. (p. 267)

Less frequently cited is the fact that Köhler went on to describe instances of what he regarded as closer to real "remembering" (p. 278), as opposed to "the plain after-effects of past experience in present actions" (p. 277). Köhler noted, "where real remembering broadens the scope of those conditions, which influence the life of the animal, this real extension of the life surveyed impresses the observer considerably: and 'free,' 'enlightened' does the ape then look, compared with the 'narrowness of time' in which lower animals live" (p. 278). (Since Köhler's time, estimates of the capacities of other animals have been drastically revised too.)

Köhler's examples of "the plain after-effects of past experience in present actions" included the observation that the chimpanzees immediately recognized familiar people and familiar group members after absences of several months. Köhler's examples of "recognition and reproduction" also included the observation that "even after long lapses of time one finds the effect of an earlier learnt discrimination test as strong as though only a few days had elapsed" (p. 277). Köhler retested four chimpanzees on a variety of size and color discrimination problems, more than a year after the end of their earlier period of learning. The chimpanzees' choices were as accurate as they had been previously. Köhler commented, "For these achievements, there was certainly no necessity whatsoever for any image of the past. The familiar situation appears again immediately in the form of apprehension acquired in the learning period, and so brings about the same direction of choice behaviour" (p. 278).

Köhler's examples that, following Hunter's (1913) terminology, "involved something like real 'remembering,' rather than the reproduction of former behaviour in a like situation" (p. 278) included the following experiments with a male chimpanzee, Sultan. While Sultan watched, Köhler buried a pear in a sandy area, 1.4 meters outside Sultan's barred enclosure. Köhler carefully smoothed over the spot and the surrounding area, so that no trace remained of the hole. Sultan could not reach the pear directly; to obtain it, he had to reach out with a stick. At first, no stick was available. After about 30 minutes, Köhler moved a stick to within reach of Sultan's enclosure. When Sultan noticed the stick, he pulled it in, ran to the bars opposite the hidden pear, and scraped the sand away at the exact location until the pear appeared. The field of possible error was approximately 10 square meters. Several tests with delays up to 16.5 hours and additional chimpanzee subjects yielded similar results. Köhler concluded, "An extension of this test to longer periods, and, above all a closer analysis of the proceedings, are both very desirable" (p. 282).

In one such variation, four chimpanzee subjects of Yerkes and Yerkes (1928) were able to respond to food, which they had seen buried in the ground, after a delay of 48 hours. In another extension, Tinklepaugh (1932) examined whether chimpanzees, macaques, human adults, and children could respond to a series of locations in which they had seen objects hidden by another agent. He arranged up to 16 pairs of containers in a circle 20 feet in diameter. The members of each pair of containers were as close to identical as possible, with the exception of one pair, but there were clear differences between the pairs. A subject was brought into the test room and made to sit on a stool in the center of the circle. The experimenter then went to each pair of containers and, while the subject was watching, placed a piece of banana (or some other type of lure for the humans) under a randomly selected member of each pair of containers. The nonhuman subjects were tested on a leash, and had to make their choices in a sequence determined by the experimenter. The subject was permitted to go around the circle to each pair and make a choice of one of the containers, taking the lure if it was correct. The subject had to return to the stool between each choice, regardless of whether the choice was correct or incorrect. The chimpanzees (a female approximately 8 years old and a male approximately 6 years old) were first tested with 8 pairs of containers (20 trials), and then the number was increased to 12 (11 trials) and 16 (18 trials).

Results were that with 8 pairs of containers, the two chimpanzees chose the correct member of the pair on 85% and 90% of pairs, respectively. With 16 pairs, the chimpanzees chose the correct member of the pair on 79% and 78% of pairs, respectively. The chimpanzees did as well as the average of five adult humans, who were run on a single trial with 16 pairs of containers; the adults' scores ranged from 44% to 100% (mean 75%). The four children, aged 7 to 9 years, had scores from 44% to 69% (mean 54%). The monkeys' choices were only slightly better than chance with 8 pairs of containers but were well above chance with 3 pairs (77% and 73% correct, respectively).

Control procedures excluded the possibility that the chimpanzees were simply detecting the food by odor. Other experimental variations showed that the chimpanzees were responding on the basis of spatial position rather than by the visual features of the containers. The focus of Tinklepaugh's (1932) study was on the spatial and visual cues used by the chimpanzees to locate individual hidden foods, rather than on how the chimpanzees organized a food-harvesting route. That is, it showed that chimpanzees could remember a large number of food locations in a given trial but left largely unanswered the question of whether the chimpanzees remembered the spatial relationships among these locations.

E. Menzel (reviews, 1978, 1984) conducted an extensive series of studies of chimpanzee memory and communication in a 1-acre field. In one study (E. Menzel, 1973a), one chimpanzee from a group of six juveniles was carried around the experimental field and shown a piece of fruit in each of 18 randomly selected sectors of the field. Unlike Tinklepaugh's study, each trial used a different set of test locations. During the cue-giving process, the chimpanzee was not allowed to do anything other than cling to his carrier and watch the hiding of the food. Thus, locomotor practice and primary reinforcement were eliminated during the cue-giving phase of a trial. The field included areas of relatively tall grass, trees, irregularities (small hills), and other visual barriers, and not all of the 18 food locations were visible to the chimpanzee from a single vantage point. After being shown the food, the experimenters returned the chimpanzee to the group. The experimenters then ascended an observation tower and within 2 minutes released the group into the field. The question was how the chimpanzee organized his route to harvest the 18 hidden food items. Four different chimpanzees were used as test animals.

Results were that the chimpanzee that had been shown the food obtained most of the hidden items, using a highly efficient route. In 16 trials, the informed (test) chimpanzee found 200 of 288 hidden foods (mean 12.5 per trial), and the five control animals that had not been shown the food found a total of 17 (0.21 per animal per trial). Usually, the test animal ran in a direct line to the exact tree stump, clump of grass, or hole in the ground where a piece of hidden food lay, grabbed and ate the food, and then ran directly to the next location, no matter how far away or obscured by visual barriers that location was. Control animals obtained food mainly by searching near the test animal or by begging from him. The test animal rarely searched the ground manually farther than 2 meters from a food pile, whereas controls did so on innumerable occasions. The itinerary that the test animal used during the recovery of food was only 64% as long as the mean of all possible $N!$ itineraries on that trial and bore no relation to the route along which the chimpanzee had been carried during cue giving. The test animals clearly took into account more than one or two food locations at a time, because on any given choice they not only generally went to one of the closer locations of all those that still contained food, but also they usually went from the outset of a trial toward larger rather than smaller clusters.

Specifically, in a further experiment, they typically went toward whichever half of the field contained three food locations versus two food locations. In other tests, the experimenters hid a piece of preferred food (fruit) in nine locations and a piece of nonpreferred food (vegetable) in nine other locations. The informed chimpanzee went first to the fruit locations and rarely reinspected a location that he had already emptied. Relevant to the topic of recall discussed earlier is that on several trials, a seeming "example of sudden recall occurred while an animal was apparently asleep. After having eaten many pieces of food and lain supine with his eyes closed for up to 30 minutes, the test animal suddenly jumped to his feet and ran 10 to 30 m straight to a hidden piece of food" (E. Menzel, 1973a, p. 944).

Other experiments in the series (E. Menzel, 1973b) showed that a knowledgeable chimpanzee could retain and transmit information to group members about object quality (fruit versus vegetable), the relative goodness or badness of object (food versus snake), quantity of food, and location. The group of chimpanzees also searched very differently after an operationally designated leader had been shown a real snake than they did after the leader had been shown a piece of food that was later removed. Not only would they use a stick to probe the last location where the snake had been seen, but they would also broaden the area searched, as if taking into account the potential of the snake for movement. In contrast, if the leader had been shown food, they restricted their search to the vicinity of the original location. These studies showed not only that chimpanzees could remember many food locations in a given trial, but also that they remembered the spatial relationships among the locations (Gallistel, 1990; E. Menzel, 1973a). The studies also demonstrated transmission of information about the nature and location of hidden objects from one chimpanzee to another at an unexpectedly high level of efficiency (E. Menzel, 1973b).

MEMORY IN SYMBOL-COMPETENT CHIMPANZEES

An extension of these delayed-response methods for studying memory in nonhumans is to examine which features of events a subject conveys to other beings through behavior or a symbol system (Herman & Forestell, 1985; E. Menzel, 1973b; Savage-Rumbaugh, McDonald, Sevcik, Hopkins, & Rubert, 1986; Tulving, 1984, p. 224). Symbol-competent chimpanzees provide a powerful method for investigating the "time in which the chimpanzee lives" and the apes' memory for events. Symbol-competent apes at Georgia State University's Language Research Center have learned lexigrams, arbitrary geometrical forms that refer to types of food and other objects. These animals have been immersed in the visual symbol system and exposed to spoken English since an early age. As a result of their rearing history, the apes can comprehend lexigrams and can use lexigrams in a productive manner, and some of them can understand spoken English at approximately the level of a very young child (Savage-Rumbaugh et al., 1993). The symbol system allows one to ask questions regarding memory that previously had not been asked by Köhler or other researchers; it is possible to obtain more information from the apes. Symbol-competent apes potentially can convey the specific events and environmental features they have seen, through use of the lexigram system. They can be tested outside the spatial and temporal contexts in which they encountered the events. Some of the Language Research Center apes can use lexigrams outside the context in which the objects were originally encountered (Savage-Rumbaugh et al., 1986, 1993; Savage-Rumbaugh, Pate, Lawson, Smith, & Rosenbaum, 1983).

Announcement of Travel Destinations in a Twenty-Hectare Forest

Savage-Rumbaugh et al. (1986) tested a 3-year-old bonobo, or pygmy chimpanzee (*Pan paniscus*), Kanzi, in a heavily wooded 20 hectare area. The area included 5.6 kilometers of trails. Kanzi had traveled with human companions in the forest daily and had learned the locations of all 17 of the food stations in the forest. Kanzi's rearing history is reported in Savage-Rumbaugh, Rumbaugh, and McDonald (1985) and Savage-Rumbaugh et al. (1986). Each station had a different food type present. Four months after food was first placed in the forest, a caregiver who had not previously entered the forest accompanied Kanzi and allowed him to lead the way from place to place. The caregiver did not know the location of any of the foods or the locations of any of the trails. At each stopping point, the person presented Kanzi with an array of 6 to 10 alternatives. The alternatives consisted of photographs and lexigrams representing food and locations. Kanzi made his selection from this array. When Kanzi was at a stopping point, he used photographs on five occasions, lexigrams on seven occasions, and both photographs and lexigrams on three occasions to indicate his next destination, with 100% accuracy. After touching a photograph or lexigram, Kanzi proceeded to guide the person to the location of the food he had selected, sometimes traveling over 30 minutes to reach the food site. Distances between the successive food sites ranged up to 600 meters. To reach his destination, Kanzi had to choose a direction at up to seven different trail crossings. Kanzi used the smallest possible number of turns and the shortest possible route along the trail on all but one occasion (Savage-Rumbaugh et al., 1986). E. Menzel (1984, p. 520) noted, "From the standpoint of 'memory proper,' it would be most interesting to see if [Kanzi] can also indicate where he has been and what he has done after such an outing."

Use of Road Signs in a Twenty-Hectare Forest

C. Menzel, Savage-Rumbaugh, and Menzel (2002) used Kanzi's lexigram competence as a tool to study his spatial memory organization when he was 4 years old. The focus of the study was on Kanzi as a receiver rather than a sender of information. In the first experiment, we showed Kanzi a "road sign" just outside his indoor sleeping area. The sign indicated, by means of lexigrams, the location where food was hidden. Only 2 of the 15 locations were visible from the sign. Distances ranged up to 170 meters from the sign. In 99 of 127 test trials, Kanzi went to the designated location on his first move. In a second experiment, we presented Kanzi with the road sign at varied points in the forest rather than at the original fixed place. In these trials, the goal was a preferred toy. Kanzi's human companions were never informed about the location of the goal, and distances ranged up to 650 meters. In all 12 trials, Kanzi led his companions to the designated location using an efficient path. In sum, Kanzi appeared to be able to move, based on the information provided by a lexigram, from almost any arbitrarily designated starting location in his 20-hectare environment to any one of the numerous goal locations.

UNPROMPTED RECALL AND REPORTING OF HIDDEN OBJECTS BY A COMMON CHIMPANZEE

Next I describe in some detail my first study (C. Menzel, 1999) on memory in a lexigram-competent female common chimpanzee (*Pan troglodytes*) called Panzee. The aim of this study was to identify some of the types of information that Panzee could recall and convey about hidden objects. Details of the procedure are given in C. Menzel (1999). In brief, Panzee was 11 years old at the outset of the experiment, and she had already learned more than 120 lexigrams (Beran, Savage-Rumbaugh, Brakke, Kelley, & Rumbaugh, 1998). Panzee had been reared by Sue Savage-Rumbaugh, Karen Brakke, and their associates; she had been given intensive early exposure to spoken English and to lexigrams that referred to foods, tools, actions, and locations in the 20-hectare forest at the Language Research Center. Panzee was exposed to lexigrams in the everyday contexts of food preparation, travel, and play, rather than taught lexigrams through discrete trial training. That is, her lexigram acquisition appeared to be based on observational learning (Brakke & Savage-Rumbaugh, 1995, 1996; cf. Savage-Rumbaugh et al., 1993). There had been no previous attempt to determine Panzee's retention time beyond about 40 seconds for visual stimuli or locations. Panzee had not been presented with objects outside her outdoor enclosure that she could later name or request indoors. Recruitment of people to the outdoor enclosure and inducing them to search the terrain was never a part of her experimental history. This is not to claim, however, that she brought no relevant experience to the experimental situation. For example, Panzee had used gestures and lexigrams in routine interactions with caregivers to request movement between cages, activities (e.g., chasing, grooming, drawing, television), foods, and other objects (e.g., blanket, clay). As a juvenile, Panzee also had played the game of hide-and-seek with caregivers, and it was in the context of searching for a hidden person that she originally used the hiding gesture described later.

During this experiment (C. Menzel, 1999), Panzee was housed in the Lanson building, an indoor-outdoor facility. When Panzee was indoors, she could not see the outdoor cage or the forest. The outdoor cage was bordered by forest, and an area of forest adjacent to the cage, measuring about 160 square meters, served as a test area for the introduction of objects. Panzee had not entered this forest for at least 6 years prior to this study. The indoor and the outdoor cage each contained a keyboard, each of which displayed 256 lexigrams. To obtain something from outside the outdoor cage in this study, Panzee had to recruit the assistance of a person and in effect tell them where to go. Panzee was not required also to tell people what type of object to look for. If she did provide this information, it would be as a result of her own initiative or due to past experience.

Design and Procedure

This initial experiment (C. Menzel, 1999) consisted of 34 trial-unique tests, each consisting of a cue-giving phase, a delay phase, and a response phase. The test objects were 26 food types and 7 types of non-food objects. During cue giving, the experimenter stood outside Panzee's outdoor enclosure, held up an object while Panzee was watching, then walked to a predetermined hiding place in the forest and placed the object on the ground. Each trial used a different location, and distances from the enclosure to the object ranged up to 8 meters. On 32 of the 34 trials, the experimenter placed the object under natural cover, so that the object was concealed from view, and then smoothed over the area. On these 32 trials, the object was buried under leaf litter and completely concealed from view, not simply placed behind a bush. On the remaining 2 trials the object was not concealed, and Panzee could see it from her outdoor cage. After placing the object, the experimenter left the area, and this began the delay phase of the trial. On 10 trials, the experimenter imposed an overnight delay between the cue-giving phase and the response phase by showing Panzee the object outdoors after all caretakers had left for the day. Panzee did not have a chance to interact with a person until the next morning. On the remaining 24 trials, Panzee had an opportunity to interact with a person indoors on the same day, typically within a few minutes after seeing the object. On any given opportunity, Panzee might or might not choose to recruit the assistance of the person to recover the hidden object. The delay phase lasted until Panzee initiated recruitment of a person (details below). Thus, Panzee determined the exact time of recruitment and the total length of delay.

In the response phase of a trial, Panzee interacted with a person inside the Lanson building. This person did not know what had gone on outside the Lanson building and did not know what the object was nor where it was located. Three different people served as "uninformed persons" during the study. On at least 24 of the 34 trials, the person did not even know in advance that a trial had been set up. Once a person was involved in the study, he or she knew that potentially a trial could happen but did not know when. Experimental trials were interspersed with nontest days on which no object was presented, over a total study period of 268 days.

The uninformed person went about his or her routine caregiving activities and let Panzee initiate any interactions regarding what had gone on outside the Lanson building. During the study period, persons made detailed notes regarding any occasion on which Panzee recruited them outdoors, regardless of whether they thought a test actually was being conducted. The person recorded on each such occasion all lexigrams that Panzee touched on the indoor and outdoor keyboards, Panzee's gestures, and her vocalizations. Gestures recorded included pointing outdoors with an extended arm, beckoning with a sweeping movement of her hand, and covering her eyes with the palm of her hand (a gesture previously associated with the game of hide and seek with caregivers). Spatial data recorded during each trial included the location at which Panzee sat when she pointed manually out of the outdoor enclosure (figure 8.1) and each location in the woods that the uninformed person inspected manually. If Panzee guided the uninformed person to a hidden food item, then the person carried the food indoors and offered it to Panzee, regardless of whether Panzee had touched the lexigram corresponding to the food.

Figure 8.1 After touching the lexigram on her keyboard (visible in background) corresponding to the type of object hidden, Panzee points toward the location of the object. See color insert. Photo by Charles R. Menzel.

Results

The uninformed persons found all 34 objects that were used in these tests as the result of Panzee's behavior. False positives occurred on only 3 of the 268 days of the experiment. That is, Panzee almost never recruited the uninformed person and caused him or her to search when there was no test object in the woods. When a test object was present outdoors, Panzee never pointed to a location that had contained an object on a previous trial. In fact, in 34 recruitment sequences with an object present in the woods, Panzee never pointed in an incorrect direction. In total, there were 57 days on which an object was present. Panzee recruited a person and pointed toward a single, specific location on 34 of these 57 days and did not recruit a person on the remaining 23 days. (Panzee did not fail to report the objects that were hidden on these 23 remaining days; she simply did not always recruit a person to the object at her first opportunity. She might wait a day or more.) In contrast, there were 211 nontest days on which no object was present in the woods, and Panzee recruited a person and pointed toward a specific location on just 3 of these 211 days (C. Menzel, 1999).

From Trial 1, Panzee was highly effective in attracting the uninformed person's attention, in conveying the type of item hidden, and in directing the person to the location of the hidden item. A summary account of how the uninformed persons described Panzee's behavior is as follows (C. Menzel, 1999). Panzee gained the person's attention by vocalization, by gesturing toward the indoor keyboard, or by moving to the keyboard when the person happened to come near her cage. She held her index finger on a lexigram until the person came over and acknowledged her lexigram use verbally. Panzee then covered her eyes with her hand, held her arm extended in the direction of the tunnel leading outdoors, moved to the tunnel, and went outdoors. If the person did not follow, then Panzee came back inside, again gestured "hide," beckoned, and pointed outdoors.

Once both Panzee and the person were outdoors, Panzee beckoned manually and moved to the edge of the enclosure, across from the hidden object. She sat facing the object and extended her index finger through the cage wire in the direction of the object. She prompted the person to search the terrain by gesturing "hide," by pointing manually toward the object location with her index finger extended (figure 8.1), by giving low vocalizations, and by staring toward the location, with interspersed looks toward the person. She might leave her position, walk to the outdoor keyboard several meters away, touch a lexigram, and then return to her original position and resume pointing. During interactions outdoors, the person was outside the enclosure; Panzee was inside the enclosure and did not have physical access to the object. Because of the orientation of Panzee's body and gaze and the persistence of her pointing in a given direction, the person restricted most of his or her searching to within 1 meter of a straight line between Panzee and the object location and found the object within a few minutes, typically within 1 minute. The person determined the distance to the object, in part, simply by following the direction of Panzee's gaze and responding to her relative degree of excitement. Panzee kept pointing, showed intensified vocalization, shook her arm, and bobbed her head or body as the person got closer to the site. Once the person found the object, Panzee stopped pointing outside the enclosure and stopped gesturing "hide."

Lexigrams Used During Recruitment

The lexigrams that Panzee touched when she recruited a person typically corresponded to the type of object she had seen (table 8.1, table 8.2). Considering just the 33 lexigrams corresponding to the 33 types of objects used in the experiment to be the relevant available choices, then 84% of Panzee's 76 lexigram touches corresponded to the specific type of experimental object presented, rather than to one of the other 32 types of experimental objects (diagonal in table 8.2). It is obvious that the observed frequency of correct lexigram touches far exceeded the frequency expected by chance. Furthermore, when Panzee recruited a person, she touched lexigrams that she rarely touched under routine conditions. On 25 of 34 trials, the lexigram corresponding to the object hidden was one that accounted for 1% or less of Panzee's routine lexigram use. Panzee used the correct lexigram on 21 of these 25 trials, and on the 4 remaining trials Panzee relied effectively on gesture (C. Menzel, 1999).

Additional findings of interest were as follows. First, Panzee indicated specific nonfood objects (snake, balloon, paper) as well as food types. Second, the method did not involve any deliberate training. Even on Trial 1, Panzee used lexigrams, the gesture "hide," arm pointing, and manual pointing toward the object to recruit and direct the person. Third, Panzee indicated object types after overnight delays; for example, on Trial 34 she touched the lexigram corresponding to the object without having seen the outdoor area in 15 hours. I have replicated this specific finding in more than 30 additional trials. Fourth, Panzee touched the lexigram *stick* on 14 of the 34 occasions on which she recruited a person to a test object. The test objects in most of the 34 trials were hidden under pine needles and sticks. Even on the first trial (Trial 3) on which Panzee touched *stick*, the person inferred correctly that "bananas were hidden under sticks" before finding the object location. Finally, on occasion Panzee did not recruit a person until 2 hours or more had passed, even when the object was

Table 8.1 Lexigrams Panzee Touched in the Context of Recruiting a Person as a Function of Which Object Panzee Had Been Shown Outdoors

| | | | Lexigrams Panzee Used in Context of Gesturing to Recruit Uninformed Person | |
| | | Delay | | |
Trial	Object Shown	(hours)	Indoor Keyboard	Outdoor Keyboard
1	Kiwi	0.17	grape, kiwi	—
2	Monster mask[b]	0.18	monster mask	—
3	Banana	3.77	stick, banana, stick	banana, banana
4	Grapes[a]	0.15	grape	grape, grape, grape, grape
5	Apple	3.33	hide, apple	apple
6	Coke[b]	1.17	Coke	Coke
7	Pineapple	0.85	pineapple	—
8	Blanket[a]	2.52	—	—
9	Orange drink (can)[b]	16.20	Coke	orange drink, peach, Coke
10	Strawberries[b]	0.88	strawberry	—
11	Snake[b]	1.62	snake	snake
12	String rope[b,c]	0.22	surprise, surprise	Coke, Coke, string rope, Coke, stick, string rope
13	Blueberries[b]	0.07	blueberries	blueberries
14	Melon[b,d]	0.22	orange	melon, melon
15	Raisins[a]	0.03	raisin	—
16	Peanuts and balloon[b]	0.17	peanut	peanut, peanut, hide, balloon
17	M&M candies[a]	15.62	M&M, M&M	M&M, M&M
18	Popsicle[b]	16.35	surprise, hide, hide, hide, hide, surprise, hide	hide, hide, hide, stick, stick
19	Pear	19.12	stick, hide, hide, stick, stick, stick	stick, hide, stick, stick
20	Orange	19.07	orange (×4); melon, orange	orange
21	Paper[a] and drawing pen[b]	90.17	—	hide (×4); stick, hide, stick, hide, hide, hide, paper
22	Kiwi	98.85	—	hide, stick, hide, stick, stick, stick, hide, kiwi, kiwi

(continued)

Table 8.1 Continued

Trial	Object Shown	Delay (hours)	Lexigrams Panzee Used in Context of Gesturing to Recruit Uninformed Person	
			Indoor Keyboard	Outdoor Keyboard
23	Cherries[b]	0.15	*stick, cherries, cherries*	*cherries*
24	Peaches[a]	90.80	*hide*	*peach, hide*
25	Jelly[b]	15.17	*jelly, stick*	*jelly*
26	Cereal[b]	304.40	*stick, stick*	*peach, peanut, pine-apple*
27	Yogurt[a]	22.50	*stick*	*yogurt*
28	Egg[a]	0.46	*stick, egg*	*stick, stick*
29	Jell-O gelatin[b]	22.25	—	*Jell-O*
30	Bread	0.88	*bread*	*bread*
31	Sugar[b]	19.97	*stick, stick, stick*	*stick, stick*
32	Juice[a]	0.05	*juice, juice*	*juice, juice*
33	Raisins[a]	0.35	*stick, stick*	*raisin*
34	Pear	15.75	*stick, stick, pear*	*pear, pear, pear, pear*

Note. Lexigrams are those that Panzee touched prior to the person finding the object. Dashes indicate that Panzee did not touch any lexigrams on the keyboard in question. Delay = time elapsed from Panzee seeing the object until she began to recruit the uninformed person.
[a]Lexigram accounted for 1% or less of Panzee's total lexigram touches in the 12-day baseline sample.
[b]Lexigram rarely used by Panzee under routine conditions and never touched in the 12-day baseline sample. Panzee had not seen strawberries, string rope, blueberries, melon, balloon, or cherries in more than 4 months.
[c]When Panzee was offered the string rope, she ignored it and again touched *Coke* on the keyboard; the person interpreted this as a request for Coke.
[d]Panzee traditionally used *orange, melon* to refer to melon.
Copyright @ 1999 by the American Psychological Association. Reprinted with permission.

a highly preferred type of food; the longest delay with correct report-ing of object type exceeded 90 hours (table 8.1).

At least five aspects of Panzee's performance suggested that her memory involved a fairly rich information retrieval process (C. Men-zel, 1999). First, Panzee, rather than the experimenters, determined the exact time of reporting, and she reported items after extended delays. Second, Panzee selected lexigrams from the whole keyboard of 256 lexigrams, rather than from a small set of alternatives as in traditional primate matching-to-sample tasks. Third, she selected the lexigrams indoors, without an immediate view of the area in which the object was hidden. Fourth, she did not simply touch lexigrams;

she pointed toward the outdoor area from the vicinity of the indoor keyboard, and she persisted in the interaction using a variety of response outputs until the person found the object outdoors. Fifth, she used the *stick* lexigram when recruiting people, and many of the test objects were covered with leaves and sticks. The findings strongly suggest that Panzee could recall which one of several dozen types of objects she had been shown from a distance (and had not been allowed to navigate to or to touch) for overnight periods of at least 16 hours.

Sample Recruitment

The map in figure 8.2 shows an example of a recruitment by Panzee. Panzee watched from Location 1 in her outdoor enclosure as an experimenter hid M&M candies, a prized food, in the woods at the point marked X. The experimenter then left the scene. After about 15 minutes, Panzee moved to her keyboard indoors (Location 2). She faced toward John Kelley (J.K.), her favorite caregiver. She held her finger on the M&M lexigram and vocalized; this attracted J.K.'s attention. J.K. did not know the type or location of the object. Panzee continued to hold her finger on the M&M lexigram until J.K. approached and acknowledged her lexigram use verbally. At that time, Panzee moved to Location 3 and extended her left arm toward the tunnel, looking back toward J.K., who agreed to go outside and search for M&Ms. Panzee went outside. Panzee held her finger on the M&M lexigram on her outdoor keyboard (Location 4) when J.K. arrived in the woods. When J.K. acknowledged her lexigram use verbally, Panzee moved to Location 5 and sat and directed J.K. into the woods to the location of the hidden M&Ms by pointing with her right hand and vocalizing. J.K. determined the distance to the object, in part, by following the direction of Panzee's gaze and by responding to her relative degree of excitement. Panzee kept pointing and vocalized more intensely as J.K. got closer to the site. Panzee also raised her hand higher to send J.K. further out. After J.K. found the M&Ms, he brought them indoors and gave them to Panzee. Figure 8.1 shows a representative view of Panzee directing J.K.

Additional Tests of Recall With Panzee

I have replicated these findings in more than 14 additional experiments, including variations in type of item hidden, the number of items hidden, the modality of cue giving (direct view versus video representation), the modality of recruitment (direct pointing versus reporting on a video representation), and the outcome of recruitment (whether or not the item was removed and given to Panzee). I now briefly describe some of the main variations. I do not give all the details; these are in preparation for publication.

Table 8.2 Lexigrams Panzee Touched in the Context of Recruiting a Person as a Function of Which Objects Panzee Had Been Shown Outdoors

| | | Lexigrams Panzee Touched | | | | | | | | | | | | | | |
Trial	Objects Shown	KI	MA	BA	GR	AP	CO	PI	BK	OD	ST	SN	SR	BB	ME	RA	PN
1	Kiwi	1	—	—	1	—	—	—	—	—	—	—	—	—	—	—	—
2	Monster mask	—	1	—	—	—	—	—	—	—	—	—	—	—	—	—	—
3	Banana	—	—	3	—	—	—	—	—	—	—	—	—	—	—	—	—
4	Grapes	—	—	—	5	—	—	—	—	—	—	—	—	—	—	—	—
5	Apple	—	—	—	—	2	—	—	—	—	—	—	—	—	—	—	—
6	Coke	—	—	—	—	—	2	—	—	—	—	—	—	—	—	—	—
7	Pineapple	—	—	—	—	—	—	1	—	—	—	—	—	—	—	—	—
8	Blanket	—	—	—	—	—	—	—	—	—	—	—	—	—	—	—	—
9	Orange drink	—	—	—	—	—	2	—	—	1	—	—	—	—	—	—	—
10	Strawberries	—	—	—	—	—	—	—	—	—	1	—	—	—	—	—	—
11	Snake	—	—	—	—	—	—	—	—	—	—	2	—	—	—	—	—
12	String rope	—	—	—	—	—	3	—	—	—	—	—	2	—	—	—	—
13	Blueberries	—	—	—	—	—	—	—	—	—	—	—	—	2	—	—	—
14	Melon	—	—	—	—	—	—	—	—	—	—	—	—	—	2	—	—
15	Raisins	—	—	—	—	—	—	—	—	—	—	—	—	—	—	1	—
16[a]	Peanuts	—	—	—	—	—	—	—	—	—	—	—	—	—	—	—	3
	and balloon	—	—	—	—	—	—	—	—	—	—	—	—	—	—	—	—
17	M&M candy	—	—	—	—	—	—	—	—	—	—	—	—	—	—	—	—
18	Popsicle	—	—	—	—	—	—	—	—	—	—	—	—	—	—	—	—
19	Pear	—	—	—	—	—	—	—	—	—	—	—	—	—	—	—	—
20	Orange	—	—	—	—	—	—	—	—	—	—	—	—	—	1	—	—
21[a]	Paper	—	—	—	—	—	—	—	—	—	—	—	—	—	—	—	—
	and draw pen	—	—	—	—	—	—	—	—	—	—	—	—	—	—	—	—
22[b]	Kiwi	—	—	—	—	—	—	—	—	—	—	—	—	—	—	—	—
23	Cherries	—	—	—	—	—	—	—	—	—	—	—	—	—	—	—	—
24	Peach	—	—	—	—	—	—	—	—	—	—	—	—	—	—	—	—
25	Jelly	—	—	—	—	—	—	—	—	—	—	—	—	—	—	—	—
26	Cereal	—	—	—	—	—	—	1	—	—	—	—	—	—	—	—	1
27	Yogurt	—	—	—	—	—	—	—	—	—	—	—	—	—	—	—	—
28	Egg	—	—	—	—	—	—	—	—	—	—	—	—	—	—	—	—
29	Jell-O gelatin	—	—	—	—	—	—	—	—	—	—	—	—	—	—	—	—
30	Bread	—	—	—	—	—	—	—	—	—	—	—	—	—	—	—	—
31	Sugar	—	—	—	—	—	—	—	—	—	—	—	—	—	—	—	—
32	Juice	—	—	—	—	—	—	—	—	—	—	—	—	—	—	—	—
33[b]	Raisins	—	—	—	—	—	—	—	—	—	—	—	—	—	—	—	—
34[b]	Pear	—	—	—	—	—	—	—	—	—	—	—	—	—	—	—	—

Note. Scores are frequencies of Panzee's lexigram touches within the trial. The dashes represent frequency scores of zero. The two-letter abbreviations correspond to the objects shown.
[a]Panzee was shown two objects per trial; the experimenter placed the two objects together in the same location.
[b]Panzee was tested with object for the second time.
Based on table 2, in C. Menzel (1999). Copyright @ 1999 by the American Psychological Association. Adapted with permission.

Lexigrams Panzee Touched

BL	MM	PS	PR	OR	PP	DP	KI	CH	PC	JE	CE	YO	EG	JO	NR	SU	JU	RA	PR
—	—	—	—	—	—	—	—	—	—	—	—	—	—	—	—	—	—	—	—
—	—	—	—	—	—	—	—	—	—	—	—	—	—	—	—	—	—	—	—
—	—	—	—	—	—	—	—	—	—	—	—	—	—	—	—	—	—	—	—
—	—	—	—	—	—	—	—	—	—	—	—	—	—	—	—	—	—	—	—
—	—	—	—	—	—	—	—	—	—	—	—	—	—	—	—	—	—	—	—
—	—	—	—	—	—	—	—	—	—	—	—	—	—	—	—	—	—	—	—
—	—	—	—	—	—	—	—	—	—	—	—	—	—	—	—	—	—	—	—
—	—	—	—	—	—	—	—	—	—	—	—	—	—	—	—	—	—	—	—
—	—	—	—	—	—	—	—	—	—	—	—	—	—	—	—	—	—	—	—
—	—	—	—	—	—	—	—	—	—	—	—	—	—	—	—	—	—	—	—
—	—	—	—	—	—	—	—	1	—	—	—	—	—	—	—	—	—	—	—
—	—	—	—	—	—	—	—	—	—	—	—	—	—	—	—	—	—	—	—
—	—	—	—	—	—	—	—	—	—	—	—	—	—	—	—	—	—	—	—
—	—	—	—	—	—	—	—	—	—	—	—	—	—	—	—	—	—	—	—
—	—	—	—	—	—	—	—	—	—	—	—	—	—	—	—	—	—	—	—
—	—	—	—	—	—	—	—	—	—	—	—	—	—	—	—	—	—	—	—
—	—	—	—	—	—	—	—	—	—	—	—	—	—	—	—	—	—	—	—
—	—	—	—	1	—	—	—	—	—	—	—	—	—	—	—	—	—	—	—
—	—	—	—	—	—	—	—	—	—	—	—	—	—	—	—	—	—	—	—
—	—	—	—	—	—	—	—	—	—	—	—	—	—	—	—	—	—	—	—
—	—	—	—	—	—	—	—	—	—	—	—	—	—	—	—	—	—	—	—
1	—	—	—	—	—	—	—	—	—	—	—	—	—	—	—	—	—	—	—
—	4	—	—	—	—	—	—	—	—	—	—	—	—	—	—	—	—	—	—
—	—	—	—	—	—	—	—	—	—	—	—	—	—	—	—	—	—	—	—
—	—	—	—	—	—	—	—	—	—	—	—	—	—	—	—	—	—	—	—
—	—	—	—	—	—	—	—	—	—	—	—	—	—	—	—	—	—	—	—
—	—	—	—	6	—	—	—	—	—	—	—	—	—	—	—	—	—	—	—
—	—	—	—	—	1	—	—	—	—	—	—	—	—	—	—	—	—	—	—
—	—	—	—	—	—	—	—	—	—	—	—	—	—	—	—	—	—	—	—
—	—	—	—	—	—	—	—	—	—	—	—	—	—	—	—	—	—	—	—
—	—	—	—	—	—	—	2	—	—	—	—	—	—	—	—	—	—	—	—
—	—	—	—	—	—	—	—	—	—	—	—	—	—	—	—	—	—	—	—
—	—	—	—	—	—	—	—	3	—	—	—	—	—	—	—	—	—	—	—
—	—	—	—	—	—	—	—	—	1	—	—	—	—	—	—	—	—	—	—
—	—	—	—	—	—	—	—	—	—	2	—	—	—	—	—	—	—	—	—
—	—	—	—	—	—	—	—	—	—	—	1	—	—	—	—	—	—	—	—
—	—	—	—	—	—	—	—	—	—	—	—	—	—	—	—	—	—	—	—
—	—	—	—	—	—	—	—	—	—	—	—	1	—	—	—	—	—	—	—
—	—	—	—	—	—	—	—	—	—	—	—	—	1	—	—	—	—	—	—
—	—	—	—	—	—	—	—	—	—	—	—	—	—	—	—	—	—	—	—
—	—	—	—	—	—	—	—	—	—	—	—	—	—	1	—	—	—	—	—
—	—	—	—	—	—	—	—	—	—	—	—	—	—	—	—	—	—	—	—
—	—	—	—	—	—	—	—	—	—	—	—	—	—	—	2	—	—	—	—
—	—	—	—	—	—	—	—	—	—	—	—	—	—	—	—	—	—	—	—
—	—	—	—	—	—	—	—	—	—	—	—	—	—	—	—	—	4	—	—
—	—	—	—	—	—	—	—	—	—	—	—	—	—	—	—	—	—	1	—
—	—	—	—	—	—	—	—	—	—	—	—	—	—	—	—	—	—	—	5

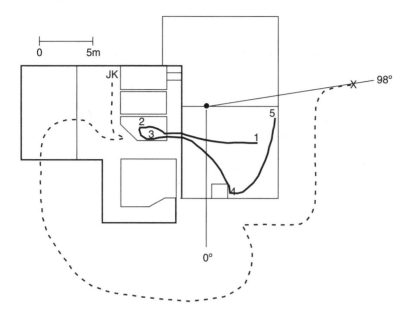

Figure 8.2 Map of Panzee's recruitment of her favorite caregiver (J.K.) to M&M candies (X) in the woods. 1 = Panzee's location during cue giving. 2 = Her position at indoor keyboard. 3 = Her position while arm pointing toward outdoor enclosure. 4 = Her position at outdoor keyboard. 5 = Her position while pointing toward the hidden M&M's. Dark line is Panzee's approximate path of travel; dotted line is J.K.'s path. The outer box around the figure is imaginary; the woods extend a large distance in all directions. Vertical line to 0 degrees = invisible west-oriented vector used as reference for computing angle to the M&M's (shown by invisible line to 98 degrees). Across 54 sample trials in which Panzee had a direct view of an object being hidden in the woods, the Pearson r between the "angle of the hidden object" and the "angle of the first location that the person searched, as a result of Panzee's pointing" was 0.99.

Use of Indirect Cues of Object Type   Panzee retained higher order, indirect signs of the type of object hidden. If she saw an experimenter hide an opaque container in the forest with a lexigram on it (corresponding to the type of food inside the container), she reliably retained the specific type of food for one or more days. Similarly, if the experimenter hid an opaque container in the forest and told Panzee in English the type of food that was inside the container, Panzee retained the type of food for at least 15 minutes (Panzee understands approximately 150 spoken English words; Beran et al., 1998). Retention of auditory cues of object type beyond even 60 seconds is considered exceptional for chimpanzees (Hashiya & Kojima, 2001a, 2001b).

Use of Televised Cues   Panzee used a video representation of the forest as a guide to locating objects in the forest. If Panzee was shown a brief videotape of a food-hiding event that had been filmed in the forest behind her enclosure, she reliably recruited an uninformed person and directed him or her to the hidden food on the next day. Panzee performed very accurately in a series of more than 30 trials, including Trial 1. She also typically reported the type of item she had seen on the cue tape. Each trial used a different location. On most of the trials, Panzee was confined indoors overnight immediately after she viewed the cue tape, and thus she did not have an opportunity to see the forest for more than 15 hours. Furthermore, the angle of the camera during the filming of the food-hiding event differed by up to 120 degrees from Panzee's familiar angle of view of the forest, and on some of the trials the video cue tape presented her with a perspective of the forest that she could not possibly have had from her outdoor enclosure.

Discrimination Between Relevant and Irrelevant Video Representations   Panzee discriminated sharply between relevant and irrelevant videotapes of food-hiding events. When Panzee was shown a videotape of a food-hiding event that had been filmed in a distant forest that she had never seen, she watched the videotape with interest, but she did not subsequently recruit a person or point toward the forest behind her own enclosure within 40 hours. These 10 control trials were intermixed with the test trials that had been filmed behind Panzee's outdoor enclosure. As usual, the caregiver did not know whether a trial was being conducted.

Reporting of Hidden Objects on a Video Representation   Panzee could transfer in the reverse direction, from real life to television. If she watched the experimenter hide an object in the forest in real life, and the experimenter then locked her indoors overnight, she was able to report the exact location of the hidden object to an uninformed person the next day by touching the corresponding location on a televised image of the forest with a stick or a joystick-controlled laser pointer. Panzee did this accurately and reliably in a series of more than 20 trials, including on Trial 1.

Use of Laser Pointer in Woods   Panzee used a laser pointer to pinpoint the location of hidden items in the woods. On overcast days, an experimenter hid an object in the woods, 3 to 20 meters from Panzee's outdoor enclosure. Each of the 20 trials used a different location. After a delay of approximately 5 minutes, a person who did not know where the object was hidden or the type of object gave Panzee access to a joystick. The joystick controlled a motorized pan head, on which a laser pointer was mounted. The laser pointer itself was located outside the cage and was not accessible to Panzee. Panzee controlled the location of the laser dot in the woods by manipulating the joystick.

The area available for error was more than 100 square meters. Panzee moved the dot to a location, then took her hand off the joystick, shook her arm and bobbed her head while looking at the person. The person then walked into the woods and manually inspected the location of the dot. On all 20 trials, Panzee put the dot within 1 meter of the hidden object (within 15 centimeters on most trials, including a trial at 20 meters) and the person found the hidden object without further search. Panzee also named all 20 hidden objects correctly using lexigrams before the person had checked the location.

Factors That Did Not Cause Panzee to Forget Hidden Objects

Panzee initiated the interactions with humans, and she did not appear to forget her intended actions when they were interrupted. For example, if she worked on a computer-presented cognitive task, or if she engaged in social interactions (e.g., grooming) during a several-hour-long retention interval, she still reported the object and directed a person to it. Similarly, if she recruited a person and pointed toward the hidden object but the person could not find the object, Panzee would break off the interaction, but she would resume the recruitment at a later time. (As mentioned earlier, Panzee was confined to her enclosure and had to rely on a person to get the object; she could not simply get the object herself.) In several trials, Panzee continued to recruit people and point toward a hidden object over a period of 2 weeks until a person finally found the object. Finally, if the person found the object but merely replaced it in the forest rather than bringing it indoors, Panzee continued to report the location at later times and to different people until the object was removed. She did so with high reliability in a series of more than 20 trials.

Inferences About Objects and Locations

Given the durability of this chimpanzee's memory for single food locations (see also Yerkes, 1943, p. 148; Tinklepaugh, 1932), maybe a more basic question than "Why does she remember?" is "Why does she forget?" or "Why does she stop reporting locations?" I have identified some of the factors that cause Panzee to stop reporting locations. If Panzee reported a hidden object and saw a person remove it from the woods, she rarely reported that location again. That is, she rarely showed false positives. Panzee also behaved as if she could infer whether an object had been removed from the forest, based on events that she had seen indoors. In one experiment, Panzee saw an experimenter hide a food item in the forest as usual. After Panzee had "named" the item and initiated recruitment of a caregiver, however, the caregiver confined Panzee indoors. Panzee then reported the location of the item on a televised image of the woods, as described earlier. The caregiver then left the building, walked to the woods, and after several minutes reentered the building, carrying the same type of item that Panzee had seen hidden in the forest. Under these conditions (more than 20 trials), Panzee did not subsequently recruit a person and point toward the location where she had seen the item hidden, despite opportunities to do so. It was as if Panzee assumed that the food item the caregiver brought back was the same item Panzee had seen hidden in the forest, even though Panzee could not see the forest or see or hear what the person was doing outside the building.

In a control series, when Panzee initiated recruitment, the caregiver locked her indoors, but then simply gave her the named type of item from the refrigerator instead of going outdoors. The refrigerator was located near Panzee's indoor cage and was visible to her. On all 20 trials of this type, Panzee subsequently recruited a person and directed him or her to the hidden item in the woods. In another experiment, two different types of objects were hidden in two different locations in the woods. When Panzee came indoors, "named" one of the objects, and initiated recruitment of a caregiver, the caregiver locked her indoors, went outdoors for several minutes, and then reentered the building carrying one item that was of the same type as one of the items that Panzee had seen hidden in the woods (but not necessarily the one that Panzee had named). Under these conditions, Panzee subsequently recruited a person and directed him or her to the location of the other type of object, that is, to the remaining type of item that the caregiver had not brought indoors. Again, it was as if Panzee assumed that the food item the caregiver brought back to the building was one of the food items Panzee had seen hidden in the woods. I am currently working with this procedure to try to determine the more specific cues and assumptions that Panzee uses to discriminate when a location in the forest has been emptied.

Massed Trials

Tulving suggested the following specific test to assess episodic memory in Panzee. I presented Panzee with a massed series of trials using just two locations and two types of objects. The delay interval between cue giving and reporting within each trial was long enough to involve long-term memory. The test was conducted indoors, to facilitate the presentation of many trials in succession. When humans are given a long series of similar trials in succession with delay intervals of several minutes, they can find it increasingly difficult to discriminate the current trial from the preceding trials. In principle, the test places demands on memory for the time of occurrence of events. The question was whether Panzee could sustain high accuracy as the test session progressed.

To begin a trial, the experimenter hid either a slice of apple or a slice of banana under one of two identical opaque containers while

Panzee watched. The containers were 1.5 meters apart and 1 meter from Panzee's cage. The experimenter left nothing under the other container and left the area. After a delay interval of 5 minutes, a caregiver entered the ape area. The caregiver knew that a trial was underway but did not know which type of item was present or which container was baited. Panzee indicated her selection of one of the two containers by pointing. Before lifting the container that Panzee had designated, the caregiver presented Panzee with a keyboard that displayed 256 lexigrams and noted which lexigram Panzee touched. If Panzee selected both the correct location and the correct lexigram (corresponding to the food type), then the caregiver removed the food and gave it to Panzee. Otherwise, the caregiver removed the food without giving it to Panzee. Intertrial intervals were approximately 1 minute. A session lasted approximately 90 minutes and consisted of 12 trials. Eight sessions (96 trials) were conducted. The type of item and the container baited varied across trials in an irregular, quasi-random sequence.

Panzee was correct on item type on 96% of trials, slightly higher than her average in outdoor tests; she was correct on location on 88%, and correct on both item and location on 84% of trials. On the last trial of the session (Trial 12), Panzee was still accurate; she was correct on Trial 12 on location on 7 of 8 sessions, correct on item on 7 of 8 sessions, and correct on both item and location on 6 of 8 sessions. Thus, Panzee appeared to be resistant to the sort of proactive interference that can impair performance in amnesics (Schacter, Moscovitch, Tulving, McLachlan, & Freedman, 1986).

New Aspects of the Study

The key empirical issue of this and many other recent studies of animal memory is how information about the environment and about the animal's own past experiences is organized. The data strongly suggest that, for Panzee, information is to a significant extent organized independently of stimulation from the environment in question and constitutes recall as opposed to recognition. The "time in which chimpanzees live" remains an open question, but Panzee could certainly recall which one of at least 30 different types of objects she had seen outdoors, after delays of more than 48 hours.

This study presents several new features compared to other work on animal memory. The most obvious respect is that Panzee used lexigrams to report hidden objects, and that she did so from locations that were visually separated from the place where the event occurred, after substantial time delays. Panzee transmitted multiple features of events, not just a single feature. In particular, she used lexigrams in conjunction with a video representation of the woods to convey both the type and the location of objects she had seen hidden in the woods on the previous day.

Second, evidence for generalized spatial skills came from the fact that Panzee used a video representation of the woods as a guide to locating objects in the woods, after overnight delays. Her use of televised spatial information far exceeded that reported for other nonhuman organisms, including juvenile chimpanzees (E. Menzel, Premack, & Woodruff, 1978), baboons (Vauclair, 1990), and dolphins (Herman, Pack, & Palmer, 1993), in regard to extracting spatial information from a video representation and using that information at a much later time in an outdoor area. What is new is the long time span over which Panzee retained televised spatial information, the large number of different locations used in the test, her ability to withstand changes in visual perspective, her use of a video representation to report locations, and her labeling of the item type by lexigram.

Another relatively novel aspect of this study compared to other research on animal memory concerns the physical separation between Panzee and the physical properties of the objects. During the information-gathering phase of each trial, Panzee was not allowed to handle the objects herself. She had to watch the object-hiding events from a distance. She did not always even see the hiding event directly; sometimes she saw only a video representation of the event. Later, she had to solicit the assistance of an uninformed person and then had to guide the person to the hidden object by pointing from a distance, or by using a stick to touch the corresponding location on a video representation of the forest. She was not allowed simply to take the person by the arm to the locations. Furthermore, she had to watch the object-removal events from a distance; and she did not always even see the removal event directly. As stated earlier, Panzee had not entered the forested area within 6 years prior to the onset of this study. Thus, her memory of the presence, type, and location of test objects in the forest was based on observations of events from a distance. These aspects of her performance seem very different from memory studies using food-storing animals. In such studies, animals usually hide the items themselves and receive proprioceptive and close visual feedback from the location during the information-gathering part of the trial, both of which can improve memory. To paraphrase Nissen (1951, pp. 379–380) and Pavlov (1904), the more attenuated the basis of association between cues and objects, the more likely we are to assume that some form of symbolic or sign process contributes to the problem solving.

Finally, an aspect of the study that is relatively unique, compared to most studies of human memory as well as animal studies, is that Panzee's recall and reporting of hidden objects were unprompted. In studies of human recall memory, the experimenter typically tells the participant when to provide information. Even in studies of "free recall," the experimenter typically tells the person when to report. In humans, the ability to recall goals, and the ability to monitor which intended actions have and have not occurred, is somewhat fragile and can be disrupted by aging and brain injuries (Einstein, McDaniel, Manzi, Cochran, & Baker, 2000; Johnson, DeLeonardis, Hashtroudi, & Ferguson, 1995). In this study, Panzee, rather than the human caregivers, initiated the exchanges of information about hidden objects, and she persisted in reporting a given location for days, if the search was interrupted by outside disturbances or if the person failed to find the hidden item.

Recall Versus Recognition Memory

The sine qua non of recall in humans is often said to be verbal or other self-generated reporting of events. In the experiments described in this chapter, Panzee initiated the exchanges of information about hidden objects, and she conveyed which one of at least several dozen types of objects she had seen hidden outdoors, by touching lexigrams. Furthermore, Panzee did not merely touch lexigrams: She used a wide range of response outputs to convey her message, and she did so from Trial 1 in a series of trial-unique experimental tests. The overall organization of her behavior suggested that she could retrieve information indoors about the presence, types, and locations of objects that she had seen outdoors hours or days earlier.

Panzee did not literally draw a lexigram or a map of the forest. She chose lexigrams from a large set of options. Thus, the relevant visual stimuli used in the reporting situation were not purely self-generated. Does this mean that Panzee's selection of lexigrams at her keyboard could be better described as a recognition task, in which there were 256 choices, rather than as a recall task? I think not. On several hundred trials, Panzee vocalized persistently, then (when the caregiver approached) rushed to the keyboard and in less than one second touched the lexigram corresponding to the type of item hidden, and then gestured toward and headed up to the tunnel that leads outdoors. In light of Panzee's nearly immediate selection of the correct lexigram on the complex keyboard, it seems likely that she already knew the type of item and/or the lexigram she was going for before she approached the keyboard. It seems doubtful that in these cases Panzee knew at best that something was outdoors but not the type of item, and that she only had this information after she had scanned the keyboard and recognized the lexigram. One might still ask whether Panzee had scanned the keyboard and had recognized the lexigram just moments before she had vocalized and attracted the caregiver's attention. However, on more than 30 trials Panzee was locked in a special cage overnight without any access to a keyboard. When the caretaker entered the building in the morning, Panzee vocalized and gestured persistently to the adjacent cage; as soon as the caregiver opened the door between the cages, Panzee rushed to the keyboard in the adjacent cage and touched the correct lexigram in less than one second, and pointed toward the tunnel. Again, Panzee's speed of touching the correct lexigram on these trials suggested that she already knew the type of object and/or the lexigram before moving to the keyboard, without having seen the outdoor area or the keyboard during the overnight retention interval.

To be sure, Panzee did not close her eyes and give a verbal report of what she had seen or heard. Regardless of whether her performance satisfies everyone's definition of "self-generated, active recall," what is important is the degree to which Panzee's memory is organized independent of stimulation from the original environment in question. The lexigrams that Panzee touched did not resemble the objects that she had seen hidden, and of course the lexigrams did not resemble the spoken English words that Panzee had heard the experimenter say aloud, in some trials, as cues of object type. The video representation of the woods on which Panzee reported object locations differed in numerous respects from a direct view of the woods itself (e.g., it did not provide motion parallax, and it presented a different visual perspective). If we envision a continuum between recall and recognition, then Panzee's performance is much farther in the direction of recall than any other animal performance of which I am aware, or at least any published experimental study.

WHAT IS ESSENTIAL IN OUR FIELD?

In this volume, Tulving suggests that there has been no essential progress on the problem of self-knowing consciousness in animals in the past 100 years. Tulving is certainly entitled to his personal opinion, and I admire him for stating it so explicitly, but when he speaks for psychology in general, I must differ.

James (1890) pointed out that the only meaning of "essence" is teleological, in the sense that it is defined in relation to a particular set of interests. James encouraged other researchers to look for themselves and decide what is essential. Insofar as one remains a naturalist or experimentalist, there is always more to learn regarding what is and what is not essential. No finite list is ever likely to be permanently exhaustive and definitive.

One hundred years ago, psychologists were disputing whether any nonhuman could be said to remember anything at all, or possess memory of any sort, or learn anything by observation, or be capable of one-trial as opposed to slow gradual learning, or communicate, or recognize themselves, or symbolize in any more profound a fashion than a dog that salivates at the sound of a dinner bell, or not merely behave but sometimes show signs of comprehension as well (Thorndike, 1898). Few current scientists would hesitate to answer any of the above questions with at least a weak affirmative. That counts as progress of sorts, especially since the debates were settled mainly by empirical data rather than polemics. The issue of what types of data, methods, and questions are permissible is currently seen in a very different way because of the information that was obtained by animal researchers. The amount of data on the topics listed above in nonhuman primates has expanded exponentially, partly as a result of research by Köhler and Yerkes, the establishment of national primate research centers, field studies, ethology, sociobiology, and cognitive studies. Many of the advances in the study of perception and cognition in human infants have been based on methods originally developed with nonverbal animals. This is progress toward meeting Tulving's challenge, because if we are not in agreement on the above questions, there is no way we can reach agreement on subsidiary issues that are far more specific, yet even more inferential and difficult to operationalize.

The boundary line of "self-reflective consciousness" is vague (Wheeler, 2000), and we cannot know in advance which phenomena of animal behavior will shed light on the main issue at hand. Progress on Tulving's problem can be made through empirical research on a broad front. Improvements in methodology will remain especially important (Rumbaugh & Washburn, 2003). Hunter's (1913) delayed-response procedure did not definitively answer Hunter's original question (whether animals have "ideas"), but it has made major contributions to our understanding of observational learning, spatial and object memory, recall, and communication among other topics. The present chapter illustrates how delayed-response procedures have clarified the operation of chimpanzee memory in situations that are somewhat loosely structured but that allow the subjects adequate space, time, environmental structures, and social options to express their interests and abilities in a well-developed form. Additional methodological improvements discussed here include the use of specialized rearing histories, lexigram competencies, and technologies (keyboards, video representations, and pointing devices) to study chimpanzee recall.

Should "Self-Knowing Consciousness" Be Taken as an Axiom, or as a Null Hypothesis to Be Tested Experimentally?

There is a difference between the point of view of a caregiver and that of a critic or an experimenter. We need both points of view. A human mother does not wait for valid evidence that her infant already has the capacity for language, memory, empathy, and self-concept before treating her infant as if it will be able to become a real, intelligent human being. She takes the capacity for self-reflective consciousness as a given, not as a hypothesis to be tested. Her faith that her infant definitely will be able to become a real, caring, intelligent human is what prevents the infant from being treated inhumanely. How accurate is a mother's assessment of an infant's perceptual and cognitive capabilities, compared to the assessment of an experimentalist? Historically, the mother has sometimes been far more accurate. Many of William James's (1890) statements about the perceptual world of human infants were flatly wrong, and he would have been the first to say that in many respects his wife had the better understanding of the consciousness of their own infants.

This raises the question: Is there any single best way to rear chimpanzees for the purposes of studies such as this one? I do not think there is. The cognitive capabilities of normally reared chimpanzees in their natural habitat are still basically unknown (Boesch & Boesch-Achermann, 2000). With regard to laboratory studies, we have learned a great deal since the home-rearing studies of Kellogg and Kellogg (1933) and Ladygina-Kohts (1935/2002), but every generation and every infant is different (Rumbaugh & Washburn, 2003). The people who reared Panzee assumed that immersing her in an enriched communicative environment would support the emergence of diverse cognitive abilities, some of which might not become apparent until years later. Several of these people, including Sue Savage-Rumbaugh, Rose Sevcik, and Elizabeth Pugh, had already reared and extensively tested two other symbol-competent chimpanzees (Sherman and Austin) and two symbol-competent bonobos (Kanzi and Malika). Their assumptions about Panzee's developmental potential were informed by daily interactions with her plus experience with the developmental end points and behavior of other individual apes.

Experimental studies (Beran et al., 1998; Brakke & Savage-Rumbaugh, 1995, 1996; C. Menzel, 1999), conducted years later and designed with attention to Panzee's particular interests, preferences, and existing daily activities have provided strong support for her mother surrogates' assumptions regarding Panzee's cognitive and developmental potential. In particular, Panzee can comprehend spoken English words (Beran et al., 1998), can perform recall in different situations and in different ways (C. Menzel, 1999), and can comprehend video representations at levels that far exceed the levels previously demonstrated experimentally in any common chimpanzee. By comparison with other adult chimpanzees, she seems exceptionally interested in humans and exceptionally eager to engage them in communication about the environment, but as yet I have not attempted to get formal data on that.

Does Panzee Possess True (Human) Episodic Memory?

Human episodic memory, as defined by Tulving (1983) and Tulving and Markowitsch (1998), includes the ability to perform recall in different situations and conscious awareness of at least some aspects of the spatial and temporal contexts of the recalled event, or "mental time travel." As stated earlier, the boundary line of these capacities is vague. The potential value of further research on nonhuman animals should not be underestimated, and it would be premature at this early stage of research to claim that chimpanzees lack these skills entirely.

With regard to her memory of the temporal (sequential) aspects of events, it can be noted that Panzee kept track accurately over days whether hidden objects had been removed from the woods, or had been replaced in the same location, or had been moved to another location. She showed few false positives, and she rarely appeared to confuse the locations or the object types of the previous trial with those of the current trial, even in a study in which she watched the experimenter hide six different types of items in six different locations per trial. It is as if she discriminated sharply between tasks that were "completed" and those that were still "uncompleted" (Zeigarnik, 1927, cited in Woodworth & Schlosberg, 1954). She also performed accurately in massed trials that used just two types of items and two locations repeatedly.

Furthermore, Panzee's use of stored information appeared to be controlled and strategic. Her decision of whether and when to recruit appeared to be based on a deliberate choice between known alternatives; she seemed almost constantly to take into account what the caregivers were doing, what they were likely to do in the near future, the availability of alternative foods indoors, and the presence, type, and location of a large number of goal objects over a large spatial extent. For example, after seeing an experimenter hide a highly prized box of juice in the woods in the afternoon, Panzee might recruit the assistance of the caregiver to recover the juice within a few minutes after seeing the event. If, however, she saw the experimenter hide a somewhat less preferred item (e.g., an orange), she might come indoors, touch the *sweet potato* lexigram, and vocalize and point toward the microwave in which she saw the caregiver put sweet potatoes earlier in the day, then use lexigrams, vocalizations, and manual pointing to request television viewing, or touch the *blanket* lexigram and point toward the laundry room where blankets (for nest making) are kept, then only on the next morning touch the *orange* lexigram, point toward the woods, and recruit a caregiver's assistance to recover the orange outdoors. To say that Panzee appears to be capable of recalling multiple features of her environment quickly and accurately, that she appears to use this recalled information strategically, that she appears throughout the day to be attempting to manipulate the outcome of anticipated events, that she controls her environment indirectly by controlling her caregivers, and that she uses a large range of behaviors flexibly and interchangeably to exert this influence is not simply a poetic metaphor. It is close to the direct impression gained by observing the interactions between Panzee and her caregivers in the daily situations and tests described earlier.

As to what exactly makes some people believe that Panzee has the same kind of autonoetic, self-knowing consciousness that humans do, and why others will remain skeptical or even scornful of that possibility, one prime variable is assuredly firsthand personal experience: with animals, with Panzee herself, with one or more live test sessions, and with the investigators themselves. The pictures, tables, figures, and written descriptions provided in this chapter are a pale representation of the real thing. If they provided all the information that anyone should ever need, then funding agencies surely would not invest so much in site visits and conferences. A person does not have to work for years as a chimpanzee researcher or caregiver to experience these things. First-time visitors, including neurobiologists and students, who see a single live test session are typically impressed with the forcefulness and clarity of Panzee's behavior and with the significance of her behavior for memory.

There are at least two approaches to the problem of self-knowing consciousness in animals. One approach is to attack the problem head on, by presenting animals with arbitrarily designed tasks in the tradition of Thorndike (1898). The other approach is indirect, by examining what the animal already does. My study of Panzee is an example of the second approach. To paraphrase Wehner (1996), I did not begin with an attempt to test a preconceived idea about how a memory system or a symbol system might work in principle. Rather, I have begun by taking a detailed look at what this particular chimpanzee does in her particular ecological and social context.

ACKNOWLEDGMENTS Thanks are due to John Kelley, Michael Beran, Stephanie Berger, Christopher Elder, Cameron Hastie, John Mustaleski, Isabel Sanchez, and Shelly Williams for their help conducting the experiments with Panzee. This research was supported by the L.S.B. Leakey Foundation, the Wenner-Gren Foundation, National Science Foundation grant SBR-9729485, and National Institute of Health grants MH-58855, HD-38051, and HD-06016.

REFERENCES

Aristotle. (1990). Memory and reminiscence. In *Great books of the western world: The works of Aristotle, Vol. 1* (pp. 690–695, J. I. Beare, Trans.). Chicago: Encyclopaedia Britannica.

Balda, R. P., & Kamil, A. C. (1992). Long-term spatial memory in Clarks's nutcracker, *Nucifraga columbiana. Animal Behaviour, 44,* 761–769.

Bayley, P. J., & Squire, L. R. (2002). Medial temporal lobe amnesia: Gradual acquisition of factual information by nondeclarative memory. *Journal of Neuroscience, 22,* 5741–5748.

Beran, M. J., & Beran, M. M. (2004). Chimpanzees remember the results of one-by-one addition of food items to sets over extended time periods. *Psychological Science, 15,* 94–99.

Beran, M. J., Savage-Rumbaugh, E. S., Brakke, K. E., Kelley, J. W., & Rumbaugh, D. M. (1998). Symbol comprehension and learning: A "vocabulary" test of three chimpanzees (*Pan troglodytes*). *Evolution of Communication, 2,* 171–188.

Bickerton, D. (1995). *Language and human behavior.* Seattle: University of Washington Press.

Bischof, N. (1978). On the phylogeny of human morality. In G. S. Stent (Ed.), *Morality as a biological phenomenon* (pp. 48–66). Berkeley: University of California Press.

Boesch, C., & Boesch-Achermann, H. (2000). *The chimpanzees of the Täi forest.* New York: Oxford University Press.

Brakke, K. E., & Savage-Rumbaugh, E. S. (1995). The development of language skills in bonobo and chimpanzee: I. Comprehension. *Language and Communication, 15,* 121–148.

Brakke, K. E., & Savage-Rumbaugh, E. S. (1996). The development of language skills in *Pan.* II. Production. *Language and Communication, 16,* 361–380.

Clayton, N. S., & Dickinson, A. (1998). Episodic-like memory during cache recovery by scrub jays. *Nature, 395,* 272–274.

Clayton, N. S., & Dickinson, A. (1999a). Memory for the content of caches by scrub jays (*Aphelocoma coerulescens*). *Journal of Experimental Psychology: Animal Behavior Processes, 25,* 82–91.

Clayton, N. S., & Dickinson, A. (1999b). Scrub jays (*Aphelocoma coerulescens*) remember the relative time of caching as well as the location and content of their caches. *Journal of Comparative Psychology, 113,* 403–416.

Clayton, N. S., Griffiths, D. P., Emery, N. J., & Dickinson, A. (2002). Elements of episodic-like memory in animals. In A. Baddeley, J. P. Aggleton, & M. A. Conway (Eds.), *Episodic memory: New directions in research.* New York: Oxford University Press.

Donald, M. (1993). Precis of origins of the modern mind. *Behavioral and Brain Sciences, 16,* 737–791.

Einstein, G. O., McDaniel, M. A., Manzi, M., Cochran, B., & Baker, M. (2000). Prospective memory and aging: Forgetting intentions over short delays. *Psychology and Aging, 15,* 671–683.

Gaffan, D. (1994). Scene-specific memory for objects: A model of episodic memory impairment in monkeys with fornix transection. *Journal of Cognitive Neuroscience, 6,* 305–320.

Gallistel, C. R. (1990). *The organization of learning.* Cambridge, MA: MIT Press.

Gallup, G. G., Jr. (1970). Chimpanzees: Self-recognition. *Science, 167,* 86–87.

Garber, P. (1989). Role of spatial memory in primate foraging patterns: *Saguinus mystax* and *Saguinus fuscicollis. American Journal of Primatology, 19,* 203–216.

Hampton, R. R. (2001). Rhesus monkeys know when they remember. *Proceedings of the National Academy of Sciences U.S.A., 98,* 5359–5362.

Hashiya, K., & Kojima, S. (2001a). Acquisition of auditory-visual intermodal matching-to-sample by a chimpanzee (*Pan troglodytes*): Comparison with visual-visual intramodal matching. *Animal Cognition, 4,* 231–239.

Hashiya, K., & Kojima, S. (2001b). Hearing and auditory-visual intermodal recognition in the chimpanzee. In T. Matsuzawa (Ed.), *Primate origins of human cognition and behavior* (pp. 155–189). New York: Springer.

Herman, L. M., & Forestell, P. H. (1985). Reporting presence or absence of named objects by a language-trained dolphin. *Neuroscience and Biobehavioral Reviews, 9,* 667–681.

Herman, L. M., Pack, A. A., & Palmer, M. (1993). Representational and conceptual skills of dolphins. In H. L. Roitblat, L. M. Herman, & P. E. Nachtigall (Eds.), *Language and communication: Comparative perspectives* (pp. 403–442). Hillsdale, NJ: Lawrence Erlbaum.

Hunter, W. (1913). The delayed reaction in animals and children. *Behavior Monographs, 2*(1), Serial No. 6.

James, W. (1890). *Principles of psychology.* New York: Holt.

Janson, C. H. (1998). Experimental evidence for spatial memory in foraging wild capuchin monkeys, *Cebus apella. Animal Behaviour, 55,* 1229–1243.

Johnson, M. K., DeLeonardis, D. M., Hashtroudi, S., & Ferguson, S. A. (1995). Aging and single versus multiple cues in source monitoring. *Psychology and Aging, 10,* 507–517.

Kawai, N., & Matsuzawa, T. (2001). Reproductive memory processes in chimpanzees: Homologous approaches to research on human working memory. In T. Matsuzawa (Ed.), *Primate origins of human cognition and behavior* (pp. 226–234). Tokyo: Springer-Verlag.

Kellogg, W. N., & Kellogg, L. A. (1933). *The ape and the child.* New York: Mc-Graw-Hill.

Köhler, W. (1925). *The mentality of apes* (E. Winter, Trans.). New York: Liveright.

Kuhlmeier, V. A., Boysen, S. T., & Mukobi, K. L. (1999). Scale model comprehension by chimpanzees (*Pan troglodytes*). *Journal of Comparative Psychology, 113,* 396–402.

Ladygina-Kohts, N. N. (2002). *Infant chimpanzee and human child: A classic 1935 comparative study of ape emotions and intelligence* (F. B. M. de Waal, Ed.). New York: Oxford University Press. (Original work published 1935)

Menzel, C. R. (1991). Cognitive aspects of foraging in Japanese monkeys. *Animal Behaviour, 41,* 397–402.

Menzel, C. R. (1999). Unprompted recall and reporting of hidden objects by a chimpanzee (*Pan troglodytes*) after extended delays. *Journal of Comparative Psychology, 113,* 426–434.

Menzel, C. R., Savage-Rumbaugh, E. S., & Menzel, E. W., Jr. (2002). Bonobo (*Pan paniscus*) spatial memory and communication in a 20-hectare forest. *International Journal of Primatology, 23,* 601–619.

Menzel, E. W., Jr. (1973a). Chimpanzee spatial memory organization. *Science, 182,* 943–945.

Menzel, E. W., Jr. (1973b). Leadership and communication in young chimpanzees. In E. Menzel, Jr. (Ed.), *Symposium of the Fourth International Congress of Primatology: Vol. 1. Precultural primate behavior* (pp. 192–225). Basel: Karger.

Menzel, E. W., Jr. (1978). Cognitive mapping in chimpanzees. In S. H. Hulse,

H. Fowler, & W. K. Honig (Eds.), *Cognitive processes in animal behavior* (pp. 375–422). Hillsdale, NJ: Lawrence Erlbaum.

Menzel, E. W., Jr. (1984). Spatial cognition and memory in captive chimpanzees. In P. Marler & H. S. Terrace (Eds.), *The biology of learning* (pp. 509–531). New York: Springer-Verlag.

Menzel, E. W., Jr., & Juno, C. (1985). Social foraging in marmoset monkeys and the question of intelligence. *Philosophical Transactions of the Royal Society of London, Series B, 308,* 145–158.

Menzel, E. W., Jr., Premack, D., & Woodruff, G. (1978). Map reading by chimpanzees. *Folia Primatologica, 29,* 241–249.

Menzel, E. W., Jr., Savage-Rumbaugh, E. S., & Lawson, J. (1985). Chimpanzee (*Pan troglodytes*) spatial problem solving with the use of mirrors and televised equivalents of mirrors. *Journal of Comparative Psychology, 99,* 211–217.

Menzel, R., Geiger, K., Chittka, L., Joerges, J., Kunze, J., & Muller, U. (1996). The knowledge base of bee navigation. *Journal of Experimental Biology, 199,* 141–146.

Mishkin, M., Suzuki, W. A., Gadian, D. G., & Vargha-Khadem, F. (1997). Hierarchical organization of cognitive memory. *Philosophical Transactions of the Royal Society of London, Series B, 352,* 1461–1467.

Nissen, H. (1951). Phylogenetic comparison. In S. S. Stevens (Ed.), *Handbook of experimental psychology* (pp. 347–386). New York: Wiley.

Olton, D. (1978). Characteristics of spatial memory. In S. H. Hulse, H. Fowler, & W. K. Honig (Eds.), *Cognitive processes in animal behavior* (pp. 341–373). Hillsdale, NJ: Lawrence Erlbaum.

Olton, D. S. (1984). Comparative analysis of episodic memory. *Behavioral and Brain Sciences, 7,* 250–251.

Parkinson, J. K., Murray, E. A., & Mishkin, M. (1988). A selective role for the hippocampus in monkeys: Memory for the location of objects. *Journal of Neuroscience, 8,* 4159–4167.

Pavlov, I. (1904). *Physiology of digestion.* Nobel lecture, December 12, Stockholm.

Roberts, A. C. (1996). Comparison of cognitive function in human and nonhuman primates. *Cognitive Brain Research, 3,* 319–327.

Roberts, W. A. (2002). Are animals stuck in time? *Psychological Bulletin, 128,* 473–489.

Ruggiero, F. T., & Flagg, S. F. (1976). Do animals have memory? In D. L. Medin, W. A. Roberts, & R. T. Davis (Eds.), *Processes of animal memory* (pp. 1–19). Hillsdale, NJ: Lawrence Erlbaum.

Rumbaugh, D. M., & Washburn, D. A. (2003). *Intelligence of apes and other rational beings.* New Haven, CT: Yale University Press.

Savage-Rumbaugh, E. S., McDonald, K., Sevcik, R. A., Hopkins, W. D., & Rubert, E. (1986). Spontaneous symbol acquisition and communicative use by pygmy chimpanzees (*Pan paniscus*). *Journal of Experimental Psychology: General, 115,* 211–235.

Savage-Rumbaugh, E. S., Murphy, J., Sevcik, R., Brakke, K. E., Williams, S. L., & Rumbaugh, D. M. (1993). Language comprehension in ape and child. *Monographs of the Society for Research on Child Development, 58*(3–4, Serial No. 233).

Savage-Rumbaugh, E. S., Pate, J. L., Lawson, J., Smith, S. T., & Rosenbaum, S.

(1983). Can a chimpanzee make a statement? *Journal of Experimental Psychology: General, 112,* 457–492.

Savage-Rumbaugh, E. S., Rumbaugh, D. M., & McDonald, K. (1985). Language learning in two species of apes. *Neuroscience and Biobehavioral Reviews, 9,* 653–665.

Schacter, D. L., Moscovitch, M., Tulving, E., McLachlan, D. R., & Freedman, M. (1986). Mnemonic precedence in amnesic patients: An analogue of the AB error in infants? *Child Development, 57,* 816–823.

Schacter, D. L., & Tulving, E. (1994). What are the memory systems of 1994? In D. L. Schacter & E. Tulving (Eds.), *Memory systems 1994* (pp. 1–38). Cambridge, MA: MIT Press.

Schwartz, B. L., Colon, M. R., Sanchez, I. C., Rodriguez, I. A., & Evans, S. (2002). Single-trial learning of "what" and "who" information in a gorilla (*Gorilla gorilla gorilla*): Implications for episodic memory. *Animal Cognition, 5,* 85–90.

Schwartz, B. L., & Evans, S. (2001). Episodic memory in primates. *American Journal of Primatology, 55,* 71–85.

Sherry, D. (1984). Food storage by black-capped chickadees: Memory for the location and contents of caches. *Animal Behaviour, 32,* 451–464.

Shettleworth, S. J. (1995). Memory in food-storing birds: From the field to the Skinner box. In E. Alleva, A. Fasolo, H.-P. Lipp, & L. Nadel (Eds.), *Behavioural brain research in naturalistic and semi-naturalistic settings* (pp. 158–179). The Hague: Kluwer Academic.

Shettleworth, S. J. (1998). *Cognition, evolution and behavior.* New York: Oxford University Press.

Squire, L. R. (1992). Memory and the hippocampus: A synthesis from findings with rats, monkeys, and humans. *Psychological Review, 99,* 195–231.

Suddendorf, T., & Corballis, M. C. (1997). Mental time travel and the evolution of the human mind. *Genetic, Social, and General Psychology Monographs, 123,* 133–167.

Thorndike, E. L. (1898). Animal intelligence: An experimental study of the associative processes in animals. *Psychological Monographs, 2*(8).

Tinklepaugh, O. L. (1932). Multiple delayed reaction with chimpanzees and monkeys. *Journal of Comparative Psychology, 13,* 207–243.

Tomasello, M., & Call, J. (1997). *Primate cognition.* Oxford, UK: Oxford University Press.

Tulving, E. (1983). *Elements of episodic memory.* Oxford, UK: Clarendon Press.

Tulving, E. (1984). Precis of elements of episodic memory. *Behavioral and Brain Sciences, 7,* 223–268.

Tulving, E., & Markowitsch, H. J. (1998). Episodic and declarative memory: Role of the hippocampus. *Hippocampus, 8,* 198–204.

Vander Wall, S. B. (1990). *Food hoarding in animals.* Chicago: University of Chicago Press.

Vander Wall, S. B. (1991). Mechanisms of cache recovery by yellow pine chipmunks. *Animal Behaviour, 41,* 851–863.

Vauclair, J. (1990). [Complex cognitive processes: Study of mental performance in baboons.] In J.-J. Roeder & J. R. Anderson (Eds.), *Primates: Recherches actuelles* (pp. 170–180). Paris: Masson.

Wehner, R. (1996). Preface. *Journal of Experimental Biology, 199,* i.

Wheeler, M. A. (2000). Episodic memory and autonoetic awareness. In E. Tulving & F. I. M. Craik (Eds.), *The Oxford handbook of memory* (pp. 597–608). New York: Oxford University Press.

Woodworth, R. S., & Schlosberg, H. (1954). *Experimental psychology* (Rev. ed.). New York: Henry Holt.

Yerkes, R. M. (1943). *Chimpanzees: A laboratory colony.* New Haven, CT: Yale University Press.

Yerkes, R. M., & Yerkes, D. N. (1928). Concerning memory in the chimpanzee. *Journal of Comparative Psychology, 8,* 237–271.

9

Do Nonhuman Primates Have Episodic Memory?

Bennett L. Schwartz

Consider the familiar image of a deposed alpha male ape, much beloved by the females of a troop, who has been overthrown by a bunch of rowdy young males eager to make their own mark. The deposed male, now an outcast, looks back at the troop he has known for years. Does he reflect on his glory days as an alpha male and recall specific episodes of his former life? Does he worry about his diminished status in times to come? If he did, he would have abilities that cognitive scientists claim are uniquely human: a sense of his self, his past, and his future.

Consider another scenario. A murder takes place at a captive primate facility. The only witness to the crime is a language-trained chimpanzee. The police have no clues, save for the agitated chatter of the chimpanzee. Could the chimpanzee recall the murderer and communicate his identity to the police? This very plot was actually used in a mystery novel (Dickinson, 1974).

Empirical questions suggested by these scenarios have only recently been posed in the scientific literature (see Griffiths, Dickinson, & Clayton, 1999; Roberts, 2002; Schwartz & Evans, 2001, for reviews). Based on the assumption that memory is a unitary phenomenon, research on animal memory addressed more tractable questions. There is, for example, a large literature on delayed matching to sample (see Dewsbury, 2000; Harper & Garry, 2000; Morris, 2002), spatial memory (e.g., Burke, Cieplucha, Cass, Russell, & Fry, 2002; MacDonald, 1994; MacDonald & Agnes, 1999; Sherry, 1984), and memory of species-typical behavior (e.g., Platt, Brannon, Briese, & French, 1996). However, none of these studies addressed the question whether animals have episodic memory.

Most cognitive psychologists consider episodic memory to be the sole domain of human beings and therefore do not consider it an appropriate topic for study in nonhuman animals (e.g., Tulving, 1983). That situation is rapidly changing. During the past few years, a number of investigators have begun to study episodic memory in a variety of species: pigeons (Zentall, Clement, Bhatt, & Allen, 2001), rats (Eichenbaum & Fortin, 2003; Morris, 2002), scrub jays (Clayton & Dickinson, 1998; Clayton, Yu, & Dickinson, 2001), chimpanzees (Menzel, 1999), and gorillas (Schwartz, Colon, Sanchez, Rodriguez, & Evans, 2002). Although the results of those studies have been suggestive, they have not provided clear evidence that episodic memory exists in nonhuman animals.

In this chapter, I evaluate evidence of episodic memory in nonhuman species, in primates in particular. I begin by discussing operational definitions of episodic memory in humans and animals and indicate how they differ. I then describe research I have conducted on the episodic memory of a western lowland gorilla and discuss the implications of that research for narrowing the gap in the study of episodic memory between humans and animals.

EPISODIC MEMORY IN THE HUMAN LITERATURE

Tulving (1972, 1983, 1993, 2002) introduced the term "episodic memory" to refer to the human capacity to recollect individual events from their personal lives. Definitions of episodic memory have varied, but all center on one idea, which is that episodic memory is a memory system that involves the conscious retrieval of events from one's personal past. Tulving and Markowitsch (1998) defined episodic memory as having to do "with the conscious recollection of previous *experiences* of events, happenings, and situations" (p. 202). They argued further that episodic memory is directed toward the past, whereas the focus of other memory systems is the present. Wheeler (2000) defined episodic memory as the "the type of memory that allows people to reflect upon personal experience" (p. 597). Cabeza (1999) observed that "episodic memory retrieval allows one to travel back in time and re-experience events that happened minutes ago or decades ago" (p. 76).

I consider three aspects of episodic memory to be important. First, the memory refers to a specific event from personal experience. Second, retrieval involves some form of "mental time travel" or reexperiencing of the past event (Roberts, 2002; Suddendorf & Corballis, 1997; Tulving, 1983). Thus, episodic memory concerns past states of the world and not the present. Third, episodes are retrieved from long-term memory rather than from working memory (Schwartz & Evans, 2001).

A wealth of data and theory support these definitions. Indeed, the past three decades of research have demonstrated that episodic memory is cognitively, neuropsychologically, and developmentally dissociable from its close cousin, semantic memory. That literature has been reviewed by Tulving (2002) and is not discussed in this chapter. Instead, I focus on a functional analysis of episodic memory.

In humans, episodic and semantic memory differ functionally. To characterize that difference, Tulving and Lepage (2000) distinguished between *proscopic* (for semantic memory) and *palinscopic* memory (for episodic memory). The function of proscopic memory is to update current knowledge. When we remember proscopically, there is no reference to particular past events. To refer to proscopic memories, we use the verb "know," as in "I know where my keys are," or "I know the scientific name of the orangutan." I need not remember the event of placing my keys on the table by the door; I merely need to know that they are there now. Similarly, I do not need to remember when and how I first learned the phrase *"Pongo pygmaeus"*; I merely need to access the term now. Proscopic memory can be broken down into procedural memory (knowledge of motor routines), lexical memory (knowledge of words), and semantic memory (knowledge of meaning) (Tulving & Lepage, 2000).

Palinscopic memory refers to memory of specific events. The mental focus of palinscopic memory is the past, not the present. Palinscopic memories are retrieved by mental time travel. To refer to palinscopic memories, we use the verb "remember," as in "I remember eating lunch with my colleagues at a Korean restaurant on Broadway" or "I remember testing an orangutan in my lab yesterday." It is important to keep in mind that the retrieval of information based on unique events does not implicate palinscopic memory. It could be proscopic memory if that memory refers to a general fact (e.g., "My keys are in the bowl by the door"). It is palinscopic memory if it refers to past events (e.g., "I remember leaving my keys in the bowl when I came home last night").

The issue of palinscopy has been examined by researchers investigating the remember/know distinction in recognition memory of words. In one experiment, for example, Gardiner and Java (1991) presented human participants with a list of words, which they were asked to study for a future memory test. Each word was presented only once. Later, they were given an "old-new" recognition test. In this test, they were presented with some words that had been presented on the earlier list and some words that were not presented on the earlier list. The participants were asked to decide "old" if the word had appeared in the list, and "new" if it had not. Most important for the current discussion, the participants were asked to distinguish whether they "remembered" the word from the list (that is, whether an experience of recollection accompanied the memory decision) or if they simply "knew" the word had been on the list. Gardiner and Java showed that human participants were accurate at deciding which words had been presented earlier and assigned many of them to the "remember" category. Subsequent studies have shown that items assigned to the "remember" category correlate with variables that affect human episodic memory (e.g., Wheeler, 2000). For example, amnesics who show selective deficits in episodic memory also show a lower proportion of remember judgments (Schacter, Verfaillie, & Anes, 1997).

DEFINING EPISODIC MEMORY IN NONHUMAN SPECIES

How do we apply the concept of episodic memory from humans to nonhumans? This is a thorny issue because of the way in which episodic memory is conceptualized in humans. Episodic memory is thought of as a distinct neurocognitive system that stores events and provides for their retrieval, but its signature is the mental experiences that accompany that retrieval, namely feelings of pastness. Moreover, the usual way of assessing episodic memory in humans is with verbal tests. In the human literature, it is easy to ask a person, "What do you recall?" or "What happened to you?" We can gather data on what kinds of information people can recall, the context and source of those memories, and qualitative aspects of memory. Obviously, these kinds of verbal tests cannot be conducted with animals, except perhaps with a small number of language-trained apes. Thus, when transferring the concept of episodic memory from humans to nonhumans, there is an immediate methodological impediment. How do you test for episodic memory functions in nonlinguistic animals?

Four operational definitions of episodic-like memory have been used in the recent animal cognition literature. Two come from work on birds (i.e., Clayton & Dickinson, 1998; Zentall et al., 2001) and two from work on apes (Menzel, 1999; Schwartz et al., 2002; also see Eichenbaum & Fortin, 2003; Morris, 2002). These definitions focus on behavioral rather than phenomenological criteria because, for obvious reasons, the issue of the mental experience of a nonhuman is not a tractable issue. Each definition focuses on a different aspect of how the human episodic memory system operates. I describe each approach, as studied in different species, and then assess how well it addresses the issue of episodic memory.

Birds

What, Where, and When Clayton and Dickinson developed criteria, based on Tulving's (1972) original conception of episodic memory, to examine episodic memory in nonhumans (Clayton & Dickinson, 1998, 1999, 2000; Clayton & Griffiths, 2002; Clayton et al., 2001; Griffiths et al., 1999). Although their work involves scrub jays, they intended their operational definition to extend to other animals as well (Griffiths et al., 1999). According to their view, episodic memory stores information about temporally dated events and the spatial-temporal relation inherent in the event. Episodic memories are not of single bits of information; they involve multiple components of an event linked (or bound) together. They sought to examine evidence of accurate memory of "what," "where," and "when" information, and the binding of this information, based on trial-unique learning events.

Clayton and Dickinson (1998) focused their research on food-storing birds, in particular, the scrub jay (*Aphelocoma coerulescens*). These birds cache extra food in the wild and return to the cache sites later when food is in short supply. Clayton and Dickinson devised an ingenious experiment to determine if jays would act similarly in the laboratory, specifically, if they would remember the location of two items of food that were cached under trial-unique conditions. Their paradigm was based on a jay's preference for fresh crickets over peanuts during short intervals of time and a shift in their preferences over time because crickets degrade more quickly than peanuts. At the start of each trial, the jays were shown an ice cube tray in which crickets were stored on one side and peanuts on the other. After varying intervals of time, the jays were allowed to choose one side of the tray. Clayton and Dickinson showed that jays preferred crickets at short-retention intervals and peanuts at long-retention intervals. That is, depending on how long ago the food was stored before testing, the birds' preference switched from crickets to peanuts. These results show that jays not only remembered what type of food was hidden, but when and where it was stored.

This methodology has proved a reliable method for exploring the remarkable memory capabilities of scrub jays exposed to unique events. The birds show an amazing ability to recognize the site in which particular foods were stored at long temporal intervals, although so far the birds have only been tested with a binary choice. However, the methodology falls short of addressing the issue of palinscopy. The birds merely have to continually update their knowledge of the world at the current moment, rather than reflect on the past. In this way, it is not dissimilar to the memory of where one's keys are. In essence, it would be perfectly reasonable to hypothesize that the jays accomplish this task with something much closer to semantic memory than to episodic memory. Thus, however compelling this research may be, the methodology and the operational definition of episodic-like memory behind it do not accord with a key aspect of human episodic memory, palinscopy.

Surprise Test After Unique Events   The next operational definition comes from the work of Zentall and his colleagues (2001). Their definition is based on tests of an animal's ability to recall a unique event when it is not expecting a test. Zentall et al. argue that an animal would not attempt to update information when trained on a paradigm on which it did not anticipate a test.

In order to apply this definition, Zentall et al. (2001) trained pigeons (*Columbia livia*) to respond to a red light if they had just pecked and to respond to a green light if they had not. This would later serve as the method by which the pigeons could demonstrate memory of an event. The pigeons were then trained to peck when presented with a yellow stimulus and not to peck when presented with a blue stimulus. The two kinds of training were not combined during the pretest period.

After these responses had been trained, Zentall et al. introduced a novel manipulation. The pigeons were given the opportunity to choose red or green after being presented with blue or yellow. Zentall et al. asked whether the pigeons would "comment" on their memory by choosing the appropriate color to indicate if they had pecked or not. The results clearly indicated that the pigeons could reliably indicate whether or not they had pecked by choosing green and red appropriately. The data from eight pigeons also indicated that they were above chance on the very first few trials, when the element of "surprise" was still present.

Zentall et al.'s study has one major drawback. The retention intervals were short enough to fall within the domain of short-term memory or working memory (Bjork & Bjork, 1992; Washburn & Astur, 1998). Thus, it is unclear if the pigeons' performance is being guided by retrieval from working memory or retrieval from long-term memory, let alone long-term episodic memory. In addition, like all studies conducted with animals to date, there is no evidence that the pigeon's choice was based on self-reflection. For that reason, the Zentall et al. (2001) study provides no conclusive evidence for an episodic-like system in pigeons.

Apes

Spontaneous Recall Menzel (1999) investigated memory of unique events in a language-trained chimpanzee (*Pan trogolodytes*) named Panzee at the Language Research Center. The unique symbolic ability of this chimpanzee allowed for the kind of experiment that cannot be done with most animals. Panzee is capable of communicating about a vast number of objects, places, and other information by using a lexigram keyboard (see Beran, Savage-Rumbaugh, Brakke, Kelley, & Rumbaugh, 1998). As such, Menzel evaluated Panzee's ability to spontaneously recall unique events by using particular symbols after long retention intervals.

In this study, an experimenter hid foods and assorted objects just beyond the fence of Panzee's outdoor enclosure. Panzee could see the food being placed outside but was moved back inside before she could get the food. The experimenter then left the area and Panzee's caretakers noted what spontaneous communications Panzee used with them. The caretakers had no knowledge of what was hidden and when it was hidden. They were also blind as to the location of the foods or objects, ruling out any form of experimenter bias. The caretakers noted the lexigrams that Panzee chose to communicate and the physical gestures that Panzee used to capture the caretaker's attention and to direct the caretakers to the hidden objects.

At retention interval as long as 16 hours, Panzee indicated both memory for the food type (by selecting the appropriate lexigram) and its location (by pointing in the general direction of where it was hidden). She was more likely to use a lexigram for a particular object during the period in which it was hidden than during control periods during which there were no hidden objects. Panzee was also more likely to elicit help from the caretakers when an object was hidden than when it was not.

Importantly, Panzee remembered both the what and where components of events that were based on unique events. Furthermore, Panzee's retrieval of this information was spontaneous, that is, unprompted by any of her caretakers. Panzee's working vocabulary was about 120 lexigrams, most of which refer to food, and therefore, her use of the keyboard to indicate the hidden item approximates a recall measure. Buchanan, Gill, and Braggio (1981) also used a recall-like measure with a language-trained chimpanzee in a list-learning paradigm. However, the retention interval between the beginning of the learning phase and the beginning of the retrieval phase lasted for a maximum of around 30 seconds. Therefore, the Buchanan et al. data are likely to have been recalled from short-term or working memory, whereas Menzel's data were retrieved from long-term memory. Finally, pointing to food hidden outside Panzee's enclosure was not a common task for Panzee. Therefore, the trials used also satisfy the trial-unique constraint of episodic memory.

Menzel's study represents a significant advance in the study of nonhuman episodic memory, but there is a problem when interpreting Menzel's results as evidence of episodic memory. The chimpanzee's memory need not have been palinscopic. It is possible that Panzee updated her memory about spatial landmarks and their contents and did not need to mentally refer to the event of watching Menzel hiding the food. In this view, retrieval would be based on the present state of the world and not on the occurrence of a past event.

Reporting on Past Events   A fourth approach comes from my own lab. I have argued that the three main features of episodic memory in humans are long-term memory based on unique and nonrepeatable events, feelings of pastness when those memories are retrieved, and a feeling of veracity and confidence about those memories (Schwartz & Evans, 2001). The last two features are extremely difficult to demonstrate in nonhuman animals. Accordingly, we have opted for an operational definition of episodic-like memory in our work with apes that has the following features. The ape's response must be based on retrieval from long-term memory of a unique event that was learned in a single trial. In addition, the animal's response should provide information about its past rather than about the current state of its knowledge. This allows us to address the issue of palinscopy without concern for the animal's ability to describe its internal mental states. Note that in the prior research described, only Zentall et al. (2001) asked their animals to report on the past, albeit at very short retention intervals. Clayton et al. (2001) and Menzel's (1999) animals were required to report the location of food that was hidden earlier on a single trial (also see MacDonald, 1994, for single-trial spatial learning in gorillas). We now turn to data collected using the "reporting on past events" definition.

KING, THE GORILLA

I have had the opportunity to study King, a lowland gorilla (*Gorilla gorilla gorilla*) who has lived at Monkey Jungle in Miami, Florida, for the past 20 years (figure 9.1). At the time I began testing him, King was 30 years old and had a long history of contact and social interactions with his human caretakers. King was wild-caught around the age of 2 in Cameroon, in western Africa. He was then sold to a Las Vegas circus, where he performed on a daily basis for nearly 8 years. Little is known now about his life in the circus, other than that he was trained to perform and his front teeth were removed (making social contact with other gorillas problematic). By the age of 10, King was too large, strong, and unmanageable for the circus, and he was sold to Monkey Jungle in 1980. For many years, he lived alongside a female gorilla, who died in 1989. Since then, King has not been in the company of other gorillas. King has received daily enrichment sessions to keep his mind active, to educate the public, and to facilitate medical exams.

Perhaps because of his extensive human contact and his limited contact with his own species, King shows behaviors uncommon to his species. Few of these abilities have ever been studied formally. They include his language comprehension of both spoken English and Spanish speech, his response to eye contact as a social bond rather than as a threat, and, indeed, his schadenfreude (we have noted but not attempted to measure his pleasure vocalizations when he witnesses someone tripping or falling). Some prior formal testing had

Figure 9.1 King knuckle-walking in his outdoor area. He occupies .6 hectares of Florida hammock forest. See color insert.

been done with King. He is the only gorilla in the scientific literature to have passed the mirror self-recognition test (see Swartz & Evans, 1994, for details). After observing the mark on his brow in the mirror, he immediately engaged in touching it and then tried to rub off the mark on the bars of his cage. For all these reasons, we considered King an excellent animal to test for evidence of episodic memory.

Before formal testing began, King was trained to associate specific cards with specific items of food. Thus, a card with a drawing of an apple on it was associated with both apples and the spoken word "apple." Five such foods were trained. Because this was done as enrichment prior to my involvement with King, there is no documentation of how many trials and how much time it took King to learn these card/food associations. However, at the start of my research, King was trained to use a particular card in the presence of three different experimenters or when the experimenter's name was spoken. Training continued until King was 90% accurate at presenting the card when either the name was mentioned or the person was present. This 90% accuracy was achieved after three sessions (30 trials).

In Experiment 2 of Schwartz et al. (2002), King was expected to make two responses, one about the "what" component (food) and one about the "who" component, that is, which experimenter gave King the food. One of the experimenters gave King a specific food. Retention intervals were either short (5 minutes) or long (24 hours). In order to be reinforced (with an unrelated food), King had to respond with a card representing both the correct food (the what component) and the correct person (the who component). King was accurate at both the short and long retention intervals at identifying both the food (what) and the person (who) (see table 9.1).

The Schwartz et al. (2002) study has one important advantage over the earlier work of Menzel (1999). In our study, the gorilla's responses were not based on the current state of the world—that is, the food had been distributed and consumed. The response that King made is therefore a reflection of what happened in the past. To be concrete, King ate an apple at Time 1. After a retention interval, the apple was eaten and gone, but remembering that action garnered a reward. We rewarded King for the correct answer, which required King to retrieve information about the past. Thus, like Zentall's study, Schwartz et al. showed that the gorilla was referring to a past event. However, unlike Zentall et al., we showed retention at long intervals (up to 24 hours).

Nonetheless, this study is not without nonepisodic interpretations. First, and most problematic, is that King was tested repeatedly in similar trials. It is therefore possible that he expected the test and that he planned the correct response by encoding the correct food and person "semantically." He could then rehearse that association (see Washburn & Astur, 1998, for a discussion of rehearsal in nonhuman primates). Like Panzee, King's responses are potentially guided by semantic as well as episodic memory. Thus, we lack the element of surprise that Zentall et al. (2001) consider so important. Second, because the tests were five-alternative recognition tests (for food) and two-alternative recognition tests, it is also possible that some responses were guided by the familiarity of the targets rather than retrieval of past events (i.e., Jacoby, 1991; Kelley & Jacoby, 2000). However, the 24-hour retention intervals suggest that it was not simply familiarity. Third, like all previous experiments with nonhumans, we

Table 9.1 King's Percentage Correct

	5 min. RI		24 hr. RI	
	"What"	"Who"	"What"	"Who"
Experiment 1	70		82	
Experiment 2	55	82	73	87

Note: 20% is chance baseline for "what" questions; 50% is chance baseline for "who" quetions. RI, retention interval. From Schwartz et al., 2002.

made no headway in examining the mnemonic experience of the go-rilla when he was retrieving the target memory.

To address some of those issues, we have completed a new series of studies with King (Schwartz, Meissner, Hoffman, Evans, & Frazier, 2004) that was based on the human eyewitness memory paradigm. In the study, King witnessed unique events. These events involved either eating novel foods (e.g., sapodilla, cactus fruit, passion fruit), seeing unfamiliar people or familiar people doing odd things (e.g., stealing a cell phone, doing jumping jacks, swinging a tennis racket), or seeing unfamiliar objects (e.g., a plastic frog, a baby's shoes, a guitar). After eating a novel food or witnessing a novel event, King was given a 5- to 15-minute retention interval. After the retention interval, three photographs were shown and then given to King. One photograph depicted an aspect of the event (e.g., the object witnessed) and the other two photographs were distractors (e.g., other objects). King's task was to select the correct photograph and pass that card through the bars of his cage to a blind tester. A trainer outside of King's view would then verify if the photograph was the correct one. If it was, King was given food reinforcement.

King's performance in this task was less than stellar (55% accurate overall). However, it was significantly higher than chance (33%). We suspect his performance was weak because some of the photographs might have been hard for him to see and some of the discriminations themselves were difficult (e.g., choosing honeydew over cantaloupe melon). The study does show that King could retrieve unique events from the past based on unique events even when he did not know what test to expect. Because 24-hour retention intervals were not tested, responses based on familiarity could not be ruled out. Thus, we cannot rule out a nonautonoetic response based on familiarity in this study. On the other hand, King's responses are based on past events, not current knowledge, and, in that sense, they satisfy the palinscopy constraint.

In another experiment in this series, we asked whether an ape's episodic memory could be manipulated in a manner similar to that observed in experiments on human episodic memory. An eyewitness to a crime sees a perpetrator engage in an illegal act. This is a unique and often exceedingly quick event involving the observation of a com-plete stranger doing something that may arouse high levels of stress in the witness (e.g., Loftus, 1979; Loftus & Hoffman, 1989). Think of witnessing a burglar climb out your window and descend the fire escape. At some point later, either to police, lawyers, or under oath in the courtroom, the eyewitness must recount the event in question. The desired memory response is a palinscopic reflection on the events witnessed. The witness must mentally time travel and recount the event from the past. We know that people are generally accurate, but that under many circumstances people are prone to errors (Dunning & Stern, 1992). For example, in the famous misinformation paradigm, witnesses often misremember events in systematic ways (see Loftus, 1979; Loftus & Hoffman, 1989).

Would a nonhuman primate be able to report who committed a particular act? This is a potentially revealing line of inquiry because the memory would necessarily be palinscopic, that is, about the past and not about the present state of the world. Thus, even if the research fails to show mechanisms common to human episodic memory, the studies would be important because of the palinscopic nature of the task. Another advantage of this paradigm is that it only requires an animal to point or otherwise select a photograph. Thus, it can be done with a range of animals in addition to primates and it does not involve language-like communication. Indeed, Harper and Garry (2000) have found that pigeons show some "misinformation" effects at short-term memory retention intervals in a delayed matched-to-sample task.

As we discussed earlier, King is able to reliably choose the correct person, object, or food from among three photographs following a unique event (Schwartz et al., 2004). We recently completed a misinformation study with King. Similar to the paradigm described earlier, King witnessed a unique event, such as a familiar person jumping rope. Shortly after the event, King either was shown a photograph of the person, the object, or food involved in the event (correct information condition), was shown another person, object, or food item (misinformation condition), or was not shown any new photograph (control condition). Thus, like misinformation experiments in humans, the misinformation condition here was intended to create the possibility of false memories in King.

The results were quite clear; whereas King was above chance at retrieving the correct photograph in the control and correct information condition (53%; chance was 33%), he was no different than chance in the misinformation condition (40%). However, his percentage correct in the control and correct conditions was not significantly above the 40% rate of the misinformation condition. Nonetheless, in the misinformation condition, King was just as likely to choose the additional distractor as he was the misinformation item. Therefore, like the eyewitness relying on episodic memory, King's memory was impaired by the presentation of misinformation.

CONCLUSION

One of the most perplexing issues of science is the evolution of human cognition and intelligence. Comparing humans and apes provides an imperfect measurement of this evolution because of the 6 to 8 million years of divergent paths. Depending on one's orientation and preferences, one can marvel at the similarity between humans and apes or skeptically nod at the profound differences. It would not be difficult to demonstrate any number of common episodic memory tasks that are far beyond the capability of a gorilla (e.g., flashbulb memories; see Conway, 1995). I think, however, that I have demonstrated some striking similarities between human episodic memory and the trial-unique learning and memory for individual events we have tested in King. Because King's memory attains the criterion of palinscopy or referential to the past, I think we may claim to have supported the contention that King has the rudiments of an episodic memory system.

QUESTIONS AND ANSWERS

Dr. Josep Call: I'm curious how you ask King the key question. Do you just present symbols?

Dr. Bennett Schwartz: The tester is experimentally blind to the food presented to King. In the initial studies, the tester asked, "What did you eat?" and "Who gave it to you?" We know that King responds appropriately to a wide variety of English words and commands, but what interests us is not his behavior in response to language, but if he can demonstrate memory. Nonetheless, at some point, we do wish to test the extent of his comprehension of English words and grammar. We have no idea to what extent he is responding to words or other cues.

King responds to us by using the cards. He has a set of cards with pictures of food on them and he has a set of cards with names of familiar people written on them. The cards are put into his cage by the trainer, and he responds by pushing his choice back out through the cage to the trainer. Please see Schwartz et al. (2002) for complete details.

Dr. David Smith: At what time point do you go from short term to long term? For example, how long would an animal have to hold on to a delay match-to-sample trial for it to move from short to long term?

Dr. Schwartz: Because my main focus is comparing this to human memory, I use human memory differences between long- and short-term memory as an initial guide. In theory, apes could have working memories that are either longer or shorter than ours (but see Washburn & Astur, 1998). We thought 5 minutes would put us safely beyond what anyone would expect possible of a short-term memory system.

Dr. Leonard Rosenblum: There is a study, I believe with baboons, which shows that after some preliminary training that animals outside of the group setting can correctly identify parent-offspring pairs as compared to adult female nonpaired similarly aged animal sitting next to them in photographs. Would you comment on where that kind of ability would fit into this framework?

Dr. Schwartz: That is what we would call semantic memory in humans, our knowledge of the world. Countless studies demonstrate that primates are expert learners and represent spatial and conspecific information quite well (see MacDonald, 1994, for an example). We also know they learn symbols in language-learning studies (e.g., Beran, Pate, Richardson, & Rumbaugh, 2000).

Dr. Herb Terrace: Can you expand on the uniqueness of the experience? Presumably there is a small and finite range of answers. Has the ape been trained on that block so that the uniqueness may be with respect to that particular block? How does the ape get the flavor of the task without previous experience?

Dr. Schwartz: When I started to test King, he had already been at Monkey Jungle for 20 years. He had been doing "enrichment" activities for nearly that long. One of his enrichment activities was learning to associate the wooden blocks with food items and people's names. Nobody was able to tell me how long he had been doing this form of enrichment, and there are no records. So much of his learning history is undocumented. We did document the rapidity with which he learned the names of new blocks, such as the block bearing my name. By the second session of learning, he was at 90% correct in providing the block with my name in response to my spoken name.

To answer the first part of your question, his ability to report on unique experiences is limited by the number of cards he can handle. Thus, in Experiment 2 of Schwartz et al. (2002) he is limited to one of two people and one of five foods. For this reason, the second set of studies described in this chapter use photographs in which we were able to test him each time with a unique event and not have to repeat stimuli.

Dr. Endel Tulving: I'd like to congratulate you on a fascinating and very interesting presentation. You reminded us all that we may be witnessing a new research area that has a potential at being successful. You understand what the issues are perfectly. In all of the history of science many people just talk past each other. A very important requirement for these kinds of experiments is that you don't let your animals pull a clever Hans trick. Earlier I told you I spent the whole day with John, who has no episodic memory because of hippocampal damage. He has become very sensitive to tests of science. Some of the things that amnesiacs can accomplish in test situations are due to very subtle cues. It is very important that when you do these tests with King, the experimenter is experimentally blind.

Dr. Schwartz: The trainer who did most of testing has little understanding of the scientific process. The biggest trick is making sure the trainer has no idea what the food is. If she did, she would try to cue him every which way. In fact, we threw out several trials in which she came by while we were giving food to King that she wasn't supposed to see.

Dr. Tulving: If so, I think you should test her as well and correlate the results.

Dr. Schwartz: In the second set of studies, the tester always guessed at the correct response. Testers did not differ from chance, nor was there a correlation between their choices and those of King.

ACKNOWLEDGMENTS I am grateful to Monkey Jungle for access to King and for employees' time. In particular, I thank Sharon Du Mond, Sian Evans, and

Steve Jacques for their continued support of this project. I thank Leslie Frazier, Chris Meissner, Lisa Son, and Herb Terrace for comments on earlier drafts of this chapter. I thank Herb Terrace, Janet Metcalfe, and the participants of the conference on the origins of self-knowing consciousness for their insight and comments.

REFERENCES

Beran, M. J., Pate, J. L., Richardson, W. K., & Rumbaugh, D. M. (2000). A chimpanzee's (*Pan troglodytes*) long-term retention of lexigrams. *Animal Learning and Behavior, 28,* 201–207.

Beran, M. J., Savage-Rumbaugh, E. S., Brakke, K. E., Kelley, J. W., & Rumbaugh, D. M. (1998). Symbol comprehension and learning: A "vocabulary" test of three chimpanzees (*Pan troglodytes*). *Evolution of Communication, 2,* 171–188.

Bjork, R. A., & Bjork, E. L. (1992). A new theory of disuse and an old theory of stimulation fluctuation. In A. F. Healy, S. M. Kosslyn, & R. M. Shiffrin (Eds.), *From learning processes to cognitive processes: Essays in honor of William K. Estes* (Vol. 2, pp. 35–67). Hillsdale, NJ: Lawrence Erlbaum.

Buchanan, J. P., Gill, T. G., & Braggio, J. T. (1981). Serial position and the clustering effect in a chimpanzee's free recall. *Memory and Cognition, 9,* 651–660.

Burke, D., Cieplucha, C., Cass, J., Russell, F., & Fry, G. (2002). Win-shift and win-stay learning in the short-beaked echidna (*Tachyglossus aculeatus*). *Animal Cognition, 5,* 79–84.

Cabeza, R. (1999). Functional neuroimaging of episodic memory retrieval. In E. Tulving (Ed.), *Memory, consciousness, and the brain* (pp. 76–90). Philadelphia: Psychology Press.

Clayton, N. S., & Dickinson, A. (1998). Episodic-like memory during cache recovery by scrub jays. *Nature, 395,* 272–274.

Clayton, N. S., & Dickinson, A. (1999). Memory for the content of caches by scrub jays (*Aphelocoma coerulescens*). *Journal of Experimental Psychology: Animal Behavior Processes, 25,* 82–91.

Clayton, N. S., & Dickinson, A. (2000). What-where-when memory in food-storing scrub jays. *Abstracts of the Psychonomic Society, 5,* 59.

Clayton, N. S., & Griffiths, D. P. (2002). Testing episodic-like memory in animals. In L. Squire & D. L. Schacter (Eds.), *The neuropsychology of memory* (pp. 492–507). New York: Guilford.

Clayton, N. S., Yu, K. S., & Dickinson, A. (2001). Scrub jays (*Aphelocoma coerulescens*) form integrated memories of the multiple features of caching episodes. *Journal of Experimental Psychology: Animal Behavior Processes, 27,* 17–29.

Conway, M. A. (1995). *Flashbulb memories.* Hove, UK: Lawrence Erlbaum.

Dewsbury, D. A. (2000). Comparative cognition in the 1930's. *Psychonomic Bulletin and Review, 7,* 267–283.

Dickinson, P. (1974). *The poison oracle.* New York: Pantheon.

Dunning, D., & Stern, L. B. (1992). Examining the generality of eyewitness hypermnesia: A close look at time delay and question type. *Applied Cognitive Psychology, 6,* 643–657.

Eichenbaum, H., & Fortin, N. J. (2003). Episodic memory and the hippocampus: It's about time. *Current Directions, 12*, 53–57.

Gardiner, J. M., & Java, R. I. (1991). Forgetting in recognition memory with and without recollective experience. *Memory and Cognition, 19*, 617–623.

Griffiths, D., Dickinson, A., & Clayton, N. (1999). Episodic memory: What can animals remember about their past? *Trends in Cognitive Science, 3*, 74–80.

Harper, D. N., & Garry, M. (2000). Postevent cues bias recognition performance in pigeons. *Animal Learning and Behavior, 28*, 59–67.

Jacoby, L. L. (1991). A process dissociation framework: Separating automatic from intentional uses of memory. *Journal of Memory and Language, 30*, 513–541.

Kelley, C. M., & Jacoby, L. L. (2000). Recollection and familiarity. In E. Tulving & F. I. M. Craik (Eds.), *The Oxford handbook of memory* (pp. 215–228). New York: Oxford University Press.

Loftus, E. F. (1979). *Eyewitness testimony.* Cambridge, MA: Harvard University Press.

Loftus, E. F., & Hoffman, H. G. (1989). Misinformation and memory: The creation of new memories. *Journal of Experimental Psychology: General, 118*, 100–114.

MacDonald, S. E. (1994). Gorilla's (*Gorilla gorilla gorilla*) spatial memory in a foraging task. *Journal of Comparative Psychology, 108*, 107–113.

MacDonald, S. E., & Agnes, M. M. (1999). Orangutan (*Pongo pygmaeus abelii*) spatial memory and behavior in a foraging task. *Journal of Comparative Psychology, 113*, 213–217.

Menzel, C. R. (1999). Unprompted recall and reporting of hidden objects by a chimpanzee (*Pan trogolodytes*) after extended delays. *Journal of Comparative Psychology, 113*, 426–434.

Morris, R. G. M. (2002). Episodic-like memories in animals: Psychological criteria, neural mechanisms and the value of episodic-like tasks to investigate animal models of neurodegenerative disease. In A. Baddeley, M. Conway, & J. Aggleton (Eds.), *Episodic memory: New directions in research* (pp. 181–203). New York: Oxford University Press.

Platt, M. L., Brannon, E., Briese, T. L., & French, J. A. (1996). Differences in feeding ecology predict differences in performance between golden lion tamarins (*Leontopithicus rosalia*) and Wied's marmoset (*Callithrix kuhli*) on spatial and visual memory tasks. *Animal Learning and Behavior, 24*, 384–393.

Roberts, W. A. (2002). Are animals stuck in time? *Psychological Bulletin, 128*, 473–489.

Schacter, D. L., Verfaillie, M., & Anes, M. D. (1997). Illusory memories in amnesic patients: Conceptual and perceptual false recognition. *Neuropsychology, 11*, 331–342.

Schwartz, B. L., Colon, M. R., Sanchez, I. C., Rodriguez, I. A., & Evans, S. (2002). Single-trial learning of "what" and "who" information in a gorilla (*Gorilla gorilla gorilla*): Implications for episodic memory. *Animal Cognition, 5*, 85–90.

Schwartz, B. L., & Evans, S. (2001). Episodic memory in primates. *American Journal of Primatology, 55*, 71–85.

Schwartz, B. L., Meissner, C. A., Hoffman, M., Evans, S., & Frazier, L. D.

(2004). Event memory and misinformation effects in a gorilla (*Gorilla gorilla gorilla*). *Animal Cognition, 7*, 93–100.

Sherry, D. (1984). Food storage by black-capped chickadees: Memory for the location and contents of caches. *Animal Behavior, 32*, 451–464.

Swartz, K. B., & Evans, S. (1994). Social and cognitive factors in chimpanzee and gorilla mirror behavior and self-recognition. In S. T. Parker, R. W. Mitchell, & M. L. Boccia (Eds.), *Self-awareness in animals and humans: Developmental perspectives* (pp. 189–206). Cambridge, UK: Cambridge University Press.

Suddendorf, T. S., & Corballis, M. C. (1997). Mental time travel and the evolution of the human mind. *Genetic, Social, and General Psychology Monographs, 123*, 133–167.

Tulving, E. (1972). Episodic and semantic memory. In E. Tulving & W. Donaldson (Eds.), *Organization of memory* (pp. 382–403). New York: Academic Press.

Tulving, E. (1983). *Elements of episodic memory.* New York: Oxford University Press.

Tulving, E. (1993). What is episodic memory? *Current Directions in Psychology, 3*, 67–70.

Tulving, E. (2002). Episodic memory and common sense: How far apart? In A. Baddeley, M. Conway, & J. Aggleton (Eds.), *Episodic memory: New directions in research* (pp. 269–288). New York: Oxford University Press.

Tulving, E., & Lepage, M. (2000). Where in the brain is the awareness of one's past. In D. Schacter & E. Scarry (Eds.), *Memory, brain, and belief* (pp. 208–230). Cambridge, MA: Harvard University Press.

Tulving, E., & Markowitsch, H. J. (1998). Episodic and declarative memory: Role of the hippocampus. *Hippocampus, 8*, 198–204.

Washburn, D. A., & Astur, R. S. (1998). Nonverbal working memory of humans and monkeys: Rehearsal in the sketchpad. *Memory and Cognition, 26*, 277–286.

Wheeler, M. A. (2000). Episodic memory and autonoetic awareness. In E. Tulving & F. I. M. Craik (Eds.), *The Oxford handbook of memory* (pp. 597–608). New York: Oxford University Press.

Zentall, T. R., Clement, T. S., Bhatt, R. S., & Allen, J. (2001). Episodic-like memory in pigeons. *Psychonomic Bulletin and Review, 8*, 685–690.

10

Studies of Uncertainty Monitoring and Metacognition in Animals and Humans

J. David Smith

HUMAN METACOGNITION

Humans feel uncertain—they know when they do not know. Moreover, they often respond intelligently in difficult situations by pausing, reflecting, and seeking help, hints, or information. These states of feeling and knowing and these adaptive coping responses anchor the extensive literatures on metacognition and the related phenomena of metamemory and uncertainty monitoring (Brown, 1991; Brown, Bransford, Ferrara, & Campione, 1983; Dunlosky & Nelson, 1992; Flavell, 1979; Hart, 1965; Koriat, 1993; Metcalfe & Shimamura, 1994; Nelson, 1992; Schwartz, 1994; Smith, Brown, & Balfour, 1991).

Metacognition can be defined as thinking about thinking, or cognition about cognition. The idea in this field is that in some minds mental activities occur at a higher "metalevel" and at a lower "object level" during cognitive processing. In these minds, there is a cognitive executive that supervises (i.e., oversees and facilitates) thought or problem solving. Figure 10.1 summarizes the functions of the cognitive executive using a framework provided by Nelson and Narens (1990). The overseeing or monitoring functions are shown at the top, and they are studied by having human participants make basic metacognitive judgments. There is an ease-of-learning judgment about whether material will be easy or hard to learn, a judgment of learning about how much has been learned, a feeling-of-knowing judgment about whether information is potentially available in memory, and a confidence judgment about a potential answer.

The cognitive executive also controls cognition, directing information processing along more productive paths. These metacognitive control processes are shown at the bottom of the figure. The executive

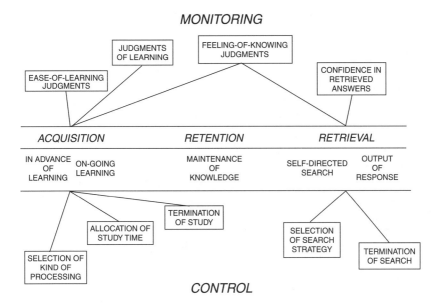

Figure 10.1 A theoretical framework for research on metacognition, showing examples of process-monitoring capacities above and process-control capacities below (after Nelson & Narens, 1990).

may devote disproportionate study time to difficult items, terminate studying when sufficient learning has been achieved, select new retrieval strategies when the present ones are failing, or abandon retrieval efforts if success seems improbable.

When humans behave metacognitively, we naturally infer some intriguing aspects of mind. We take metacognition to be about hierarchical tiers of oversight in mind (i.e., the meta- and object levels of cognition). We take it to demonstrate our awareness of the processes of mind. We link metacognitive states to our self-awareness in a reflexive sense, because uncertainty and doubts are personalized (i.e., I know that I am uncertain). We even link metacognitive states to declarative consciousness (Nelson, 1996) because we so naturally introspect about those states and speak about them to one another. It is no wonder that we take metacognition to be one of humans' most sophisticated cognitive capacities and one of those most likely to be humanly unique. For all these reasons, it is an intriguing question whether animals have analogous or homologous metacognitive capacities. The purpose of this chapter is to review some research that has attempted to answer this question and to evaluate the progress and prospects of the new research area that explores metacognition comparatively.

THE PROBLEM OF COMPARATIVE METACOGNITION RESEARCH

In beginning this exploration, comparative metacognition researchers faced obstacles that slowed initial progress. For one thing, human metacognition paradigms were not appropriate for animal participants. Their phenomena relied too heavily on introspection and on verbal reports about feelings and judgments of knowing and learning. Instead, researchers faced the problem of constructing a behavioral (i.e., nonverbal) metacognition or uncertainty-monitoring paradigm that could be used comparatively.

One key element of such a paradigm is that it must systematically cause difficulty for animals. The difficulty is what will create something like an uncertainty state that the animal may monitor or respond to adaptively. For example, psychophysical procedures accomplish this because they let one reduce the contrast between two stimulus input classes (e.g., faint sounds vs. silence) until the threshold is reached at which perceptual discriminations become very difficult (Au & Moore, 1990; Schusterman & Barrett, 1975; Yunker & Herman, 1974).

However, causing animals difficulty is not sufficient for studying their uncertainty. Illustrating this point, figure 10.2A shows a bottlenosed dolphin's performance near threshold in a difficult auditory discrimination task (Smith et al., 1995). Pressing the *high* paddle was correct when the animal heard a 2100-Hz tone. Pressing the *low* paddle was correct when the animal heard any tone that was lower in pitch. The dolphin was often able to make the response *high* for 2100-Hz tones and to make the response *low* for tones below about 2075 Hz. But the trials surrounding 2085 Hz, his known psychophysical threshold relative to 2100 Hz (Herman & Arbeit, 1972), produced chance performance and many errors. This task caused the animal the difficulty it was meant to; however, it did not show whether the ani-

---

FACING PAGE

Figure 10.2 A. Frequency discrimination performance by a bottlenosed dolphin (*Tursiops truncatus*) in the procedure of Smith et al. (1995). The horizontal axis indicates the frequency (Hz) of the tone. The response *high* was correct for tones at exactly 2100 Hz, and these trials are represented by the rightmost data point for each curve. All lower tones deserved the response *low*. The percentages of trials ending with the *high* response (dashed line) or *low* response (dotted line) are shown. B. The dolphin's performance in the same auditory discrimination when he was also given the response *uncertain*. The solid line represents the percentage of trials receiving the uncertainty response at each difficulty level. The error bars show the lower 95% confidence limits. C. The intensity of the dolphin's incidental hesitation and wavering behaviors for tones of different frequencies (Hz). See color insert.

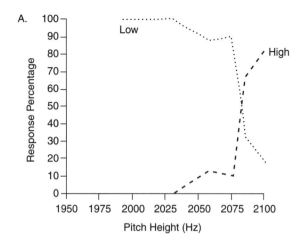

A.

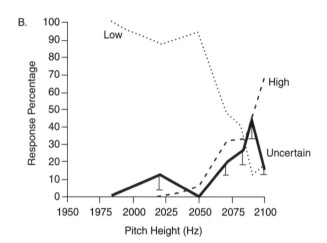

B.

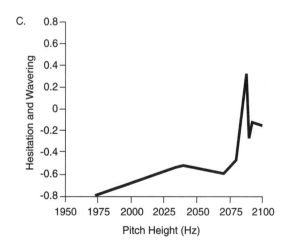

C.

mal sensed this difficulty. In fact, it was not suited to show the animal analogues of confidence and doubt or anything about the animal's system for coping with uncertainty. There were only the two primary perceptual responses, *high* and *low*, so this task denied the animal any way to demonstrate something like uncertainty by coping with it.

Therefore, a second key element of a comparative uncertainty paradigm is to give animals a third, uncertainty response that lets them cope with difficulty by declining the trials they do not choose to complete. Then one can ask if animals sense the difficulty caused by the task and respond adaptively to it.

THE UNCERTAINTY RESPONSE IN HUMAN PSYCHOPHYSICS

One sees from this discussion that one potential paradigm for studying animals' uncertainty monitoring would combine the perceptual difficulty caused by psychophysical procedures with an uncertainty response that animals could use to report on and cope with their uncertainty. I soon realized that this paradigm had a long history in human experimental psychology that was friendly to the possibility of studying metacognition comparatively.

Humans in the founding psychophysical studies were often allowed to respond Uncertain when they felt unable to classify an event into one of the two primary input classes (sound-silence, lighter than–heavier than, etc.; Angell, 1907; Fernberger, 1914, 1930; George, 1917; Watson, Kellogg, Kawanishi, & Lucas, 1973; Woodworth, 1938). However, some came to question this approach (Fernberger, 1914; Woodworth, 1938, pp. 419–427) after noting what they took to be the special psychological status of the response *uncertain*. That response had longer latencies (Angell, 1907; George, 1917; Woodworth, 1938). It was strongly affected by instructional set (Brown, 1910; Fernberger, 1914, 1930; Woodworth, 1938). It seemed to be linked to participants' temperamental tentativeness (Angell, 1907; Fernberger, 1930; Thomson, 1920). It seemed to be more reflective and cognitive than the two primary discrimination responses (Angell, 1907; Fernberger, 1930; George, 1917).

Theorists also came to believe that uncertainty responses were meta to the primary discrimination and were a comment on the participant's failure to assign a stimulus to one of the primary input classes. For example, Boring (1920) suggested that doubt was an attitudinal seducer that distracted observers from the series of mental states that are a continuous function of the series of stimuli. Similarly, George (1917) concluded that doubtful responses disrupted the constant attitude required for psychophysical judgments because they introduced "extra-serial" attitudes into a task that depended on intraserial, sensory attitudes.

The concerns the early theorists had about the uncertainty response—its special psychological status; its metarole in the performance of the psychophysical task—make this response interesting in the context of exploring metacognition comparatively. For we shall soon see that animals can respond *uncertain* in psychophysical tasks. Given this fact, it is possible that the uncertainty response plays a metarole in their performance, too. It is possible that it is for them, too, a comment on or a response to indeterminacy and difficulty in the primary discrimination.

Weiskrantz (1986, 1997) saw the same possibility. In a provocative thought experiment, he considered giving blindsight animals a commentary key with which they could report on knowing or not knowing, or on seeing or not seeing. Cowey and Stoerig (1992) considered a similar gedanken procedure. They proposed to use psychophysical procedures to bring animals to threshold (where they could be only 50% correct) in a light–no light discrimination, but also to give the animal a third lever reinforced on a 75% schedule. Then adaptive animals could report on their state of not knowing whether a light was seen by choosing the third lever selectively on threshold trials.

These converging ideas suggested that a psychophysical task combined with an uncertainty response might constructively initiate the comparative study of metacognition and uncertainty monitoring. In the next section, I discuss the results when a dolphin, monkeys, and humans were placed into uncertain perceptual situations and asked to make difficult threshold judgments while also being allowed to respond *uncertain*.

As I discuss these results, readers will naturally consider both metacognitive and lower level interpretations of performance. For example, it is possible that a dolphin trainer might cue the animal to respond *uncertain* on difficult trials. For another example, the animal might respond *uncertain* not to cope adaptively with uncertainty but simply to avoid those stimuli that are associated with errors and lean reinforcement. Additional research in the domain of memory monitoring is discussed below, and it addresses some alternative accounts. Moreover, in the last sections of this chapter, I try to address carefully the appropriate psychological interpretation of animals' performances in these procedures. Meanwhile, I invite readers to read on with both healthy skepticism and an open mind.

ANIMALS' USE OF THE PSYCHOPHYSICAL UNCERTAINTY RESPONSE

Dolphin Uncertainty Responses

To evaluate animals' capacity to respond *uncertain* in a psychophysical task, Smith et al. (1995) gave a bottlenosed dolphin (*Tursiops truncatus*) the auditory discrimination task that was described above. Pressing the paddles *high* or *low*, respectively, was correct for a 2100-Hz tone or for any lower-pitched tone. The third paddle, *uncertain,* advanced the animal into an easy, low-pitched trial that was rewarded when answered correctly. Initially, the animal was stabilized on an easy discrimination between 2100-Hz and 1200-Hz trials. Then the difficulty of the discrimination was gradually increased by raising the pitch of the lower tones until the dolphin was trying to distinguish trials of 2100 Hz and 2085 Hz. At mature performance, trial difficulty was adjusted dynamically based on performance within a session to maintain difficulty at a high level.

Figure 10.2A shows the dolphin's performance with the response *uncertain* disallowed. *High* and *low* responses mapped generally to 2100-Hz and lower-pitched tones, respectively, with these response curves crossing (signifying chance performance) at the dolphin's threshold. However, this two-response procedure denied the animal any way to cope with his uncertainty on threshold trials. To study uncertainty processes, one must map the confidence landscape more finely by providing a third response alternative.

Figure 10.2B shows the dolphin's use of this uncertainty response. Against the backdrop of the same primary discrimination performance as before, he used the uncertainty response selectively for the difficult trials surrounding his discrimination threshold.

The dolphin amplified his primary evidence of uncertainty responding through his incidental confidence and uncertainty behaviors. When the trial was easy, he swam toward the response paddles so fast that he created a bow wave that required us to cover our electronics in condoms to prevent their being soaked. When the trial was uncertain, we observed him to slow his approach to the response paddles or to waver among them. To formalize these observations, raters judged the intensity of these hesitation and wavering behaviors during the trials seen in videotaped sessions. Figure 10.2C shows the overall intensity of these behaviors for trials at different pitch levels. These behaviors were most intense at 2087 Hz and were distributed like the uncertainty response was (figure 10.2B).

Behaviors like these—which Tolman (1938, p. 27) called "lookings or runnings back and forth"—were always challenging to behaviorists because they hinted at mental turmoil in animals and because they were intuitive symptoms of uncertainty states. Indeed, Tolman (1927) offered these behaviors as a "behaviorist's definition of animal consciousness." Given the time and theoretical climate, this was an extraordinary statement. In a limited sense, therefore, the dolphin's ancillary behaviors reinforced an uncertainty interpretation of the animal's uncertainty responses. However, the concrete uncertainty response is more easily measured and compared across situations and species than are incidental waverings.

Monkey Uncertainty Responses

In a companion study, Smith, Shields, Schull, and Washburn (1997) placed two rhesus monkeys (*Macaca mulatta*) in a visual density-discrimination task. The animals (tested using the Language Research Center's Computerized Test System, LRC-CTS; Washburn & Rumbaugh, 1992) used a joystick to move a cursor to one of three objects on a computer screen (figure 10.3A). Moving the cursor to the box was correct if it contained exactly 2,950 illuminated pixels. Choosing the S was correct if the box contained any fewer pixels. Choosing the star allowed participants to decline the trial and move into a new, guaranteed-win trial. Initially, animals were stabilized on a dense-sparse discrimination involving 2,950-pixel and 450-pixel boxes. As training progressed, the difficulty of the discrimination was increased by increasing the density of the sparse boxes until participants' performance faltered (i.e., at about 2,950 vs. 2,600 pixels). At mature performance, trial difficulty was adjusted based on animals' performance within a session to maintain difficulty at a high level.

Figures 10.3B and 10.3C show the monkeys' performance. Box responses predominated on dense trials and the most difficult sparse trials. S responses predominated on the sparser trials. The primary discrimination was performed at chance where these two response curves cross, and the star was used most in this region of maximum uncertainty. Both monkeys assessed accurately when they were liable to make an error in the primary discrimination, and they bailed out of those trials selectively and adaptively. Figure 10.3D shows that humans did, too. In fact, the graphs in figure 10.3 show one of the strongest performance similarities between humans and animals in the comparative literature.

Humans' descriptions of performance were revealing about the cognitive and decisional organization of the task. They said that their responses *sparse* and *dense* were cued by the objective stimulus conditions (i.e., sparseness or denseness) on a trial. Notice that they mapped the task's two primary responses to the task's two stimulus input classes. In contrast, they said that their uncertainty responses were prompted by feelings of uncertainty and doubt about the correct answer on a trial. Notice that they mapped the uncertainty response to monitored uncertainty. It is also interesting that humans stated the uncertainty and doubt personally (I was uncertain; I didn't know). They understood that the trial was still either sparse or dense—they just felt they could not tell. Thus humans' uncertainty responses may also be showing reflexive self-awareness in the sense that humans are aware of themselves as cognitive monitors.

Given this interpretation of the uncertainty response, many humans underuse it because they are overconfident or because they feel

A. Trial Screen

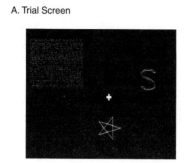

B. Monkey Abel

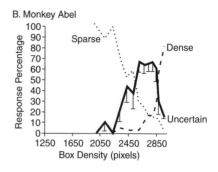

C. Monkey Baker

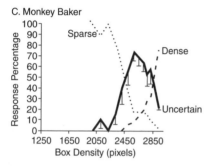

D. Humans

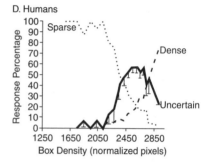

Figure 10.3 A. The screen from a trial in the dense-sparse discrimination of Smith et al. (1997). B. The performance of monkey Abel in the dense-sparse task. The response *dense* was correct for boxes with exactly 2,950 pixels—these trials are represented by the rightmost data point for each curve. All other boxes deserved the response *sparse*. The horizontal axis indicates the pixel density of the box. The solid line represents the percentage of trials receiving the uncertainty response at each density level. The error bars show the lower 95% confidence limits. The percentages of trials ending with the *dense* response (dashed line) or *sparse* response (dotted line) are also shown. C. The performance of monkey Baker in the dense-sparse discrimination depicted in the same way. D. The performance of seven humans in the dense-sparse discrimination. To equate discrimination performance across participants, the data have been normalized to place each participant's discrimination crossover at a pixel density of about 2,700. The horizontal axis indicates the normalized pixel density of the box. See color insert.

they should try or because they want to know if they can be right. They think escaping from the trial is lame or a copout. Humans have underused the response *uncertain* for these reasons for nearly 100 years. Psychophysicists have sometimes agreed with them that responding *uncertain* amounts to shirking and mental inertia (Brown, 1910, p. 32) or an admission of weakness (Fernberger, 1930, p. 110). Recently, Washburn, Smith, Baker, and Raby (2001) found that there are sex differences in this area—males are especially overconfident and tend to think they know even when they do not. Apparently, males are unlikely to stop and ask for directions even in a psychophysical discrimination.

Given the strong analogy in the data patterns produced by humans and monkeys, one wonders whether monkeys' uncertainty responses are also indicative of some form of cognitive monitoring. If so, the response *uncertain* would be a very important behavioral ambassador.

Individual Differences in Uncertainty Responding

The cross-species behavioral analogy is made stronger by the fact that there are parallel individual differences in how individual members of the two species use the uncertainty response. In a related experiment, Smith et al. (1997) gave humans and monkeys another common type of psychophysical task (Woodworth, 1938). Instead of dynamically adjusting the level of sparse trials to hold perceivers at their sparse-dense threshold, we created a sparse-dense break point at the density continuum's center and then continuously tested perceivers on a wide range of densities from sparse to dense including the difficult and uncertain region near the discrimination's break point.

Figures 10.4A and 10.4B, respectively, show the results from eight humans and one particular human. In both graphs, the discrimination responses *sparse* and *dense* were used in the same way. However, whereas humans generally responded *uncertain* most often to the difficult trials near the discrimination's break point, the one human did not. Figures 10.4C and 10.4D, respectively, show the performance of monkeys Baker and Abel. Both animals used the *sparse* and *dense* discrimination responses in the same way as each other and as humans did. However, whereas Baker selectively declined the indeterminate trials near the discrimination's break point, Abel did not. The vanishing error bars in Abel's graph make plain how long and hard we tried to get him to behave like Baker.

Everyone (humans and monkeys) in both dense-sparse tasks used the *dense* and *sparse* discrimination responses in the same way. This suggests that the two primary responses in a discrimination task have a transparent and highly stable function. Probably this is because these two responses are mapped to the two stimulus input classes. In contrast, the uncertainty response showed strong differences across individuals and tasks. The pronounced changeability of the uncertainty response persuaded early psychophysicists that it was not mapped to a stimulus input class, that it was a report on the failure to assign a stimulus to an input class, that it was related to uncertainty, extraserial attitudes, and decisional temperaments (Angell, 1907; Fernberger, 1930; Thomson, 1920). It is interesting that monkeys' use of the response *uncertain* shows this changeability, too.

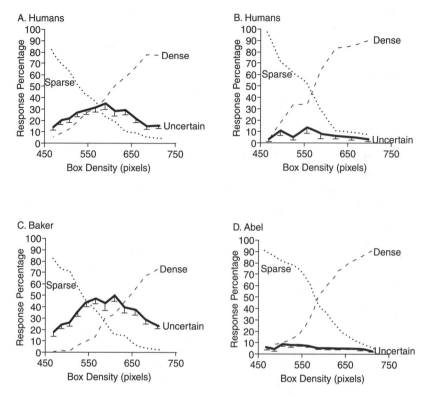

Figure 10.4 A. The performance of eight humans in the second kind of dense-sparse discrimination used by Smith et al. (1997). The lower and upper half of a range of densities deserved the *sparse* and *dense* response, respectively. The percentage of trials receiving the uncertainty response at each density are shown by the solid line. The error bars show the lower 95% confidence limits. The percentages of trials ending with the *dense* response (dashed line) or *sparse* response (dotted line) are also shown. B. The performance of one human in the same dense-sparse discrimination. C. The performance of monkey Baker in this discrimination. D. The performance of monkey Abel in this discrimination. See color insert.

COMPARATIVE STUDIES OF MEMORY MONITORING IN A SERIAL PROBE RECOGNITION TASK

There are other kinds of difficulty than perceptual difficulty. In fact, memory tasks that cause memory difficulty are a sharp focus in studies of human metacognition. Accordingly, comparative researchers have also asked whether animals can monitor their memory and respond adaptively when the state of their memory does not justify completing a memory test—that is, whether animals have cognitive capacities that are analogous to humans' memory monitoring.

For example, Smith, Shields, Allendoerfer, and Washburn's (1998) exploration of these capacities took advantage of the fact that memory performance changes in predictable ways across the serial positions of a memory list. The predictability tells the experimenter which memory trials are difficult and uncertain and lets him or her ask whether animals decline those trials selectively. Smith et al. adopted the serial probe recognition (SPR) task that is ubiquitous in comparative memory research (Castro & Larsen, 1992; Roberts & Kraemer, 1981; Sands & Wright, 1980; Wright, Santiago, Sands, Kendrick, & Cook, 1985). In their procedure, the animal saw a "list" of four pictures and then was asked whether a fifth probe picture had been in the list or not. Working from left to right at about 1 second each, scan the four shapes in figure 10.5 to get an idea of what the presentation of a memory trial was like. If you think this kind of trial is too easy, go pick on someone your own brain size—the participants were monkeys. Monkeys made a *there* or *not there* response as the probe was judged to have been in the list or not. But we also gave animals the response *uncertain* that let them decline any memory tests of their choosing. (Robert Hampton's closely related research on memory monitoring by monkeys is discussed in chapter 11, this volume.)

Figure 10.6A shows a monkey's performance in this task. When he chose to complete the memory tests, he showed classic primacy and recency effects. Most important, though, he used the uncertainty response in the mirror image of those effects. That is, he declined trials selectively when his worst serial positions were probed. Figure 10.6B shows that the same was true for 10 humans under similar conditions (though these conditions were not the right ones for producing a robust human primacy effect). The similarity between the human and animal graphs is made more compelling by the fact that humans were told explicitly to use the uncertainty response to report on and cope with memory indeterminacy. Thus, humans declined memory tests when they felt uncertain. Monkeys behaved like humans.

Figure 10.5 An example of the memory lists Smith et al. (1998) presented to monkeys in a serial probe recognition task. The pictures would have been presented to monkeys successively for about 1 second each, by computer and in different colors.

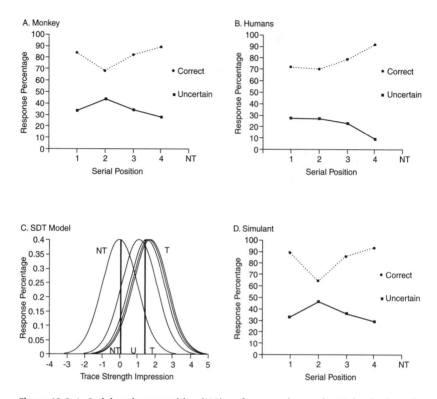

Figure 10.6 A. Serial probe recognition (SPR) performance by monkey Baker in the task of Smith et al. (1998). NT denotes *not there* trials. The serial position (1–4) of the probe in the list of pictures is also given along the x-axis for the probes on *there* trials. The percentage of trials of each type that received the uncertainty response is shown (bold line). The percentage correct (of the trials on which the memory test was attempted) is also shown (dotted line). B. Performance by 10 humans in a similar SPR task used by Smith et al. C. A signal detection theory (SDT) portrayal of monkey Baker's decisional strategy in the SPR task of Smith et al. (1998). Unit-normal trace-impression distributions are centered at the locations along the trace-strength continuum corresponding to the animals *d* for probes of the four serial positions in the memory lists (*there*, T), and at 0.0 for the NT probes. These normal curves are overlain by the decision criteria that define the animal's three response regions (from left to right, NT, *uncertain* [U], and T). D. Performance by the SDT simulant that fit best monkey Baker's performance. See color insert.

On some occasions, Smith et al. ran monkey Baker without the uncertainty response available. This condition let us test an additional prediction that arises from a memory-monitoring interpretation of monkeys' performance. The prediction is that animals should perform better when they choose to complete the memory test than when they are forced to complete it. This prediction follows because the monkey should accept memory tests when the probe picture encounters either quite strong or quite weak traces, and he will often be able to give these probes a correct *there* or *not there* response, respectively. In contrast, if the animal is forced to complete all memory tests, his performance will include those memory tests he would have declined because he monitored indeterminate traces. He will often be wrong on these trials and so his overall percentage correct will fall. Smith et al. found that Baker's performance did deteriorate substantially when he was denied the uncertainty response. Baker was clearly sensing something real about his memory that was rationally attended to in deciding whether to accept or decline memory tests. In fact, evidently Baker was using the uncertainty response adaptively to avoid errors when he monitored an indeterminately available memory.

A Formal Model of Uncertainty Monitoring

Signal detection theory (SDT) provides a constructive framework for thinking about the psychological organization of the animal's performance in this and the perceptual threshold tasks considered earlier. Regarding the memory-monitoring task, one can assume that the list items create memory impressions that lie along a continuum of trace strength (the x-axis in figure 10.6C). Then the probe picture queries the strength of one trace. Probes on *not there* trials will generally point to weak traces, perhaps averaging 0.0 plus or minus the scatter of memory variability (the normal distribution NT in the figure). Probes on *there* trials will point to stronger traces on average (though still with memory variability), especially for the primacy and recency list items (the four T normal distributions in the figure). These four distributions would be centered at the memory sensitivity (d) appropriate to the performance that the animal showed at each serial position (MacMillan & Creelman, 1991, pp. 209–230). The overlap between the *not there* and *there* distributions is what makes the SPR task difficult and uncertain, because it means that probes on *there* and *not there* trials often feel equally strongly remembered to the animal. Facing this difficult memory situation, the animal needs to find a way to divide the memory continuum into three response regions using response criteria, hopefully being able to respond *not there*, *there*, or *uncertain* when the probe contacts a memory trace that is weak, strong, or ambiguous/indeterminate. These criterion lines are also shown in the figure.

To feel this model in your mind, think which of the two probe pictures in figure 10.7 contacts a stronger trace in memory. Many will say that the probe on the left does. It was the fourth item in the sample trial given previously and so received a recency boost of activation from being in that position in the list. The animals would likely respond *there* to this probe item. The probe on the right may have made a dimmer impression on memory because it was presented in the sec-

Figure 10.7 Two probes that might have followed the memory list given in figure 10.5. Both would be *there* probes. The item on the left reprises the item in the list that occurred at the final, strongest, recency-advantaged serial position. The item on the right reprises the item in the list that occurred at the weakest, second serial position. The monkeys' memory probes were computer-presented in color.

ond, weakest serial position. The animals would often respond *uncertain* to this probe item.

I conducted simulations to evaluate the SDT model of monkeys' memory-monitoring performances and to find out what decisional strategy (i.e., what placement for the two criterion lines) they were probably using. To do so, I evaluated the data patterns produced by many thousands of simulated creatures (simulants), who placed their decision criteria at different points along the trace-strength continuum. Each simulant completed 8,000 trials in a virtual version of the SPR task. On each trial, the simulant received one of five trial types (*not there* or a *there* probe of one of four serial positions), assessed (with memory variability) the trace strength this probe item contacted (following the five probability-density functions shown in figure 10.6C), and responded according to its criterion placements. I summarized the simulant's performance over the 8,000 trials and compared its performance pattern mathematically to monkey Baker's observed performance pattern. The criterion of best fit was the sum of the squared deviations (SSD) between the observed and simulated percentages. On average, the best-fitting response percentages were within about 3% of their observed targets. Thus the performance of this model was competitive with the performance of other formal models in the experimental literature (Smith & Minda, 1998, 2000). Figure 10.6D shows the performance of the simulant that most closely reproduced Baker's performance (compare figure 10.6A). Figure 10.6C shows the criterion placements of this simulant. One sees intuitively that Baker found an adaptive decisional strategy. He took the memory tests (i.e., he responded *not there* or *there*) that presented with weak or strong traces. He responded *uncertain* for indeterminate, ambiguous trace strengths that could easily have been caused by either a *there* or a *not there* probe. In fact, in additional simulations I was able to establish that Baker's decisional strategy in the task was essentially optimal in terms of its reward efficiency.

CONSIDERING THE PSYCHOLOGY OF UNCERTAINTY RESPONSES AND UNCERTAINTY-MONITORING PERFORMANCES

The data patterns produced by the dolphin and monkeys in the perceptual and memory tasks are noncontroversial matters of fact. However, there remains the problem of interpreting these performances psychologically. What representations underlie performance? What level do animals' decisional processes occupy in their cognitive system? How close to consciousness do they lie? How close is the performance of animals to those performances of humans that we comfortably call metacognitive? Difficult questions like these have sparked theoretical tensions throughout a century of scholarship within comparative psychology. In the present discussion, I raise six points that help me think psychologically about animals' use of the response *uncertain* and that may help readers of this volume, too.

1. The Parsimony Embodied in Morgan's Canon Is Sometimes False

Actually, it is easy to get theoretical sparks to fly regarding this research. For example, consider the dolphin's and monkeys' perceptual threshold tasks that began the exploration of animals' metacognitive capacities and that were discussed earlier. In these cases, one could explain performance using behaviorist constructs like stimulus control or reinforcement history. One might say that stimuli of intermediate (threshold) pitch or density were mildly aversive for being associated with errors and timeouts and that uncertainty responses were conditioned in these stimulus contexts. In this case, the uncertainty response would be poorly named and would have nothing to do with metacognition. This low-level description of animals' responses in perceptual threshold tasks would have a distinguished pedigree. It would defend the principle of parsimony embodied in Morgan's Canon (Morgan, 1906, p. 53) that one should always interpret an organism's behavior at the lowest possible psychological level. Thus, given performances by animals that might be about uncertainty monitoring, there is a 100-year-old urge to dismiss them as low-level associative phenomena. I suspect that many readers felt this urge as they read about those results. The first point in my discussion is to caution readers sharply that this urge is inappropriate in the present instance. The parsimony embodied in Morgan's Canon is false in this case.

To see why, consider the graphs in figure 10.3 that show humans and monkeys using the uncertainty response identically in the dense-parse threshold task and that show one of the strongest existing parallels between human and animal performance. These graphs make it clear that one cannot interpret the monkeys' performance in a vacuum. Humans perform the same way. Moreover, humans report that they are consciously uncertain and reflexively (i.e., personally) self-aware as they produce these graphs. Humans and monkeys have shared much of their evolutionary histories, and probably shared the set of adaptive pressures that could have led to the emergence of an adaptive uncertainty-resolving cognitive system. Humans and monkeys even share homologous brain structures. Thus it is unparsimonious to interpret the same graph produced by humans and monkeys in qualitatively different ways—consciously metacognitive versus low-level associative. It uses two opposed behavioral systems to produce the same phenomenon when one might do.

In fact, this duality of interpretation would even be an inappropriate scientific stance in this case. Imagine if, in any other domain, a researcher showed identical graphs by two populations (older and younger children, nondepressed and depressed individuals, etc.) and then nonetheless offered qualitatively different high-level and low-level interpretations to explain them. This would cause a peer-review massacre. If it were older and younger children, or individuals with and without depression, the researcher would have no warrant to make this dual interpretation. Likewise, in the case of humans and animals, there is no warrant to do so, either. It is extraordinary that this duality of interpretation is given momentary credence when the two populations are humans and animals. However, this is an accident of the history of comparative psychology that serves the field poorly. To the contrary, scientific inference in this case would require that the two graphs be provisionally interpreted as instances of the same phenomenon—a phenomenon that humans describe very clearly—until other evidence required the monkey graph to be given a qualitatively different and lower interpretation. Thus, given identical graphs by humans and animals, a significant part of the burden of proof falls on the behaviorist who would interpret the monkeys' performances in a dismissive way. The dismissive interpretation is not the scientifically appropriate default assumption, though it may be the historically preconceived notion.

2. Associative Interpretations Are Not Sufficient for Explaining Animals' Performances in Uncertainty-Monitoring Tasks

Given this historical context, it is a helpful consideration that a variety of low-level interpretations that concern the control of behavior by stimulus cues are insufficient to explain the performances described in this chapter. For example, in the memory-monitoring task of Smith et al. (1998), all stimuli, across trials, became targets and foils and were rewarded and nonrewarded following both primary responses. No stimulus cue indicated any response. Only the presence or absence of the probe in the preceding list was ever relevant. The psychological action in this experiment occurred along an internal continuum of subjective trace strength, with the animals responding *uncertain* when probes met memory traces that were indeterminately strong or weak. Thus, the signals for behavior in this study were cognitively derived, abstract, and subjective. These memory-based assessments are profoundly different from the signals available in many traditional operant situations, wherein a tone or a keylight comes over many trials to stably, predictably signal rich or poor reinforcement. Accordingly, one sees that the animals' behavior in the memory task lies far from traditional senses of stimulus control.

This is an important theoretical and psychological interpretation. In essence, the animals are monitoring the contents of memory on each trial. In essence, they are realizing a capacity for metamemory, though further research might be able to draw distinctions between what humans and monkeys are capable of in this area, and between what the two species know, feel, and experience consciously in the tasks.

A similar conclusion would apply to the uncertainty-monitoring task used by Shields, Smith, and Washburn (1997). Shields et al. asked whether monkeys could recruit adaptive uncertainty responses when pushed to their psychophysical limit in a same-different task. The same-different task requires one to go beyond the absolute stimulus qualities in order to make a judgment about the relation between two stimuli. The abstractness of this task explains why same-different performance is so hard to train, why it is so fragile when placed into opposition with absolute stimulus qualities, and why true same-different performance is so phylogenetically restricted. Shields et al. found that monkeys did respond *uncertain* adaptively when they were presented with stimulus relations that were near their threshold of discriminating same from different. The monkeys' data pattern was once again essentially identical to that of humans. Yet behavior in this task was not controllable by absolute stimuli, whether through the generalization gradients surrounding them or the reinforcement histories associated with them. As within the memory task, the cues were more cognitively derived. In the same-different task, they represented a decision about the (indeterminate) status of the relation assessed on a trial.

The principal conclusion of this section—that associative interpretations do not suffice for the memory-monitoring task or for Shields et al.'s (1997) same-different task—feeds back to provide an additional reason why an associative interpretation of animals' perceptual threshold performances is unparsimonious. One cannot consider the perceptual threshold results in a vacuum because they do not exist alone. That animals can base uncertainty responses on derived cognitive states (e.g., indeterminate same-different relations, indeterminately available memory traces) already grants them a sophisticated form of cognitive monitoring. Now, if one explains their threshold performances using a low-level associative mechanism, one grants them (unparsimoniously) two different indeterminacy-resolution systems, one of which is already fairly high level. However, one could explain the data more simply just by invoking one uncertainty-resolution system that applies to indeterminate memories, same-different relations, and threshold events. Readers might want to consider, if they find themselves resisting the idea that animals would have a generalized indeterminacy-resolution system of this kind, why they think it is implausible. Later I discuss the possible benefits animals might derive from having such a system.

3. A Failure of Uncertainty Monitoring by Rats

Additional data suggest indirectly that monkeys' and the dolphin's performances at threshold were not ascribable to associative mechanisms. Smith and Schull (1989) gave a perceptual threshold uncertainty-monitoring task to rats. A repeating 400-Hz tone deserved one response. A 400-Hz tone alternating with any other deserved another response. The third, uncertainty response let the animal wave off any trial and begin a new one. Animals knew the effect of this response because they also used it to initiate trials. Once rats had mastered an easy discrimination between 400–400 Hz tone pairs and 400–700 Hz tone pairs, the discrimination's difficulty was increased until animals were struggling to distinguish 400–400 Hz tone pairs from tone pairs of about 400–410 Hz.

Figure 10.8 shows that rats mastered well the two primary discrimination responses. They made the *alternating* and *repeating* responses mainly on alternating and repeating trials, respectively, though of course the discrimination was performed at chance where these two response curves cross at threshold. However, unlike humans, monkeys, and a dolphin, the rats did not selectively make the uncertainty response at threshold. They could not tell when they were at risk for error in the primary discrimination and could not decline those trials selectively, even though Smith and Schull tried for months to coax this monitoring capacity from them.

Yet rats could certainly learn a reinforcement contingency attached to a middle stimulus class between two others and have a response brought under the control of those middle stimuli. If this were all there is to the threshold task, rats would escape from threshold trials

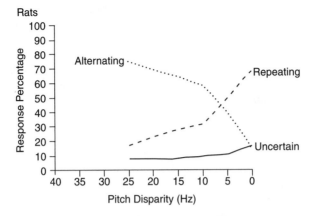

Figure 10.8 Performance by six rats in the frequency discrimination used by Smith and Schull (1989). The horizontal axis
indicates the frequency difference between the alternating
pitches on a trial. The repeating response was correct for trials
with a frequency difference of 0, and these trials are represented by the rightmost data point for each curve. All other
trials deserved the alternating response. The solid line represents the percentage of trials receiving the uncertainty response at each pitch disparity. The percentages of trials ending
with the repeating response (dashed line) or alternating response (dotted line) are also shown. See color insert.

naturally and easily. They do not. This suggests that uncertainty responses in perceptual threshold tasks are not just about middle-stimu-
lus avoidance. The threshold tasks seem to be psychologically structured in some way that leaves rats out (insofar as the methods were
sufficient to elicit the crucial capacities from them) but leaves humans,
monkeys, and dolphins in.

An additional manipulation supported this interpretation. We were
concerned that the rats' null result arose because, for the rats, the uncertainty response doubled as a trial-initiation response. To evaluate
this possibility, we examined how rats responded to an occasional
higher, faster repeating tone that the computer rewarded randomly
so that rats could only be 50% correct (just as they are at threshold).
The rats declined these trials three times as often as they declined
threshold trials. So rats did bail out of the objective, stimulus-borne
50:50 contingency, but not the subjective, threshold-borne 50:50 contingency. Once again, this suggests that the two kinds of behavior
have a different underlying psychological organization. Moreover, it
reinforces the idea that the capacity to sense threshold is relatively
inaccessible in the rat's cognitive system (inaccessible to the rat and

to the experimenter), whereas we know from earlier sections of this chapter that this capacity is easily accessible in the cognitive systems of humans, monkeys, and dolphins.

4. Tests of Uncertainty Monitoring Foster Controlled Cognitive Processes Because They Ensure Inconsistent Mappings Between Stimulus Inputs and Behavioral Outputs

One can make two principled statements about the psychological organization of the capacity for monitoring threshold perceptions and memories and for responding adaptively to them. This section considers the first of these. All the tasks described in this chapter trade on the scatter and variability that accompany all acts of perceiving and remembering by humans and animals. For example, the perceptual threshold tasks deliberately challenge the observer's discrimination ability. Given the variable impression made by the same objective perceptual event on different occasions, true dense trials and threshold sparse trials (for example) will often produce the same subjective psychological impression. Likewise, the same memory event on different occasions (e.g., a second-serial-position presentation) will create a distribution of trace strengths (this is why the T and NT distributions in figure 10.6C have widths). Consequently, the trace strength monitored on a trial could be caused by either a *there* probe or a recently seen *not there* probe (this is why the T and NT distributions in figure 10.6C overlap).

Therefore, neither the impression of density nor the monitored trace strength can reliably tell the animal what to do. These perceptual/memorial impressions are inherently ambiguous. Shiffrin and Schneider (1977, pp. 167–168) discussed the information-processing consequences of this ambiguity. In their description, indeterminate mental representations of stimuli necessarily mapped inconsistently onto behavioral responses, making those representations poor indicators of what the organism should do, and ruling out that an adaptive response could safely be automatically associated to them. Instead, higher levels of controlled cognitive processing would be needed to resolve the indeterminacy and produce a decision about behavior. All the uncertainty-monitoring tasks described in this chapter are inconsistently mapped in Shiffrin and Schneider's sense. All would require this higher-level form of controlled cognitive processing. From this perspective, the uncertainty response would be one manifestation of the controlled indeterminacy-resolution processes that are necessary near threshold. It might represent a decision that the trial should be declined because the primary perceptual or memory process had failed. Note that this description applies to both human and animal cognition. Psychophysical procedures and uncertainty-monitoring tasks ensure indeterminate stimulus-response mappings and encourage controlled decision-making processes no matter the participant species. This realization provides a theoretically gentle but principled way to grant animals' uncertainty responses some of the cognitive sophistication that is due them.

An everyday example can clarify the contrast between stimulus-controlled and decisionally controlled processes. Many humans perform the following conditional discrimination daily—green-go; red-no go. This task is consistently mapped. The underlying perceptual representations (green and red) are not confuseable and they point absolutely consistently and reliably to the appropriate behavior. This task needs no fine discriminations, no decision criteria, and no decision making. In fact, behavior in the stoplight task may be triggered automatically, reflexively, fast, and effortlessly simply because the task's consistent mapping allows stimulus and response to associate very strongly. This is the reason that stoplights worldwide present the same consistent mapping.

In contrast, imagine the decisional nightmare we would all face if traffic lights gradually morphed between red and green, so that drivers had to decide whether their light was green enough to go. This situation would require decision making and decision criteria. It would involve controlled processing—slow, attentional, and capacity intensive. The situation would also be dangerous, as behind-schedule businesswomen and soccer dads cheated on their green criterion at the same crossing. It is an important fact that all of the uncertainty-monitoring paradigms described in this chapter represent this latter kind of controlled, decisional task. Once again, this claim applies to both humans and animals. Humans and animals must decide if the box is dense or sparse enough to try, if the tone's pitch is high or low enough, if the memory trace is weak or strong enough.

I point out that this kind of information-processing analysis, done deliberately to include both species, can serve a constructive purpose in comparative psychology. Too often our comparisons of human and animal performance are polarizing. We describe humans' conscious, verbal metacognition in a way that excludes animals. We try to describe animals' similar performances using low-level, behaviorist descriptions that do not apply to humans. (The same thing happens in discussions about tool use, language, and so forth.) But these issues do not have to reduce to either elevating humans or denigrating animals. Rather, given true comparative data like those shown in figure 10.3 and the strong cross-species analogy between the performance of humans and animals, it is possible to pursue a reasoned middle ground that in my view is preferable to a clash between divergent explanatory frameworks at different psychological levels. The real parsimony in our explanation of the situation may lie in being able to explain simply the performance of several species using a single, structural information-processing description. Such multiple-species descriptions are still a rarity in comparative psychology, because so many laboratories, research programs, and articles are single-species driven. But they may become an increasingly important feature of comparative psychology as it gains in maturity and in information-processing comfort and sophistication. To me, an important possibility for the next decade of comparative research is that we may come to treat cognition and behavior more integratively and more truly comparatively by attending systematically to strong cross-species similarities in performance and by seeking the information-processing middle ground. Of course, this reasoned middle ground could consider both common processing principles across species while also acknowledging possible experiential differences across species in whatever way the whole empirical picture warranted.

5. Animals May Share With Humans a Theoretically Important Construal of the Threshold and Memory-Monitoring Tasks

One can make another principled statement about the psychological organization of the capacity for monitoring threshold perceptions and memories and for responding adaptively to them. Humans understand the grammar of uncertainty-monitoring tasks in a distinctive way that explains their data patterns and their self-descriptions of performance. Humans know that these tasks have two primary input classes (dense-sparse, there-not there). They know that one of these two input classes is instantiated on every trial, so that every trial has a correct answer if they could only discover it. The consequence is that humans map the two stimulus input classes to the two primary responses, use these responses when they think they know which event occurred, and use the uncertainty response when they cannot tell.

Given this understanding of this task, the uncertainty response is not associated with a stimulus input class. Instead, it is a judgment about the probable failure of the primary discriminatory process on a trial. In this sense, it is structurally outside the discrimination and meta to it. For humans, it seems clear that the uncertainty response is also linked to conscious uncertainty states that can be verbalized and that reveal personal self-awareness.

This understanding of the uncertainty-monitoring task sheds a clear light on why the uncertainty response feels less stimulus-based (it is!), and why it can feel like mental shirking or like an admission of weakness (I should be able to discover the answer and should try!). This understanding explains why the uncertainty response can be naturally excluded from the task's structure, and why some humans choose to do so because of their scruples against it or because of their unwarranted bravado in the face of the difficult threshold task. The other two responses cannot be omitted, and humans would not do so. This understanding also justifies the special psychological status that psychophysicists always accorded the uncertainty response.

There are strong reasons for suggesting that animals share with humans their understanding of the perceptual and memory uncertainty-monitoring tasks, though animals' understanding of the task will of course be more tacit and less verbal. First, we generally train animals extensively in the primary discrimination before giving them an uncertainty response in the task. The uncertainty response joins as an extra, optional response a mature discrimination that has the two input classes and the two primary responses already established, mapped to one another, and sufficient for performance. Second, we generally provide animals a daily warm-up in which they receive easy discrimination trials that then gradually increase in difficulty. This warm-up, during which animals do not choose to use the uncertainty response, reestablishes the idea that the task has two input classes and two primary response. Third, we sometimes give animals sessions in which they perform the mature discrimination without the uncertainty response available. This reinforces again the understanding of the task I am discussing here. Fourth, in our tasks the uncertainty response never earns a direct reward, never earns a timeout penalty, and always has the same neutral function and result in every stimulus context. These things are not true of the two primary responses in the task. This also helps the animal differentiate the uncertainty response from the two discrimination responses. All in all, I believe that my animals are highly trained to have tacitly just the task understanding that humans have explicitly.

To summarize Points 1 to 5, the identity between the data patterns of humans and animals in figure 10.3 suggests a strong homology between the behavior of the two species. Given this, one does not want to interpret the human performance in a qualitatively high-level metacognitive way, while interpreting the monkey performance in a qualitatively low-level associative way. There is no warrant for this duality of interpretation (indeed, the graphs provide a negative warrant), and the duality is unparsimonious because a common information-processing description might explain both data patterns and their identity (Point 1).

Fortunately, one can show that low-level associative interpretations are not sufficient to explain the animals' performances. They certainly do not work for the serial probe recognition task. They would not work for Shields et al.'s same-different paradigm either. Though they might work for the perceptual threshold tasks, it is unparsimonious again to explain the animals' memory data in a high-level way but then insist on an associative interpretation of the same animals' threshold data. The two performances could be explained in just the same way if only the animal were granted a generalizable uncertainty-resolution system (Point 2). Moreover, it is interesting that rats failed to use the uncertainty response at threshold as humans, monkeys, and a dolphin did, though probably they would have succeeded if low-level associative cues had been available at threshold (Point 3).

Given the failure of an associative account, it is constructive to consider a reasoned, information-processing middle ground that addresses aspects of the task and its decisional processes that apply to performance across species. One element of this middle ground is that the uncertainty-monitoring tasks are inherently inconsistently mapped and will require of humans and animals a more decisional, controlled brand of cognitive processing to disambiguate perception or memory and to adaptively choose behavioral options (Point 4). A second element of this common ground is that humans and animals probably share an abstract understanding of the uncertainty-monitoring task in which the uncertainty response is sharply differentiated from the two primary discrimination responses so that it serves the function of a negative judgment about the outcome of the primary discriminatory process (Point 5).

It seems to us that these five points lay the groundwork for a psychological understanding of humans', monkeys', and a dolphin's successful performances in uncertainty-monitoring tasks. They offer a balanced psychological interpretation of uncertainty responses, granting them the cognitive sophistication they deserve without burdening them with consciousness or with equally heavy behaviorist assumptions. These points also suggest the possibility of integrating findings from humans and animals into an overall information-processing framework instead of the polarizing descriptions that are more common.

6. Do Controlled Decisional Processes Set the Stage for Conscious Cognition?

Smith et al. (1998), in considering monkeys' memory-monitoring performance in an SPR task, noted that "one could scale back the claims of consciousness while preserving something of the sophisticated, memory-based, flexible, controlled mediational processes that do represent a higher level of choice and decision making and that are needed to explain how monkeys cope with (and escape) indeterminate memory events" (p. 245). This statement let Smith et al. give animals' uncertainty responses considerable cognitive credit without prematurely engaging the nettlesome question of the role that consciousness plays in memory monitoring and uncertainty responding.

I close by engaging this nettlesome question briefly, first regarding human cognition, then regarding animal cognition. Humans encounter situations daily in which their automatic and habitual behavior patterns are thwarted and they enter difficult and uncertain straits. It is worth reflecting on how cognition meets these challenging situations. Simply put, when the going gets tough, the tough get conscious. Times of difficulty and uncertainty seem to shift the mind into conscious overdrive as humans ask themselves that all-important question—so what do I do now?

This is not my original intuition. In fact, it is a beloved idea in cognitive science that cognitive indeterminacy and difficulty inherently elicit higher level and even conscious modes of cognition and decision making in the organism. James (1890/1952, p. 93) noted that consciousness provides extraneous help to cognition when nerve processes are hesitant. "In rapid, automatic, habitual action it sinks to a minimum." In contrast, he added, "Where indecision is great, as before a dangerous leap, consciousness is agonizingly intense" (p. 93). Dewey (1934/1980, p. 59) also argued that in habitual, well-learned behaviors, the behavioral impulses are "too smooth and well-oiled to admit of consciousness." Tolman (1932/1967, p. 217) noted that "conscious awareness and ideation tend to arise primarily at moments of conflicting sign-gestalts, conflicting practical differentiations and predictions." Karoly (1993, p. 25) emphasized that uncertain, conflicted conditions are the ones that initiate self-regulation. Gray (1995) described the special neural circuits that may arrest behavior, increase arousal, and redirect attention and mental resources toward the causes of difficulty (see also Smith, 1995).

There is a structural, almost logical, reason why mind needs to be so composed that it responds to difficulty and uncertainty in this way. Difficulty and uncertainty imply that the well-learned behavior, the well-oiled habit, will not work and could be dangerous. Instead, a close cognitive call has to be made and a behavioral solution chosen online. To do so, the human has to gather together within some immediate/current information-processing resource—that is, within working memory or working consciousness—his or her situation, goal, possible approaches, and their risks, benefits, costs, and prospects. The elements that enter cognition as a human resolves indeterminacy and chooses a behavioral solution I call a decisional assemblage. This is the multidimensional pool of knowledge, situational perception, reasoning, and evaluation that lets him or her maximize within the difficult problem space or at least satifice safely.

I hope that I have communicated successfully a theme in this chapter that there are sometimes structural similarities in the information-processing situations that humans and animals face, in the task construals they make, and in the character of their information-processing approaches. The idea of the decisional assemblage provides a final case in point. As with humans, animals will encounter difficult and uncertain situations in which their well-learned associations and automatic behavioral patterns cannot help them because a finely balanced judgment call is required or because there is no existing template for an appropriate behavior. Then, in the immediate moment, animals too will have to rethink the problem, to assemble together what they know, what they remember, what the goal is, what the choices are, and their prospects and risks. Interestingly, animals have faced this same immediate need to rethink their situation in many classic comparative paradigms. For example, Rumbaugh (see Rumbaugh & Pate, 1984) would suddenly reverse animals' discrimination contingencies to see if they could use an environmental signal mediationally and change behavior quickly. For another example, Harlow (1949) would suddenly instantiate a qualitatively new contingency to see if animals had a learning set that would let them respond to a single error insightfully.

As with humans, something like a working consciousness could be especially appropriate for holding the cognitive and decisional assemblage that allows the momentary rethinking in which the animal deals in its own tacit way with the question of what to do now. If a working consciousness is especially useful or appropriate, it would have substantial fitness utility and phylogenetic breadth. In that case, one cognitive utility serving difficult and uncertain decisions by animals would be a working consciousness that is the functional parallel of human declarative consciousness.

Therefore, I hope that readers will reflect on the long-lived intuition in cognitive science that the highest levels of information processing and especially consciousness present themselves when difficulty and indeterminacy are encountered. I would suggest, though, that this may not be just a human phenomenon but rather a functional property of adaptive cognitive systems more generally. Thus it is potentially important that all the tasks considered in this chapter create decisional difficulty and indeterminacy. This makes it possible that these tasks are well suited to elicit higher-level and possibly conscious regulatory processes in animals. If so, then they and additional tasks that others will contrive may eventually ground the systematic study of animal consciousness. This would be what Tolman hoped for so long ago when he saw animals poised in decisional conflict at the choice point of a maze and he wondered at their lookings and runnings back and forth.

ACKNOWLEDGMENTS Correspondence concerning this chapter should be addressed to J. David Smith, Department of Psychology, Park Hall, State University of New York at Buffalo, Buffalo, NY, 14260, or to psysmith@buffalo.edu. The preparation of this chapter was supported by NIH grant HD-38051, which also funds ongoing research in this area. I thank my collaborators, Wendy E. Shields and David A. Washburn, for their important contributions to all phases of this research. I also thank Kenneth Allendoerfer, Roian Egnor, Linda Erb, Katerina Guttmanova, Kelli Mcgee, Joshua Redford, Jonathan Schull, Jared Strote, the staff and trainers of the Dolphin Research Center, colleagues at the Language Research Center, and many laboratory RAs at the University at Buffalo for their contributions to this research.

REFERENCES

Angell, F. (1907). On judgments of "like" in discrimination experiments. *American Journal of Psychology, 18,* 253.

Au, W. W., & Moore, P. W. (1990). Critical ratio and critical bandwidth for the Atlantic bottlenose dolphin. *Journal of the Acoustical Society of America, 88,* 1635–1638.

Boring, E. G. (1920). The control of attitude in psychophysical experiments. *Psychological Review, 27,* 440–452.

Brown, A. L., Bransford, J. D., Ferrara, R. A., & Campione, J. C. (1983). Learning, remembering, and understanding. In J. H. Flavell & E. M. Markman (Eds.), *Handbook of child psychology* (Vol. 3, pp. 77–164). New York: Wiley.

Brown, A. S. (1991). A review of the tip-of-the-tongue experience. *Psychological Bulletin, 109,* 204–223.

Brown, W. (1910). The judgment of difference. *University of California Publications in Psychology, 1,* 1–71.

Castro, C. A., & Larsen, T. (1992). Primacy and recency effects in nonhuman primates. *Journal of Experimental Psychology: Animal Behavior Processes, 18,* 335–340.

Cowey, A., & Stoerig, P. (1992). Reflections on blindsight. In D. A. Milner & M. D. Rugg (Eds.), *The neuropsychology of consciousness: Foundations of neuropsychology* (pp. 11–37). London: Academic Press.

Dewey, J. (1980). *Art as experience.* New York: Perigee Books. (Original work published 1934)

Dunlosky, J., & Nelson, T. O. (1992). Importance of the kind of cue for judgments of learning (JOL) and the delayed JOL effect. *Memory and Cognition, 20,* 374–380.

Fernberger, S. W. (1914). The effect of the attitude of the subject upon the measure of sensitivity. *American Journal of Psychology, 25,* 538–543.

Fernberger, S. W. (1930). The use of equality judgments in psychophysical procedures. *Psychological Review, 37,* 107–112.

Flavell, J. H. (1979). Metacognition and cognitive monitoring: A new area of cognitive-developmental inquiry. *American Psychologist, 34,* 906–911.

George, S. S. (1917). Attitude in relation to the psychophysical judgment. *American Journal of Psychology, 28,* 1–38.

Gray, J. A. (1995). The contents of consciousness: A neuropsychological conjecture. *The Behavioral and Brain Sciences, 18,* 659–722.

Harlow, H. F. (1949). The formation of learning sets. *Psychological Review, 56,* 51–65.

Hart, J. T. (1965). Memory and the feeling-of-knowing experiments. *Journal of Educational Psychology, 57,* 347–349.

Herman, L. M., & Arbeit, W. R. (1972). Frequency difference limens in the bottlenose dolphin: 1–70 kc/s. *Journal of Auditory Research, 2,* 109–120.

James, W. (1952). *Great books of the western world: Vol. 53. The principles of psychology.* Chicago: University of Chicago Press. (Original work published 1890)

Karoly, P. (1993). Mechanisms of self-regulation: A systems view. *Annual Review of Psychology, 44*, 23–52.

Koriat, A. (1993). How do we know that we know? The accessibility model of the feeling of knowing. *Psychological Review, 100*, 609–639.

MacMillan, N. A., & Creelman, C. D. (1991). *Detection theory: A user's guide.* Cambridge, UK: Cambridge University Press.

Metcalfe, J., & Shimamura, A. (1994). *Metacognition: Knowing about knowing.* Cambridge, MA: Bradford Books.

Morgan, C. L. (1906). *An introduction to comparative psychology.* London: Walter Scott.

Nelson, T. O. (Ed.). (1992). *Metacognition: Core readings.* Toronto: Allyn and Bacon.

Nelson, T. O. (1996, February). Consciousness and metacognition. *American Psychologist, 51*, 102–116.

Nelson. T. O., & Narens, L. (1990). Metamemory: A theoretical framework and new findings. *The Psychology of Learning and Motivation, 26*, 125–141.

Roberts, W. A., & Kraemer, P. J. (1981). Recognition memory for lists of visual stimuli in monkeys and humans. *Animal Learning and Behavior, 9*, 587–594.

Rumbaugh, D. M., & Pate, J. L. (1984). The evolution of cognition in primates: A comparative perspective. In H. L. Roitblat, T. G. Bever, & H. S. Terrace (Eds.), *Animal cognition* (pp. 569–587). Hillsdale, NJ: Lawrence Erlbaum.

Sands, S. F., & Wright, A. A. (1980). Primate memory: Retention of serial list items by a rhesus monkey. *Science, 209*, 938–939.

Schusterman, R. J., & Barrett, B. (1975). Detection of underwater signals by a California sea lion and a bottlenose porpoise: Variation in the payoff matrix. *Journal of the Acoustical Society of America, 57*, 1526–1537.

Schwartz, B. L. (1994). Sources of information in metamemory: Judgments of learning and feelings of knowing. *Psychonomic Bulletin and Review, 1*, 357–375.

Shields, W. E., Smith, J. D., & Washburn, D. A. (1997). Uncertain responses by humans and rhesus monkeys (*Macaca mulatta*) in a psychophysical same-different task. *Journal of Experimental Psychology: General, 126*, 147–164.

Shiffrin, R. M., & Schneider, W. (1977). Controlled and automatic human information processing: II. Perceptual learning, automatic attending, and a general theory. *Psychological Review, 84*, 127–190.

Smith, J. D. (1995). The homunculus at home: Commentary on J. A. Gray, The contents of consciousness: A neuropsychological conjecture. *The Behavioral and Brain Sciences, 18*, 697–698.

Smith, J. D., & Minda, J. P. (1998). Prototypes in the mist: The early epochs of category learning. *Journal of Experimental Psychology: Learning, Memory, and Cognition, 24*, 1411–1436.

Smith, J. D., & Minda, J. P. (2000). Thirty categorization results in search of a model. *Journal of Experimental Psychology: Learning, Memory, and Cognition, 26*, 3–27.

Smith, J. D., & Schull, J. (1989). *A failure of uncertainty monitoring in the rat.* Unpublished data.

Smith, J. D., Schull, J., Strote, J., McGee, K., Egnor, R., & Erb, L. (1995). The uncertain response in the bottlenosed dolphin (*Tursiops truncatus*). *Journal of Experimental Psychology: General, 124*, 391–408.

Smith, J. D., Shields, W. E., Allendoerfer, K. R., & Washburn, W. A. (1998). Memory monitoring by animals and humans. *Journal of Experimental Psychology: General, 127*, 227–250.

Smith, J. D., Shields, W. E., Schull, J., & Washburn, D. A. (1997). The uncertain response in humans and animals. *Cognition, 62*, 75–97.

Smith, S. M., Brown, J. M., & Balfour, S. P. (1991). TOTimals: A controlled experimental method for studying tip-of-the-tongue states. *Bulletin of the Psychonomic Society, 29*, 445–447.

Thomson, G. H. (1920). A new point of view in the interpretation of threshold measurements in psychophysics. *Psychological Review, 27*, 300–307.

Tolman, E. C. (1927). A behaviorist's definition of consciousness. *Psychological Review, 34*, 433–439.

Tolman, E. C. (1938). The determiners of behavior at a choice point. *Psychological Review, 45*, 1–41.

Tolman, E. C. (1967). *Purposive behavior in animals and men.* New York: Meredith. (Original work published 1932)

Washburn, D. A., & Rumbaugh, D. M. (1992). Testing primates with joystick-based automated apparatus: Lessons from the Language Research Center's Computerized Test System. *Behavior Research Methods, Instruments, and Computers, 24*, 157–164.

Washburn, D. A., Smith, J. D., Baker, L. A., & Raby, P. R. (2001). Responding to uncertainty: Individual differences and training effects. *Proceedings of the 45th annual meeting of the human factors and ergonomics society* (pp. 911–915). Santa Monica, CA: HFES.

Watson, C. S., Kellogg, S. C., Kawanishi, D. T. & Lucas, P. A. (1973). The *uncertain* response in detection-oriented psychophysics. *Journal of Experimental Psychology, 99*, 180–185.

Weiskrantz, L. (1986). *Blindsight: A case study and implications.* Oxford, UK: Oxford University Press.

Weiskrantz, L. (1997). *Consciousness lost and found: A neuropsychological exploration.* Oxford, UK: Oxford University Press.

Woodworth, R. S. (1938). *Experimental psychology.* New York: Holt.

Wright, A. A., Santiago, H. C., Sands, S. F., Kendrick, D. F., & Cook, R. G. (1985). Memory processing of serial lists by pigeons, monkeys, and people. *Science, 229*, 287–289.

Yunker, M. P., & Herman, L. M. (1974). Discrimination of auditory temporal differences by the bottlenose dolphin and by the human. *Journal of the Acoustical Society of America, 56*, 1870–1875.

11

Can Rhesus Monkeys Discriminate
Between Remembering and Forgetting?

Robert R. Hampton

As I entered the study, I flipped the light switch and was startled by a loud "pop!" and an electric flash. There was a loose connection that was shorting. I was headed for the fuse box to remove the fuse when the phone rang. Another annoying telemarketer! I went upstairs and got a screwdriver. As I began to remove the switch cover, I thought, "Did I remove the fuse?" I could not bring to mind a memory of having done it, so I put down my screwdriver and checked the fuse box. Sure enough, the fuse for the study was still in place. I removed it before proceeding to open the switch and tighten the loose wire.

A form of self-reflective cognition saved me from getting a shock. Like most humans, I can tell the difference between knowing and not knowing, or between remembering and forgetting. While we take such memory awareness for granted, there is surprisingly little compelling evidence that it exists in nonhuman species. The difficulties in demonstrating memory awareness in nonhuman species stem from the existence of unconscious memory in humans. In the absence of awareness, humans show classical conditioning (Clark & Squire, 1998), word priming (Hamman & Squire, 1997; Tulving & Schacter, 1990), and learn new skills (Cohen, Eichenbaum, Deacedo, & Corkin, 1985; Knowlton, Ramus, & Squire, 1992; Knowlton & Squire, 1993). Given that these behaviors can occur without awareness in humans, isn't it possible that unconscious, inaccessible forms of memory and cognition can account for all nonhuman behavior? Indeed, it is rightly argued that we do not need to invoke concepts like consciousness or memory awareness to account for most, possibly all, of nonhuman behavior (e.g., Shettleworth, 1998, pp. 5–10). In this chapter, I outline a framework that makes tests for memory awareness in nonhumans possible, and describe some of the few observations of nonhuman behavior that are difficult to explain without reference to memory awareness.

AN ASSUMPTION OF ADAPTATION

I assume that self-reflective cognition evolved by natural selection. Most readers probably do not find this position radical. Some conclusions that follow from this assumption may be more controversial, but they suggest a way to make the problem of detecting self-reflective cognition in nonhuman animals tractable. The central working hypothesis of an evolutionary approach, and a point that distinguishes it from many more philosophical approaches, is that self-reflection is not epiphenomenal but is instead *functional* (Dennett, 1992). Self-reflective cognition evolved because it enabled organisms to behave overtly in adaptive ways that would not be possible without it. The behaviors enabled by self-reflection were the basis on which natural selection acted to increase the occurrence of self-reflection in subsequent generations. Self-reflection is therefore a mechanism that supports a set of potentially identifiable adaptive behaviors. Like other cognitive mechanisms, it can be inferred from overt, nonverbal behavior, without reference to private experience.

In studies of human cognition, it is convenient to ask subjects about their experiences as they carry out cognitive tasks. To confirm the occurrence of episodic memory, for example, subjects might be asked whether memory was accompanied by the "experience of having been there," or whether they "remembered" or just "knew" the correct answer (Tulving, 1985, 1993). But emphasizing these verbal reports of private phenomenology is problematic for the wider effort of comparative cognition. Defining cognitive systems in ways that depend on verbal reports of private experience creates a rift between studies of cognition in humans and nonhumans because such reports cannot be obtained from nonhumans. Furthermore, the definition of phenomena like episodic memory, declarative memory, and metacognition may become so dependent on reported phenomenology that the most important feature of these cognitive mechanisms, their function, is obscured. As a result, it can appear impossible, even in principle, to demonstrate the existence of these cognitive phenomena in nonhumans, simply for lack of verbal behavior.

I argue that verbal reports are not necessary to demonstrate self-reflective cognition. It can be inferred instead from the nonverbal abilities it confers on a human or nonhuman animal (see also Inman & Shettleworth, 1999; Smith, Shields, Washburn, & Allendoerfer, 1998; Weiskrantz, 2001). By treating self-reflection as a biological phenomenon that resulted from the mechanistic action of natural selection, we can define self-reflective cognition by what it accomplishes for an organism, rather than by how it is experienced. Investigations of self-reflective cognition in nonhumans can then focus on the same material that natural selection acts on—overt behavior. If self-reflective cognition was naturally selected on the basis of overt behavior, then the occurrence of self-reflection can be identified on the basis of those same, or related, overt behaviors.

MENTAL CONTENTS AND BEHAVIORAL CAPABILITY

In over a century of scientific study of animal cognition, well-designed experiments have allowed investigators to infer some of the contents of animal information processing systems. Pigeons demonstrate that they mentally represent specific rewards when they peck. When pecking a response key associated with water reward, pigeons peck with a "nibbling" motion like that used when drinking. In contrast, when pecking a key associated with grain, they peck with the beak open, as is done when actually pecking at grain (Jenkins & Moore, 1973). Rats represent the durations of sounds and will appropriately press levers associated with long and short sounds (Meck, 1983). Scrub jays represent which foods they have hidden, where they hid them, and even when they did the hiding, demonstrated by their avoidance of the locations of perishable foods stored long enough to have spoiled (Clayton & Dickinson, 1999). In each of these cases, the animals behaved in a way that would not be possible had they not mentally encoded the types of reward, the durations of the tones, and the locations of the foods. The observed behavior requires the inference of mental representations of these particular features of events or stimuli. In other words, these experiments show that nonhuman animals, in some sense, remember. The success of this behavioral approach, in which the unobservable features of memory are logically inferred from the observable properties of behavior, encourages emulation.

However, while these clever experiments do show that animals remember, there is nothing in these findings to indicate that the animals were aware of having their memories the way that humans are aware of many memories. The experiments provide no basis for discriminating between memories that are like human conscious declarative memory and those that are unconscious or implicit. That is, they do not demonstrate memory awareness. However, that does not mean that other experiments could not provide relevant data. I argue that it is possible to treat memory awareness as another feature of a memory, like the type of reward, duration of a tone, or location of a seed. It follows that observable behavior, if measured under appropriately controlled conditions as in the preceding examples, can be sufficient to demonstrate memory awareness in a nonverbal animal.

A FUNCTIONAL DEFINITION OF MEMORY AWARENESS

The conceptual approach used to demonstrate memory in nonhuman animals may be adapted to generate tests for memory awareness as well. The presence of memory is inferred when a subject demonstrates behavior that cannot be explained without reference to memory (see Shettleworth, 1998). For example, a monkey might be presented with an object overlaying a candy. It removes the object and eats the candy. The object is then taken out of sight for a minute, after which the monkey is presented with the object it just saw, plus another object. In many trials, the monkey shows that it can select the rewarded object and avoid the object that had not been paired with a candy. The monkey can "match to sample," correctly identifying a recently seen object. In order for the monkey to do this, some representation, or memory, of the object must persist in the brain after the object is removed from view to later control behavior. Under similar circumstances, humans could not only respond correctly, but could also predict their ability to respond correctly. Thus, humans not only have *primary mental states of memory* about events or objects in the world, they also have *secondary mental states about memories*—for instance, states indicating the presence or absence of memory. That is, we can often know whether or not we know the correct answer. How could a nonhuman animal demonstrate such a secondary mental state without the use of language?

Conventionally, nonhuman memory is assessed in forced-choice situations. In the case of our monkey looking for the candy, the rewarded object and the distracter object are presented simultaneously, and the monkey has to choose between them. If it is unsure, the monkey has to guess. A human confronting uncertainty in such a situation might say he was uncertain, or state that he was guessing. But the monkey is afforded no opportunity to do this in conventional tests of memory (Inman & Shettleworth, 1999; Smith et al., 1998; Weiskrantz, 2001). We can accurately measure how well the monkey remembers, but we have no measure of whether it knows it remembers, or is uncertain. To get such a measure, we need to explicitly posit what memory awareness might afford an organism.

Memory awareness can make it possible to determine whether or not the information required to successfully perform a particular task is available. Consider the example of making a phone call to order take-out food from a restaurant you have used several times. Before starting, you would likely attempt to retrieve a memory of the number. If you successfully recall the number, you go ahead and dial. If retrieval fails, you look up the number before dialing. Awareness of the presence or absence of a memory of the number permits you to choose appropriately between dialing immediately or looking up the number. It should be noted, though, that awareness of the memory is not the only way you could accurately determine whether or not to look up the number. If you call every day to order food, you would likely cease to check whether you know the number, and simply assume that you do—not necessarily on the basis of memory awareness, but rather on the basis of your knowledge that you have succeeded many times in dialing correctly. Nonetheless, normal humans are indeed capable of making this sort of judgment on the basis of memory awareness.

The alternatives to evaluating knowledge states through memory awareness can be quite clumsy. Imagine being unable to introspect about your memory of a phone number. You would either have to look up the number every time you call, or use trial and error to determine whether or not you remembered the correct number. In the case of phone calls, this could be embarrassing. If you were unable to determine whether or not you know how to rewire a fuse box, or need to hire an electrician for the job, trial and error testing could have more serious consequences. Humans can sometimes avoid putting themselves in dangerous or futile situations through accurate self-reflective assessments of knowledge.

One can imagine similar situations in which memory awareness would be helpful to nonhuman animals. Consider a rabbit that detects a fox in the field. It faces a choice between freezing, possibly avoiding detection, or running for shelter. The ability to assess whether it knows the location of a shelter would be helpful to the rabbit in making an adaptive choice. If the rabbit knows of a shelter, nearby but out of sight, running to it might be the best option. In contrast, making itself conspicuous by dashing around the field at random searching for shelter would be a bad choice. Thus the rabbit could adaptively choose to freeze or run based on awareness, or lack of awareness, of a memory for a nearby shelter. Of course, the fact that it would be useful for a rabbit to have memory awareness does not mean that rabbits have it. It would also be useful for the rabbit to sprout wings and fly away from danger, yet rabbits do not fly. Nonetheless, thinking about how memory awareness would be useful suggests how to design experiments to test for it. Speculation can then be replaced by experimentation.

A SIMPLE MODEL

Awareness of the presence of memory can permit an animal to choose adaptively between behavioral options when the success of one or more of the options depends on remembered information, as when the rabbit's decision to run or freeze should be contingent on knowing of a good place to run toward. Humans can choose between dialing a number and looking it up, first by assessing whether or not we remember the number. We can either choose to undertake a home repair ourselves, or hire a professional, based on an assessment of our own knowledge relevant to completion of the repair. Of course, in initially testing for this ability in nonhuman animals, a simple situation and a simple model are desirable. Such a simple model of memory awareness is diagrammed in figure 11.1. A prerequisite for a metacognitive or self-reflective system is a cognitive system in which stimuli in the world are mentally represented. Modern cognitive theory posits that mental representations link events outside the organism to behavior emitted by the organism (Terrace, 1984). For example, without mental representations of objects, the monkey in our earlier example could not correctly choose the rewarded object. In figure 11.1, seeing the stimulus object (S) causes a mental representation of the object (M) to be formed. This representation persists after the object is removed from sight and later guides the response (R). We can therefore infer the existence of M because it makes a logically necessary link between S and R.

Accepting the existence of M in figure 11.1 admits the possibility of another, secondary or *meta* mental representation (m), as shown in the lower part of figure 11.1. While M is a cognitive representation of an object in the world, m is a metacognitive representation about M.

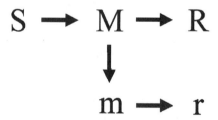

Figure 11.1 Measuring memory awareness behaviorally. Viewing an object (S) causes the formation of a mental representation, or memory, of the object (M) that persists in the brain even when the object is removed from view. The memory later guides the response (R) to the remembered object in a memory test. In the same way that M is about the object in the world, m is a secondary mental representation that is about the memory M. A secondary response (r) is required to infer the presence of m. A procedure for doing so is shown in figure 11.2. See color insert.

It is a thought about a thought (Nelson, 1996). To test for the existence of m, an experimental situation must be created in which a second response (r) allows us to infer the presence or absence of m, just as R allows us to infer M.

THE EXPERIMENTS

A schematic of the experiment used to test for metacognitive representation is shown in figure 11.2 (Hampton, 2001). Matching to sample was the primary task, which requires first-order mental representations, such as M in figure 11.1. At the beginning of each trial, monkeys saw a centrally located image on a touch-sensitive computer monitor (figure 11.2, top panel). They touched the image, demonstrating that they had viewed it. The screen was then blank for a delay period over which monkeys should remember the image. At the end of the delay, monkeys were presented with four images, one occupying each of the four corners of the computer monitor (lower left panel). In order to receive a reward, monkeys had to touch the image that was identical to the one seen at the beginning of the trial. The task was made difficult by increasing the delay to a point at which the monkeys often made mistakes. Thus, on some trials they remembered while on other trials they had forgotten (see figure 11.2).

In the secondary, or metacognitive, task, the monkeys were given a choice between taking the memory test and receiving a favored reward for correct responses, or declining the test and receiving a less desirable but guaranteed reward (middle panels). This choice phase occurred at the end of the delay on each trial, and *before the monkey saw the test array.* Facing these contingencies, a monkey could maximize reward by choosing to take the memory tests when memory for the studied image was good, and avoiding the test (settling for the lesser but guaranteed reward) when memory was relatively poor.

An important feature of this procedure is that it requires a prospective judgment of memory, that is, the monkeys had to decide whether to take or decline the memory test before being presented with the test. A prospective judgment addresses two concerns. First, because the test stimuli were absent when the judgment was made, the choice to decline tests could not be based on familiarity or perceptual fluency of the correct test image (Verfaelli & Cermak, 1999; Wagner & Gabrieli, 1998). Second, a prospective judgment also precludes a decision to decline tests based on direct experience with the difficulty of a given test. Previous studies using pigeon subjects showed that the distinction between prospective and concurrent memory judgment can be critical (Inman & Shettleworth, 1999; J. E. Sutton & S. J. Shettleworth, personal communication, February 12, 2003). Pigeons offered the option of declining tests concurrently with presentation of the test dis-

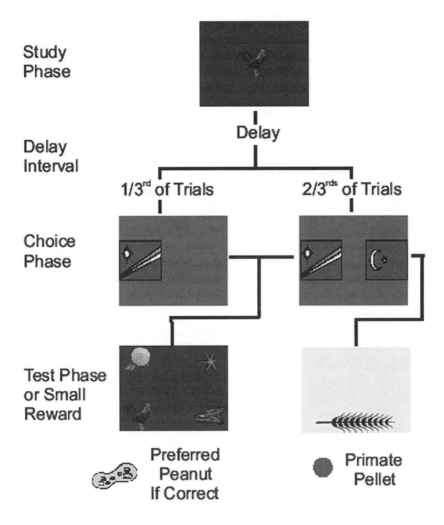

Study Phase

Delay Interval

Delay

1/3rd of Trials   2/3^{rds} of Trials

Choice Phase

Test Phase or Small Reward

Preferred Peanut If Correct

Primate Pellet

Figure 11.2 Method for assessing whether monkeys know when they remember. Each colored panel represents what monkeys saw on a touch-sensitive computer monitor at a given stage in a trial. At the start of each trial, subjects studied a randomly selected image. A delay period followed, during which monkeys often forgot the studied image. On two thirds of trials, animals chose between taking a memory test (right panel, left-hand stimulus) and declining the test (right panel, right-hand stimulus). On one third of trials, monkeys were forced to take the test (left panel). Better accuracy on chosen memory tests than on forced tests indicates that monkeys know when they remember and decline tests when they have forgotten, if given the option. See color insert.

play behaved as if they knew when they remembered. However, when these same birds were required to judge memory prior to presentation of the memory test, they were unable to discriminate trials on which they remembered from those on which they had forgotten the sample.

In earlier training, two monkeys, Shepard and Gagarin, were familiarized with the significance of the choice phase stimuli (figure 11.2, middle panels). Preference for peanut over pellet rewards was also established earlier and confirmed throughout the experiments. The monkeys were tested on matching to sample with four new images used each day. On each trial, one of the four images was randomly selected to serve as the sample for that trial; the other three images served as distracters, yielding a chance rate of 25%. Initially, the monkeys were given only the primary matching task, without the secondary choice phase in which they could decline memory tests. The delay over which the monkeys were required to remember the sample on each trial was gradually increased until they made errors on approximately 35% of trials. Thus, the monkeys were sure to be experiencing a substantial number of trials on which they forgot the identity of the sample. Shepard was tested at a delay of 34 seconds and Gagarin at 38 seconds.

The choice phase stimuli were then incorporated into testing. At the end of the delay period on each trial, one of two choice phase arrays was presented. On one third of trials, the "choice" consisted of only the stimulus associated with taking the memory test. On these forced-test trials, monkeys had to touch this stimulus in order to proceed to the memory test. At test, correct responses were rewarded with highly desirable peanuts, while a distinctively colored error screen and no reward followed incorrect choices. These trials were therefore almost identical to the normal matching-to-sample trials, except the monkeys had to touch the stimulus associated with tests before proceeding to the test. On the other two thirds of trials, monkeys were given a choice between taking the test and declining the test. If they selected the stimulus associated with taking the memory test, the trial proceeded as just described. If they chose the stimulus associated with avoiding the memory test, an escape response screen appeared. The monkeys were rewarded with less desirable primate pellets after they touched the image on this screen, which was unrelated to the other test images and presented in a location not used for other images.

If monkeys can accurately assess whether or not they remember the studied image, they should choose to take the test when they remember and avoid the test when the studied image is forgotten. Reliable discrimination between trials on which memory was good and trials on which memory was poor should result in higher accuracy on chosen tests compared to forced tests. Both monkeys were more accurate on trials in which they freely chose memory tests than they were on forced-test trials in which they were not given the option of declining the test (figure 11.3, paired t tests: Shepard, $t_9 = 3.91$, $p < .01$; Gagarin, $t_9 = 4.51$, $p < .01$). However, accuracy on these tests does not directly reflect the accuracy expected on trials in which the monkeys declined the memory test.

Unfortunately, it is difficult to get a direct measure of accuracy on trials on which the monkeys declined to take the test, for two reasons. The first is that the contingencies of the experiment, by which the monkeys learned the significance of taking and declining memory tests, would be undermined by any reasonably large number of probe tests in which the monkey was forced to take a memory test, even though it had declined to do so. Second, performance on such trials is unlikely to reflect memory accurately. This is because the monkeys expect a small, reliable reward after declining the test. If they were forced to take the test instead, they would likely be surprised and possibly frustrated by the unexpected change. Surprise or frustration could disrupt performance and impair accuracy. Thus, forced tests following the decline response do not provide a good measure of memory on declined trials. Instead, we have to rely on a less direct measure, as follows.

Accuracy on forced tests is a weighted average of accuracy on tests subjects would have declined, given the choice, and those they would freely have chosen to take anyway. The expected accuracy on declined trials is substantially lower than this weighted average, and avoiding

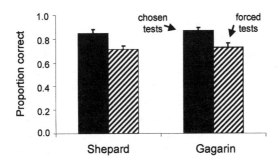

Figure 11.3 Accuracy on freely chosen tests and forced tests. Dark bars represent accuracy on tests the monkeys chose to take. Striped bars represent performance on trials in which the animals were not given the choice of declining tests. Scores for the two monkeys are the means of 10 daily sessions. Error bars are standard errors. Subjects would be correct 25% of the time if guessing.

these tests is of considerably more value than it at first appears. Because accuracy on freely chosen tests is known, as is the proportion of tests taken and declined on free-choice trials, the expected accuracy in trials on which the monkeys declined the memory test can be determined. Using the proportions of tests monkeys declined when given the opportunity (Shepard, 0.51; Gagarin, 0.36), and the accuracies shown in figure 11.3, expected accuracies on the trials monkeys declined are determined to be 58.1% and 46.8%, respectively. The accuracy of memory on trials the monkeys declined is thus substantially lower than it is on other trials, and monkeys experience a substantial increase in reward rate by avoiding these tests.

How Did the Monkeys Know That They Had Forgotten?

The relevance of these findings to memory awareness depends on determination of the discriminative stimulus used by monkeys to guide their choice to decline some of the memory tests. The working hypothesis is that it is awareness of the memory that serves as the discriminative stimulus. Therefore, the critical concern is that some factor other than the absence of memory per se might control the choice to decline memory tests. There are many candidate alternatives. Events that might occur during the delay interval, such as noises, bouts of grooming, or changes in motivation, might result in forgetting by distracting the animal or interrupting a memory process. These events themselves could therefore cue animals to decline tests and yield a false impression that the animals attended to their own memory states. To rule out the possibility that monkeys' decisions to decline tests were controlled by such external cues, monkeys were presented with infrequent randomly distributed probe trials. These unpredictable probe trials were identical to normal trials in every way except that no image was presented for study (figure 11.4). When the absence of memory was experimentally controlled in this way, a priori prediction of which tests the monkeys would decline was possible. After an intertrial interval, and a delay period equivalent to that on normal trials, animals were given the choice of declining or taking a memory test, just as would occur on normal trials.

If the absence of memory causes the monkeys to decline tests, they should decline tests on these no-sample probe trials, treating them like trials on which they have forgotten the studied image. If, however, the decision to decline tests is controlled by some environmental or behavioral event, subjects should decline normal and probe trials with equal probability, because such events are evenly distributed among the randomly intermixed normal trials and the no-sample probe trials. In six test sessions with no-sample probe trials, both monkeys were much more likely to decline tests if no image was presented for study than they were to decline tests on normal trials (figure 11.5; Shepard:

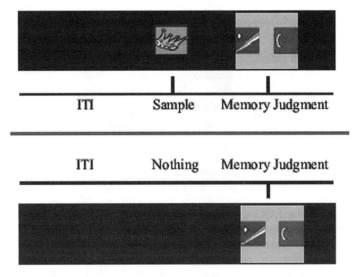

Figure 11.4 Schematic of a normal trial (upper panel) and a no-sample probe trial (lower panel). The white lines represent the passage of time. During the intertrial interval (ITI), the screen was black. On normal trials, a sample appeared and the monkeys had to touch it to advance the trial. After a delay, the monkeys could choose to either take or decline the memory test. Probe trials were identical, with the exception that no sample appeared, and the monkey did not have to touch the screen to advance the trial. See color insert.

$t_5 = 24.34$, $p < .01$; Gagarin: $t_5 = 10.19$, $p < .01$). Shepard declined the memory test on 49% of normal trials, and 100% of the probe trials where no sample was presented. Gagarin declined 18% of normal trials and 63% of probe trials. These results, following the experimental manipulation of memory, provide compelling support for the hypothesis that the choice to decline tests was based on the absence of memory per se, rather than due to some external event correlated with forgetting.

Monkeys might have gradually learned to base the decision to decline tests on some distinguishing feature of probe trials, rather than on the absence of a memory per se. The first session of probe trials was therefore analyzed separately. Both monkeys declined probe tests from the first session of testing (Shepard, $\chi^2_{1,n=66} = 7.66$, $p < .01$; Gagarin, $\chi^2_{1,n=69} = 7.88$, $p < .01$), indicating that learning did not take place after the onset of probe trials. Additionally, Shepard declined every probe trial presented and could never have learned the negative consequences of choosing a memory test on such trials. The high probability with which monkeys declined the no-sample probe trials therefore

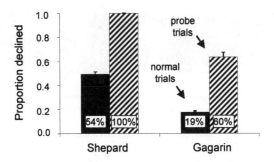

Figure 11.5 Probability of declining tests on normal trials and on probe trials lacking an image to study. Dark bars show the proportion of normal trials on which monkeys declined tests; striped bars represent this proportion on probe trials. Error bars are standard errors. Inset in each bar is the percentage of each test type declined in the first session of testing only. These results indicate that it is the absence of a memory that causes the monkeys to decline tests. If some factor other than the absence of memory per se, such as distracting noises, variation in motivation, or fatigue, controlled the decision to decline tests, normal and probe trials would be affected equally.

reflects spontaneous generalization to these probes as equivalent with trials on which the sample was forgotten.

Monkeys might have used delay, or a correlate of delay, as a cue to decline tests. In these experiments, the computer controlled when the monkey could first respond, but the monkey could respond at any time after that point. Thus, on some trials the monkey might complete the choice phase promptly, and other times slowly. Because performance deteriorates as the delay before the memory test increases, the monkeys could theoretically have produced the pattern of results observed by choosing to take the memory test when they completed the choice phase promptly, and choosing to avoid the test when this phase was completed more slowly. Indeed, the monkeys responded slightly more quickly when choosing to take the test than they did when choosing to decline the test (Shepard, mean difference 0.29 seconds, $t_9 = 2.09$, $p < .10$; Gagarin, mean difference $= 0.46$ seconds, $t_9 = 3.7$, $p < .01$). However, these differences of a fraction of a second in response latency, added to mean delays of about 36 and 40 seconds respectively, are hardly enough to produce the difference in accuracy between freely chosen and forced memory tests. It is rather more likely that this small difference in latency to complete the choice phase reflects a slightly longer decision process preceding the decision to avoid the memory test. Apparently, when the monkeys are sure they remember, they decide quickly and surely to take the test. But when they are less certain, it takes slightly longer to make a decision. This difference may reflect a search of memory conducted at the time the monkey is choosing to take or decline the memory test. On trials in which a memory is located, the search is terminated and the monkey chooses to take the test. On trials on which the sample is forgotten, the search continues for some time without a memory being located. Eventually the search of memory is terminated and the monkey declines the test. Thus longer latencies are associated with failure to find the item in memory (Briggs & Blaha, 1969; for review, see Van Zandt & Townsend, 1993).

Forgetting as Time Passes

Varying the delay over which the monkeys were required to remember the studied image provides a second way of directly manipulating memory in these experiments. Because memory declines as time passes, monkeys should decline tests more often after long than after short delay intervals. Each monkey was tested with five delay intervals, which were randomly intermixed in test sessions so that the monkeys could not anticipate the delay on a given trial. For Shepard, the delay intervals ranged from 12.5 to 200 seconds; for Gagarin the range was 15 to 240 seconds. Accuracy on forced tests was high for both monkeys at short delays, but declined as the delay interval increased (figure 11.6, filled circles; Shepard: $F_{4,116} = 45.66$, $p < .01$; Gagarin: $F_{4,116} = 44.72$, $p < .01$). As would be expected if monkeys declined tests when memory was poor, both monkeys declined tests more often after long delays than after short delays (figure 11.6, filled squares; Shepard: $F_{4,116} = 196.02$, $p < .01$; Gagarin: $F_{4,116} = 30.76$, $p < .01$). The first 100 free-choice trials with these variable delays were analyzed separately to test whether monkeys generalized immediately to the delays or learned gradually with experience. Trials were divided into two groups: those with delays shorter than the mean and those with delays longer than the mean. Shepard declined 85% of these long-delay trials, compared with 43% of short-delay trials ($\chi^2_{1,n=100} = 17.34$, $p < .01$), while Gagarin declined 32% and 16% of these trials, respectively ($\chi^2_{1,n=100} = 3.72$; $p = .05$).

By selectively declining tests when they had forgotten the studied image, both monkeys were significantly more accurate overall on chosen tests than they were on forced tests (Shepard: 88% vs. 67%, $F_{1,29} = 152.62$, $p < .01$; Gagarin: 78% vs. 69%, $F_{1,29} = 21.20$, $p < .01$). But in addition to improving overall accuracy, monkeys able to detect the absence of memory with high sensitivity should also be able to improve memory performance at each delay at which substantial forgetting occurs. No difference between free- and forced-test accuracy is

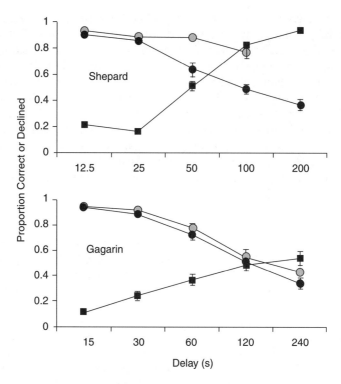

Figure 11.6 Accuracy and the probability of declining tests after randomly intermixed variable delay intervals. Filled squares depict the probability of declining tests. Shaded circles represent accuracy on freely chosen tests, and filled circles accuracy on forced tests. Error bars are standard errors.

expected at delays at which animals rarely forget, and accuracy is high, because there is little room for improvement. However, as the delay interval increases, and forced-choice accuracy declines, a difference between accuracy on chosen tests and forced tests should emerge. Shepard clearly showed this pattern (figure 11.6, shaded circles; $F_{1,23} = 53.66$, $p < .01$; only the first four delays were analyzed, because at the longest delay Shepard declined nearly 100% of tests and did not choose any of these trials in over half of test sessions, thereby precluding an accurate estimate of accuracy). Gagarin was also more accurate on freely chosen tests at longer delays, but this difference was not statistically significant ($F_{1,25} = 3.17$, $p < .09$).

Together, these findings indicate that rhesus monkeys know when they know. In addition to often retaining a representation of a recently seen image, the monkeys were able to discriminate between the presence and absence of such a representation in memory. Competence in this discrimination allowed the monkeys to choose appropriately to take memory tests when memory for the studied image was strong and to decline the test when memory was weak, thus increasing the total number of rewards received in a session. The ability of the monkeys to generalize performance to the no-sample probe trials and to the sessions with variable delays rules out many "simpler" accounts of this behavior, such as a discrimination based on some external event rather than attention to the presence or absence of memory per se. Thus, monkeys are aware of at least some of their memories. Memory awareness is a form of metacognition, or thinking about thinking (Nelson, 1996). For metacognition to occur, two types of mental state are required, an object-level state and a metalevel state. In the present case, memory for the recently seen image constitutes the object-level state, M in figure 11.1. The metalevel is in some way contingent on the object-level memory, and is represented by m. This contingency relationship between the object level and the metalevel is often referred to as *monitoring*, reflecting the fact that the meta-level state is indicative of the condition of the object level, for example, indicating the quality, vividness, or, in the most basic case, presence or absence of the object-level state. The metalevel state can thereby provide the basis for a discrimination between remembering and forgetting, by reflecting the presence or absence of memory.

CANDIDATE PSYCHOLOGICAL MECHANISMS

I have argued that monkeys are aware of the presence of memory and have bolstered this position by eliminating many other possible explanations for the behavior of declining memory tests. But narrowing the field to some sort of memory awareness leaves a great deal of explanatory terrain to cover. Of what aspects of a memory can monkeys be aware? Can we determine any more about the psychological mechanism underlying memory awareness? Future work might discriminate among several candidate mechanisms (figure 11.7).

Before describing these candidate mechanisms, it should be said that it is not certain whether monkeys were using short-term memory or long-term memory in these tests, and so it may be premature to analyze performance in terms specific to either type of memory. However, several facts suggest that the monkeys were using a long-term memory mechanism. Monkeys were completing the memory tests about 40 seconds after the offset of the sample, and in subsequent experiments, delays of up to 240 seconds were used. These delays far exceed what are often considered the temporal limits of short-term memory for monkeys (e.g., Alvarez-Royo, Zola-Morgan, & Squire, 1992). While neurobiological evidence was not collected in these experiments, many experiments have shown that monkeys performing

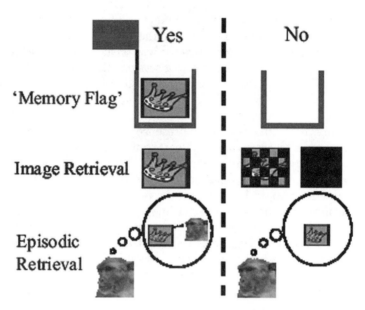

Figure 11.7 Cartoons of candidate processes underlying memory aware-ness. The left column represents the contents of cognitive processing dur-ing trials on which monkeys choose to take the memory test. The right column depicts the same on trials on which the test is declined. The mem-ory flag hypothesis posits an indicator for the presence of memory. Mon-keys can respond on the basis of the indicator but are not aware of the memory itself. In the case of the other two hypothetical mechanisms, the decision to take the memory test is based on the richness of the memory retrieved. See text for more details. See color insert.

very similar memory tasks, at delays shorter than 40 seconds, are im-paired following lesions of the medial temporal lobe (Mishkin & Mur-ray, 1994; Squire & Zola-Morgan, 1991). Thus, performance on the tests described here almost certainly depends on the medial temporal lobe memory system, and falls in the category of long-term memory. Nonetheless, depending on the criteria adopted for distinguishing be-tween working and long-term memory, the data described could fall in either category.

Here I suggest three candidate mechanisms to account for the per-formance of monkeys in these experiments. The first account, the "memory flag" hypothesis, posits a mental representation of memory strength. Such a representation might be as simple as a binary signal representing only the presence or absence of memory. This represen-tation would encode nothing about the context of the study episode or the features of the image being remembered. The activity of the memory flag could merely reflect the presence or absence of *something* in memory, and monkeys would choose to take the test when the flag was active. Because activation of the flag is contingent on the presence of a memory, monkeys would be more accurate at test if the flag was active than when it was inactive.

A more elaborate decision process could be based on the richness of the recalled memory. If a retrieval attempt results in a very detailed representation of a studied image, including its shape and color for example, this could guide the monkey to choose to take the memory test on that trial. In contrast, if few or no features of the item could be recovered, the monkey would choose to decline the memory test. At the extreme of the richness of recall account would be episodic retrieval, in which the monkey recalled a sufficient amount of detail from the study episode to reexperience it (Tulving, 1985). In any case, the monkeys could base their decision on the number of features of the study episode or the studied image that could be successfully retrieved. When retrieval is rich, the monkey chooses to take the memory test. When the retrieved memory is impoverished, the test is declined.

To determine which mechanism underlies memory awareness in this case, we need to know more about what the monkey is thinking when making the decision to take or decline the memory test. What are the contents of the representation guiding the monkey's choice? Is the representation binary, encoding only two possible states—memory present and memory absent—or does it include many features of the remembered item? Experiments in which the monkeys are required to make delayed categorization decisions about the studied image might provide the answer. For example, after choosing to take or decline the memory test, the monkey might be required instead to categorize the image on the basis of color or shape (e.g., red vs. blue, animal vs. plant). If the choice to take the test were based entirely on a memory flag, there should be no basis on which to make the categorization, because the activity of the flag does not reflect the specific contents of the memory. In contrast, if the monkey calls the image to mind and assesses the richness of the memory before choosing to take or decline tests, it will have information about the properties of the image available to guide categorization following "remember" responses but not following "forget" responses. Recall that the monkey has to choose to take or decline the memory test before seeing the test. Therefore the tests just described could be used to determine which features of the image the monkey can freely recall (see Menzel, 1999; chapter 8, this volume).

Less elaborate mechanisms may be sufficient to account for similar data collected under different conditions than those described here. Pigeons declined tests selectively when memory was poor only if they viewed the memory test at the time the choice to take or avoid the test was made (Inman & Shettleworth, 1999; J. E. Sutton & S. J. Shettleworth, personal communication, February 12, 2003). Given the success of pigeons under conditions of simultaneous presentation and the failure of the same birds when the judgment to decline memory tests preceded the presentation of the memory test, it is likely that the two types of test differ in the mechanisms required to solve them. Pigeons apparently cannot judge the strength of a memory for an absent image by "calling it to mind," although some other mechanism does allow them to choose to decline tests when memory is weak when the test is present (see Inman & Shettleworth, 1999). In related work with monkeys, subjects similarly made the choice to take or decline tests in the presence of the test discriminanda (Smith et al., 1998; chapter 10, this volume). In the innovative work of Call and Carpenter (2001; chapter 13, this volume), apes and children collected more information when confronted with a problem they lacked the necessary information to solve. Because these primates were not required to judge their memory before seeing the memory test, they could have been using a mechanism similar to that used by Shettleworth and Inman's pigeons. While it remains to be determined what this mechanism is, apparently it does not require free recall (Menzel, 1999) of the memory. This does not mean that the subjects were not engaged in metacognition. The metacognition may not have been based on direct access to a mental representation, but rather on indirect evidence (Flavell, 1979). In constrast, the prospective memory judgment used in the experiments described in this chapter, and other control procedures, made it very unlikely that monkeys based their judgments of memory strength on indirect evidence. The monkeys most likely based their decision to take or decline tests on a direct assessment of a recalled memory.

MEMORY AWARENESS

Neurobiology of Memory Awareness

Our understanding of the neurobiology of memory in rhesus monkeys has advanced dramatically in the last 15 years (Murray, 1996). Studies continue to focus on the medial temporal lobes, but new emphasis has been placed on areas adjacent to the hippocampus, including the perirhinal, entorhinal, and parahippocampal cortices. It has also become clear that the function of these medial temporal lobe structures is often dependent on interaction with other areas, including the frontal cortex (Easton, Parker, & Gaffan, 2001; Gaffan, Parker, & Easton, 2001; Parker, Wilding, & Akerman, 1998). Despite these advances in the localization of memory function, the animal models used to date do not capture a conspicuous feature of human declarative memory, memory awareness. As described in the introduction to this chapter, this failure to capture memory awareness stems from the exclusive use of forced-choice memory tests, which do not provide any opportunity for subjects to demonstrate awareness of memory or metacognitive ability. Instead, investigators have necessarily relied on a largely circular argument to justify animal models of declarative memory. This argument posits that because human declarative memory depends on medial temporal lobe structures, and memory deficits have been observed in monkeys following damage to these same structures, the tests used to detect these deficits measure declarative memory or amnesia (e.g., Gaffan et al., 2001; Squire & Zola-Morgan, 1991). While this logic has permitted work to move forward on the localization of structures necessary for memory in monkeys, it does not provide much help in discriminating between declarative memory and implicit memory in nonhuman animals. With the new techniques described here and elsewhere (Call & Carpenter, 2001; Hampton, 2001; Smith et al., 1998) comes the promise of directly studying the neurobiology of memory awareness and declarative memory in non-human animals for the first time.

Evolution of Memory Awareness

The ability of these monkeys to appropriately decline memory tests when they were unlikely to choose the correct image indicates that they know when they remember. The monkeys demonstrated a form of self-reflective cognition that I have referred to as memory awareness in this chapter. Awareness is one of the properties of declarative memory, strongly suggesting that the monkeys used declarative memory, at least in part, to identify the correct images in these experiments. This work reinforces other experiments with nonhuman primates (Call & Carpenter, 2001; Smith et al., 1998; chapters 10 and 13, this volume). In each of these cases, nonhuman primates appear to demonstrate the ability to make judgments about their own knowledge states. In striking contrast to these observations of primates, pigeons tested under similar conditions appear to lack memory awareness, suggesting that it may not be widely distributed among species (Inman & Shettleworth, 1999; J. E. Sutton & S. J. Shettleworth, personal communication, February 12, 2003). However, considerably more comparative work with pigeons and other species will be required to substantiate the presence of memory awareness in some, but not other, animals. For one thing, further work will be required to determine the importance of methodological differences, such as whether the subject makes a memory judgment before being presented with the memory test, or in the presence of the test.

One central question to be answered about the evolution of self-reflective cognition is phylogenetic. When in our evolutionary history did it originate? The existence of memory awareness in many species would suggest an early emergence in our ancient pre-primate ancestors. In contrast, a more restricted distribution among our closer relatives would indicate a more recent emergence of memory awareness (Riley & Langley, 1993). Answering the phylogenetic question thus requires testing many species under similar conditions. To start, it would be interesting to test more species of nonhuman primates. Currently there is evidence for memory awareness in apes (Call & Carpenter, 2001) and in Old World monkeys (Hampton 2001; Smith et al., 1998). Old World monkeys and apes shared a common ancestor 20 to 25 million years ago (Tomasello & Call, 1997, p. 15). This suggests that memory awareness likely first evolved at least 20 to 25 million years ago in an ancestor apes share with the Old World monkeys. Should memory awareness be shown to occur in New World monkeys (capuchins or marmosets, for example), or in the prosimians (such as lemurs), that would suggest pushing back the date for the emergence of memory awareness even farther.

A related question about the emergence of self-reflective cognition is ecological. What selection pressures promote the evolution of self-reflective cognition (e.g., Povinelli & Cant, 1995)? One approach to this problem is to think of self-reflective cognition as a set of component functions, such as memory awareness, body awareness, emotional awareness, and so on, rather than as a unified capacity. Because an animal demonstrates self-reflective cognition in one domain does not necessarily mean that it possesses it in other domains. Types of information processing that are particularly crucial to a given species, or which have to be carried out in a way only possible with self-reflective processing, may be selectively subject to awareness (see Kamil, 1988, for a discussion of this view on the evolution of cognition). In this scenario, self-reflective cognition might be widespread among species, but restricted to particular ecologically relevant information processing domains in each species. Alternatively, a domain-general form of self-reflective cognition may have arisen more than once, independently, for example, in primates and cetaceans (Reiss & Marino, 2001). Comparisons between these groups could identify life history variables that are common to them but are not shared by groups lacking self-reflective cognition.

Critique of Memory Awareness in Monkeys

There are both experimental and conceptual issues regarding the validity of the concept of memory awareness in nonhuman animals. The experimental difficulties consist of the possibility that the experimental procedures used are not adequate to discriminate memory awareness per se from other explanations of the behavior observed in these and other experiments. These threats are addressed using experimental manipulations, as described in the preceding sections. New control procedures will likely be required as new critiques of these results emerge. In contrast, conceptual criticisms are much more resistant to solution by technical innovation. These have to do with the definition of memory awareness and whether we can agree on a definition that allows for the inclusion of nonverbal animals. I have adhered to a functional definition of memory awareness in this chapter and have argued that a functional account can capture the essential features of memory awareness (see Dennett, 1992, for related views). For others, a functional account of self-reflective cognition, one that strictly eschews phenomenology in the sense of private experience, will be unsatisfying (Chalmers, 1996; see Zeman, 2001, for review of these issues).

Although we are sure to learn more about what nonhuman species know, it is unlikely that procedures can be developed to directly measure the experience of memory in a nonhuman animal. It will therefore always remain a matter of conjecture whether monkeys experience conscious states of knowing like our own. No amount of functional convergence between rhesus monkey and human will convince the hardened skeptic of similar experience in the two groups of animals. Such a skeptic holds that conscious experience, Descartes's one certainty, is the essence of self-reflection. However, I argue that emphasizing experience over function relegates memory awareness to an epiphenomenal domain and undermines its significance. Furthermore, the phenomenological position may be irrelevant to the endeavor of understanding the evolution of self-reflective cognition. For this, we need to put aside introspection, treat self-reflection as a biological mechanism, and focus on what self-reflection does for us and may have done for our ancestors. The evolution of self-reflective cognition cannot be understood by delving further into our own thoughts, or by wondering what it is like to be a monkey. Rather we need to adopt the performance-based view of natural selection, a vantage from which cognition is seen through what it does, not through how it is experienced. Paradoxically, by avoiding the allure of our private experience, we might learn something new about ourselves.

ACKNOWLEDGMENTS The writing of this chapter was supported by the NIMH Intramural Research Program. I thank Cindy Buckmaster and Kristen Hampton for helpful discussions and comments on a draft.

REFERENCES

Alvarez-Royo, P., Zola-Morgan, S., & Squire, L. R. (1992). Impairment of long-term memory and sparing of short-term memory in monkeys with medial temporal lobe lesions: A response to Ringo. *Behavioural Brain Research, 52,* 1–5.

Briggs, G. E., & Blaha, J. (1969). Memory retrieval and central comparison times in information processing. *Journal of Experimental Psychology, 79,* 395–402.

Call, J., & Carpenter, M. (2001). Do apes and children know what they have seen? *Animal Cognition, 4,* 207–220.

Chalmers, D. J. (1996). *The conscious mind.* Oxford, UK: Oxford University Press.

Clark, R. E., & Squire, L. R. (1998). Classical condition and brain systems: The role of awareness. *Science, 280,* 77–81.

Clayton, N. S., & Dickinson, A. (1999). Scrub jays (*Aphelocoma coerulescens*) remember the relative time of caching as well as the location and content of their caches. *Journal of Comparative Psychology, 113,* 403–416.

Cohen, N. J., Eichenbaum, H., Deacedo, B. S., & Corkin, S. (1985). Different memory systems underlying acquisition of procedural and declarative knowledge. In D. S. Olton, E. Gamzu, & S. Corkin (Eds.), *Memory dysfunction: An integration of animal and human research from preclinical and clinical perspectives* (pp. 54–71). New York: New York Academy of Sciences.

Dennett, D. C. (1992). *Consciousness explained.* Boston: Little, Brown.

Easton, A., Parker, A., & Gaffan, D. (2001). Crossed unilateral lesion of medial forebrain bundle and either inferior temporal or frontal cortex impair object recognition memory in rhesus monkeys. *Behavioural Brain Research, 121,* 1–10.

Flavell, J. H. (1979). Metacognition and cognitive monitoring: A new area of cognitive-developmental inquiry. *American Psychologist, 34,* 906–911.

Gaffan, D., Parker, A., & Easton, A. (2001). Dense amnesia in the monkey after transection of fornix, amygdala, and anterior temporal stem. *Neuropsychologia, 39,* 51–70.

Hamman, S. B., & Squire, L. R. (1997). Intact perceptual memory in the absence of conscious memory. *Behavioral Neuroscience, 111,* 850–854.

Hampton, R. R. (2001). Rhesus monkeys know when they remember. *Proceedings of the National Academy of Sciences U.S.A., 98,* 5359–5362.

Inman, A., & Shettleworth, S. J. (1999). Detecting metamemory in nonverbal subjects: A test with pigeons. *Journal of Experimental Psychology: Animal Behavior Processes, 25,* 389–395.

Jenkins, H. M., & Moore, B. R. (1973). The form of the autoshaped response with food or water reinforcers. *Journal of the Experimental Analysis of Behavior, 20,* 163–181.

Kamil, A. C. (1988). A synthetic approach to the study of animal intelligence. In D. W. Leger (Ed.), *Nebraska Symposium on Motivation: Vol. 35. Comparative perspectives in modern psychology* (pp. 257–308). Lincoln: University of Nebraska Press.

Knowlton, B. J., Ramus, S., & Squire, L. R. (1992). Intact artificial grammar learning in amnesia. *Psychological Science, 3,* 172–179.

Knowlton, B. J., & Squire, L. R. (1993). The learning of categories: Parallel brain systems for item memory and category knowledge. *Science, 262,* 1747–1749.

Meck, W. H. (1983). Selective adjustment of the speed of internal clock and memory processes. *Journal of Experimental Psychology: Animal Behavior Processes, 9,* 171–201.

Menzel, C. R. (1999). Unprompted recall and reporting of hidden objects by a chimpanzee (*Pan troglodytes*) after extended delays. *Journal of Comparative Psychology, 113,* 426–434.

Mishkin, M., & Murray, E. A. (1994). Stimulus recognition. *Current Opinion in Neurobiology, 4,* 200–206.

Murray, E. A. (1996). What have ablation studies told us about the neural substrates of stimulus memory? *Seminars in the Neurosciences, 8,* 13–22.

Nelson, T. O. (1996). Consciousness and metacognition. *American Psychologist, 51,* 102–116.

Parker, A., Wilding, E., & Akerman, C. (1998). The von Restorff effect in visual object recognition memory in humans and monkeys: The role of frontal/perirhinal interaction. *Journal of Cognitive Neuroscience, 10,* 691–703.

Povinelli, D. J., & Cant, J. G. H. (1995). Arboreal clambering and the evolution of self-conception. *Quarterly Review of Biology, 70,* 393–421.

Reiss, D., & Marino, L. (2001). Mirror self-recognition in the bottlenose dolphin: A case of cognitive convergence. *Proceedings of the National Academy of Sciences U.S.A., 98,* 5937–5942.

Riley, D. A., & Langley, C. M. (1993). The logic of species comparisons. *Psychological Science, 4,* 185–189.

Shettleworth, S. J. (1998). *Cognition, evolution, and behavior.* New York: Oxford University Press.

Smith, J. D., Shields, W. E., Washburn, D. A., & Allendoerfer, K. R. (1998). Memory monitoring by animals and humans. *Journal of Experimental Psychology: General, 127,* 227–250.

Squire, L. R., & Zola-Morgan, S. (1991). The medial temporal lobe memory system. *Science, 253,* 1380–1386.

Terrace, H. S. (1984). Animal cognition. In H. L. Roitblat, T. G. Bever, & H. S. Terrace (Eds.), *Animal cognition* (pp. 7–28). Hillsdale, NJ: Lawrence Erlbaum.

Tomasello, M., & Call, J. (1997). *Primate cognition.* New York: Oxford University Press.

Tulving, E. (1985). Memory and consciousness. *Canadian Psychology, 26,* 1–12.

Tulving, E. (1993). What is episodic memory? *Current Directions in Psychological Science, 2,* 67–70.

Tulving, E., & Schacter, D. L. (1990). Priming and human memory systems. *Science, 247,* 301–306.

Van Zandt, T., & Townsend, J. T. (1993). Self-terminating versus exhaustive processes in rapid visual and memory search: An evaluative review. *Perception and Psychophysics, 53,* 563–580.

Verfaelli, M., & Cermak, L. S. (1999). Perceptual fluency as a cue for recognition judgments in amnesia. *Neuropsychology, 13,* 198–205.

Wagner, A. D., & Gabrieli, J. D. E. (1998). On the relationship between recognition familiarity and perceptual fluency: Evidence for distinct mnemonic processes. *Acta Psychologica, 98,* 211–230.

Weiskrantz, L. (2001). Commentary responses and conscious awareness in humans: The implications for awareness in non-human animals. *Animal Welfare, 10,* S41–S46.

Zeman, A. (2001). Consciousness. *Brain, 124,* 1263–1289.

12

Metaconfidence Judgments
in Rhesus Macaques:
Explicit Versus Implicit Mechanisms

Lisa K. Son & Nate Kornell

To date, psychological research on human metacognition centers on whether and to what extent people know what they know. For example, feeling-of-knowing judgments ask people how certain they are that they know an answer that they are unable to retrieve. Judgments of learning ask how certain they are that they will be able to remember a recently learned item in the future. Confidence judgments ask people how certain they are that their response to a question is correct. In this chapter, we focus on confidence judgments, which in humans are typically made verbally. Our chapter describes an experiment on confidence judgments in rhesus macaque monkeys. Because of their obvious lack of verbal ability, the monkeys were given the opportunity to express their confidence by placing bets on the accuracy of their responses in a cognitive task.

BACKGROUND ON HUMAN METACOGNITION

Until recently, the experimental study of metacognition had generally been limited to the human species. We begin by summarizing the major theories of human metacognition before discussing their extension to nonhuman species. The term "metacognition" has been associated with uniquely human qualities such as introspection, self-reflection, frontal lobe function, theory of mind, and even consciousness (Flavell, 2000; James, 1890; Janowsky, Shimamura, & Squire, 1989; Shimamura & Squire, 1986; Tulving, 1994; Tulving & Madigan, 1990). For example, Tulving (1994) says that metacognitive researchers use "behavioristically safe expressions, such as memory 'monitoring,' mnemonic 'behavior,' memory 'search,' tip-of-the-tongue 'states,' and feeling of knowing 'experience' ... possibly to avoid the big bad 'C' word" (p. ix), "C" being consciousness. Metcalfe and Kober (chapter 2, this volume) say that metacognition is associated with having a self-reflective "inner eye" that can look at other cognitive functions and content. Thus, the ability to self-reflect, or introspect on one's internal mental representations, has been considered a foundation for human consciousness (see Metcalfe & Shimamura, 1994, preface).

Metacognitive processes, which have been more formally specified by Nelson and Narens (1990, 1994), consist of a basic structure containing two interrelated levels, an object-level and a meta-level. The two levels are shown in figure 12.1A. The object-level may include an

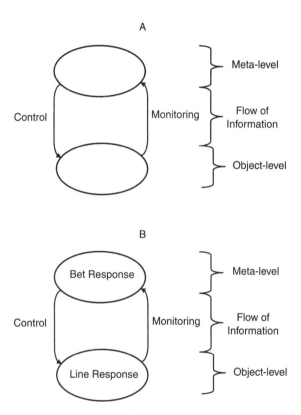

Figure 12.1 A. An overview of the two separate, but interacting, processes during learning as illustrated by Nelson and Narens (1990, 1994). During metacognitive monitoring, the meta-level is informed by the object-level of the present state, and, in turn, during metacognitive control, the meta-level modifies the object-level. B. The current investigation: A meta-level confidence judgment, as measured by risk response, assessing an object-level line task.

individual's memories, cognitions, and behaviors, and describes the state of the present situation. The meta-level monitors (and sometimes can control) the object-level. The interaction between the two levels has generally been thought of as being one of self-reflection. Nelson and Narens (1994) described people as "systems containing self-reflective mechanisms for evaluating (and re-evaluating) their progress and for changing their ongoing processing" (p. 7). The results of processing at the meta-level are judgments and feelings, such as confidence judgments and other expressions of certainty.

One important line of research within the area of metacognition is the issue of how the metacognitive judgments, or meta-judgments, are made. Two categories of mechanisms have been proposed to underlie meta-level judgments in the human literature: direct-access mechanisms and inferential mechanisms (see Nelson, Gerler, & Narens, 1984; Schwartz, 1994). Direct-access mechanisms rely on the accessibility of the internal memory trace. An example is the metacognitive judgment of being in a tip-of-the-tongue state (TOT)—in a TOT, people can often retrieve part of the target memory (e.g., only the first letter), causing a state of frustration. But it is the state of being "close" to accessing the internal memory that causes the high feeling of knowing in a TOT, and the more features of the memory one is able to retrieve, the stronger the meta-judgment of certainty.

Some of the earliest studies of metacognition were interpreted as supporting the direct-access view. For example, in the first investigation of feeling-of-knowing judgments (FKJs), Hart (1965) asked participants trivia questions, and then asked for FKJs on those items the participants could not answer. Then a final recognition test was given. Results showed that people's judgments were positively correlated with recognition on the final test—items given high judgments were more likely to be recognized than items given low judgments. The results indicated that people's judgments were probably based on an accurate assessment of what was in memory. Underwood (1966) conducted a similar study, presenting participants with three-letter trigrams. The trigrams varied from common three-letter words to difficult consonant syllables. Participants had to judge the difficulty of learning the items, after which they were all given a recall test. Results showed that individuals predicted their own recall with high accuracy. Also, Arbuckle and Cuddy (1969) presented participants with lists of paired associates, and asked them to predict whether they would be able to recall each pair. After giving the judgment, the participants were given a memory test. Results showed that the predictions were accurate—those paired associates given lower ratings were recalled less well than those given higher ratings. The main conclusion from these early studies was that people's meta-judgments were based on the amount of information they had been able to retrieve, or directly access, from an internal memory representation at the time of judgment.

Unlike the direct-access view, the inferential view posits that meta-judgments are based on cues that are external, rather than internal, to the memory trace. For example, a judgment may be made based on how familiar the topic of the question is (e.g., giving a high judgment to the question, "Who is the tallest basketball player in the NBA?" because basketball is a familiar topic). Or a judgment may be based on how quickly the answer comes to mind (e.g., giving a higher judgment following a quickly retrieved answer than a slowly retrieved answer). Both of these can predict the accuracy of a memory, but neither relies on directly accessing information about the internal representation.

Schwartz and Metcalfe (1992) compared the direct-access and inferential accounts in an experiment by comparing the relative contribution of the memory strength of the cue and target in making FKJs. They presented participants with paired associates and asked for FKJs in presence of only the cue. Prior to presenting the list, they also manipulated the accessibility of some of the cues by preexposing them in a pleasantness-rating task, and they did the same for a different set of target items. Their results showed that priming cues influenced FKJs, but priming targets did not. They concluded that the strength of the memory trace did not influence meta-judgments, as a direct-access account would predict; instead the judgment was inferred from the familiarity of the cue (see also Glenberg, Sanocki, Epstein, & Morris, 1987; Metcalfe, 1993a, 1993b; Metcalfe, Schwartz, & Joaquim, 1993; Miner & Reder, 1994; Reder, 1987; Reder & Ritter, 1992).

Benjamin, Bjork, and Schwartz (1998) found further evidence for inferentially based meta-judgments. They had participants answer general information questions, such as "What is the color of topaz?" Participants were also told that the time it took them to answer each question was of primary interest, and to press the Enter key as soon as they knew the answer to the question. After answering each question, participants gave a judgment predicting how well they would be able to remember their answer on a later test on a scale from 0 (no chance of later recall) to 100 (certain later recall). The data showed what was called a retrieval fluency effect—participants' judgments were negatively correlated with response times for answering the questions. The researchers concluded that the speed or ease with which one is able to come up with an answer seems to be a source of information for making meta-judgments—even though, in this case, it led to very inaccurate judgments. Furthermore, the judgments could not have been based on the amount of information directly accessed from the memory trace, because all of the answers were fully retrieved. Based on these studies, then, there is ample evidence that meta-judgments can be based on inferential or external cues—cues other than those based on an assessment of an internal representation.

The results of these studies point out that meta-judgments need not be based on introspection of the internal memory trace. Instead, a host of inferential or external cues may be the basis of our judgments. An interesting question, then, might be to ask whether awareness of such cues is necessary in order to make the judgment—some think not (see Cary & Reder, 2002, an article titled, "Metacognition . . . Giving Consciousness Too Much Credit"). Below, we present data that suggest that meta-judgments need not be based on decisions that one is aware of, but instead may be based on implicit mechanisms.

IMPLICIT METACOGNITION

Outside of psychology laboratories, people are not asked to verbally provide meta-judgments very often. However, we believe that they may, nevertheless, be made frequently and, more important, without our awareness. To illustrate, most people, if asked what Lyndon Johnson had for dinner on February 23, 1958, would probably feel uncertain and say, "I don't know." When asked their own name, they would feel very certain and would state their name immediately. It seems rather absurd that meta-judgments such as "I'm quite sure that I know my name" would or should reach awareness. Yet, merely responding "I don't know" might contain a tacit meta-judgment of uncertainty. Here is another example: On the game show *Jeopardy*, a successful contestant only rings her buzzer when she feels fairly certain that her answer is correct (or in *Jeopardy* terms, she feels fairly sure that her question is correct). Her decisions to press the buzzer must be made very quickly, perhaps even more quickly than the time needed to become aware of her decisions. Still, each of those decisions may consist of several different tacit meta-judgments.

In several experiments using a game-show paradigm similar to *Jeopardy*, Reder and colleagues (e.g., Reder, 1996) asked participants a series of trivia questions. They were told to imagine that they were competing against another contestant, and to say as quickly as possible whether they knew the answer to the question. Only then would they be able to answer the question to earn points. Results showed that these meta-judgments could be made more quickly than participants could retrieve the answers. Furthermore, the judgments were usually accurate in predicting subsequent accuracy of the answer. Reder (1996) also found that priming words in the question led to increased subjective estimates of knowing the answer, despite the fact that this exposure did not improve actual rates of producing the correct answer. Reder and her colleagues concluded that some meta-judgments operate at an implicit level (Reder, 1996; Reder & Schunn,

1996). We believe that certainty and uncertainty are feelings that can occur to us even when we cannot explain them and can result from implicit cues that are always present. For the most part, it is only when we are asked about our level of certainty that we become aware of that certainty. As we will see later in the chapter, the implications of animals making judgments of uncertainty depend very much on whether one views the judgments as being an implicit, nonverbal process or a conscious experience.

In this chapter, we relate explicit mechanisms with that which pertains to an assessment of an internal representation, mainly because this requires that one directly access retrieved pieces of information from the memory trace. The notion that meta-judgments are based on explicit mechanisms fits nicely with the original, more philosophical definition of metacognition of labeling humans as self-reflective machines. On the other hand, we relate implicit mechanisms with meta-judgments made on the basis of external cues that are currently present, mainly because these judgments may be made without any internal monitor. These judgments transform continuously as a result of the constantly changing external cues and transient events that people are typically unaware of. Based on the data in the human literature summarized above, we would argue that people use both explicit and implicit metacognitive processes. The question of whether any metacognitive processes exist in nonhuman species remains.

ARE METACOGNITIONS SPECIAL TO HUMANS?

As mentioned earlier, metacognition is considered a very high-level mental function unique to humans. "Machines without consciousness, and animals whose consciousness is different from that of human beings, could not perform many of the tasks that human subjects in metacognitive experiments, and others of the same general kind, can and do perform" (Tulving, 1994, p. ix). Tulving and Madigan (1970) state that metacognition is "one of the truly unique characteristics of human memory: knowing about knowing" (p. 477). Metcalfe and Shimamura (1994) begin their book by saying, "The ability to reflect upon our thoughts and behaviors is taken, by some, to be at the core of what makes us distinctively human" (p. xi).

One obvious difference between humans and animals is the ability to speak. A question, then, is whether it is the ability to verbalize thoughts and feelings that grants humans the ability of self-reflection. And if one did not—or more pertinently, could not—verbally express one's feelings, does that then rule out the possibility that meta-judgments can occur? We think not. Thoughts or feelings, after all, are not synonymous with verbal speech. Judgments that are based on the familiarity of a question or cue, for instance, do not seem too cognitively advanced for an animal. After all, animals can easily discriminate more familiar stimuli from less familiar ones. In addition, anyone who has seen a dog hesitate before jumping into a high truck bed, or a monkey waver between two choices in a psychological task, is likely to imagine that the animal is experiencing some sort of uncertainty. Of course, there is a difference between behaving in a way that appears uncertain and being able to report feelings of uncertainty about cognitions. The latter is analogous to answering the question, "Can you give me a judgment about the certainty of your response?" and only it qualifies as metacognitive.

A few empirical studies have shown that monkeys and dolphins are able to make uncertainty responses (Hampton, 2001; Shields, Smith, & Washburn, 1997; Smith et al., 1995; Smith, Shields, Allendoerfer, & Washburn, 1998; Smith, Shields, Schull, & Washburn, 1997; also see chapters 10 and 11, this volume). In an early study of uncertainty in animals conducted by Smith et al. (1995), human and dolphin subjects were asked to respond *high* when a 2100-Hz tone was played, and *low* for tones less than 2100 Hz. Then they were tested with tones ranging from 1200 Hz to 2100 Hz, with the correct response being *low* for any tone but the 2100 Hz tone. However, in addition to the *high* and *low* choices, a third choice, *escape*, was offered simultaneously, which, when pressed, returned a guaranteed reward, which was smaller than the reward for a correct *high* or *low* answer. The results showed that both humans and dolphins responded *high* for 2100-Hz tones and *low* for low tones up to about 2080 Hz. Most interestingly, they chose *escape* on trials with tones in between. Presumably these were the most difficult trials, where the subjects would have felt the most uncertain about their answers. Follow-up studies showed similar evidence of uncertainty in monkeys.

No one would question that human participants chose to escape difficult trials because they felt uncertain. But is this conviction based on the fact that people can verbalize the feelings by saying, "I chose to escape because I was uncertain"? Or is the behavior (pressing the escape response) enough for us to assume feelings of uncertainty in human participants? If so, then we could grant those same abilities to animals that behave similarly. However, when animals do behave similarly, the immediate reaction often is to ask whether the results might be based on external cues, or whether the learning was based on simple stimulus-response associations, or whether these behaviors did not require any internal monitoring at all. For example, could the animals have simply learned that to maximize reward, high tones should be followed by *high*, low tones should be followed by *low*, and middle-level tones should be followed by the escape response? In this case, no meta-level process is necessary; object-level processes suffice.

Hampton's procedure (see Hampton, 2001; chapter 11, this volume) investigated prospective judgments in monkeys by using a modified escape procedure. He presented two monkeys with a picture. Following a variable delay, the monkeys were given a forced recognition test in which they had to identify the picture that they had been shown among three distractors. However, on some of the trials, rather than being forced to take the test, the monkeys were free to either choose to take the test (for a big reward only if correct) or escape the test (for a guaranteed smaller reward). If the monkey chose to escape, the trial ended without the test being taken. This decision was made prospectively, before the test was presented. His results showed that both monkeys performed better on tests that they freely chose to take than on tests that they were forced to take, suggesting that the monkeys chose to take the test when they were certain. The improvement in this procedure over the original escape procedure is that the test was not present simultaneously with the escape choice. However, a few issues remain. For example, when the monkey chooses to escape the trial, the trial ends, and no object-level response is made. Thus, on a given trial, there is no way of knowing the monkey's actual performance on the test and his certainty of taking the test. In the rest of this chapter, we present findings using a new paradigm in which meta-judgments can be measured separately from object-level responses in nonhuman animals.

META-CONFIDENCE JUDGMENTS IN ANIMALS

Is there a way to measure meta-level judgments, as in Nelson and Narens' (1990) framework in animals? We decided to investigate this question using confidence judgments made about previous responses. Using confidence judgments seemed like the obvious next step, particularly since others, mentioned above, had already shown that animals could report uncertainty by using the escape response efficiently. In our task, two responses were required, representing the two levels in the Nelson and Narens (1990, 1994) framework. If an analogous task were conducted on a person, the response at the object-level would be to answer a question such as, "Who painted the Sistine Chapel?" Then, after giving the response, he or she would make the meta-level judgment about the correctness of the answer on a confidence rating scale. Several studies have shown that humans can make accurate confidence judgments (Koriat, Lichtenstein, & Fischhoff, 1980; Perfect & Hollins, 1996; Shaughnessy, 1979). A schematic of our task in the framework of Nelson and Narens is provided in figure 12.1B.

Our experiment was designed to test, in rhesus macaque monkeys, the existence of true meta-judgments (explicit or implicit) about their previous cognitive responses. The monkeys were first asked to touch the longest of nine lines (analogous to a trivia question for a human). After making their response, they were asked for their judgment of certainty of their response by making a high or low bet. Unlike making an escape response, where there is only one response, the difficulty of our task was that the monkey had to remember the object-level response he had just made, but he would also have to connect that response to a subsequent meta-judgment. Furthermore, unlike the escape procedures, the benefit of asking for both object-level and meta-level responses is that we could tell on a given trial both whether the monkey knew the answer and how sure he was. Of course, a monkey confidence judgment could not be a simple rating of 0 to 100 as it would be for humans. Instead, the betting paradigm was used, in which the monkey could wager a lot on a response (in terms of reward), or play it safe and risk only a little.

EXPERIMENT 1: THE BETTING PARADIGM

Two male rhesus macaques (*Macaca mulatta*), named Ebbinghaus and Lashley, were tested in a chamber containing a touch-sensitive computer screen. On each trial, they were presented with nine lines positioned vertically on the screen, in a 3 × 3 array. Their task was a psychophysical task, in which they had to press the longest of the nine lines. Trials were either easy or difficult: On easy trials, one of the nine lines was noticeably longer than the other eight, which were all the same length. On difficult trials, all nine lines were the same length, but one line was arbitrarily designated as correct, so the monkeys were correct on one out of nine trials by chance. For each touch, a green border appeared around the item briefly. Then the screen cleared and the monkeys were asked to make a bet by touching one of two icons: a high-risk icon and a low-risk icon. Figure 12.2 displays the four possible outcomes that could occur for the two risk responses. If high risk was selected, the reinforcement was the gain of two tokens given a correct response on the line task, or the loss of two tokens given an incorrect response (the tokens were later exchanged for pellets). If the low-risk icon was touched, the reinforcement was always a gain of one token regardless of accuracy on the line task. The token reservoir was located on the bottom right-hand side of the screen. Tokens appeared to fly out of or into the reservoir with noticeable noises. Once the number of tokens in the reservoir reached or exceeded 12, the monkeys received two real banana-flavored food pellets and the token reservoir reset to 9 tokens. Using the tokens allowed us to calibrate the amounts of reward for each level of risk, so as to minimize bias toward one of the risk options. Toward the same end, when a monkey developed a bias toward one of the risk choices, that

Correct   Incorrect

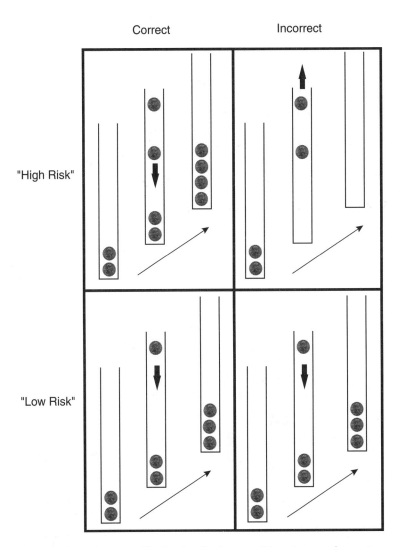

"High Risk"

"Low Risk"

Figure 12.2 Contingency table showing the four possible outcomes of correct or incorrect response to the line task and high- and low-risk bets, starting with two tokens already present in the reservoir. When high risk was pressed, two tokens fell into the reservoir after correct responses, but flew out of the reservoir after incorrect responses. When low risk was pressed, one token fell into the reservoir regardless of whether the line response was correct or incorrect. Note that in Experiment 2, choosing high risk resulted in a gain or loss of three, rather than two, tokens. See color insert.

risk icon began to appear only after a delay, which ensured that the monkeys chose both levels of risk with some frequency. A sample trial is presented in figure 12.3A.

The hypothesis was that on easy line-discrimination trials, the monkeys would get the answer correct, presumably feel certain about it, and consequently bet high risk. On difficult (impossible) trials, though, they would (usually) get the answer incorrect, presumably feel uncertain, and bet low risk. Again, an advantage of this paradigm was that two responses were required: the line discrimination at the object-level, and a judgment of that response—the bet—at the meta-level.

Training

Typically, it is advantageous to reward animals immediately following a response. This keeps the animal motivated. Furthermore, imme-

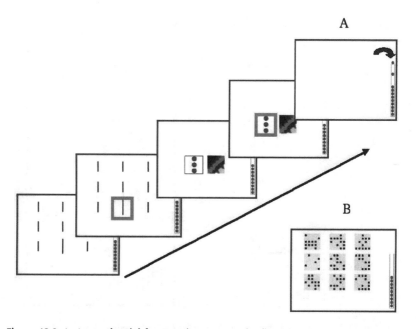

Figure 12.3 A. A sample trial for Experiment 1. In the first phase, nine lines appeared on the screen. A token reservoir appeared in the bottom right-hand corner of the screen, set at nine at the beginning of each session. The monkey's task was to press the longest line. For each touch, a green border appeared around the pressed item. Then the lines disappeared, and two risk icons appeared. The monkey's task was to report his confidence by betting either low or high risk. Once he made his bet, the token reservoir changed accordingly. In this sample trial, the monkey has bet high risk, and was correct on the line task. Thus, two tokens were added to the reservoir. B. Sample numerical stimuli for Experiment 2. The task was to press the stimulus with the most (Lashley) or the least (Ebbinghaus) items in them. Otherwise, the general methods remain the same as those in Experiment 1. See color insert.

diate feedback is most easily associated to the one and only most recent response that has been made. Thus, an animal should have little
trouble understanding what response is being rewarded. However,
this was not the case in the current paradigm. Rather than immediate
feedback, the monkeys learned that feedback occurred only after making two separate responses. Never before had these monkeys been
asked to perform two separate tasks in a single trial. Essentially, after
the monkey made his first response, the screen went blank and a new
question appeared. The monkey's task was not only to make a second
response but also to understand that the feedback he received not
only depended on that second response but reflected two past responses—the bet response in addition to the earlier line response. We
believe this was perhaps the most challenging aspect of the experiment. In addition, we required that the monkey remember four different contingency combinations and respond accordingly. Finally, the
monkey needed to learn that accumulating a certain number of tokens
on the computer screen resulted in a food reward after a criterion had
been reached. Thus, because of the novelty of the paradigm for these
participants, a substantial amount of training was involved prior to
the actual initiation of the experiment. This included training of three
distinct aspects: the main task, the tokens (including reward and punishment), and the betting icons.

The monkeys were first trained on the psychophysical task alone. At
the start of training, Ebbinghaus and Lashley were presented with two
vertical lines of different lengths on the screen. Their task was to press
the longer of the two lines. A food pellet was earned only after correct
responses. Both participants learned the task very quickly, after only a
few sessions. Gradually, the number of lines presented for each question was increased, to three, then four, until they were presented with
a total of nine vertical lines. All sessions were 20 minutes in length.

About a year after the beginning of training on the line task, a
token reservoir was added on the bottom right-hand side of the screen
during the entirety of each session. (During that year, we tried a similar betting procedure using food pellets as rewards and time-outs as
punishments. Specifically, a high-risk response resulted in either a big
food reward or a long time-out, whereas a low-risk response resulted
in a small food reward or a short time-out. However, using this paradigm, both monkeys had a significant bias for pressing high risk. We
thought that this might have been because the aversion to the time-
outs was not nearly as salient as the attraction of the food rewards.
We attempted to fix the problem by tweaking the contingencies—increasing the length of the high-risk time-out period—but there was
no evidence that the monkeys understood the connection between the
line task and the risk contingencies, and so we gave up.) Following
each correct response to the line task, a token flew into the reservoir.

After each incorrect response, the token reservoir remained empty. At the start of token training, the criterion for receiving real food pellets was set at one token, so that whenever the monkey responded correctly, a token would fly into the reservoir and then would disappear at the bottom, simultaneously with the delivery of a food pellet. Gradually, the criterion was increased. Thus, the monkeys learned that an accumulation of these tokens was a positive feature that would eventually earn them food reward. At this time, the line trials were kept at a fairly easy level, so that the monkeys would not get frustrated and would continue to be motivated during each session. (We would experience motivation difficulties several times over the course of the research.) Then the number of starting tokens in the reservoir was varied. For example, for some sessions, the reservoir started at a level of three, with six as the criterion—meaning that in order to receive food, the monkeys needed to get three trials correct. We had the start number begin at a number greater than zero because the next step of training would be to introduce punishment, or the loss of tokens. We were also interested in having the monkeys connect the tokens to actual food pellets, which they did. In fact, throughout training, both Ebbinghaus and Lashley spent some time licking the tokens on the screen, and attempting to push the tokens down, as though they could force the tokens to come out as real food pellets. In the meantime, the trials were made gradually more difficult (the ratio of difficult to easy trials increased).

The next major training step was to introduce the punishment—in our paradigm, a loss of tokens—to the monkeys. We were not sure how aversive such a punishment would be. (We only hoped that this time, the punishment would be more effective than the time-out punishment that we had attempted to use prior to incorporating the token economy.) Never had any food pellets, tokens, or other rewards been "snatched away" from the monkeys prior to this experiment. Here, when an incorrect response was made, a token (only if there were already at least one in the reservoir) would fly up and out of the reservoir, making a "negative" noise, and disappear. Of course, by this time, the monkeys knew that fewer tokens in their reservoir meant they were farther away from reaching criterion or winning a food pellet. Thus, on the first session of punishment training, both monkeys seemed almost stunned, staring at the reservoir on the screen for a while and showing obvious frustration behaviors. Lashley, after a couple minutes of frustration, soon settled in again, performing some more trials and continuing on in training. Ebbinghaus, on the other hand, stopped working, forcing us to put him on a period of remedial training with easier trials without punishment for a while. Slowly, Ebbinghaus got back on track and learned to work consistently even with the punishment. Although we were happy to know that the punishment using the token paradigm was adequately aversive for the monkeys, one future interest of ours is to investigate the differences in salience for rewards and punishments by manipulating the contingencies.

Following punishment training, both monkeys were trained to respond at a stable pace during 20-minute sessions, with a mixture of both easy and difficult trials. For each session, the reservoir began with 9 tokens, while the criterion was set at 12. Finally, the risk icons were introduced. Both icons were presented on the screen after the line response was made. One worry was that up until this point using the token procedure, the monkeys had always received feedback immediately after making their line response. This would be the first time they would not receive immediate feedback. The risk icons that we chose were two pictures, each symbolizing the number of tokens that would be risked if pressed. For example, the high-risk icon was a picture of a square with two tokens and the low-risk icon was a picture of a square with one token. The contingencies, set up like a logical gamble, were as follows: For betting high risk, they earned two tokens after a correct line response and lost two tokens after an incorrect line response. For betting low risk, they earned one token after a correct line response and lost one token after an incorrect line response. The monkeys soon learned that each of the pictures resulted in different contingencies. Whether they knew that it had anything to do with their previous line response was not yet known. In fact, again, both monkeys acquired an early bias for pressing high risk. This led us to increase the number of difficult trials during the session. We also changed the low-risk contingencies to always gaining a token regardless of previous line accuracy (changed from the previous low-risk contingencies of gaining a token when correct and losing a token when incorrect). When we still had difficulties in encouraging the monkeys to select the low-risk option more often, we changed the low-risk icon to an arbitrary picture (see figure 12.3A, the middle picture of the row of five) because we were concerned that the original low-risk icon had become unattractive. At the end of training, then, which was approximately 7 months after the tokens had first been introduced, the betting procedure was one in which a high bet meant risking two tokens, while a low bet was gaining one token regardless of previous line accuracy. Furthermore, due to the high-risk bias, a time delay was added prior to the appearance of one—the more biased one—of the risk icons (i.e., the more biased they were toward high risk, the longer they had to wait before the high-risk icon appeared). Starting from this point, we were able to obtain 41 subsequent sessions of data for both Ebbingaus and Lashley.

Results

The data were analyzed over a total of 41 sessions for each monkey. The average number of trials completed in each session was 87 and 60 for Ebbinghaus and Lashley, respectively (each session lasted 20 minutes). The mean percentage of easy trials answered correctly was 94% for Ebbinghaus and 88% for Lashley, and the mean percentage of difficult trials answered correctly was 12% for both monkeys (11.1% is chance with nine items to choose from). This is slightly higher than chance, but the difference was not significant for either monkey.

For each session, a phi correlation was computed between accuracy (correct vs. incorrect) and bet (high risk vs. low risk). We expected the monkeys to bet high risk on correct trials and low risk on incorrect trials, which would result in positive correlations. The correlations, blocked in sessions of four, are presented in figure 12.4. As shown, the correlations were generally positive.

In general, although Ebbinghaus took a little longer to achieve high correlations, both monkeys were able to report stable positive correlations by the end of training. For all 41 sessions, the mean correlations

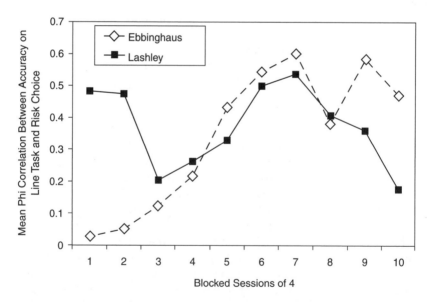

Figure 12.4 The mean phi correlations between accuracy of the object-level line task and the meta-level risk choice for the final 41 sessions of training, in blocks of four. A positive correlation indicates that on trials that were correct, the monkeys more often bet high risk, whereas on trials that were incorrect, they more often bet low risk.

were significantly above zero for both Ebbinghaus, $M = 0.33$, $t(40) =$ 8.43, $p < .0001$, and Lashley, $M = 0.37$, $t(40) = 13.37$, $p < .0001$. We also calculated the percentage of correct and incorrect trials on which the monkeys chose high risk. As figure 12.5A indicates, both monkeys chose high risk significantly more often after correct trials than after incorrect trials—for Ebbinghaus, $t(40) = 8.44$, $p < .0001$; for Lashley, $t(40) = 13.31$, $p < .0001$.

We also calculated reaction times (RT) for the difficult and easy trials (for all RT analyses, we excluded trials over 10 seconds long). The results showed that both monkeys took longer to respond to the line-discrimination task on difficult trials than on easy trials. Ebbinghaus took an average of 1.24 seconds to respond on difficult trials, but only 1.07 seconds on easy trials, which significantly differed from each other, $t(40) = 3.19$, $p < .01$. Lashley also took significantly longer to respond on difficult trials, averaging 2.00 seconds as compared to 1.66 seconds on easy trials, $t(40) = 2.55$, $p < .05$. In general, a longer response time could be interpreted as resulting from more uncertainty.

In summary, using a betting paradigm that included both an object-level task and a meta-level task, it appeared that both Ebbinghaus and Lashley were able make accurate confidence judgments. When they responded correctly on the object-level task, they were able to report that they were certain by tending to bet high risk. Similarly, after responding incorrectly, they bet low risk more often. If they were human, this chapter could now conclude without much controversy by saying that "Ebbinghaus and Lashley were able to express feelings of certainty and uncertainty about their cognitions, thus showing metacognitive abilities."

Discussion

However, the reader may be curious, as we were, to know whether these responses were based on judgments resulting from direct or explicit access of internal representations, or from inferential mechanisms. Regardless of what the basis was, both of these mechanisms, according to the human literature, would indicate that the monkeys possess metacognitive abilities. Given this, several questions arise. To begin with, perhaps the monkeys relied on cues that did not require any feelings of uncertainty. For example, the monkeys could have been relying on their own response times to guide their bets. This seems plausible, since easy and difficult trials resulted in a difference in response latencies—they might have simply bet low risk when they observed that they had taken a long time to make their response during the line task, and high risk when they had been fast. Alternatively, they could have relied on pattern recognition to make their bets. For example, they might have responded low risk when they recognized

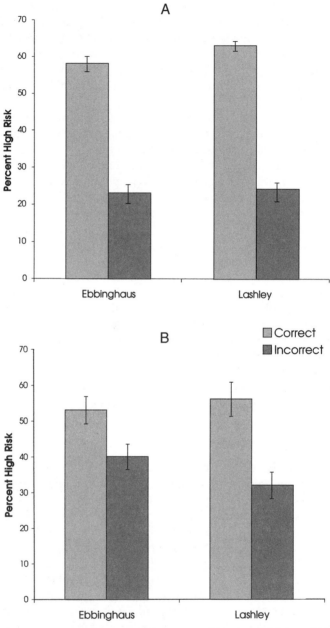

Figure 12.5 Mean percentage of correct and incorrect trials on which high risk was chosen in (A) Experiment 1 and (B) Experiment 2. These means were calculated for each monkey over the final 41 sessions for the line task in Experiment 1 and over the first 4 sessions for the numerosity task in Experiment 2.

that all of the lines were the same length, without actually feeling uncertain. If either of these was the case, then one hesitates to say that the monkeys were responding based on explicit mechanisms.

It is interesting to note that these two possibilities are quite similar to two inferential mechanisms in relation to human metacognition: retrieval fluency and cue familiarity. As described at the beginning of this chapter, in retrieval fluency, the faster one arrives at an answer, the higher the judgment will be. The cue familiarity hypothesis states that meta-judgments are based on how recognizable the cue is (Metcalfe, 1993a). For example, a person may give a high judgment for the question "What was the name of Batman's butler?" because of high familiarity in the subject of Batman and not because of any actual memory of the answer. Cue familiarity as a metacognitive cue has been supported by many experimental results (Glenberg et al., 1987; Metcalfe, 1993a, 1993b; Metcalfe et al., 1993; Miner & Reder, 1994; Reder, 1987; Reder & Ritter, 1992; Schwartz & Metcalfe, 1992). In both retrieval fluency and cue familiarity, metacognition is inferred from factors other than the explicit assessment of memory itself. Still, in the above-mentioned literature, when these judgments were found to be based on such inferential mechanisms, they were classified as meta-cognitive judgments. Based on this, if Ebbinghaus and Lashley were using cue-based pattern recognition or their reaction time as a basis for their uncertainty judgments, one reaction is to say that they still do possess metacognitive abilities. Furthermore, they would be a lot like humans if they did either of these.

To investigate these possibilities, we first explored the question of whether retrieval fluency predicted risk choice for our monkeys. To do so, we calculated mean point-biserial correlations between response time to the line-discrimination task and the bet choice. If the monkey bet low risk when he was slow on the line task and bet high risk when he was fast, the mean correlation across the 41 sessions would be negative, and it was for both Ebbinghaus, $M = .12$, $t(40) = 4.43$, $p < .0001$, and Lashley, $M = .17$, $t(40) = 5.64$, $p < .0001$. Based on this finding, it seems that response latencies could have helped guide the monkeys confidence judgments. This opens up the possibility that the monkeys behavior can be explained without positing that they made judgments based on explicitly assessing internal representations. However, we had not yet investigated whether there was any evidence that the monkeys might have, in fact, been making their risk judgments based on something internal.

To explore the question of whether the monkeys were monitoring an internal representation, we reanalyzed the data, factoring out the effect of both trial difficulty and RT. First, we analyzed only the easy trials, which were all equally difficult, meaning the monkeys could not use difficulty as a cue, which even for a human makes meta-judgments much more difficult. We then computed Pearson correlations (although the Pearson correlations are standard for continuous variables, we used them here because there was no standard way of computing partial correlations between binary and continuous data) between accuracy of the line task and risk choice, partialing out the effect of RT, separately for each session. A positive correlation would indicate that the judgments were attributable to mechanisms other than those based on trial difficulty or RT. The mean correlations were significantly positive for both Ebbinghaus, $M = 0.07$, $t(35) = 2.67$, $p < .05$, and Lashley, $M = 0.20$, $t(29) = 4.24$, $p <; .001$, although more so for Lashley than for Ebbinghaus. These results reveal that both monkeys might be making meta-judgments based on something more than implicit cues such as assessments of internal representations.

Another way to investigate whether the monkeys were not merely basing their confidence judgments on external pattern recognition, relying on features specific only to the line task, was to present the monkeys with a novel question, a transfer task. Transfer tasks are widely used, typically to ensure that the tested skill—in this case, the reporting of accurate confidence judgments through bets—has not been learned as an automated response to the external stimulus that was presented, and can be generalized to other tasks. Thus, in Experiment 2, we presented an experiment similar to Experiment 1, except that the line task was replaced with a new task. First the monkeys were trained on the new task until performance was stable, and then the risk choices were added. If they could make appropriate risk choices immediately, we reasoned that their ability to make confidence judgments had generalized and was not based on features specific to the line task in Experiment 1.

EXPERIMENT 2: TRANSFER

The purpose of Experiment 2 was to test whether the ability to make accurate meta-level confidence judgments would generalize to a numerosity task in which the monkeys had to differentially choose one correct picture out of nine presented on the screen (see figure 12.3B for a sample stimulus). Both Ebbinghaus and Lashley had previous experience with a numerical task in which pictures containing varying numbers of items (e.g., a yellow square containing 12 black dots) were presented simultaneously. Ebbinghaus had learned to press the pictures in an ascending order, and Lashley had learned to press the pictures in a descending order. We modified our task so that the monkeys were presented with nine pictures, each containing some number of items. The monkeys had to press only the one picture that contained either the most items (in Lashley's case) or the fewest items (in Ebbinghaus's case). For both monkeys, each of the eight incorrect choices contained the same number of dots. As in Experiment 1, trials varied in difficulty, but instead of only two levels of difficulty, there were four levels (none of them being impossible as one was in Experiment 1): On the very easy trials, one of the nine pictures consisted of noticeably more (or fewer) items than the other eight choices. As the trials became increasingly difficult, the correct answer became less and less distinguishable from the distractors. All sessions were 20 minutes in length. Once the monkeys had been trained on this paradigm (which took three sessions for Ebbinghaus and seven sessions for Lashley), the risk choice was added. After the numerical response was made, the computer screen cleared and the monkeys were asked to make their bet. The reinforcement contingencies were slightly modified from Experiment 1, in which the monkeys gained or lost two tokens when they bet high risk. Here, in order to increase the number of pellets the monkeys received, the contingency was changed to a gain or loss of three tokens following high-risk choices. Our hope was that, starting with the very first sessions, both Ebbinghaus and Lashley would behave metacognitively, by risking more when they were correct than when they were incorrect. These results would suggest that the monkeys had understood the meaning of the bet choices, rather than choosing them in response to patterns of the line task.

Results and Discussion

In Experiment 1, we were interested in investigating whether the monkeys acquired a metacognitive skill through training on the betting paradigm. Here, though, we were not interested in whether the monkeys could acquire the metacognitive skill. Rather, our interest lay in the very beginning of training, to examine whether immediate transfer of the betting skill occurred for a new task. Thus, in Experiment 2, we analyzed the first four sessions of training. To analyze the relationship between accuracy and risk, we again calculated phi coefficients, which allowed us to compute Fisher's exact p-values for a small number of observations. Both monkeys showed positive correlations almost immediately. For Lashley's first four sessions combined, $\varphi = 0.24$, $p < .0001$. For Ebbinghaus's first four sessions combined, $\varphi = 0.14$, $p < .05$. We also calculated the percentage of trials on which high risk was chosen separately for correct and incorrect trials, again combining the first four sessions, as shown in figure 12.5B. As in Experiment 1, high risk was chosen more often on correct trials than on incorrect trials.

The transfer task showed that both monkeys began making good risk decisions directly upon being introduced to their new task. They did not need training to make confidence judgments on the new task—unlike in the line/risk task, which took many months to learn. Instead, they showed enough flexibility to generalize the risk response to the new task. This makes sense if they were making their risk responses as meta-judgments. Such judgments about cognitions should occur for virtually any cognition, and it appears that what the monkeys had learned was how to respond with accurate *meta*-cognitions.

We were aware of the fact that although the transfer results make a stronger case for us, there are still similarities between the numerical task and the line task, the most obvious being that both involve some trials where all the stimuli look very similar, and other trials where one stimulus is quite different than the others. Thus, the monkeys could have succeeded by responding to the risk choices based solely on whether the stimuli were the same or different, in both experiments. We answered this criticism earlier by showing that risk choices were appropriate even when only easy trials (which are all the same) were included in the analysis. But it might be argued that on incorrectly answered easy trials, the monkeys simply did not notice the correct answer, and therefore thought that all of the stimuli were the same. In that case, even on easy trials, they would choose low risk and get the answer incorrect without necessarily relying on uncertainty. In short, one of the concerns of the present tasks is that they are both perceptual tasks that may not have required internal representations. So, although we think our findings are convincing, the best way to answer criticisms about stimulus cues is to use a task where nothing about the stimuli themselves makes it possible to make the risk choice successfully. One way to address this concern would be by using the betting paradigm with a memory task (e.g., Hampton, 2001; Smith et al., 1998; chapter 11, this volume), not a perceptual task.

Tasks that rely on the monkeys' memory make it difficult for a meta-judgment to be made on the basis of external cues. For example, Smith et al. (1998) used a serial probe recognition task, in which monkeys were shown four pictures in sequence and then a probe, and had to indicate whether the probe had been in the preceding list. If the probe had been presented in the list, the participants were to press the probe. If the probe was new, they were to press a second option that represented the idea of "new." If they were unsure whether the probe was old or new, they were to press a third option, the escape response. In this paradigm, when the monkey is faced with the probe, the only thing that indicates to him whether the trial is easy or difficult is the strength of his memory trace. The appearance of the stimuli offers no hints. Combining the serial probe recognition task with the current confidence-judgment task would have the advantage that on each trial the monkeys would make a response before placing their bet. As a result, we would know which trials were difficult for them. Also, when using only the escape response, if the item is very familiar or very unfamiliar, the monkeys will have a strong urge to respond either *old* or *new*. On difficult trials, if they have no strong urge they might simply respond randomly, or choose the escape response by default, and as a result choose the escape response relatively frequently. Confidence judgments do not allow such a strategy. Neither does the match-to-sample task used by Hampton (2001; chapter 11, this volume): By forcing the monkey to choose between high and low risk and then perform the task, he ensured that his monkeys could not choose low risk randomly or by default.

Memory tasks avoid certain criticisms, but there is a deeper reason to favor them. Our monkeys' estimations of size and number are cognitions, and thus their performance fits the traditional definition of metacognition. However, metacognitive research has been traditionally associated with judgments and assessments about memory. Thus, our next step is to test our monkeys' ability to make confidence judgments using a memory task, namely, one similar to the serial probe recognition task.

CONCLUSION

The current definition of metacognition is associated with many different functions, some of which (e.g., theory of mind) go far beyond making smart risk choices. For example, Nelson (1992) defines it as a form of self-reflective consciousness, in which we are able to consciously observe the workings of our own minds. This type of metacognition is thought to be a high-level process that entails privileged access into one's own internal mind and may be impossible to observe in nonverbal animals. However, another definition of metacognition takes a different view—that many of the mechanisms involved in making metacognitive judgments need not be open to conscious awareness (Cary & Reder, 2002; Reder & Schunn, 1996). According to this view, we make metacognitive judgments constantly and without explicit knowledge of them. These implicit metacognitions can be based on internal factors, but may also be based on ongoing external factors that we are not aware of.

A link can be drawn between direct-access mechanisms and conscious metacognition, in that both involve inward reflection. Feelings of uncertainty that are inferential and based on cue familiarity (for example) do not necessarily require self-reflection any more than a simple familiarity judgment does. Yet it is also clearly possible to feel uncertain based on the familiarity of a cue and, at the same time, be quite aware of that feeling. Likewise, it is also the case that an animal (or human) might have a feeling of uncertainty based on a direct access mechanism and not be aware of the process. In fact, some researchers have claimed that people have little or no direct introspective access to mental processes such as those affecting judgments (Koriat, 1993; Nisbett & Bellows, 1977; Nisbett & Wilson, 1977). For example, Koriat (1993) provides evidence supporting an accessibility mechanism of metacognition which states that, although people may access internal representations and base their judgments on those representations, they have no direct awareness of the accuracy of the internal representations. Instead, people's meta-judgments are based on both correct and incorrect pieces of information that were purportedly retrieved from an internal memory trace.

Given these issues, although it may seem that there could be a correspondence between direct access and consciously aware metacognition, it cannot be confirmed. If the process of accessing internal information from memory is not necessarily open to conscious awareness, then we see no reason why the result of the process has to be either. Thus, neither explicit mechanisms nor implicit mechanisms are "more metacognitive" than the other. Regardless of how humans, or our monkeys, made their judgments, it does not take away from the fact that the meta-judgments were made.

In this chapter, we have presented evidence that two rhesus macaque monkeys were able to display metacognitive abilities by reporting high- and low-risk bets about their own cognitions. If metacognition is taken to mean self-reflective consciousness, then our conclusion is, of course, endlessly arguable. However, we believe that the monkeys were making the type of metacognitive judgments that occur in people all the time, with or without awareness. We readily concede that because they cannot verbally express their judgments, we do not have evidence of awareness of their judgments. If we did, we would then have evidence of *meta*-metacognition (which people express when they verbalize their metacognitions). The results from the present experiments allow us to conclude that our monkeys are able to reflect upon their cognitions, indicating that they possess at least one level of metacognition. And that suffices for granting them metacognitive abilities.

REFERENCES

Arbuckle, T. Y., & Cuddy, L. L. (1969). Discrimination of item strength at time of presentation. *Journal of Experimental Psychology, 81,* 126–131.

Benjamin, A. S., Bjork, R. A., & Schwartz, B. L. (1998). The mismeasure of memory: When retrieval fluency is misleading as a metamnemonic index. *Journal of Experimental Psychology: General, 127,* 55–68.

Cary, M., & Reder, L. M. (2002). Metacognition in strategy selection: Giving consciousness too much credit. In M. Izaute, P. Chambres, & P. J. Marescaux (Eds.), *Metacognition: Process, function, and use* (pp. 63–78). New York: Kluwer.

Flavell, J. H. (2000). Development of children's knowledge about the mental world. *International Journal of Behavioral Development, 24,* 15–23.

Glenberg, A. M., Sanocki, T., Epstein, W., & Morris, C. (1987). Enhancing cali-
bration of comprehension. *Journal of Experimental Psychology: General, 116*,
119–136.

Hampton, R. R. (2001). Rhesus monkeys know when they remember. *Proceedings of the National Academy of Sciences U.S.A., 98*, 5359–5362.

Hart, J. T. (1965). Memory and the feeling-of-knowing experience. *Journal of
Educational Psychology, 56*, 208–216.

James, W. (1890). *Principles of psychology*. New York: Holt.

Janowsky, J. S., Shimamura, A. P., & Squire, L. R. (1989). Memory and metamemory: Comparisons between frontal lobe lesions and amnesic patients.
Psychobiology, 17, 3–11.

Koriat, A. (1993). How do we know that we know? The accessibility model
of the feeling of knowing. *Psychological Review, 100*, 609–639.

Koriat, A., Lichtenstein, S., & Fischhoff, B. (1980). Reasons for confidence.
Journal of Experimental Psychology: Human Learning and Memory, 6, 107–118.

Metcalfe, J. (1993a). Novelty monitoring, metacognition, and control in a composite holographic associative recall model: Implications for Korsakoff amnesia. *Psychological Review, 100*, 3–22.

Metcalfe, J. (1993b). Monitoring and gain control in an episodic memory
model: Relation to the P300 event-related potential. In A. F. Collins & S. E.
Gathercole (Eds.), *Theories of memory* (pp. 327–353). Hove, UK: Lawrence
Erlbaum.

Metcalfe, J., Schwartz, B. L., & Joaquim, S. G. (1993). The cue-familiarity heuristic in metacognition. *Journal of Experimental Psychology: Learning, Memory,
and Cognition, 19*, 851–864.

Metcalfe, J., & Shimamura, A. P. (1994). *Metacognition: Knowing about knowing*.
Cambridge, MA: MIT Press.

Miner, A. C., & Reder, L. M. (1994). A new look at feeling of knowing: Its
metacognitive role in regulating question answering. In J. Metcalfe & A. P.
Shimamura (Eds.), *Metacognition: Knowing about knowing* (pp. 47–70). Cambridge, MA: MIT Press.

Nelson, T. O. (1992). *Metacognition: Core readings*. Boston: Allyn and Bacon.

Nelson, T. O., Gerler, D., & Narens, L. (1984). Accuracy of feeling-of-knowing
judgments for predicting perceptual identification and relearning. *Journal
of Experimental Psychology: General, 113*, 282–300.

Nelson, T. O., & Narens, L. (1990). Metamemory: A theoretical framework
and new findings. In G. H. Bower (Ed.), *The psychology of learning and motivation* (Vol. 26, pp. 125–141). New York: Academic Press.

Nelson, T. O., & Narens, L. (1994). Why investigate metacognition? In J. Metcalfe & A. P. Shimamura (Eds.), *Metacognition: Knowing about knowing* (pp.
1–25). Cambridge, MA: MIT Press.

Nisbett, R. E., & Bellows, N. (1977). Verbal reports about causal influences on
social judgments: Private access versus public theories. *Journal of Personality and Social Psychology, 35*, 613–624.

Nisbett, R. E., & Wilson, T. D. (1977). Telling more than we know: Verbal
reports on mental processes. *Psychological Review, 84*, 231–279.

Perfect, T. J., & Hollins, T. S. (1996). Predictive feeling of knowing judgements
and postdictive confidence judgements in eyewitness memory and general
knowledge. *Applied Cognitive Psychology, 10*, 371–382.

Reder, L. M. (1987). Strategy selection in question answering. *Cognitive Psychology, 19,* 90–138.

Reder, L. M. (1996). Different research programs on metacognition: Are the boundaries imaginary? *Learning and Individual Differences, 8,* 383–390.

Reder, L. M., & Ritter, F. E. (1992). What determines initial feeling of knowing? Familiarity with question terms, not with the answer. *Journal of Experimental Psychology: Learning, Memory, and Cognition, 18,* 435–451.

Reder, L. M., & Schunn, C. (1996). Metacognition does not imply awareness: Strategy choice is governed by implicit learning and memory. In L. M. Reder (Ed.), *Implicit memory and metacognition* (pp. 45–77). Mahwah, NJ: Lawrence Erlbaum.

Schwartz, B. L. (1994). Sources of information in metamemory: Judgments of learning and feelings of knowing. *Psychonomic Bulletin and Review, 1,* 357–375.

Schwartz, B. L., & Metcalfe, J. (1992). Cue familiarity but not target retrievability enhances feeling-of-knowing judgments. *Journal of Experimental Psychology: Learning, Memory, and Cognition, 18,* 1074–1083.

Shaughnessy, J. J. (1979). Confidence-judgment accuracy as a predictor of test performance. *Journal of Research in Personality, 13,* 505–514.

Shields, W. E., Smith, J. D., & Washburn, D. A. (1997). Uncertain responses by humans and Rhesus monkeys (*Macaca mulatta*) in a psychophysical same-different task. *Journal of Experimental Psychology: General, 126,* 147–164.

Shimamura, A. P., & Squire, L. R. (1986). Memory and metamemory: A study of the feeling-of-knowing phenomenon in amnesic patients. *Journal of Experimental Psychology: Learning, Memory, and Cognition, 12,* 452–460.

Smith, J. D., Schull, J., Strote, J., McGee, K., Egnor, R., & Erb, L. (1995). The uncertain response in the bottlenosed dolphin (*Tursiops truncates*). *Journal of Experimental Psychology: General, 124,* 391–408.

Smith, J. D., Shields, W. E., Allendoerfer, K. R., & Washburn, D. A. (1998). Memory monitoring by animals and humans. *Journal of Experimental Psychology: General, 127,* 227–250.

Smith, J. D., Shields, W. E., Schull, J., & Washburn, D. A. (1997). The uncertain response in humans and animals. *Cognition, 62,* 75–97.

Tulving, E. (1994). Foreword. In J. Metcalfe & A. P. Shimamura (Eds.), *Metacognition: Knowing about knowing* (pp. vii–x). Cambridge, MA: MIT Press.

Tulving, E., & Madigan, S. A. (1970). Memory and verbal learning. In P. H. Mussen & M. R. Rosenzweig (Eds.), *Annual review of psychology* (pp. 437–484). Palo Alto, CA: Annual Reviews.

Underwood, B. J. (1966). Individual and group predictions of item difficulty for free-recall learning. *Journal of Experimental Psychology, 71,* 673–679.

13

The Self and Other: A Missing Link in Comparative Social Cognition

Josep Call

The research area of mental state attribution has experienced great change in recent years. Topics such as the understanding of intention, knowledge, and belief are receiving increasing research attention (see Heyes, 1998; see also Call & Tomasello, 2003, for a recent review). However, the area that has developed most in the last few years is the study of the understanding of visual perception in others, particularly in chimpanzees. Studies show that chimpanzees follow the gaze of conspecifics and humans, follow it past distractors and behind barriers, "check back" with humans when gaze following does not yield interesting sights, use gestures appropriately depending on the visual access of their recipient, and select different pieces of food depending on whether their competitor has visual access to them (see Call & Tomasello, in press, for a review). These results, which cannot be explained by invoking a conspecific's line of sight or orientation as a discriminative stimulus, show that, at a minimum, chimpanzees know what others can and cannot see.

Interest in mental state attribution in others contrasts with the meager research devoted to the study of mental attribution in the self. Since chimpanzees appear to know about what others can and cannot see, one can also ask whether they also know about what they themselves have seen. Partly, an explanation for the little development of this research area can be found in the methods that have been used to answer questions about the self in comparative social cognition. Two approaches have traditionally dominated the study of the self in nonhuman animals: imitation and mirror self-recognition. Although these two paradigms have offered some valuable information about the self, I argue that these two paradigms have exhausted their explanatory power regarding the self. This is particularly true of the conceptual self as opposed to the ecological self. Neisser (1988) defines the ecological self as that who interacts with the environment and receives information about it via the senses, whereas the conceptual self consists of the mental representation of the individual's personal features including his or her knowledge.

Recently, however, new paradigms to investigate metacognition in nonhuman animals have contributed significantly to the renewed interest in this area (as this volume testifies). These paradigms are broadly based on presenting animals with uncertain situations and measuring their responses in an attempt to gauge how much an animal knows about what it knows and whether it can apply that knowledge to exercise control over the information it seeks to obtain (Call & Carpenter, 2001; Hampton, 2001; Smith et al., 1995; Smith, Shields, Schull, & Washburn, 1997). The goal of this chapter is to depict these methods as valid alternatives to more traditional methods and to indicate the significance of studying the self and others for understanding comparative social cognition.

This chapter is organized as follows. First, I present the main findings produced by the imitation and the mirror self-recognition paradigms in relation to the question of the self in social cognition, and I highlight their limitations. Second, I describe some new methods that use uncertainty as alternatives and extensions of the imitation and self-recognition paradigms. I concentrate on the findings of a paradigm based on presenting incomplete information to see if subjects seek additional information before making a choice. Third, I discuss the possibility that the seeking-information paradigm can be used to gauge metacognitive functioning across various species. I then return to the questions I raised at the beginning of the chapter about mental state attribution in others and propose a closer connection, both empirically and theoretically, between the study of mental attribution in the self and in others.

TWO TRADITIONS IN THE STUDY OF THE SELF IN NONHUMAN ANIMALS

The comparative study of the self has been based on two paradigms: imitation and mirror self-recognition. Each of these paradigms comes from two different traditions, developmental and comparative psychology, respectively. Due to their different origins, each tradition has imprinted its particular features on the comparative study of the self. Consequently, the questions that each tradition seeks to answer are not the same, even though they bear some resemblance. Here I review the main findings of each field in relation to the self and note some of their limitations.

Imitation

Copying someone else's actions involves making a correspondence between the observed actions and producing actions on the self (Mitchell, 1993). In other words, imitation involves a translation of the visual information (observed actions of others) into kinesthetic information (produced actions by the self). For that reason, imitation is commonly used as evidence of self-recognition (Lewis, 1994) or self-concept (Hart & Fegley, 1994). Moreover, many developmental psychologists see in the imitation of others one of the most fundamental processes by which individuals construct their self-concept (Baldwin, 1902; Lewis & Brooks-Gunn, 1979). This process may be initiated at a very early age when very young infants imitate the facial expressions of others. Gopnik and Meltzoff (1994) have argued that by imitating the facial expressions of others, very young infants get to experience what emotions are associated with certain facial expressions, thus giving them a glimpse of what others feel when they display those facial expressions. Later, the reproduction of others' behavior through imitation will give children additional information about other aspects of others' minds that children will eventually assimilate into their concept of self, and by extension to others will form their mental state attribution abilities (theory of mind).

Some authors have extended the connection between imitation and self-concept to the great apes (Parker & Milbrath, 1994). However, the evidence that apes copy actions is fragile (see Tomasello, 1996, for a review). Currently, there is no consensus regarding whether chimpanzees or other apes spontaneously imitate the actions of others. Some studies suggest that the most likely learning mechanism is for one observer to attempt to reproduce an outcome similar to that produced by a demonstrator rather than copying the demonstrator's actions (Call, Carpenter, & Tomasello, 2002; Call & Tomasello, 1995; Myowa-Yamakoshi & Matsuzawa, 1999; Nagell, Olguin, & Tomasello, 1993; Tomasello, Davis-Dasilva, Camak, & Bard, 1987). Others claim that chimpanzees and other apes are capable of spontaneously copying actions of others to solve problems, although these studies do not effectively distinguish actions from results (Stoinski, Wrate, Ure, & Whiten, 2001; Whiten, 1998; Whiten, Custance, Gómez, Teixidor, & Bard, 1996). It is true that apes raised by humans are more skilled at copying the actions of others (Bering, Bjorklund, & Ragan, 2000; Bjorklund, Yunger, Bering, & Ragan, 2002; Tomasello, Savage-Rumbaugh, & Kruger, 1993). However, these actions usually involve some sort of result such as a noise or a change of state in an object, so that it is hard to know precisely what is the contribution of actions or results to the reproduction of the target behaviors. Some studies have eliminated the objects altogether and focused on the reproduction of gestures (Call, 2001; Custance, Whiten, & Bard, 1995; Miles, 1990). After extensive training, apes can reproduce novel body movements on command, but their accuracy is far from perfect, and there is some indication that apes reproduce those actions with some tangible result more readily than those without results (Call, 2001).

Mirror Self-Recognition

From its inception, the mirror self-recognition paradigm has been closely linked to self-awareness and a concept of self (Gallup, 1970, 1982). According to Gallup, self-directed mirror inspection is evidence for self-awareness (Gallup, 1982), or a representational self (Anderson & Gallup, 1999). The empirical evidence that has been used to support this claim is as follows (see Anderson, 1999; Anderson & Gallup, 1999, for reviews). When confronted with a mirror, chimpanzees and orangutans show social responses first, followed by contingent behavior in front of the mirror, and finally mirror-guided self-directed inspection of body parts not visible otherwise (Lethmate & Ducker, 1973; Suarez & Gallup, 1981). When administered the mark test, in which subjects are anesthetized and an odorless dye is applied to some body part that is not directly visible, these species touch the mark more often in the presence of a mirror than in its absence. Developmentally, the ability to show self-directed behavior appears between 3 and 5 years of age, with adolescents and young adults showing the highest levels of self-directed behavior in front of the mirror. In contrast to orangutans and chimpanzees (and bonobos, for whom there is also some positive evidence; see Hyatt & Hopkins, 1994), most gorillas tested have produced no clear evidence of mirror self-directed inspection. Two possible exceptions to these negative results are two human-reared gorillas that also seem to have passed some version of this test (Patterson & Cohn, 1994; Swartz & Evans, 1994).

Similar tests done with monkeys have produced negative results (see Anderson & Gallup, 1999, for a review). Monkeys also produce social responses to the mirror image, but they do not show clear evidence of self-directed mirror-guided behavior despite the numerous studies that have attempted to find self-recognition in monkeys. Nevertheless, monkeys, like apes, can use mirrors to find hidden food that cannot be observed directly (Anderson, 1986).

Although there has been continued controversy regarding the procedural details of the mirror self-recognition paradigm across the years (e.g., Epstein, Lanza, & Skinner, 1981; Heyes, 1994), the basic findings are generally accepted. Nevertheless, the question of what the mirror self-recognition experiments show regarding self-awareness is still a matter of intense debate. While some authors maintain that mirror self-recognition experiments cannot answer questions about self-awareness (Heyes, 1994), others see mirror self-recognition as evidence of self-awareness (Gallup, 1982), a representational self (Anderson & Gallup, 1999), or a concept of me (Lewis, 1994). I argue that no major advances in answering this question have been made in the last 20 years, even though there is more information about more species. Particularly lacking are answers for the question of the more psychological self rather than the perceptual self. Mirror self-recognition (and imitation) experiments are eerily silent regarding what the self knows, remembers, or sees. But this is not surprising, because these paradigms were not designed to answer such questions in the first place. In my view, these traditional paradigms have offered as much as they can regarding the question of the psychological self, and I agree with other authors (Anderson, 1999; Gallup, 1994; Itakura, 2001) that novel approaches should complement these more traditional approaches. These novel approaches, however, should not merely be covert mirror self-recognition tests. The study of shadow reflections (e.g., Cameron & Gallup, 1988), video representations of the self (Anderson, 1999), or the use of computer joysticks (Jorgensen, Suomi, & Hopkins, 1995), though interesting in themselves, are not enough. A truly novel approach to the question of the psychological self is needed. Only recently have new studies attempted to get some answers on the more psychological level of the self. Next, I review these studies.

RECENT APPROACHES TO THE STUDY OF THE UNDERSTANDING OF THE SELF

Research on human metacognition is burgeoning. In general, researchers have used two methods to explore this area in nonhuman animals. One is to create uncertainty and measure escape responses. The other is to provide incomplete information and measure whether subjects seek additional information. Unfortunately, most studies with humans are not applicable to nonhuman animals because they rely heavily on language. Recently, however, two lines of research have used nonverbal measures to assess escape responses in cetaceans and primates, including humans.

Smith et al. (1995) presented an auditory discrimination task to dolphins and humans. They presented subjects with auditory stimuli that varied between 1200 Hz and 2100 Hz. For a given stimulus, subjects had to decide whether the stimulus was low or high pitch. If the stimulus was between 1200 and 2099 Hz, they had to press the low key, whereas if the stimulus was 2100 Hz (the highest pitch) they had to press the high key. For stimuli at the low end of the distribution this discrimination was easy, but as stimuli drew closer to the 2100 Hz mark, the discrimination became increasingly difficult. Subjects were only rewarded for correct responses. Incorrect responses produced a time-out period of 9 to 12 seconds. In addition to the low or high key choice, subjects had a third option: the escape key. Subjects could press this key to skip the current trial and go to the next one, which was always reinforced. However, to avoid excessive use of this key, the computer gradually delayed the presentation of trials on which reinforcement was guaranteed if the escape key was used too frequently. Results showed that dolphins and humans increased the use of the escape key when the discrimination became increasingly difficult. They rarely used the escape key for low-pitch stimuli, and the percentage of escape responses also decreased for the highest pitch stimulus. Thus, the distribution of escape responses was an inverted U-shaped curve that peaked slightly before the 2100-Hz mark.

In another study, Smith et al. (1997) tested rhesus monkeys and humans with a visual discrimination task and found results similar to those of the previous study. The stimuli varied in the density of pixels presented, and subjects had to discriminate low-density boxes (450–2,949 pixels) from high-density boxes (2,950 pixels). Subjects also had the option of the escape key available. The contingencies for correct and incorrect responses and for the use of the escape key were analogous to those of the previous study. The pattern of results was nearly identical to that found in the previous study. Rhesus macaques and humans increased the use of the escape key when the discrimination became increasingly difficult. They rarely used the escape key for low-density stimuli, and the percentage of escape responses also decreased for the highest pitch/density stimuli. The distribution of escape responses was an inverted U-shaped curve that peaked before the 2,950-pixel mark. Smith and colleagues argued that these studies show that dolphins, rhesus monkeys, and humans behave in similar ways in uncertain situations. All species showed some control over their decision to avoid a given trial under perceptual uncertainty.

Hampton (2001; see chapter 11, this volume) used a different approach to study metacognition in a nonverbal animal. Two rhesus monkeys were trained on a delayed matching-to-sample task that was presented on a touch-sensitive computer screen. Following the presentation of a sample stimulus and a delay of 30 seconds, the subject was presented with the sample and three distractors. On one third of the trials, a desirable reward (a peanut) was contingent on selecting the sample. Incorrect choices resulted in no reward and a time-out period. On the remaining two thirds of the trials, subjects were offered the option of declining the test. Choosing that option resulted in the delivery of monkey chow, a less desirable reward. Whereas declining a test always produced a reward, opting to take the test produced a peanut only if the subject was correct. Hampton observed that monkeys performed better on those trials in which they were free to decline a test compared with the forced test. This suggested that monkeys may have known when they had forgotten the correct answer.

Two additional tests reinforced this conclusion. In a second experiment, Hampton increased the delay interval between the presentation of the sample and the alternatives. This was done to foster forgetting in the monkeys. Results showed that monkeys' performance declined proportionally to the amount of delay between the sample and the alternative stimuli. This was expected. More important, the proportion of trials on which the monkeys chose to decline the trial increased as the delay between the sample and the alternatives increased. In a third experiment, Hampton presented some trials without a sample (a blank picture, to be exact). As expected, the monkeys declined a high proportion of tests when no sample had been offered. Hampton concluded that rhesus monkeys know when they have forgotten and that they can remedy this lack of information by escaping the situation.

An Initial Study on Seeking Information

The two previous studies showed that cetaceans and primates can escape situations of uncertainty. They knew when stimuli were too hard to discriminate or when they did not have information about the sample stimuli. Another avenue to explore metacognition in nonhuman animals consists of presenting incomplete information and seeing whether individuals seek additional information. Call and Carpenter (2001) presented chimpanzees, orangutans, and 2.5-year-old children with a situation in which they had to choose one of two containers to obtain a reward. Previous to this study, subjects had been presented with two opaque containers, and they had to displace one of them to indicate their choice. In this study, however, we replaced the opaque containers with hollow 30-cm tubes that were placed perpendicular to the subject. We hid food in the side of the tube closest to the experimenter so that the subjects were not able to see the food from their location. However, subjects could see the food inside the tube if they bent down and looked through the tube (see figure 13.1). Using this

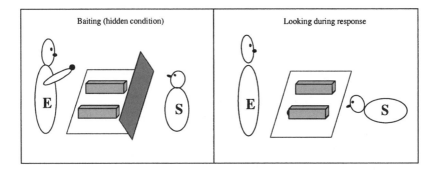

Figure 13.1 Experimental setup to investigate whether subjects will look inside the tubes before selecting one of them when subjects are prevented visual access to the baiting procedure. E, experimenter; S, subject. From Call and Carpenter (2001). Copyright © Springer-Verlag.

setup, we presented two conditions. In the visible condition, subjects had visual access to the baiting procedure so that they could see in which tube the experimenter had placed the reward. In the hidden condition, the baiting process was conducted behind a screen so that subjects were prevented from seeing in which tube the experimenter had placed the reward. We recorded which tube they selected, but more important, we recorded whether they looked inside the tube before choosing.

Results indicated that subjects looked significantly more often inside the tubes when they had been prevented from witnessing the baiting process. Typically, in hidden trials, subjects looked inside the tube, and if they saw the reward they stopped their search and selected that tube. If they did not see the reward inside the tube, they checked the second tube and then made their choice (figure 13.2). Although in most trials apes chose after seeing the food, in approximately 20% of the trials in which their first inspection revealed an empty tube, they selected the other tube without inspecting it. This means that subjects' choices (and their looking behavior) were not rigidly and solely controlled by the sight of food. Instead, they could make some inferences regarding the location of food without having seen it. Interestingly, children rarely used this inferential strategy but preferred to inspect all tubes until they found the reward. We also observed that if subjects were not allowed to choose one of the tubes right away, that is, when a 5-second delay was inserted between the end of the baiting and the opportunity to choose, subjects looked significantly more often inside the tube.

Extending the Initial Findings to Other Species

The previous study showed that chimpanzees, orangutans, and children looked more often inside the tubes on trials in which they had not seen the location of the reward than on trials in which they saw where the experimenter placed the reward. Thus, they had access to information regarding the location of the reward, and when they did not have such information, they sought it before they selected a container. This initial finding prompted us to probe this skill further. We saw two ways of broadening the scope of these initial findings. One way consisted of probing further the mechanism responsible for this performance. A second way was to study other species, both closely and distantly related to orangutans, chimpanzees, and children. We chose to start broadening the scope by comparing species.

From a comparative point of view, it was not surprising that chimpanzees and orangutans solved this problem, because they also pass the mirror self-recognition test. A more interesting comparison is gorillas because, unlike chimpanzees and orangutans, they do not readily pass mirror tests and do not show mirror-guided self-directed

Figure 13.2 Typical sequence of events in the hidden and the visible conditions. In the hidden condition, the reward is hidden inside one of the tubes behind a screen (A), the orangutan looks inside the empty tube (B), then the baited tube (C), and makes a choice (D). In the visible condition, the reward is placed inside one of the tubes in full view of the subject (E), and the subject chooses (F). Note the absence of looking behavior in the visible condition compared to the hidden condition. See color insert.

behavior. Povinelli (1993) has argued that gorillas may have lost the capacity for self-recognition (but see Patterson & Cohn, 1994; Swartz & Evans, 1994), whereas Gallup (1994) has claimed that gorillas may differ in cognition from the other great apes. In addition to studying gorillas, we completed the investigation of the great ape clade by studying bonobos. In particular, we studied 5 orangutans, 12 chimpanzees, 6 gorillas, and 4 bonobos housed at the Wolfgang Köhler Primate Research Center in Leipzig. There were 18 females and 9 males ranging from 4 to 30 years of age. All the bonobos except the female and all the adult chimpanzees were nursery reared, whereas all other subjects were mother reared. All subjects lived in social groups of various sizes, with access to indoor and outdoor areas. Subjects were individually tested in their indoor cages and were not food or water deprived.

We followed the delayed procedure used in the initial experiment (Call & Carpenter, 2001) with both visible and hidden trials. Thus, the experimenter placed two tubes on the platform and either baited them while the subject watched (visible trials) or conducted the baiting behind a screen (hidden trials). After the baiting was completed, the experimenter held the tubes in view but outside the reach of the subject for 5 seconds. The experimenter then pushed the platform toward the subject so that it could select one of the tubes. All subjects had learned prior to this experiment to touch one of the two objects available to request that container. Subjects received a total of 24 visible and 24 hidden trials presented in four 12-trial sessions. Each session consisted of 6 visible and 6 hidden trials. All trials were videotaped and later coded by the experimenter. We measured two variables across trials: (1) looking inside the tube, and (2) tube selection. A second coder who was unaware of the experimental conditions blindly coded 20% of the trials for reliability purposes on each of the two measures used in this study. Reliability for both measures was excellent (looking inside the tube: Cohen's kappa = 0.87; choosing the tube: Cohen's kappa = 1.0).

Figure 13.3 presents the percentage of trials in which subjects looked inside the tubes for each of the two conditions. The four great apes looked significantly more in the hidden than in the visible condition, $F(1,23) = 38.7$, $p < .001$. There were no differences across species and no interaction effects. Thus, gorillas were indistinguishable from the rest of the apes.

Table 13.1 presents the individual performances of each of the apes in the hidden trials, with particular attention devoted to the pattern of responses across trials. We distinguished three types of acquisition of looking inside the tubes: no acquisition, gradual acquisition, and sudden acquisition. No acquisition consisted of failing to look consistently during testing. Gradual acquisition consisted of progressively

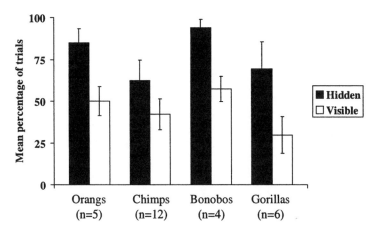

Figure 13.3   Mean percentage of trials in which apes looked inside the tube as a function of the baiting condition and the species.

increasing the looks inside the tube across trials. This type of acquisition included a period of alternation between trials, with and without looks, until the looking response appeared in every trial. Sudden acquisition consisted of looking inside the tube from the first trial (i), or, if subjects did not look in the first trial, once they started to look they looked consistently for the remaining trials (ii). Eighteen of the 27 subjects (67%) showed sudden acquisition of the looking behavior. Of those 18 subjects, 13 (48%) looked from the first trial, whereas 5 others (19%) first did not look, but once they started they did not stop looking. Five subjects acquired the looking response gradually (19%), whereas four other subjects showed no acquisition.

The search pattern was analogous to that found in our initial study (see figure 13.4). Upon finding a baited tube after their first look, subjects stopped their search and selected that tube in the great majority of trials. In contrast, if they found no food after their first look, they continued looking. Nevertheless, in a sizeable number of trials (16–38%, depending on the species) subjects selected the other tube upon finding an empty one, without looking into it. These "blind" choices resulted in a performance that was above chance, $t(15) = 2.80$, $p = .014$.

In sum, we found the same search pattern as before, and gorillas were undistinguishable from the other apes. Thus, the ape clade presents a homogenous performance when seeking information in uncertain situations. One question is how much this skill extends across other taxa. To answer this question, we contrasted the ape results with those of another species distantly related to the apes but which shows some ability to solve problems that require the use of gaze following, visual communication, or sensitivity to the state of the human's eyes

Table 13.1 Subject Information and Percentage of Trials in Which Subjects Look Inside the Tube in Hidden Trials.

Species/Name	Sex	Age (yrs)	% Trials w/Looks	Acquisition Pattern	Looks Across Trials
Gorillas					
Bebe	F	22	46	Gradual	NNNNYNNNYYNNNYNYYYNNYYYY
Viringika	F	6	100	Sudden(i)	YYYYYYYYYYYYYYYYYYYYYYYY
Vizuri	F	6	83	Sudden(ii)	NNNNYYYYYYYYYYYYYYYYYYYY
Ruby	F	4	88	Sudden(i)	YYNNNYYYYYYYYYYYYYYYYYYY
Gorgo	M	20	0	No	NNNNNNNNNNNNNNNNNNNNNNNN
Vimoto	M	6	100	Sudden(i)	YYYYYYYYYYYYYYYYYYYYYYYY
Orangutans					
Dunja	F	30	100	Sudden(i)	YYYYYYYYYYYYYYYYYYYYYYYY
Pini	F	13	96	Sudden(i)	YYYYYYYYYYYYYYYYYYYYNYYY
Toba	F	7	92	Sudden(ii)	NYYYYYYYYYYYYYYYYYYNYYYY
Padana	F	4	54	Gradual	NNNNNNYNYYYYYYYYYNNYYNN
Bimbo	M	21	83	Sudden(i)	YYYYNYYYYYYYYNYYYYNNYYYY
Chimpanzees					
Fraukje	F	25	100	Sudden(i)	YYYYYYYYYYYYYYYYYYYYYYYY
Riet	F	25	88	Sudden(i)	YYYYYYYYNYYYYNNYYYYYYYYY
Ulla	F	24	75	Gradual	NNNYNYYNYYYYYYYYNYYYYYYY
Natascha	F	21	71	Gradual	NNYNYYYYYYYYYYYNYNNYYYNY
Dorien	F	21	100	Sudden(i)	YYYYYYYYYYYYYYYYYYYYYYYY
Jahaga	F	8	88	Sudden(ii)	NYYYYYYYYYYYYYYYYYYYYNYN
Gertruida	F	8	0	No	NNNNNNNNNNNNNNNNNNNNNNNN
Fifi	F	8	100	Sudden(i)	YYYYYYYYYYYYYYYYYYYYYYYY
Sandra	F	8	17	Sudden(ii)	NNNNNNNNNNNNNNYNNNNNNYYY
Robert	M	26	8	No	NNNNNNNNYYNNNNNNNNNNNNNN
Frodo	M	8	100	Sudden(i)	YYYYYYYYYYYYYYYYYYYYYYYY
Patrick	M	4	0	No	NNNNNNNNNNNNNNNNNNNNNNNN
Bonobos					
Ulindi	F	8	79	Gradual	NNNYYNNYYYYYYYYYYYYYYYYY
Joey	M	19	96	Sudden(ii)	NYYYYYYYYYYYYYYYYYYYYYYY
Limbuko	M	6	100	Sudden(i)	YYYYYYYYYYYYYYYYYYYYYYYY
Kuno	M	5	100	Sudden(i)	YYYYYYYYYYYYYYYYYYYYYYYY

Notes. Includes the acquisition pattern and whether the subject looked on each of the 24 trials. Y, Yes; N, No. Sudden(i) indicates that subjects looked inside the tube in the first trial; Sudden(ii) indicates that looks began after the first trial.

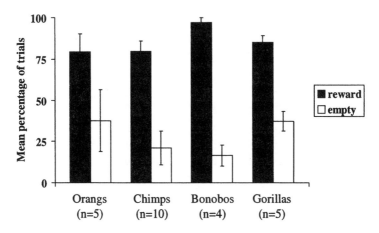

Figure 13.4 Mean percentage of trials in which apes made a choice after their first look as a function of what they saw inside the tube and the species.

(see Call, 2004, for a review). This species is the domestic dog. Bräuer, Call, and Tomasello (in press) presented dogs with the same problem that we used with apes but with a modified apparatus. Food was hidden inside a box that subjects could designate by pressing a lever with their paw. Opposite the lever was a window with holes through which dogs could look and smell the contents of the box before selecting it. As with the apes, there were visible and hidden trials. Figure 13.5 presents the percentage of trials in which dogs inspected the contents of the box (either by looking into it or sniffing it) and the percentage of correct trials. Unlike the apes, dogs did not look (or sniff) before choosing significantly more often when they had not witnessed

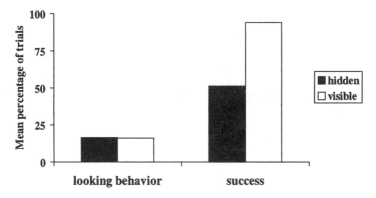

Figure 13.5 Mean percentage of trials in which dogs looked inside the tube as a function of the baiting condition.

the baiting. The percentage of correct choices in each condition reflects this fact because they were above chance when they saw the food location but not when they did not see it. So, unlike apes, dogs did not seek information before making a choice.

SEEKING INFORMATION AS A METACOGNITIVE INDEX

Recent studies have shown that our initial finding that chimpanzees, orangutans, and children seek information when they have not seen the baiting of the reward are replicable with another group of subjects of the same species and can also be extended to bonobos and gorillas. Thus, apes and children (unlike dogs) preferentially seek information when this information is missing. It is important to emphasize that the behavior they use to seek information is not the same that they use to select one of the alternatives present on the platform. They choose by touching the container, not by bending down to look through it. In fact, bending down to look is not a behavior that they usually display in our testing situation. When they are presented with opaque containers on a platform, they do not bend down or engage in other behaviors that may produce information that they do not currently have. Yet one can ask whether this seeking behavior is evidence of metacognition or can be explained by means of other mechanisms.

Two mechanisms that do not require a metacognitive explanation could explain the apes' performance. One mechanism is that subjects simply use an automatic hard-wired search routine based on executing search responses when information about the food location is missing. Thus subjects would search for food until they found it, then stop their search and select the appropriate container. There are some problems with this explanation, however. First, sometimes subjects stopped searching and made appropriate choices even without seeing the food. Gorillas and orangutans selected the container they had not inspected in 38% of the trials in which they did not see the food after their first look. In addition, recent experiments have shown that when subjects are forced to choose between two stimuli and only partial visual or auditory information is offered, they can still infer the location of food (Call, in press). This argues against a rigid algorithm for food finding. Moreover, not all subjects executed this routine, since some of them never sought information, and some of them that had seen where the food was located still looked inside the tube, albeit less often than on trials in which they had not seen the location of the food.

Another alternative that may explain our results is that subjects may have learned (rather than having a hard-wired response) some fixed rule that has produced positive consequences in the past.

Namely, in the absence of food subjects may have produced a variety of search responses indiscriminately and once some of those responses were rewarded, they became established. For instance, during the test subjects may have learned to bend down when a barrier was present during the baiting because that increased the chances of selecting the correct tube. Unlike the previous explanation, this could account for the individual differences observed. However, this explanation cannot account for the successful performance of those subjects who showed no evidence of learning during the test.

Of course, one can argue that learning took place before the experiment began. Note that we have no way to verify this possibility, but invoking the learning of some fixed rule is often postulated but rarely demonstrated. Although it is true that chimpanzees can associatively learn conditional discriminations based on the presence of a certain cue, it is not a foregone conclusion that they always do so. In fact, apes may not be as skillful as commonly thought about learning such discriminations in social and nonsocial problems (e.g., Call, Hare, & Tomasello, 1998; Tomasello, Call, & Gluckman, 1997). Moreover, note that subjects had never before experienced the tubes and barrier combination as it was presented in the current test. Although one could argue that subjects may have experienced similar situations in the past and they transferred those experiences to adapt to the new situation, this explanation opens the possibility that subjects' choices are guided by the properties of the stimuli rather than the particular stimuli themselves. In other words, subjects may encode information as "when my visual access is blocked, then do something appropriate to gain visual access to it" rather than "when a cardboard screen (or a log, wall, or rock) is present, then do X."

This more interpretive and flexible rule is a far cry from the initial fixed rule of "when the cardboard barrier is present during baiting, then bend down." Unlike a fixed rule, it is based on knowledge that was created by experiencing a variety of situations, none of which matched exactly the one that we presented in our test. Additional experiments will be needed to specify more precisely the kind of knowledge that underlies these rules. For instance, what would happen if subjects witnessed the baiting and, once it was completed, a barrier was interposed between the subject and the tubes? Or what would happen if the baiting occurred behind a barrier, but instead of hollow tubes the experimenter used opaque cups? If subjects were using this more interpretive strategy, we would not expect subjects to bend down and look for the food.

A final argument against merely learning fixed rules: Dogs are skillful in other domains of visual perception in social situations, even more than chimpanzees (Call, 2004; Hare, Brown, Williamson, & Tomasello, 2002), but they do not pass this test. Clearly, dogs' failures do not convert apes' successes into metacognition, but it shows that an animal who can learn cues to find food does not seek information when it is ignorant regarding the exact location of food. In any case, the dog-ape comparison highlights the contrast between these species and perhaps indicates a difference between the cognitive mechanisms that govern these two different animal clades.

Thus, I argue that the recourse to fixed rules such as "bend down in the presence of a barrier" is not likely to explain some of the evidence presented here. This does not mean that past experience and learning are unimportant in developing novel solutions to novel problems. On the contrary, past experience is probably crucial to develop appropriate solutions to novel problems. What it is disputed here is the validity of using fixed rules to explain phenomena to the detriment of flexible rules based on knowledge accumulation created through multiple experiences, none of which exactly matches our test situation.

In sum, neither of the previous two explanations seems fully satisfactory. One key feature in which both explanations falter is that subjects show flexibility of action in their seeking behavior. This means that subjects have some access to what they have and have not seen, and this access is not likely to be controlled by a rigid program or learned after trial and error. The nature of this access is still unclear, and additional research is needed to pinpoint the exact mechanism responsible for the behavior here described and its scope. Some additional experiments could probe the effect of increasing delays between witnessing a baiting and choosing (like Hampton, 2001), increasing the quality of the reward, the cost of choosing wrong, or the need to take intermediate steps to find out the location of the reward. For instance, subjects could lift lids to peek inside tubes and once the food has been found, they would have to use tools. One of the advantages of this method is its simplicity. It does not require any training (besides training to touch an object to select) because it capitalizes on spontaneous behavior.

THE SELF AND THE OTHER IN SOCIAL COGNITION

Positive evidence is accumulating regarding what chimpanzees know about what others can and cannot see. They follow gaze, look around barriers, use visual gestures mostly when others are looking, are sensitive to the body orientation and the faces of others when using visual signals, and know what others have and have not seen in competitive situations. The findings described in this chapter add another piece to the social cognition puzzle. Chimpanzees and the other great apes also know what they themselves have and have not seen. It is therefore possible to begin to establish a link between mental attribution in others and the self. For instance, the cognitive mechanism that gives rise to following the gaze of another individual behind a barrier to see what the other individual is looking at may be the same as the cognitive mechanism that gives rise to looking through the tubes when one has not seen where the experimenter has deposited the food. Future research will bring about a closer connection between these two complementary aspects of research on mental state attribution.

When discussing the attribution of psychological states to others (and to the self), it is important to be precise about what has been shown. I argue that these studies have shown that at least chimpanzees (and presumably other apes) know what they have seen, and they know what others can or cannot see. Some may be tempted to translate this into meaning that they know what they know and what others know or do not know. Currently, however, there is no study that can tease apart seeing from knowing. In any case, both seeing and knowing are psychological states (see Call & Tomasello, in press, for a more detailed discussion). Yet they differ in the degree of abstraction that they entail. Whereas perceptual information is a key component of seeing, such perceptual support is less relevant in the case of knowing. Individuals may represent the idea of seeing by visualizing someone facing in a certain direction and observing a given event. Knowing is harder to represent at such a perceptual level. This is why knowing is often described as a more opaque mental state than seeing. An analogy with the area of categorization may help to clarify the distinction between seeing and knowing and the different levels of abstraction that they represent. Perceptual categories would be analogous to seeing, whereas conceptual (or functional) categories would be analogous to knowing.

Despite its lower abstract load, it is important to emphasize that seeing should not be equated to purely observable behavior. Seeing, like knowledge, is a psychological state, not just observable behavior. Again, using the analogy with categories can help illustrate the difference between seeing and observable behavior. Seeing, like perceptual categories, allows individuals to solve problems with new exemplars of a given category, whereas purely observable behavior, like rote memory, only allows individuals to remember previously seen exemplars. Although seeing falls within the realm of psychological states, it is also important to recognize that it is not equivalent to other psychological states such as knowledge or belief. It is also important to recognize that various psychological states follow different developmental trajectories. For instance, some theorists argue that beliefs owe their special status to the property that the individual can entertain the possibility that a given fact may be false, and that individuals may be induced to hold false beliefs by supplying them with inaccurate information (Perner, 1991). Note that seeing does not afford this "duplicity" property. Individuals either see or do not see a particular event, but they do not necessarily entertain the possibility that what they saw may be false. One of the most critical advances in the study of the attribution of psychological states has been the realization that different species or members of a same species at different ages vary in their ability to attribute the various psychological states to themselves and others. From a comparative perspective, we still do not know whether nonhuman animals attribute knowledge to themselves or others (let alone beliefs) or just visual perception. Moreover, even within the area of visual perception, many questions remain unresolved. As mentioned before, previous studies have shown that chimpanzees know what others can and cannot see. Yet other aspects such as perspective taking (how an individual would see an object from a given perspective) or whether individuals recognize that others can be attending to two different aspects of an object (e.g., color vs. shape) remain totally unexplored. Future studies should be devoted to develop this field and strengthen the link between the self and the other in comparative social cognition.

ACKNOWLEDGMENTS This manuscript benefited tremendously from my discussions with Malinda Carpenter and Mike Tomasello on this topic. I also want to thank the participants of the conference on the evolution of self-reflective consciousness for their valuable comments on this work.

REFERENCES

Anderson, J. R. (1986). Mirror-mediated finding of hidden food by monkeys (*Macaca tonkeana* and *Macaca fascicularis*). *Journal of Comparative Psychology, 100*, 237–242.

Anderson, J. R. (1999). Primates and representations of self. *Cahiers de Psychologie Cognitive, 18*, 1005–1029.

Anderson, J. R., & Gallup, G. G., Jr. (1999). Primates and representations of self. *Cahiers de Psychologie Cognitive, 18*, 1005–1029.

Baldwin, J. M. (1902). *Social and ethical interpretations in mental life*. New York: Macmillan.

Bering, J. M., Bjorklund, D.F., & Ragan, P. (2000). Deferred imitation of object-related actions in human-reared juvenile chimpanzees and orangutans. *Developmental Psychobiology, 36*, 218–232.

Bjorklund, D. F., Yunger, J. L., Bering, J. M., & Ragan, P. (2002). The generalization of deferred imitation in enculturated chimpanzees (*Pan troglodytes*). *Animal Cognition, 5*, 49–58.

Bräuer, J., Call, J., & Tomasello, M. (in press). Visual perspective taking in dogs (*Canis familiaris*) in the presence of barriers. *Applied Animal Behaviour Science*.

Call, J. (2001). Body imitation in an enculturated orangutan. *Cybernetics and Systems, 32*, 97–119.

Call, J. (2004). The use of social information in chimpanzees and dogs. In L. Rogers & G. Kaplan (Eds.), *Are primates special?* (pp. 263–286). New York: Kluwer Academic.

Call, J. (in press). Inferences about the location of food in the great apes. *Journal of Comparative Psychology.*

Call, J., & Carpenter, M. (2001). Do chimpanzees and children know what they have seen? *Animal Cognition, 4,* 207–220.

Call, J., Carpenter, M., & Tomasello, M. (2002). Focusing on outcomes and focusing on actions in the process of social learning: Chimpanzees (*Pan troglodytes*) and human children (*Homo sapiens*). Manuscript submitted for publication.

Call, J., Hare, B. H., & Tomasello, M. (1998). Chimpanzee gaze following in an object-choice task. *Animal Cognition, 1,* 89–99.

Call, J., & Tomasello, M. (1995). The use of social information in the problem-solving of orangutans (*Pongo pygmaeus*) and human children (*Homo sapiens*). *Journal of Comparative Psychology, 109,* 308–320.

Call, J., & Tomasello, M. (2003). Social cognition. In D. Maestripieri (Ed.), *Primate psychology* (pp. 234–253). Cambridge, MA: Harvard University Press.

Call, J., & Tomasello, M. (in press). What chimpanzees know about seeing revisited: An explanation of the third kind. In N. Eilan, C. Hoerl, T. McCormack, & J. Roessler (Eds.), *Joint attention.* Oxford, UK: Oxford University Press.

Cameron, P. A., & Gallup, G. G., Jr. (1988). Shadow recognition in human infants. *Infant Behavior and Development, 11,* 465–471.

Custance, D. M., Whiten, A., & Bard, K. A. (1995). Can young chimpanzees (*Pan troglodytes*) imitate arbitrary actions? Hayes & Hayes (1952) revisited. *Behaviour, 132,* 837–859.

Epstein, R., Lanza, R. P., & Skinner, B. F. (1981). "Self-awareness" in the pigeon. *Science, 212,* 695–696.

Gallup, G. G., Jr. (1970). Chimpanzees: Self-recognition. *Science, 167,* 86–87.

Gallup, G. G., Jr. (1982). Self-awareness and the emergence of mind in primates. *American Journal of Primatology, 2,* 237–248.

Gallup, G. G., Jr. (1994). Self-recognition: Research strategies and experimental design. In S. T. Parker, R. W. Mitchell, & M. L. Boccia (Eds.), *Self-awareness in animals and humans: Developmental perspectives* (pp. 35–50). Cambridge, UK: Cambridge University Press.

Gopnik, A., & Meltzoff, A. N. (1994). Minds, bodies, and persons: Young children's understanding of the self and others as reflected in imitation and theory of mind research. In S. T. Parker, R. W. Mitchell, & M. L. Boccia (Eds.), *Self-awareness in animals and humans: Developmental perspectives* (pp. 166–186). Cambridge, UK: Cambridge University Press.

Hampton, R. R. (2001). Rhesus monkeys know when they remember. *Proceedings of the National Academy of Sciences U.S.A., 98,* 5359–5362.

Hare, B., Brown, M., Williamson, C., & Tomasello, M. (2002). The domestication of social cognition in dogs. *Science, 298,* 1634–1636.

Hart, D., & Fegley, S. (1994). Social imitation and the emergence of a mental model of self. In S. T. Parker, R. W. Mitchell, & M. L. Boccia (Eds.), *Self-awareness in animals and humans: Developmental perspectives* (pp. 149–165). Cambridge, UK: Cambridge University Press.

Heyes, C. M. (1994). Reflections on self-recognition in primates. *Animal Behaviour, 47*, 909–919.

Heyes, C. M. (1998). Theory of mind in nonhuman primates. *Behavioral and Brain Sciences, 21*, 101–134.

Hyatt, C. W., & Hopkins, W. D. (1994). Self-awareness in bonobos and chimpanzees: A comparative perspective. In S. T. Parker, R. W. Mitchell, & M. L. Boccia (Eds.), *Self-awareness in animals and humans: Developmental perspectives* (pp. 248–253). Cambridge, UK: Cambridge University Press.

Itakura, S. (2001). The level of self-knowledge in nonhuman primates: From the perspective of comparative cognitive science. In T. Matsuzawa (Ed.), *Primate origins of human cognition and behavior* (pp. 313–329). Berlin: Springer-Verlag.

Jorgensen, M. J., Suomi, S. J., & Hopkins, W. D. (1995). Using a computerized testing system to investigate the preconceptual self in nonhuman primates and humans. In P. Rochat (Ed.), *The self in infancy: Theory and research* (pp. 243–256). Amsterdam: Elsevier.

Lethmate, J., & Ducker, G. (1973). Untersuchungen zum selbsterkennen im spiegel bei orangutans und einigen anderen affenarten. *Zeitschrift für Tierpsychology, 33*, 248–269.

Lewis, M. (1994). Myself and me. In S. T. Parker, R. W. Mitchell, & M. L. Boccia (Eds.), *Self-awareness in animals and humans: Developmental perspectives* (pp. 20–34). Cambridge, UK: Cambridge University Press.

Lewis, M., & Brooks-Gunn, J. (1979). *Social cognition and the acquisition of self.* New York: Plenum.

Miles, H. L. W. (1990). The cognitive foundations for reference in a signing orangutan. In S. T. Parker & K. R. Gibson (Eds.), *"Language" and intelligence in monkeys and apes* (pp. 511–539). Cambridge, UK: Cambridge University Press.

Mitchell, R. W. (1993). Mental models of mirror-self-recognition: Two theories. *New Ideas in Psychology, 11*, 295–325.

Myowa-Yamakoshi, M., & Matsuzawa, T. (1999). Factors influencing imitation of manipulatory actions in chimpanzees (*Pan troglodytes*). *Journal of Comparative Psychology, 113*, 128–136.

Nagell, K., Olguin, R. S., & Tomasello, M. (1993). Processes of social learning in the tool use of chimpanzees (*Pan troglodytes*) and human children (*Homo sapiens*). *Journal of Comparative Psychology, 107*, 174–186.

Neisser, U. (1988). Five kinds of self-knowledge. *Philosophical Psychology, 1*, 35–59.

Parker, S. T., & Milbrath, C. (1994). Contributions of imitation and role-playing games to the construction of self in primates. In S. T. Parker, R. W. Mitchell, & M. L. Boccia (Eds.), *Self-awareness in animals and humans: Developmental perspectives* (pp. 108–128). Cambridge, UK: Cambridge University Press.

Patterson, F. G. P., & Cohn, R. H. (1994). Self-recognition and self-awareness in lowland gorillas. In S. T. Parker, R. W. Mitchell, & M. L. Boccia (Eds.), *Self-awareness in animals and humans: Developmental perspectives* (pp. 273–290). Cambridge, UK: Cambridge University Press.

Perner, J. (1991). *Understanding the representational mind.* Cambridge, MA: MIT Press.

Povinelli, D. J. (1993). Reconstructing the evolution of mind. *American Psychologist, 48,* 493–509.

Smith, J. D., Schull, J., Strote, J., McGee, K., Egnor, R., & Erb, L.. (1995). The uncertain response in the bottlenosed dolphin (*Tursiops truncatus*). *Journal of Experimental Psychology: General, 124,* 391–408.

Smith, J. D., Shields, W. E., Schull, J., & Washburn, D. A. (1997). The uncertain response in humans and animals. *Cognition, 62,* 75–97.

Stoinksi, T. S., Wrate, J. L., Ure, N., & Whiten, A. (2001). Imitative learning by captive western lowland gorillas (*Gorilla gorilla gorilla*) in a simulated food-processing task. *Journal of Comparative Psychology, 115,* 272–281.

Suarez, S. D., & Gallup, G. G., Jr. (1981). Self-recognition in chimpanzees and orangutans, but not gorillas. *Journal of Human Evolution, 10,* 175–188.

Swartz, K. B., & Evans, S. (1994). Social and cognitive factors in chimpanzee and gorilla mirror behavior and self-recognition. In S. T. Parker, R. W. Mitchell, & M. L. Boccia (Eds.), *Self-awareness in animals and humans: Developmental perspectives* (pp. 189–206). Cambridge, UK: Cambridge University Press.

Tomasello, M. (1996). Do apes ape? In C. M. Heyes & B. G. Galef, Jr. (Eds.), *Social learning in animals: The roots of culture* (pp. 319–346). New York: Academic Press.

Tomasello, M., Call, J., & Gluckman, A. (1997). Comprehension of novel communicative signs by apes and human children. *Child Development, 68,* 1067–1080.

Tomasello, M., Davis-Dasilva, M., Camak, L., & Bard, K. (1987). Observational learning of tool-use by young chimpanzees. *Human Evolution, 2,* 175–183.

Tomasello, M., Savage-Rumbaugh, E. S., & Kruger, A. C. (1993). Imitative learning of actions on objects by children, chimpanzees, and enculturated chimpanzees. *Child Development, 64,* 1688–1705.

Whiten, A. (1998). Imitation of the sequential structure of actions by chimpanzees (*Pan troglodytes*). *Journal of Comparative Psychology, 112,* 270–281.

Whiten, A., Custance, D. M., Gómez, J. C., Teixidor, P., & Bard, K. A. (1996). Imitative learning of artificial fruit processing in children (*Homo sapiens*) and chimpanzees (*Pan troglodytes*). *Journal of Comparative Psychology, 110,* 3–14.

Author Index

Subject Index

Page numbers in italics refer to figures and tables.